W9-BSZ-578

EMBATTLED REASON

EMBATTLED REASON

Essays on Social Knowledge

VOLUME I

REINHARD BENDIX

Transaction Books
New Brunswick (U.S.A.) and Oxford (U.K.)

Copyright © 1988 by Transaction, Inc.
New Brunswick, New Jersey 08903

Library of Congress Catalog Number: 86-24892
ISBN 0-88738-110-3
Printed in the United States of America

Library of Congress Cataloging-in-Publication Data

Bendix, Reinhard.
  Embattled reason.

  1. Sociology. 2. Social change. 3. Social structure. 4. Social history. I. Title.
HM51.B394   1987   301   86-24892
ISBN 0-88738-110-3 (v. 1)

For my sister Dorothy

Contents

Preface ix

Acknowledgments xiii

Part I: Conditions of Knowledge 1

Introduction 3

  1. Social Science and the Image of Man 7

  2. The Age of Ideology, Persistent and Changing 23

  3. Sociology and the Distrust of Reason 61

  4. Science and the Purposes of Knowledge 83

Part II: Theoretical Perspectives 105

Introduction 107

  5. Images of Society and Problems of Concept Formation
     in Sociology (with Bennett Berger) 111

  6. Social Theory and the Break with Tradition 133

  7. Culture, Social Structure, and Change 151

  8. Reflections on Modern Western States and Civil Societies
     (with John Bendix) 179

  9. Changing Patterns of Authority in Relation to
     Industrialization and Social Protest 203

Part III: Studies of Modernization 231

Introduction 233

10. Industrialization, Ideologies, and Social Structure 237

11. Social Stratification and the Political Community 251

12. Tradition and Modernity Reconsidered 279

13. The Special Position of Europe 321

14. The Intellectual's Role in the Modern World 339

Index 355

PREFACE

About fifteen years ago I republished a dozen essays selected from among ca. eighty articles written along with the books I have authored or co-authored. That earlier volume is the basis of this two-volume edition of selected essays. But these volumes differ from the earlier publication in content and format. A number of the earlier articles have been replaced by others, and each section and article is prefaced by introductory notes, containing ideas or reflections as well as supplementary information associated in my mind with the material that follows. A glance at the table of contents shows that the articles republished here (or published for the first time) are *not* arranged in chronological order. The sequence of presentation has a rationale of its own.

Books of selected essays should have reasons that go beyond the convenience of bringing widely scattered publications together. My reason for these two volumes is that they allow me to outline the intellectual position I have developed over the years, so that consecutive content seemed more important than chronological sequence. The reader who comes to these essays afresh would, therefore, be better advised to peruse or study them in the sequence I have arranged rather than picking and choosing among them, as he might be inclined to do otherwise. Still, these are separate essays, written on different occasions. I have not been interested in formulating my position in a separate treatise. Given the choice of spending a number of years in working out such a treatise or getting on with my socio-historical and institutional studies, I have preferred to do the latter. No doubt, that choice was prompted by personal inclination and/or limitations. However, the choice was also based on the conviction (call it an intuition if you prefer) that "a little bit of theory goes a long way." Since some colleagues have published this remark, I should explain why I have used it on occasion.

We want to understand the social world in which we live. In the past and in the foreseeable future, that understanding has had (and will have) to be built in part on the ideas ordinary people form of that world, because these ideas are aspects of our common experience. Scholars use abstractions, of course, but in the social sciences even these are part of common experience and derive from ordinary usage, however much they go beyond it. When Talcott Parsons coined a phrase like "boundary maintenance," he could no more get away from the ordinary denotations of those words than Max Weber, in defining "charisma," could get away from the use of that term in the New Testament. True, mathematicians, theoretical physicists and econometricians use languages of their own. But most social scientists, and certainly the kind of scholar I have tried to be, employ words which *also* have an ordinary meaning. One reason why this use of common words persists is that the world we want to understand is inhabited by people who use ordinary language to describe their experience which is part of that world. In a common-sense way, quite ordinary words like *house* or *rock*, *child* or *bicycle* are generic and the language supplies us with all sorts of ways in which we can specify what kind of house, rock, child or bicycle we have in mind. The social scientist engages in a similar operation, only now the analogy breaks down, because the specifications he needs are no longer provided by ordinary usage.

Take the term "feudalism" which derives from "feud" and everyone knows what that means. Feudalism is a form of governing based on landholding, associated rights and verbal agreements, the latter sanctified by solemn ceremony. Here we are well beyond common usage. If we consult the article on "feudalism" in *Geschichtliche Grundbegriffe*, a multi-volume work containing articles tracing the changing meaning of such terms over the centuries, we discover the many ways in which a given word has been used. But leaving that difficulty aside, everyone can still understand the underlying idea that the violation of solemnly achieved agreements leads to feuds. So, if social scientists use words in a technical sense or coin new ones, their intention is, nevertheless, to refer back to general understandings. They are pulled really in two divergent directions. Their analytic interests prompt them to subdivide human experience beyond where ordinary understanding can follow. But the utility of their concepts (those subdivisions) is tested in good part by the possibility of referring back to human experience.

When single words pose that difficulty, elaborate theories compound it. That is why a little bit of theory goes a long way. For every term used in the social sciences specifies, or implies, a unit of analysis and advances the proposition that we refer to the same phenomenon every time we use that word. In this way, even single terms are "mini-theories." Applying such terms to diverse experiences that "look alike" and are to be referred to "in the same way" always runs the risk of cutting off part of the evidence so that it will fit the term we have chosen. This Procrustean procedure may not be entirely avoidable. But its obvious dangers should be minimized as far as possible.

It has been my endeavor to follow these precepts by using a few categories like bureaucracy, ideology, authority, kingship, public mandate, citizenship etc. and exploring in detail what diversities of experience over time these terms encompass. My overall interest has been the changes of ideas and institutions (social structures, for short) which have helped to shape the world of the twentieth century. That is one reason why Max Weber's *Economy and So-*

ciety has appeared to me not as a dull cataloguing of definitions, but rather as a rich storehouse of suggestions for research, which I have hardly begun to utilize, as I think it should be utilized. Although the tasks ahead along these lines are beyond my capacity, I do not regret the lines of inquiry I have followed. They have helped me, as I hope they have helped and can help others, to understand the world in which we live a little better.

The essays collected in these two volumes contain reflections on my way of viewing the social world, and they present some of the explorations in comparative institutions, social and intellectual history to which that way has led me.

ACKNOWLEDGMENTS

I acknowledge, with thanks, permission to reprint the following articles (or chapters) from the publishers in whose publications the material appeared for the first time, or from co-authors and editors where appropriate. Since I am the author or co-author of each article, my name has been omitted to avoid repetition. The articles, for which permission to reprint has been granted, are listed in the order in which they appear in Volumes I and II of *Embattled Reason* (2nd edition).

"Social Science and the Image of Man," in Reinhard Bendix, *Embattled Reason* (1st edition; New York: Oxford University Press, 1970), 3-17. Copyright © 1970 by Oxford University Pres, Inc. Used by arrangement.

"The Age of Ideology, Persistent and Changing," in David Apter, ed., *Ideology and its Discontents* (Glencoe: The Free Press, 1964), 294-327. Copyright © 1964 by David Apter, Yale University.

"Sociology and the Distrust of Reason," *American Sociological Review* (1970), vol. 35, 831-43.

"Science and the Purposes of Knowledge," *Social Research* (Summer, 1975), 331-59.

With Bennett Berger, "Images of Society and Problems of Concept Formation in Sociology," in Llewellyn Gross, ed., *Symposium on Sociological Theory* (Evanston: Row, Peterson & Co. [now Harper & Row, New York], 1959), 92-118. Copyright © 1959 by Harper & Row and Bennett Berger.

"Social Theory and the Break with Tradition," in Fred Eidlin, ed., *Constitutional Democracy* (Festschrift for Henry Ehrmann; Boulder: Westview Press, 1983), 131-52. Copyright © 1983 by Westview Press.

"Culture, Social Structure and Change," in Reinhard Bendix, *Embattled Reason* (1st edition; New York: Oxford University Press, 1970), 129-71. Copyright © 1970 by Oxford University Press, Inc. Used by arrangement.

With John Bendix, "Reflections on Modern Western States and Civil Societies." A larger version of this essay appears in Reinhard Bendix, John Bendix and Norman Furniss, "Reflections on Modern Western States and Civil Society," in Richard G. Braungart (ed.), *Research in Political Sociology*. Volume 3. Greenwich, CT: JAI Press, Inc., 1987. Copyright © 1987 by JAI Press, Inc. Reprinted by permission.

"Introduction" to second edition of *Work and Authority in Industry* (Berkeley: University of California Press, 1974), vii-1.

"Industrialization, Ideologies and Social Structure," *American Sociological Review* (1959), vol. 24, 613-23.

"Social Stratification and the Political Community," *European Journal of Sociology* (1960), vol. I, 181-210.

"Tradition and Modernity Reconsidered," *Comparative Studies in Society and History* (1967), vol. 9, 292-346. Copyright © 1967 by the Society for the Comparative Study of Society and History, and reprinted with the permission of Cambridge University Press.

"The Special Position of Europe," *Scandinavian Political Studies* (1986), vol. 9, 301-16. The article was delivered as the Stein Rokkan Memorial Lecture at the University of Bergen in 1986 and printed subsequently in Scandinavian Political Studies.

"The Intellectual's Role in the Modern World," *Society* (November-December, 1987), vol. 25.

"A Memoir of my Father," *Canadian Review of Sociology and Anthropology* (1965), vol. 2, 1-18.

"Values and Concepts in Max Weber's Comparative Studies." A shorter version of this essay appears in Reinhard Bendix, "Values and Concepts in Max Weber's Comparative Studies," *European Journal of Political Research* (1987), vol. 15/4. Copyright of the shorter version © 1987 by Martinus Nijhoff Publishers, Dordrecht, Holland.

"Inequality and Social Structure: Marx and Weber," *American Sociological Review* (1974), vol. 39, 149-61.

"Two Sociological Traditions: Durkheim and Weber," in *Scholarship and Partisanship*, with Guenther Roth (Berkeley: University of California Press, 1971), 282-98.

"Max Weber and Jacob Burckhardt," *American Sociological Review* (1965), vol. 30, 176-84.

"A Case Study in Cultural and Educational Mobility: Japan and the Protestant Ethic," in Neil J. Smelser and S.M. Lipset (eds.), *Social Structure and Mobility in Economic Development* (Chicago: Aldine Publishing Company, 1966), 262-79. Copyright © 1978 by Neil J. Smelser and S.M. Lipset.

"The Cultural and Political Setting of Economic Rationality in Western and Eastern Europe," in Gregory Grossman (ed.), *Value and Plan* (Berkeley: University of California Press, 1960), 245-70.

I thank Kathleen Thelen and Martha Norkunas for their expeditious and thoughtful help in preparing these two volumes for publication. They have not only done the typing of Volume I (Thelen) and Volume II (Norkunas) on a word processor, but helped me with their editorial judgment. Thelen translated the original German version of Vol. I, chapter 13 into English. Thanks are also due to the Institute of International Studies, University of California, Berkeley, for their financial assistance in preparing these volumes for the press.

PART I

Conditions of Knowledge

Introduction to Part I

All human achievements are conditioned, even the simplest or most elementary. All men need food, clothing and shelter, but the conditions of satisfying these needs change and so does the meaning of "need." The methods and materials are altered as time goes by, and so are the judgments as to how much is enough and what kinds of food, clothing and shelter are good for our well-being. Even at any one time, human wants are clouded by ambiguity. How much and what kind of our basic means of subsistence do we need or want—really?! The question is impossible to answer definitively, because the answer depends on the kind of people we have in mind and their particular circumstances. Also, even food, clothing and shelter can be used for purposes other than the commonly accepted ones. Some children play with their food instead of eating it, even grownups do. Some people use clothing to appear different from anyone else, like a clown in a department store, or a wealthy man in rags at a fancy dinner party. Or a house may be used to store arms and as a hideout for terrorists. Recent political terminology in German has introduced an untranslatable term for this anti-ordinary or counter-cultural or criminal manipulation of ordinary objects: *umfunktionieren*. In the case of ordinary objects and activities such manipulation is the exception rather than the rule. Exceptions can increase, of course, but too many clowns in department stores or too many terrorist hideaways begin to alarm us.

The need for knowledge is not as evident to large masses of people as is the need for food, clothing and shelter. The question of how much and what kind of knowledge we need has become more troubling and unanswerable, as knowledge has expanded. The people who make it their business to advance knowledge cannot count on as much consent from the general public as can peasants, garment workers, and masons, and even these basic trades are beset by controversy.

The quest for knowledge is elitist. People at large feel only intermittently that they need knowledge when they consult a doctor, lawyer or architect. They want applied knowledge. They are not really concerned with the experiments and theories on which that knowledge rests. Also, people often want a kind of knowledge which the minority of scholars and scientists cannot, or do not want to, provide. I belong to the minority of knowledge-seekers. My background may have made me more aware than others just how conditioned and conditional the quest for knowledge is. In due course I will

3

describe that background in these essays in Vol. II, Part One. My first task is to explain the phrase "conditions of knowledge" and how I came to explore them.

My motto is this sentence from the autobiography by J.R. von Salis, the Swiss historian and political commentator during World War II. "Man muss zuerst die Dinge kennenlernen, ehe man anfangen kann zu erforschen, was *hinter* den Dingen ist."[1] One should get to know things first, before one can begin to investigate what lies *behind* them. It took me a long while to get to that point.

Before I did, I had to work my way through Marx's assertion that "a portion of the bourgeois ideologists... have raised themselves to the level of comprehending theoretically the historical movement as a whole." This statement of the *Communist Manifesto* implies that historical truth (and by vulgar extension: any truth) is class-bound. Knowing the truth depends on a solid, if sometimes devious or manipulative interest in it. Since according to Marx the workers are the wave of the future, they possess the truth, whether they know it or not, just as in the late medieval period the rising bourgeoisie had possessed the truth. Identification with the proletariat put one in possession of the truth about the future and hence (!) in possession of the future—a heady incentive for certain kinds of knowledge-seekers.

I also had to work my way through the complexities of Karl Mannheim to whom my father introduced me at an early age. In the midst of the Weimar Republic I learned a lot from Mannheim's adaptation of Marx's views. While I was struggling with Mannheim, the daily papers were reporting on thirty-five political parties contending for power, each with a *Weltanschauung* of its own. In effect, Mannheim was writing about political philosophies, not about knowledge in the broader sense of that term. In *Ideology and Utopia* (1929) there is hardly a reference to the natural sciences and precious few to serious humanistic and social studies. These represent knowledge as ordinarily understood. So, Mannheim's program of a sociology of knowledge was not in the end persuasive, because it ignored the knowledge which is most clearly identifiable as such.

Louis Wirth, my teacher at the University of Chicago, used to teach a challenging course on the "Sociology of Intellectual Life." He had translated Mannheim's book (together with Edward Shils), but covered much material that went beyond Mannheim's theoretical concerns. Two points from that course belong in this context. Wirth used to say, there is not a fact in the social sciences, however well established, which is not controversial from someone's point of view. He was also adamant that no amount of inquiry into the conditions of knowledge can either validate or invalidate a proposition. This is quite similar to Karl Popper's view that scientific objectivity results from adherence to the norms of scholarly research and communication, not from a scholar's identification with an interest group, or from his lack of such identification. I find both points persuasive, but they do not invalidate a concern with the conditions of knowledge, properly conceived.

Like other human activities, the quest for knowledge has all kinds of conditions worth investigating. Max Weber's "Science as a Vocation" represents a classic statement of these conditions and remains a source of inspiration and research projects. For my own work in this field I have found two of his remarks of special importance. He writes that "truth is only that which *claims* to be valid for all those who *want* truth." The statement points up that all knowledge is provisional, subject to correction as more becomes known, that the quest for knowledge is elitist because it is confined to those who want truth, and that it requires of all knowledge-seekers a personal commitment to the search for truth. Weber adds that this commitment "chains [us] to the idea of progress."

> It is not self-evident that something subordinate to such a law [of progress] is sensible and meaningful in itself. Why does one engage in doing something that in reality never comes, and never can come, to an end?[2]

I shall have occasion to refer to this passage again. It is cited here to convey the sense in which I shall use the phrase "purposes of knowledge." The people who make food, clothing and shelter have straightforward purposes. As long as their products are wanted, it makes little sense to ask them why they work at what they do; the question would be redundant. But this is not so in the case of knowledge-seekers. Quite often, they are challenged about what they do. When they are, they try to explain what their kind of knowledge is all about. And to explain their activities is tantamount to defending them, because it is not obvious that the knowledge they seek is "needed."

For men to be scholars, they must believe in the value of knowledge, even when the need for it is obscure. Usually, they go on evidence from the past that apparently useless knowledge proved constructive in the end. This absence of a self-evident and widely acknowledged need puts knowledge-seekers in an awkward position. They cannot pursue knowledge on the condition that their results will only be applied in humane ways the way a cook can be sure that the food he prepares will be eaten. Efforts to determine how the results of knowledge-seeking will be used always founder on the impossibility of knowing in advance what can be known and how knowledge will be used once it is available. The pursuit of knowledge wherever it may lead, and hence the suspension of specific guidelines, can be justified by this unpredictability of scholarly work. The use of food, clothing and shelter is not that unpredictable, even though counter-cultural manipulation remains possible. The ordinary purposes of scholarly knowledge are much more difficult to specify.

In the face of that uncertainty most scholars pursue their work in the general belief that it will enhance the vague goals shared by thinking men of good will. Such commitments to scholarly work only make sense if there is the hope or expectation that in the long run the constructive uses of knowledge will prevail. Scholarship presupposes a belief in progress through knowledge and in the perfectibility of man. It does not flourish where men become preoccupied with the potential evil of knowledge and, therefore, doubt that knowledge will have value in the long run.[3]

For these reasons the following essays deal specifically with the faith needed to pursue knowledge. They do not deal except incidentally with all the other conditions which make the quest for knowledge possible.

NOTES

1. J.R. von Salis, *Grenzüberschreitungen, Ein Lebensbericht* (Zürich: Orell Füssli Verlag, 1975), I, 126.
2. Max Weber, *Gesammelte Aufsätze zur Wissenschaftslehre* (Tübingen: J.C.B. Mohr (Paul Siebeck), 1968), 184.
3. The preceding wording is taken from Reinhard Bendix, "Changing Foundations of Scholarly Detachment," in *Embattled Reason* (New York: Oxford University Press, 1970), 70. The article has been omitted from this volume of selected essays.

1

SOCIAL SCIENCE AND THE IMAGE OF MAN

Introductory Note

In 1938 I arrived at the University of Chicago to begin my college training, an aging freshman of twenty-two and a refugee from Hitler's Germany. My earlier reading in Marx and Mannheim was part of the intellectual baggage with which I entered the university. As an enemy alien I was ineligible for the draft when America entered the war in 1941. When I did become eligible through naturalization, I was barred for reasons of health from joining the war against Hitler in which I wanted to participate. Destined to stay on the sidelines, I remained puzzled and concerned, as I had been under the Hitler regime, with the relation between knowledge and action. Then, in 1945, shortly before the end of the war, the problem was brought to world-wide attention through use of the atomic bomb over Hiroshima and Nagasaki. In one of my first publications I wrote:

> We fear the forces which science has unleashed, but we admire its ability to do so. And while we 'monopolize the secret' for a little while with a bad conscience, we indulge in fantasies about its future benefit to mankind.[1]

Re-reading that statement after forty years I notice the unconscious ambiguity which had slipped in, perhaps because of my uncertain command of written English. For the bad conscience I had in mind referred to the scientists who had developed the bomb as a patriotic service and now found themselves appalled at the use to which their discoveries were put. But ''bad conscience'' could also refer to keeping their discoveries a secret, when the whole ethos of science demanded prompt disclosure and open discussion. In any case, I proceeded to discuss the ''ethical implications of scientific pursuits'' in historical perspective, well aware that I came to no definite conclusions and rather uncomfortable at the thought that my competence concerned the social sciences, which had ethical implications of their own.

The questions I had raised did not let me rest. For my Master's Thesis I had struggled (on far too many pages) with the development of German sociology. On the working assumption that sociology stood for a rational study of society, I wanted to know how scholars had come to favor such an approach and, just as important, how ruling groups within German society had come to support academic studies which were bound to be critical of that society. My findings were inconclusive, I was dissatisfied with my work, but the question would not go away. At the Chicago Sociology Department I had observed how my teachers seemed to be at one in their "scientific approach" to sociology, but sharply divided among themselves over the interest in occupational sub-cultures studied by participant observation and the interest in methodological rigor through the analysis of opinion questionnaires. When I joined the Department of Sociology and Social Institutions at the University of California (Berkeley) in 1947, I encountered an analogous conflict, though in a different field. Frederick Teggart, the retired head of my new Department, had left the History Department some years earlier, because he was dissatisfied with the idea of history as narrative. He wanted to put the study of history on a scientific basis by a systematic analysis of dated events. Later on, I discovered that many other academic disciplines were split along similar lines, putting the burden of knowing both approaches on the students in each case. I did not like this imposition on the students, there was something to be said for both sides, and I did not want to make my intellectual choices in terms of such alternatives. The result was my essay "Social Science and the Distrust of Reason" (1951), of which this chapter and the next are later and better written versions.

These essays deal with the idea that knowledge-seekers do not start with an empty slate. Any quest for knowledge starts with tacit assumptions about the prospect of increased knowledge "for the benefit and use of life," as Francis Bacon put it in the early seventeenth century. Since the outcome of research is uncertain and the results will be known only in the future, the proper attitude is one of hope and fear, with hope prevailing. If fear prevailed we would not make the attempt; if hope alone prevailed we would be foolish. Consequently, the pursuit of knowledge must be undertaken, whether this is acknowledged or not, with some image of man in mind which gives us courage to venture into the unknown. That image is not the result of research, but one of its conditions.[2]

LEGACIES OF THE ENLIGHTENMENT

Some two hundred years ago, in his *Philosophical Dictionary*, Voltaire declared that God had to create man with self-esteem, but that self-esteem misleads him most of the time. Passions are necessary, for mankind cannot propagate itself without desire. But passions also lead to quarrels and wars. Still, Voltaire thought his time the "most enlightened century that ever was." God or nature has established a "few invariable principles" of morals and justice underneath all the customs and evils which have "diffused variety over the face of the universe." The office of man's reason is to discover these principles, make them his code of conduct, and teach them to his children. In this view truth and virtue are synonyms. God has so ordered the world that proper inquiry will lead to their discovery.

Social philosophers and social scientists have presupposed a secular version of these beliefs ever since the eighteenth century. By using their reason men can discover regularities of human behavior much as natural scientists have discovered laws of nature. Society, like nature, is uniform underneath the diversity of appearance; man can discover these uniformities; and the resulting knowledge will be "for the benefit and use of life"

From the Age of Voltaire to that of the social scientists of the present, writers have assumed some order in nature and society which is not man made. At one time this abstract assumption involved the idea of a divinely created order. Marx posited the theory of a predictable interrelation between an economic substructure and an ideological superstructure. Freud held that the human personality is formed in accordance with the individual's history of pleasures and pains. Economists employ laws of supply and demand in an idealized market as a useful approximation of the aggregate behavior of real men in real markets. At other levels of abstraction sociologists assume more generally that the order of society is a system of correlated factors to be analyzed by scientific methods. Theories of society as a system, or as a pattern of interaction are typical variants of this assumption.[3]

Every social scientist endeavors to clear away the bias and error that would obstruct his inquiry. But he also stands in some personal, affective relation to the society he investigates. This inquiry depends on a prior analysis of bias and error and of what can be done to minimize their distorting effects. The paradox is that the very effort to advance the study of society has deepened our understanding of human fallibility. As a result, man's efforts to understand society have been marked by increased social knowledge and by an increased distrust of reason.

Consider this sequence. In the seventeenth century, Francis Bacon believed that man could free his understanding from distortion (idols), once he understood the nature of these distortions. Man's capacity to reason was divinely ordained and the unhampered pursuit of knowledge would be rewarded by discovering the truth. In the eighteenth century, philosophers of the French Enlightenment shared this belief but saw the pursuit of knowledge endangered by the church. They advocated educational reforms and developed a scientific pedagogy as means towards the emancipation of man. For Marx, in the nineteenth century, knowledge itself was a part of society and history. In his view there is no escape from the distortions of ideology because these serve man's most vital interests. The shackles of bias and self-interest can be thrown off only when society as a whole has been reorganized. Revolution rather than elimination of bias or educational reform appears as the safeguard of human reason. With Freud, in the twentieth century, we move still further away from the tradition of the Enlightenment. Now man's quest for knowledge appears as a sublimation or rationalization of his basic organic drives. In this view all knowledge, but especially the knowledge of self and society, appears as an epiphenomenon of the human condition. Therapy rather than educational reform or revolution must safeguard what little room is left for the constructive possibilities of human reason. Freud takes a last precarious stand on the side of human improvement.

No social scientist today can match the sweep and penetration of Marx's or Freud's theoretical constructions. At the same time sophisticated methodologies are available for the elimination of bias. The elaboration of research tools may be considered an extension of Marx's or Freud's insights into the sources of error. But one cannot overlook that in the process terms like "man" or "reason" have gone out of fashion. They involve philosophical concerns which social scientists eschew as "pre-scientific." Yet these larger concerns are implicit in the very drive to be scientific.

Our awareness of human fallibility has increased as the methods to eliminate bias have become more sophisticated. By implication, these advances cast doubt upon the rational abilities of the many who cannot rid themselves of their prejudices and achieve an understanding of society. Since interests, emotions, and cultural patterns tend to obstruct the pursuit of knowledge, it requires uncommon ability to keep inquiry free of these obstructions. Inadvertently social scientists have made an invidious distinction between themselves and people at large. They have contributed their share to the decline of the Enlightenment—sometimes through the very effort to continue its traditions.

VULGARIZATION OF THE DISTRUST IN REASON

Marx and Freud have had commanding influence upon modern social thought. Both helped to destroy a naive belief in reason by insight into bias and by analyses which revealed the social and emotional foundations of culture. But neither Marx nor Freud believed that reasoning is futile or improvement by reasoning impossible.

There is a striking parallel between Freud's and Marx's belief in reason. Marx analyzed the impersonal and inadvertent operation of historic forces. Freud analyzed the organic, unconscious operation of human drives. Marx desired a society in which production could be rationally planned for the benefit of mankind. Freudian therapy aims at an individual who is able to subject his organic drives to the control of his cognitive and moral faculties.[4] Marx believed that some bourgeois intellectuals could overcome their class interest and, by comprehending the "historical movement," become leaders of the proletariat. Similarly, Freud believed that by undergoing psychoanalysis therapists could master their emotional involvements and thus become able to help patients achieve a similar emancipation.[5] Thus, the Marxian and Freudian elites depend on individual choices arising from a cathartic experience.

Neither Marx nor Freud dwelt upon *this* aspect of their belief in reason. Marx did not explain why some "bourgeois ideologists have raised themselves to the level of comprehending the historical movement." As Professor Perlman has pointed out, the workers do not ask to be guided by middle-class intellectuals; it is the latter who feel that it is their historic duty to do so.[6] Similarly, Freud did not explain why certain persons attain an exceptional level of self-knowledge and why they should see the cure of souls as their vocation. These unexplained residues suggest that the tradition of the Enlightenment requires a will to believe in reason, and that Marx and Freud were its genuine heirs. When this will to believe is absent, skepticism becomes vulgar and the distrust of reason turns into a distrust of man.

Vulgarization may be the eventual fate of all great ideas.[7] In vain did Marx state, "Je ne suis pas un Marxiste." His theory of ideology held that ideas are embedded in self-interest. He explored the relation between ideas and actions because their convergence could become an important lever of social change. In the tradition of the Enlightenment Marx was concerned with man and his perfectibility, but many of those who followed him neglect this purpose. Marx's insight becomes pedestrian when his philosophy of history is abandoned and individuals are seen primarily as products of their group affiliations. This vulgarization omits Marx's passionate concern with the paradox that the organization of production increasingly prevents the full utilization of productive capacities. It omits his attempts to relate political action to this discrepancy and thus fails to see the present as a step towards a future reorganization of society. Where this larger context of change is abandoned, our interests become restricted to what ideas reveal about man's social experience. Such inquiry may have value in certain contexts, but its humane aspirations fall short of those which motivated Marx's work.

Freud once paraphrased Marx: "Moi, je ne suis pas un Freudiste," probably because his ideas have not escaped a similar vulgarization.[8] Much of what prompts man to think and act as he does lies hidden in his unconscious. Psychoanalytic theory provides a framework for interpreting the unconscious impulses inadvertently revealed in a person's conscious life. Freud's therapeutic prescription is detachment towards the self, particularly where this is most painful. There is no guarantee of therapeutic success, but therapy aims at the individual's emancipation from his uncontrolled drives. To this end men must come to terms with their hidden feelings and ideas. Here again, great insights become pedestrian once their context is abandoned. The concept of the unconscious is vulgarized when a man's ideas are judged by the motives which prompted him to express them. Ideas are degraded to symptoms when a man's conscious experience is interpreted as a compensatory verbalization of unresolved emotional conflicts. When all knowledge is an epiphenomenon in this sense, we have no reason to expect positive results from a man's painful achievement of self-knowledge.[9]

The vulgarization of Marx and Freud is further support for the distrust of reason which has developed since the eighteenth century. The perfectibility of man is an illusion, if human fallibility is a basic obstruction to the pursuit of knowledge, rather than an impediment that can be removed. If social relations are only a breeding ground of error and prejudice, men cannot hope to profit from the use of knowledge in society. Nor can an individual benefit from education if his every action is a repercussion of emotional conflicts sustained in early childhood. These statements only extrapolate the underlying pessimism of the social sciences today.

The ramifications of this problem are explored in this volume. But at this point I shall state the resulting paradox in simplified terms. In the social sciences two contradictory views of the nature of man are asserted simultaneously. On the one hand we are told that it is possible to increase our understanding of man and society. Such knowledge promotes intellectual clarity. It can enlarge man's control of human affairs; it can reduce unhappiness and misery; it can increase the joy and fullness of life. Social scientists subscribe to Bacon's stirring denunciation of that "factitious despair, which not only disturbs the auguries of hope, but also cuts the sinews and spur of industry . . . for the miserable vain-glory of making it believed that whatever has not yet been discovered . . . can never be discovered hereafter." But on the other hand we are told that man is a creature of his drives, habits, and social roles in whose behavior reason and choice play no decisive part. As evidence for this view accumulates, it becomes difficult to see why social scientists continue a work that "disturbs the auguries of hope." If all men are mere creatures of circumstance, then social scientists are not exempt from this condition. If all men are subject only to passions, then knowledge of this fact will not prompt us to search for man's reason. Hence we will find less reason than there may be, our hopes will be diminished, and the question will be raised what passions social scientists obey in making their inquiries. A quest for social knowledge which merely expresses the impact of social and psychological determinants can give no promise of enlightenment. Why continue the work of social science, when our view of human nature becomes incompatible with the belief in the constructive possibilities of knowledge?

THE SOCIOLOGICAL PERSPECTIVE

The paradox has special relevance for sociological theory. Sociologists look to Emile Durkheim as a pioneer of their discipline. Durkheim approached the age-old problems of moral philosophy from an empirical stand-point and proposed thereby to lay the foundations of the new discipline. The sociological study of moral facts rests on two assumptions. All actions of the individual must be reduced to their elementary components. Once this is done, questions of morality and politics can be brought nearer a solution.

According to Durkheim, man is born unformed and amoral. The individual acquires the moral standards of his group and culture through interaction with peers and adults as well as through formal education. But in modern society moral standards no longer provide the individual with the guidelines he needs. Under these conditions Durkheim considers the sociological study of moral facts the only resource left to us. That study reveals the sacred character of all morality and the moral authority of the collective over the individual mind, even where secularism and individualism prevail. Durkheim expected the emergence of a new morality, once we have a well-grounded understanding of its collective nature.[10]

This approach contrasts with that of Sigmund Freud at every point. Where Durkheim assumes that other ages possessed a sound collective morality in contrast to our own, Freud asserts that the morality of all ages is impaired. Where Durkheim assumes that the individual is born with an unformed nature, Freud asserts that human nature is endowed with definite instincts demanding satisfaction (libido and the death wish). As a result a basic discontent is the mark of civilization. Aggression and license prevail if man's amoral instincts break through the cake of custom and culture. But frustration and neurosis increase if moral rules inhibit or repress man's instinctive drives. Like Durkheim, Freud asserts that the religious beliefs of the past cannot be restored to their former place in human culture. Both scholars consider science the only remedy left to us.[11] But Durkheim sees religion and science as collective representations controlling the individual mind, whereas Freud contrasts the wish fulfillment of religious beliefs with the detached and skeptical approach of science. For Freud religious beliefs and rituals are one of many resolutions to man's internal conflicts, making it possible for men to achieve some balance among their drives (Id), the demands of reality (Ego), and the demands of conscience (Superego). But such balances are precarious, internal conflicts unavoidable, and man's happiness at best a tenuous achievement.

Freud believed that with the aid of therapy the individual may achieve heightened awareness and reduce his anxiety and sense of guilt. He would have had no use for the Durkheimian view that unhappiness rises as the individual's group integration declines, or for the idea that greater integration with the aid of science is the road to happiness. Indeed, in the Freudian view Durkheim evaded the problems of morality by elevating the group at the expense of the individual. To which a Durkheimian might reply that Freud's approach downgrades society's positive contribution to the life orientation of the individual. The two approaches are in conflict because Durkheim considers the mores of society a main buttress of individual morality and mental health while Freud sees them as one source of our mental ills.

Yet both theories appeal to us, because they are scientific in intention and reductionist in procedure. Durkheim (1858-1917) and Freud (1856-1939) belong to a generation of scholars that wanted to put the study of man on a scientific basis, but in opposition to the crude materialism of the nineteenth century.[12] Through a lifetime of research Durkheim analyzed the moral framework which the group provides for the individual. Yet eventually he turned his attention to those aspects of experience which this initial assumption had left out of account. He came to insist that state intervention had rescued the individual from the despotism of the group to which he belonged, though he never relinquished his belief in the superiority of the collective conscience.[13] Durkheim considered the two views compatible because individualistic beliefs as well as state intervention are collective representations.

One can discern an analogous change of emphasis in Freud's work. In each individual there are instinctual drives which undergo a history of release or inhibition. We can understand the personality of an adult only if we trace that cumulative history back to its beginnings in early childhood. However, within this framework Freud emphasized eventually that the resulting personality structure has to be understood in its own right, a view which Anna Freud elaborated in her analysis of ego defenses.[14] Thus both writers began with a completely reductionist analysis of the individual but subsequently qualified this reductionism in the interest of balance and comprehensiveness.

Durkheim and Freud are heirs of the Enlightenment. They came to see, though perhaps not explicitly, that a completely reductionist view of human nature is incompatible with sociology and psychoanalysis as intellectual disciplines. For such disciplines cannot remain free of contradiction if steps forward in the analysis of man are steps backward from the belief in knowledge "for the benefit and use of life."

DISTRUST AND INQUIRY

As a social scientist I am concerned with the intellectual fashions implicit in this paradox. We are committed to scholarly and scientific pursuits because we want to achieve clarity and hope to discover regularities of behavior and social development. We want to go forward with efforts to ensure that the consequences of discovery will be benign, in the spirit of hope if not always of confidence. But in the last third of the twentieth century we are not sure that the constructive use of knowledge will prevail over its destructive potential. This uncertainty is long overdue. The opinion is gaining ground that human benefit may not be the only or automatic end product of advancing knowledge.

Such doubts apply to the social sciences in a special way. The uses of social knowledge will not be comparable very soon to those of knowledge in the natural sciences. Yet the social sciences have had massive consequences of their own, over and above their contributions to the management of public affairs. A conception of human impotence is the paradoxical by-product of advancing social knowledge. If physiological drives, emotional involvement, cultural legacies, and the expectations of others compel men to act as they do, they are not likely to make reasoned choices. This image of man is a popular version of theoretical ideas rather than the direct result of scholarly work, but it is still the unwitting by-product of the social sciences. As such it contributes to the antirationalist tendencies of our time, much as the vulgarization of Marx and Freud contributed to the destruction of the Enlightenment tradition.

Social scientists must try to safeguard their work against such ideological contamination. They must be able to explore the analytic utility of a theoretical perspective on the assumption that "all other things are equal." They will be aware that any theoretical perspective leaves residues which are neglected for the time being. The pluralism of theoretical perspectives provides a corrective for this neglect. And general assertions about man and society can be treated as provisional abstractions. But such conditions of the tentative and the provisional do not exist in the context of action. Here the abstractions of scholarly inquiry are general assertions about man and society which affect our lives.

The scholar and the ideologist are distinguished by a difference of commitment. In a scholarly context every theoretical scheme involves a twofold obligation. The implications of the scheme should be pursued with all the devotion of the true believer. But the scheme should be abandoned when its intellectual utility is exhausted. Evidence of this point will be proximate at best, and the productivity of theories continues to be a matter of debate. Therefore, scholars only approximate the terms of their mandate, while the academic community helps to preserve the conditions under which they can continue to do so. By contrast, in an ideological context ideas are linked to action, and commitment to a theoretical scheme is complete. Considerations which challenge the scheme may modify the details, but the theory will remain intact. For a commitment to action demands that we take a stand and make our view of the world a matter of principle, however adaptable we are in practice.

The scholarly intent of social theories is safeguarded only when the distinctions indispensable to scholarship are recognized as arbitrary and abstract, a view typically rejected by ideologists. As an analytic tool the sociological perspective emphasizes the importance of group life, and this restricts our observation of the individual. The social sciences as a whole take account of this dilemma by emphasizing the individual's integration with the group in one discipline, and choice or decision making in another. Individual scholars are in a more difficult position, however, and some of their conceptual devices have become ideological manifestos. To avoid this dilemma we should learn from Marx, Durkheim, or Freud that a reductionist analysis of the individual, carried to its extreme, comes to contradict even the rational capacities of men in science.[15]

As scholars we must guard the insights of the reductionist perspective by close attention to the role of reason and the individual in human association.[16] A lively interest in the history of ideas is a useful methodological safeguard in this respect. It provides a guide to diverse theoretical standpoints and hence a ready corrective for the distortions endemic in each. Disciplines which possess an impressive cumulation of knowledge may consider the history of the discipline a secondary interest. Disciplines which lack such cumulation do so at their peril.

IMAGES OF MAN

In the second half of the twentieth century the term "reason" does not have as widely accepted a meaning as it did for the philosophers of the eighteenth century. Indeed, empirical scholars do not concern themselves with the philosophical questions suggested by the term. Yet I do not see how we can be social scientists and not commit ourselves, tacitly at least, to some image of man and hence to a concept of reason. Knowledge may be the result of inquiry. But inquiry itself is initiated by our hopes and fears concerning the promise of knowledge for the good or ill of man. Hence we are bound to make some assumption about a discoverable order that is not man made and some estimate of what men are and what they are capable of becoming. The term *reason* refers to our estimate of the role of knowledge in human affairs. Images of man are different intellectual constructions which arise from the basic assumptions of social inquiry.[17]

For present purposes, three images of man may be distinguished. The Marxist image arises from a belief in reason as a by-product of history. The social scientist's image attributes reason to a quest for knowledge which obeys certain evolutionary regularities. Admittedly, this image is an artifact attributed to social scientists who rarely reflect on these matters. The third image also attributes reason to the quest for knowledge but emphasizes the dependence of that quest upon historical and institutional preconditions. This position is derived from a concern with the conditions of knowledge.

1. *In Marx's view the question of reason is historical.* In the long run and

in its main outlines culture is determined by the organization of production and the class struggle arising from it. Marx argues that theologies, philosophies, the sciences, and the arts reflect the all-pervasive influence of man's material life, albeit often indirectly. Not only man's conception of the world or of his place in it, but the pursuit of knowledge in all its specific developments are affected in this sense. No logic, epistemology, or scientific methodology can free our thinking from mental preoccupations which arise quite unwittingly from the way we make our living. Thus, accurate knowledge is not a simple product of correct thinking.

Marx's insights into the causes of ideology might make it appear that he was preoccupied with *un*reason as a product of history. This is misleading. His lifework was devoted to an analysis of capitalist society and this makes no sense without a belief that knowledge is attainable and can contribute to the emancipation of mankind. Marx had a conception of reason in two phases. He believed that under capitalism people cannot attain a true conception of man and society. As the contradictions of capitalism mount, so does the unreason of the many. Only a few can attain a scientific understanding of society, though it takes a Promethean conception of knowledge to attribute this attainment to the same contradictions. On the other hand, reason will prevail in the socialist society of the future. Classes and the division of labor will be abolished and with them the cause of deceit and illusion in human society. When the exploitation of man by man has ceased, then people at large will enjoy untrammeled human relations, characterized by candor and lucidity. Thus, history is the cause of reason and unreason, since the changing structure of society is the root of all theoretical and practical activity. Marx denies the distinction between theory and practice. As a result, reason in the sense of scientific knowledge and reason in the sense of honest and creative human interactions are presented as closely related aspects of one historical process.[18]

2. *The belief in reason as an attribute of the quest for knowledge is widely diffused, but not clearly identified with the work of any one scholar*. For purposes of orientation a composite view is presented here.[19]

Man's pursuit of knowledge is beset by impediments which can be removed by constant, self-critical awareness. The spirit of this Baconian position is alive today, though a great deal has been added to the early formulations, and important parts of it have been modified. Scholars constitute a community engaged in the steadfast pursuit of knowledge. On the alert against all sources of error they are dedicated to utmost candor, the accurate public disclosure of their methods and results, and the critical assessment of each other's work. The great strength of this position lies in its self-corrective mechanisms. No single evidence of error, misdirected effort, dogmatism, etc. can argue against it. Time and again scholars have shown the capacity to eradicate error, redirect their efforts, and prevent the perpetuation of dogma. There are many scholarly communities; they vary in the degree to which they apply these built-in correctives and approximate the ideal.[20]

Here is the point where the Baconian ideal is linked with an evolutionist conception of knowledge. The history of the natural sciences is marked by the cumulation of knowledge since the seventeenth century. Disciplines which lack a comparable record of cumulation take this history as their precedent. Sociology is obviously among them. If today a discipline is beset by unresolved methodological problems, dogmatic controversies, or personal polemics we are reminded that like conditions characterized disciplines like physics and chemistry at an earlier time. Redoubled efforts will overcome these defects, much as they were overcome in the more advanced disciplines. This inference assumes that the history of science provides not only an arsenal of models worthy of imitation, but also that sooner or later the pursuit of knowledge will traverse roughly similar phases of cumulative growth. The criteria of successful advance are unequivocal and the progress achieved in this way is endless.[21]

3. *My concern with the conditions of knowledge suggests a third position which differs from the evolutionist and the Marxian perspectives.* A full recognition of the achievements of the natural sciences is compatible with the observation that there are different kinds of knowing and that the term "reason" can apply to many of them. It may serve our purpose to analyze different types of knowledge and consider the growth of knowledge in that light.[22] We do not know what cannot be known and to this extent subscribe to the idea of progress. But we do not know either that knowledge, steadfastly pursued, will traverse all the phases of growth exemplified, say, by the history of physics. The pursuit of knowledge is indeed often open-ended, but its success is not assured.

One can recognize the historical conditioning of knowledge and yet deny that history is the cause of reason. The pursuit of knowledge is affected by factors extraneous to that pursuit, strictly speaking. It depends on an a priori belief in the value of knowledge. The direction of inquiry is affected by many social conditions, though these need not determine or bias its results. Intramurally, the pursuit of knowledge is affected by the social relations of a scholarly community at work, with their fashions, personality clashes, and approximations of the scholarly ideal. To deny the impact of these factors is incompatible with the evidence. To assert that they must lead to the prevalence of unreason is contradicted by the continuation of constructive scholarly inquiry. Thus, reason is the result of pragmatic approximations which may be favored or obstructed by the historical conditions of knowledge.

These considerations pose special problems for the pursuit of knowledge in the sciences, social as well as natural. The following essays explore these problems with special emphasis on the beliefs and doubts concerning the value of knowledge. In "The Age of Ideology" I consider the assumptions with which social theorists have approached the quest for social knowledge. In "Sociology and the Distrust of Reason," my Presidential address before the 1970 meeting of the American Sociological Association, I present an intellectual defense of scholarly inquiry in a period of political turmoil. And in "Science and the Purposes of Knowledge" I try to respond to the cultural dilemma of the natural sciences in a period of rising scepticism concerning the long-run balance of costs and benefits resulting from the advance of knowledge.

NOTES

1. Reinhard Bendix, "Social Science and Social Action in Historical Perspective," *Ethics*, LVI (April, 1946), 208.
2. This introductory essay draws on three earlier publications, namely, "Social Theory and Social Action in Historical Perspective," *Ethics*, LVI (1946), pp. 208-18; *Social Science and the Distrust of Reason* (Berkeley: University of California Press, 1951); and "The Image of Man in the Social Sciences," *Commentary*, II (February 1951), pp. 187-92.
3. The point is elaborated in Chapter 5 of this volume. For a comparison with parallel assumptions in the natural sciences cf. the discussion in Ernst Cassirer, *Substance and Function and Einstein's Theory of Relativity* (New York: Dover Publications, 1953), pp. 364-66, 389-93.
4. Cf. Sigmund Freud, *New Introductory Lectures to Psychoanalysis* (New York: W. Norton, 1933), pp. 111-12: "Where Id was, there shall Ego be."
5. A separate study is needed to explore the implications of recruitment. Opinion among practitioners has changed often with regard to the "proper" attitude of the analyst to the patient. Apparently, the training analysis is not sufficient as an index of competence, and indeed many conscientious analysts submit themselves to analysis at regular intervals. Since psychoanalysts had to fight for recognition, they have a vigorous professional association that watches the recruitment process in a manner encouraging to orthodoxy. As with Marxism there is much here which encourages "the self-confirming hypothesis." Cf. also Kurt Mittenzwey, "Zur Soziologie der psychoanalytischen Erkenntnis" in Max Scheler, ed., *Versuche zu einer Soziologie des Wissens* (Munich: Duncker and Humblot, 1924), pp. 365-75.
6. Selig Perlman, *Theory of the Labor Movement* (New York: Macmillan, 1928), pp. 5-9, 41-42, 68.
7. The use of this invidious term is intentional. By it I want to refer to the common practice of taking a profound idea out of the context of thought in which it had its place without considering the effect this has on the meaning of the idea itself.
8. See Theodor Reik, *Listening with the Third Ear* (New York: Farrar, Strauss and Company, 1949), p. 513.
9. It is perhaps as a reaction against this vulgarization that the neo- Freudian school has emphasized the importance of the self-system during recent years. See the writings of Karen Horney, Erich Fromm, Heinz Hartmann, Erik Erikson, David Rapoport, and others.

10. I base the preceding characterization on my reading of Emile Durkheim, *Sociology and Philosophy* (Glencoe: The Free Press, 1953), pp. 63-97 and *Education and Sociology* (Glencoe: The Free Press, 1956), pp. 113- 34. Other writings of Durkheim are also relevant, but the two volumes cited contain Durkheim's more programmatic pronouncements.
11. For Freud's statement of faith in science see his *The Future of Illusion* (Garden City: Doubleday & Co., 1957), pp. 98-102.
12. For an instructive characterization of this "generation of intellectuals" cf. Stuart Hughes, *Consciousness and Society* (New York: A.A. Knopf, 1958).
13. See Emile Durkheim, *Professional Ethics and Civic Morals* (Glencoe: The Free Press, 1958).
14. See Anna Freud, *Ego and the Mechanisms of Defense*, rev. ed. (New York: International Universities Press, 1967).
15. Cf. the further discussion of this point in Chapter 2.
16. The distinction between theories of the middle range and general social theory, introduced by Robert K. Merton, is similar in intent, by noting the difference between hypothesis construction for the explanation of specific causal relations and theory construction for cataloguing the dimensions of societies as social systems. The strategy suggested in the text is designed with reference to this second interest, as spelled out in the following essays.
17. Since aspects of this problem with special reference to Marx, Tocqueville, Durkheim, and Weber are explored in "The Age of Ideology" reprinted in this volume, I confine myself at this point to a brief characterization.
18. Cf. the argument for the unity of Marx's thought in Robert Tucker, *Philosophy and Myth in Karl Marx* (Cambridge: University Press, 1965), Chp. xi, and passim. Marx's views are analyzed in the larger historical context by Nicholas Lobkowicz, *Theory and Practice* (Notre Dame: Notre Dame University Press, 1967), passim. See also the illuminating article by Lewis Feuer, "Karl Marx and the Promethean Complex," *Encounter* XXXI (December 1968), pp. 15-32.
19. Scientists reject the view that knowledge is a by-product of history to which Marxists would rejoin that it is inseparable from the conditions of human existence. Of course no one denies that the pursuit of knowledge is affected by society and history. But there is little agreement on how this is to be assessed.
20. A workable degree of approximation can ensure the productive continuation of scientific inquiry and is thus a pragmatic criterion.
21. See the telling exposition of this evolutionist approach to the growth of knowledge by Robert K. Merton, "The Precarious Foundations of Detachment in Sociology," in Edward Tiryakian, ed., *The Phenomenon of Sociology* (New York: D. Appleton-Century, 1970), passim. By way of contrast cf. Karl Popper, *The Poverty of Historicism* (London: Routledge and Kegan Paul, 1961), passim, where the unpredictable growth of knowledge is made the basis of an anti-evolutionist and

22. The earlier distinction between natural science and *Geisteswissenschaft* or *Kulturwissenschaft* has clearly become obsolete in this respect. German philosophers like Wilhelm Dilthey or Heinrich Rickert who emphasized the difference in the objects studied by these two kinds of disciplines, worked with a nineteenth-century conception of science. In the light of more recent developments the idea of a "unity of knowledge" has been restored by showing that in the natural sciences knowledge also has an indispensable subjective component. Some implications of this development are discussed below in Chapter 5. For an outstanding exposition

of this view see Michael Polanyi, *Personal Knowledge* (London: Routledge and Kegan Paul, 1958), passim. The subjective dimension which for Dilthey distinguished the cultural from the natural sciences, is now claimed as a characteristic of the latter as well.

2

THE AGE OF IDEOLOGY, PERSISTENT AND CHANGING[1]

IDEOLOGY AS A HISTORICAL PHENOMENON

About three centuries ago, Francis Bacon observed that words become idols and obstruct our understanding. Words in common usage designate what is "most obvious to the vulgar." Men of learning, therefore, alter the common meaning of words in order to achieve accuracy through definition. Nevertheless, they often end up in dispute about words among themselves, since definitions also consist of words and these "words beget others." Bacon concluded that "it is necessary to recur to individual instances."[2] In the social sciences, his observations and advice are still valuable and nowhere more so than with regard to the phenomenon of ideology.

Modern scientists—like the earlier men of learning—tend to be impatient with words in their common usage which, as Bacon put it, "stand in the way and resist change." Like Humpty Dumpty in *Through the Looking Glass*, they want the words to mean what they say the words mean. If clarity is obtained thereby, it is well worth the artificiality that results. An artificial terminology, however, has its own risks, even aside from the problem of getting other scientists to agree to it. In order to clarify definitional problems, it is often advisable to refer to "individual instances," and such references are obscured when the terms used have been formulated deductively. In addition, it must be kept in mind that the ambiguous or multiple meanings of words, as they are ordinarily used, are an important part of the evidence. Social scientists should consider this evidence with clear heads, but should not clarify it out of existence. The scientist's legitimate quest for clarity can subtly distort such evidence by supposing that, once the confusions of a term are cleared up, the problems to which it refers have disappeared also.

"Ideology" is a case in point. The word is in such bad repute that writers on the subject are either apologetic about using it or prefer to substitute another term like "belief-system." At the same time, there are writers who continue to use it as if its meaning were well understood. Among them are those who speak of an "end of ideology," by which they mean the decline of political ideas in Western countries. This decline is attributed to the rise of totalitarianism, which diminishes controversy in the antitotalitarian camp; the

23

rise of the welfare state, which institutionalizes the drive toward equality; and the resulting consensus on a "pluralistic" society in which power is sufficiently decentralized to leave room for individual freedom.[3] These factors probably account for the sharp reduction of ideological disputes over some aspects of domestic policy, but there is also evidence of a sharp increase of ideological disputes in other respects. We may be witnessing a change in the arena of ideological conflict, rather than an "end of ideology," even in the Western context. For if intense ideological conflict has declined domestically in some respects, it has probably increased in others, in race relations, for example. While the secret diplomacy of the nineteenth century sought to obviate ideological differences, the "diplomacy" of the Cold War has accentuated them. Again, the waning imperialist doctrines of the nineteenth century have now been replaced by the anticolonial and anti-Western doctrines of the twentieth century. These considerations suggest that the phenomenon of "ideology" has an historical and structural dimension.

A Nonideological World View. If one can speak—even in a restricted sense—of an "end of ideology," then the phenomenon of ideology must also have had a beginning. Is there a common element in all the diverse uses of ideology, by reference to which one can distinguish one cultural epoch from another? Can one speak meaningfully of a "pre-ideological" epoch?[4] The answer is, I believe, that the term is not properly applicable in Western civilization prior to the seventeenth or eighteenth centuries, somewhat in the way that terms like "economy" or "society" or "intellectuals" do not fit the "premodern" period either. All these terms are applicable to the ways in which men think about their society. The shift is one of cultural pattern and intellectual perspective rather than of social or political structure. In practice, it is sometimes difficult to distinguish the earlier world view from that more characteristic of the subsequent, "ideological" epoch—especially during the long transitional period that began in the Renaissance when the earlier conviction became attenuated. But this difficulty does not invalidate the distinction. A culture based on belief in the Supreme Deity differs from one in which man and society, along with nature, are viewed as embodying an "ultimate reality" of discoverable laws. As Carl Becker has put it:

> In the thirteenth century the key words would no doubt be God, sin, grace, salvation, heaven and the like; in the nineteenth century, matter, fact, matter-of-fact, evolution, progress. . . . In the eighteenth century the words without which no enlightened person could reach a restful conclusion were nature, natural law, first cause, reason, sentiment, humanity, perfectability (these last three being necessary only for the more tender-minded, perhaps).[5]

This substitution of nature for God is especially important for an understanding of ideology as a distinctive intellectual perspective.

The ramifications of the earlier world view are observable in many different realms. In literature, for example, "reality" had been represented in a heroic and a satiric-comic mode since antiquity, a contrast that disappeared only in the realistic or naturalistic representations of nineteenth-century literature. The object of the older literature was poetic representation of reality as it should be, in terms of ideal contrasts between virtues and vices, between heroes and fools or knaves. Similarly, the facts of economic life were treated in the context of estate-management, in which instruction concerning agriculture, for example, occurred side by side with advice on the rearing of children, marital relations, the proper management of servants, and so forth. The moral approach to human relations was not at all distinguished from the economic and technical considerations of the household. Again, premodern historiography—if the word is not indeed a misnomer—consisted in what we consider a moralistic chronicling of events, an entirely unselfconscious assessment of history in terms of a moral standard accepted as given and unchanging. The basis for this moral standard was belief in a divinely ordered universe, and the common element in these premodern perspectives was therefore the effort to discover "the moral law," which had existed from the beginning of time as the central fact of a world created by God.[6] One may speak broadly of a premodern or pre-ideological epoch as long as this perspective remained intact, as long as even the most passionate controversialists did not question the existence of the moral law and the divine ordering of the universe.

In this view, history consists in the unfolding of the divine law and of man's capacity to understand it and follow its precepts. To be sure, men cannot fully understand the providential design. But through their thoughts and actions, men reveal a pattern or order of which they feel themselves to be vehicles or vessels, even though they understand it only dimly. Man's capacity to reason is not questioned, even though his development of that capacity remains forever partial, precisely as the ends of human actions are not in doubt although in an ultimate sense they remain unknown. It is when human reason and the ends of action are questioned that "ideology" comes into its own.

Sources of Error and the Ends of Action. In ordinary usage, "ideology" refers to:

1. The body of doctrine, myth, and symbols of a social movement, institution, class, or large group.
2. Such a body of doctrine, etc. with reference to some political and cultural plan, as that of fascism, along with the devices for putting it into operation.
3. *Philos*. (a.) the science of ideas. (b.) a system which derives ideas exclusively from sensation.
4. Theorizing of a visionary or unpractical nature.[7]

To relate these definitions to the present discussion, it is only necessary to distinguish their several elements. In the sociopolitical and philosophical realms, the definitions refer ideas back to a non-ideational basis, whether it be a social movement, an institution, a class, or a physiological and psychological substratum called "sensation." In this view, ideas are derived from some extra-ideational source, however the source or the process of derivation may be conceived. I shall use the term *reductionism* to characterize this approach. Second, the definitions specify that doctrine, myth, symbol, or theory is oriented to the future, in the sense that it embodies a political or cultural plan of action. In this sense, ideology is a type of goal-orientation, a special aspect of the teleology that is characteristic of much human action. I shall speak of *goal-orientation* or *the ends of action* when I refer to this attribute. The last definition refers to theorizing as visionary or impractical, thus raising a question about *the uses of theories*. The accent is polemical, setting up an invidious contrast between a visionary and a realistic approach, the latter term referring presumably to theories and truths (or statements of fact) that are practical or concrete. Here "ideology" is used in its pejorative sense, about which we shall say more presently.

The distinction between the "ends of action" and the "uses of theories and truths" requires comment. The action primarily considered here is the pursuit of knowledge, so that in the present context the "ends of knowledge" are distinguished from the "uses of knowledge." The distinction is necessary even though the relationship between the ends and uses of knowledge is sometimes close. But for the men of knowledge, the pursuit of truth is often a large and ill defined good, which is never fully realized by the uses of truths even in the ideal case, since all knowledge is proximate. Furthermore the "uses of theories and truths" are often in the hands of men of affairs, and even where theories and truths are abused from the point of view of the scientist as a citizen, such abuse does not invalidate the value of knowledge in his eyes, since, under favorable conditions and in the hands of wise men, the same knowledge can be put to constructive use as well. It is advisable, therefore, to refer to the *ends* and *uses* of knowledge as separate, though related, aspects of the action-involvement of ideas.

These three aspects together—the reductionist tendency in the analysis of ideas; plans of action for man and society, including the pursuit of knowledge for the sake of human progress; and the invidious contrast between realism and illusion—are the constituent elements of ideology as I shall use the term.

Historically, the Age of Ideology came into its own when critical questions were raised concerning man's ability to reason and to define and realize the ends of his actions. Reductionism in the analysis of ideas and concern with the ends of knowledge are important elements in Francis Bacon's programmatic statements. Critical questions about the use of theories, especially in society, arose much later toward the end of the eighteenth and the beginning of the nineteenth century.

Bacon's declaration of independence from the scholastic learning of an earlier age has the stirring power of all acts of emancipation. His manifesto seeks to guard scientific inquiry against the errors that typically obstruct human understanding. In his "theory of idols," analysis of the sources of error becomes an important part of the quest for knowledge. We must guard against the influence of interests and wishful thinking that is found in all men (idols of the tribe); against the individual's character and experience, which prompt him to dwell on some ideas with peculiar satisfaction (idols of the cave); against the "ill and unfit choice of words" (idols of the market-place); and against the received systems of philosophy (idols of the theater). In thus classifying recurrent sources of error, Bacon intends only to safeguard the pursuit of truth, and he approaches these critical questions in a spirit of optimism.

> Human knowledge and human power meet in one; for where the cause is not known the effect cannot be produced. Nature to be commanded must be obeyed; and that which in contemplation is as the cause is in operation as the rule.

Accordingly, Bacon refers to the *kingdom of man*.[8] Still basing his thought on the traditional world view, Bacon believes in man's capacity to discover the divine order. He wishes only to emancipate the men of this age from a world view which considers all wisdom already contained in the divine word. He intends "the investigation of truth in nature" as a new and better means of discovering the divine wisdom.

But when he considers the ends of human action and admonishes men to seek knowledge "for the benefit and use of life," Bacon is totally at variance with the traditional view. He reminds men to seek knowledge for charity rather than for such inferior ends as profit, fame or power,[9] but this does not alter the secular trend of his thought. Bacon is aware that the pursuit of knowledge must be safeguarded against the apprehension that it will undermine the authority of religion and the state. He claims that investigations of nature are "the surest medicine against superstition, and the most approved nourishment of faith," rather than a danger to religion as some people fear. And he argues against those who fear for the power of the state, declaring that investigations of nature can only enhance that power, while "matters of state" are not a proper subject for science—"these things resting on authority, consent, fame, and opinion, not on demonstration."[10] The very act of emancipation thus raises questions about human reason and the ends of human knowledge. Rather than relying on faith in man's God-given capacity to discover the truth, it becomes necessary to protect this human capacity by rationally devised safeguards against error. And instead of faith in a providential design, which is revealed through human action whether men know it or not, it becomes necessary to make the ends of the pursuit of knowledge (and more generally, of all actions) a conscious object that must be protected against base motives, misinterpretations and unintended consequences.

No scientific inquiry can dispense with the two concerns Bacon formulated in his "Novum Organum." The possible sources of error must be understood and guarded against; this concern is a part of the scientific enterprise. In addition, by the act of engaging in research or inquiry, scientists commit themselves to a line of action that cannot be clearly separated from its social context. The "ends of knowledge" that they pursue are a matter of belief, not of proof. We saw that Bacon raises the hopes of men for the new science but also tries to anticipate and offset the apprehensions of those who fear it. For scientific work depends upon men of affairs and the general public, and Bacon discerns some consequences of this dependence.

> It does not rest with the same persons to cultivate sciences and to reward them. The growth of them comes from great wits; the prizes and rewards of them are in the hands of the people, or of great persons, who are but in very few cases even moderately learned. Moreover, this kind of progress is not only unrewarded with prizes and substantial benefits; it has not even the advantage of popular applause. For it is a greater matter than the generality of men can take in, and is apt to be overwhelmed and extinguished by the gales of popular opinions.[11]

To be successful, the scientific enterprise requires special assistance from its sponsors and the public. Yet, neither the errors to which inquiry is subject nor its dependence upon public support has proved an ultimate bar to a properly conducted inquiry. On the contrary, critical awareness of the scientists' fallibility has helped to promote scientific knowledge, and the public's conditional support has not impeded its gradual advance.

At the threshold of the modern world, the task was to emancipate men from unthinking acceptance of received opinion, stimulate the critical scrutiny of ideas, and encourage the investigation of nature in the hope of benefiting mankind. Bacon initiated an era in which reason replaced faith among the mental and psychological conditions of inquiry, while the ends of that inquiry were defined in terms of "human utility and power," rather than the greater glory of God. In the natural sciences, the Baconian program proved extraordinarily successful. As methods of research were developed and its findings proved reliable, the utility of these findings became an article of secular faith that was questioned less with each advance in scientific knowledge. The appeal of this faith quickly dispelled the remaining commitments of scientists to the earlier world view, as well as Bacon's rather defensive declaration that "matters of state" are outside the province of scientific inquiry.[12]

The new intellectual perspective came to be applied to man and society. There also reason replaced faith, as the mental and psychological conditions of inquiry were subjected to critical scrutiny. Yet the result was a paradox. The search for the sources of error proceeded apace as an indispensable means for the advancement of social knowledge. But the ends of inquiry remained uncertain, resting as they do on the borrowed belief, rather than the proven fact, that social knowledge serves "human utility and power." Accordingly, "ideology" came to be used in a pejorative sense, when the scientific approach was applied to man and society. Here also knowledge can be advanced only if the sources of error are known and guarded against. But such knowledge of error has been used as a means of discrediting an opponent, rather than as a methodological safeguard. Here also the advance of knowledge depends on public support. But in the absence of manifest utility that support becomes precarious and provides ready arguments for those who would discredit an opponent's views as "visionary and unpractical."

These questions came to the fore as confidence in progress was extended to those "matters of state" that Bacon had cautiously excluded from his program. I need not here review these extensions in psychology, education, political theory, and philosophy except to note that in philosophy the optimistic search for truth eventually found expression in a science of ideas entitled "ideology."[13] In his *Eléments d'idéologie* (1801, 1803, 1805) Destutt de Tracy gave a systematic exposition of this science intended for use in the schools. He stated in his preface that "ideology is a part of zoology," since human intelligence is a phenomenon of animal life and must be analyzed accordingly.[14] Tracy felt, as did his ideologue colleagues, that such a reductionist analysis of ideas—"studies on the formation of our ideas" as he called it—had arrived at the truth and no longer left room for doubt or perplexity.[15] Yet this perspective was directly associated with the republicanism and atheism of t! e ideologues. During Napoleon's ascendance to supreme power, a conflict developed between the Emperor and these philosophers, whose association he had cultivated a short time before. The pejorative meaning of "ideology" originated in Napoleon's repeated denunciations of the men who had coined this term to identify a philosophical school.[16] With Napoleon's phrases like "obscure metaphysic" and "idealistic trash" to characterize the work of *les idéologues*, we have the third constituent element of "ideology," one that questions the truth, the utility, and the political repercussions of ideas about man and society.[17]

The implications of this pejorative meaning are illuminated in the work of Edmund Burke, although he wrote before Tracy had coined the term and Napoleon had used it in polemic fashion. Burke opposes the reductionist analysis of ideas with his affirmation of sentiment and prejudice as indispensable bases of the community.

   . . . In this enlightened age I am bold enough to confess that we are generally men of untaught feeling; that instead of casting away all our old prejudices, we cherish them to a very considerable extent, and, to take more shame to ourselves, we cherish them because they are prejudices. . . . We are afraid to put men to live and trade each on his own private stock of reason; because we suspect that this stock in each man is small, and that the individuals would do better to avail themselves of the general bank and capital of nations and of ages. Many of our men of speculation, instead of exploding general prejudices, employ their sagacity to discover the latent wisdom which prevails in them. . . . Because prejudice, with its reason, has a motive to give action to that reason, and an affection which will give it permanence. Prejudice is of ready application in the emergency; it previously engages the mind in a steady course of wisdom and virtue, and does not leave the man hesitating in the moment of decision, sceptical, puzzled and unresolved. Prejudice renders a man's virtue his habit; and not a series of unconnected acts. Through just prejudice, his duty becomes a part of his nature.[18]

This famous passage states the case for conservatism, but it is cited here because it illuminates the pejorative meaning of "ideology."

Burke sets out to shock his readers by using "prejudice" as a word of praise. In the eighteenth century, the philosophers of the French Enlightenment sought to discredit and unmask prevailing opinions of church and state, by theoretical reduction of all ideas to the basic "sensations" out of which they have been formed.[19] Accordingly, when Burke praises "prejudice," he seeks to put a stop to that inquiry into the "sources of error" that the Enlightenment was extending from the natural sciences to philosophy, political theory, and education. At the same time, he provides an impressive analysis of the hiatus between theory and action. Theory means detachment, while practical things are accomplished by commitment; theory deals with principles, while action involves compromises and modifications in detail; theory enlarges the horizon and endangers action by revealing its contingencies, while action is limited in its aims; theory makes provisional statements, while actions are irreversible; theory involves no presumption in favor of precedent, while action is limited by past behavior; and where theory rejects errors, prejudices, or superstitions, the statesman puts them to use.[20]

Burke thus denounces all inquiries into the conditioning of knowledge as presumptuous and unnatural, a fatal disruption of the "untaught feelings" and inherited sentiments that alone provide a basis of morality. Similarly, he denounces all theories in politics because they will jeopardize the "art of the possible." Such theories project visionary plans, state impractical principles, and undermine the resolution to act in the face of contingencies. As a conservative who seeks to preserve the older world view, Burke thus gives a pejorative meaning to critical inquiries into the "formation of our ideas" as well as to abstract political theories that define the ends of social action for the nation as a whole. The lot of men can be improved only gradually and then only if sentiments and the ends of action remain undisturbed by rational inquiry—though in making this argument he advances a theory of his own based on a concept of reason as an outgrowth of experience and tradition. In Burke's view, the position of the philosophers of the Enlightenment has wholly pernicious repercussions, and a position that gives rise to such consequences must be false. In this type of argument the truth of an idea is confused with its social and political effects so that the test of truth and evaluation of the effects become interchangeable. Burke's position is, therefore, an early example of the ideologizing tendencies, against which he fought vigorously but which he helped to initiate nevertheless. By the time he wrote, the old world view had lost its hold over the minds of men; it had become difficult to look upon man's reason and the ends of his action as an ultimately unknowable part of the providential design. Even Burke, who sought to uphold this view, was forced to do so with arguments that were at variance with its basic assumptions.[21]

IDEOLOGICAL DIMENSIONS OF SOCIAL THEORY

In the social sciences, men have not accepted the value of knowledge to nearly the same extent as in the natural sciences. It can be said that men should explore such knowledge and its possible benefits to the limit, since they never know enough to determine that limit. There was resistance to the advance of knowledge in the natural sciences as well, and in the absence of constructive alternatives the problems before us must be solved by all available avenues of detached inquiry. But these considerations, valid as they may be, do not enable us to ignore the ideological dimensions of social theory.

It is difficult to keep studies of man and society distinct from considerations of purpose and utility. Scholars who inquire into the sources of error in order to enhance social knowledge must do so in the face of considerable uncertainty. They are not in the position of natural scientists who could point to increasing utility as traditional faith declined. Accordingly, in the social sciences, every new insight into human fallibility raises questions about the role of reason in human affairs. Here also inquiry into the sources of error is indispensable. But this inquiry tends to be linked with efforts to allay uncertainty, to state the case for the value of knowledge, and to ensure that it will serve human progress.

In the twentieth century, terms like "prudence" and "reason" no longer possess a widely accepted meaning. The first term refers to the "reason of Everyman," which Hobbes defines as "learning begot by experience which equal time bestows equally on all men." Related to this concept is "cumulative experience" in the sense in which Burke saw institutions embody the judgments exercised by successive generations of men of affairs. Hobbes and Burke refer to "prudence" as the word is used here. Such prudence is distinguished from reason acquired by specialized experience, which Coke defined with reference to the common law as "an artificial reason acquired by much study." The paradox faced by the social sciences can be summed up in the statement that our general estimate of prudence has declined, while our estimate of reason acquired by "much study" has increased greatly.

Distrust of Prudence and Belief in Science. The history of social thought since the Enlightenment is characterized by exaggerated confidence, inspired by progress in the natural sciences. If it is possible to increase our knowledge of nature, then it must be possible to increase our knowledge of man and society. Such knowledge has value as a means of enhancing intellectual clarity and of enlarging man's control of human affairs.[22] Properly employed, knowledge of society can improve the human condition. In this way, many social scientists might subscribe to Bacon's stirring declarations about the "kingdom of man," were it not for their reticence in propounding a borrowed belief for which supporting evidence in their own fields is equivocal.[23] More common perhaps is the approach that emphasizes scientific method, contrasts that method with mere opinion, and urges that the ends and uses of knowledge be considered once our knowledge is sufficiently advanced and secure.[24]

On the other hand, social thought since the Enlightenment has developed an image of man as a creature in whose behavior prudence and choice play no decisive part. In this view the investigation of social life would itself be a product of social and psychological conditioning. But knowledge conceived solely as a product of social life can hold no promise for the improvement of the human condition. The paradox is an ancient one.[25] If we assume that all men are products of their passions, then we shall not search for prudence and shall consider what looks like prudence a mere by-product of passion. Our hopes will be diminished. The question becomes: What passions do we obey in making these inquiries? Unlike their fellows in other disciplines, social scientists are subject to the restriction that their general assertions about man and society affect society directly and apply significantly to themselves as well.

All social inquiry leads to a heightened awareness that easily turns into skepticism, or into the anti-intellectualism of intuition or of technical empiricism. But awareness is also an intellectual tool. Properly handled, it may protect social research against unexamined influences to which social scientists are subject as members of their societies. To this end, it is useful to explore in some depth the ideological implications arising from our inquiries into the sources of error, from our conception of the ends of knowledge, and from our uses of theories.

Since the time of Bacon, inquiry into the sources of error has greatly advanced our knowledge of men and in the process has greatly lowered our estimate of the effect of prudence on human affairs. To appreciate this development, it is necessary to recall the eighteenth-century belief in progress through science. In the view of philosophers like Condillac, Cabanis, Tracy, Helv—etius, and Holbach, the good society is the product of man's quest for knowledge. The powers of the altar and the throne stand in the way of this achievement. Representatives of these powers believe they must blind the people and exploit their prejudices in order to keep them subject. To this end, religious fanatics and political rulers interfere with freedom of thought. In the interest of humanity they must be opposed by a deliberate unmasking of prevailing prejudices and by scientific inquiry into the principles of morality which are innate in man. To the philosophers of the Enlightenment, the discoverable order of society consists of these principles, which will be revealed by knowledge of ideas and natural law. In the battle for enlightenment this knowledge is a great power feared by those who stand for the prejudices that obscure the moral order. In this view, prejudices are no longer obstructions of the mind, as they were for Bacon, but weapons with which the leaders of established institutions defend the status quo. Vices and crimes, says Helvétius, are errors of judgment closely akin to prejudices. There must be freedom of thought to combat them; such freedom encourages discussions and disputes, which bear fruit in the advance of truth. And it is God's will that truth results from inquiry.[26]

The truths to be discovered are laws of the human mind like those that Tracy and Cabanis sought through their inquiries into the "formation of our ideas." The ideologues left the use of these discoveries rather vague, content in the belief that their philosophical ideas would be used in the schools once the needed educational reforms had been instituted. Their work contributed to the transition from philosophy to the modern sciences of man and society and became widely influential through the writings of Henri de Saint-Simon (1760-1825). Following the ideologues, Saint-Simon also makes physiology the basic scientific discipline because it involves theories based on observations that can be verified in contrast to the conjectural sciences.[27] This idea of Saint-Simon actually adds little substance to earlier speculations. But—like Bacon before him—he raises men's hopes in the promise of the new science.

> Politics will become a positive science. When those who cultivate this important branch of human knowledge will have learned physiology during the course of their education, they will no longer consider the problems which they have to solve as anything but questions of hygiene.[28]

The implications of this idea are far-reaching, although its generic interest is negligible. Bacon had proposed a reductionist analysis (his theory of "idols") as a safeguard against error; now physiology rather than logic is the discipline appropriate for analysis of the human mind. Since men are animals, their physical attributes provide the clues for a scientific understanding of human qualities. Saint-Simon believes that, in the future, human affairs will be as easily manageable as personal cleanliness. Rarely perhaps has so low an estimate of man been linked with so high an estimate of science and of what scientists can accomplish.

A century and a half after Saint-Simon's death our knowledge of man has increased greatly, but our hopes for the use of knowledge have diminished. While Saint-Simon remains noteworthy as an initiator, Freud's work is relevant here as the most far-reaching development of the reductionist tradition. Where the Enlightenment philosophers sought the laws of the human mind in "sensation," Marx in the organization of production, and Nietzsche in the struggle for power, Freud sought them in man's biological make-up. All human behavior leads to pleasure or pain. Man's subjective efforts to increase the first and diminish the second are primarily reflections of a character that is formed through prior experience of drive-satisfactions (or frustrations) in the growing child's relations with his parents. Character is the product of what has happened to each individual's organic drives of sex and aggression. The satisfaction or frustration of these drives is the medium through which the individual forms his patterned responses, sees himself, and relates to his significant others. All cultural activities and values are secondary compared with these primary sources of gratification and frustration.

Freud is an heir to the eighteenth-century tradition. Based on a theory of personality-formation, his therapy aims at the improvement of the individual. Patients may find a way out of their emotional difficulties when they have opportunities to reassess especially the repressed experiences of early childhood. But common prudence is of minor importance in avoiding such difficulties and of no importance in finding solutions for them, since prudence is at a discount when a person is emotionally involved. Although Freud believes men capable of reassessing their personal histories and—to a degree—reorganizing their lives on that basis, this therapeutic use of cognitive and moral faculties depends on a cathartic experience. And catharsis depends upon a therapeutic transaction in which the patient becomes dependent upon his analyst, while the latter—with a detachment achieved through training and control analysis—seeks to help the patient master himself.

Freud does not offer psychoanalytic interpretations of the quest for psychoanalytic knowledge; he rests his case upon belief in progress through science. In his arguments against defenders of traditional religion, Freud puts the case of scientific inquiry in the following terms:

1. It is difficult indeed to avoid illusions, and perhaps the hopes men have for science are illusions also. But men suffer no penalties for not sharing the belief in science—in contrast to religion—and all scientific statements, though uncertain, are capable of correction.

2. Defenders of religion and science may agree that the human intellect is weak in comparison with human instincts. But the voice of the intellect, though soft, does not rest until it has gained a hearing. One may be optimistic about the future of mankind, for by its gradual development and despite endless rebuffs the intellect prevails. If, as a defender of religion,

> you confine yourself to the belief in a higher spiritual being, whose qualities are indefinable and whose intentions cannot be discerned, then you are proof against the interference of science, but then you will also relinquish the interest of men.

In the name of this Baconian ideal, Freud states his belief that "in the long run nothing can withstand reason and experience."[29]

3. The illusions of religions are basically infantile; once they are discredited, believers must despair of culture and of the future of mankind. The champions of science are free of this bondage. True, secular education probably cannot alter man's psychological nature. But if we acknowledge this fact with resignation, we do not thereby lose interest in life.

> We believe that it is possible for scientific work to discover something about the reality of the world through which we can increase our power and according to which we can regulate our life. . . . Science has shown us by numerous and significant successes that it is no illusion.[30]

Those who are skeptical should remember that science is still young; in judging its results we tend to use a foreshortened time perspective. The frequency with which previously established scientific statements are replaced by closer approximations to the truth is a strong argument for the scientific procedure. "It would be an illusion to suppose that we could get anywhere else what [science] cannot give us."[31] Compared with the confidence of Saint-Simon, Freud's advocacy of science is skeptical and subdued. For him, the solution of human problems is highly complex, and no advance of science will reduce the management of affairs to a question of hygiene.[32]

Saint-Simon and Freud's inquiries into the "foundation of our ideas" are linked with their concepts of the ends of knowledge. But neither writer is directly concerned with the steps taken to guard knowledge against error, or with the purpose and use of knowledge which these steps imply. These ideological implications of social theory are a central theme in the writings of Karl Marx, Alexis de Tocqueville, Emile Durkheim, and Max Weber. Each of these theorists analyzes the social conditioning of knowledge, but each also believes in progress through knowledge and thus faces the task of protecting that belief against the corrosive effects of his own insights.

THE QUEST FOR OBJECTIVITY AND THE USES OF IDEAS

Karl Marx (1818-1883). The philosophers of the Enlightenment believed that a just social order can be established through human reason, as long as discussion is free and once education is reorganized on the basis of the "science of ideas." To these men, prejudice has its source in vested interests, while the correct understanding of society results simply from unprejudiced inquiry. This easy optimism was abandoned by Marx.

He conceives of man's intellectual history as a reflection of class struggles. Ideas about society are weapons wielded by contending social classes to attack their enemies and defend their friends. Classes are formed on the basis of the organization of production, which engenders common interests and ideas among individuals who make their living in similar life-situations as capitalists, shop-keepers, craftsmen, wage-earners or others. Each individual lives under circumstances not of his own choosing and shares with others life-experiences arising from the organization of production. It is from this source that awareness of social relations and ideas about society lead to the formation of classes which affect all other aspects of consciousness as well. Accordingly, for Marx, all aspects of cultural life reflect the class struggle. Men of ideas differ among themselves only in the degree to which they are subject to the compulsions of class struggle and the manner in which they transform these compulsions intellectually. In Marx's view, knowledge of man and society depends upon and changes with the class structure. This dependence must be analyzed anew in each case. Inquiry into the "foundations of our ideas" (reductionism) is no longer a means to knowledge; it has become a type of knowledge in its own right.

Marx distinguishes social structures like feudalism, capitalism, and socialism, not only in terms of their respective class structures, but also in terms of the religious beliefs and the knowledge of social reality that "correspond" to these structures. In the feudal period, men are easily swayed by the fantastic images of mythology and religion. Because technology is backward, the masses of the people suffer great deprivations and unwittingly exchange spiritual for material satisfactions. In feudal society, social relations are marked by a pervasive personal dependence, of which the members of that society are fully aware, because it is not "disguised under the shape of social relations between products of labor."[33]

This disguise of social relations arises because capitalist society is

> based upon the production of commodities, in which the producers in general enter into social relations with one another by treating their products as commodities and values, whereby they reduce their individual private labor to the standard of homogeneous human labor—for such a society, Christianity with its

cultus of abstract man, more especially in its bourgeois developments, Protestantism, Deism, etc., is the most fitting form of religion.[34]

Religion prevents men from actively changing the world in which they live. But under feudalism technology is backward and the promise of change small, while under capitalism the real satisfaction of material needs is possible. On the basis of modern technology, capitalism has created an unprecedented productive potential, but its exploitative system of production has also created unprecedented misery because—for the first time in history—misery has become unnecessary. Religion prevents men from seeing that their misery can be abolished; it is an opiate of the people in that sense. In addition, everything is reduced to the status of a commodity that is judged in terms of its price rather than its intrinsic value. The relations between one man and another are obscured, if their transaction appears to them in terms of its price. Thus the "personal" dependence of the worker on his employer appears to both in terms of the wage agreed upon. All human values become quantified and homogeneous, when social relations are mediated by the mechanism of the market. Christianity, however, obscures and perpetuates this alienation.

Under socialism, these conditions are radically altered. Marx's critique of capitalism becomes clearer by means of this contrast. He never speaks in detail about the socialist society of the future, but he claims that religion will disappear along with the reasons for its previous importance—namely, the alienation of men from the product of their labor and from their fellow men.

> Let us now picture to ourselves . . . a community of free individuals, carrying on their work with the means of production in common, in which the labor-power of all the individuals is consciously applied as the combined labor-power of the community. All the characteristics of Robinson [Crusoe's] labor are here repeated, but with this difference, that they are social, instead of individual. Everything produced by him was exclusively the result of his own personal labor, and therefore simply an object of use for himself. The total production of our community is a social product. One portion serves as fresh means of production and remains social. But another portion is consumed by the members as means of subsistence. A distribution of this portion among them is consequently necessary.

While the mode of this distribution will vary with the productive organization and the historical development of the producers,

> The social relations of the individual producers, with regard both to their labor and to its products, are in this case perfectly simple and intelligible, and that with regard not only to production but also to distribution. . . .[35]

Since alienation arises from social relations mediated by trading on a market, alienation will be abolished once men re-establish direct, unmediated relationships with their work and their fellows through control over the processes of production and distribution. Under modern conditions, such control must be collective. Once such collective control is established, the conditions that favored religious ideas and appeals will disappear.

> The religious reflex of the real world can, in any case, only then finally vanish, when the practical relations of everyday life offer to man none but perfectly intelligible and reasonable relations with regard to his fellow men and to nature.

> The life-process of society, which is based on the process of material production, does not strip off its mystical veil until it is treated as production by freely associated men, and is consciously regulated by them in accordance with a settled plan.[36]

Once it is so treated, the need for illusions has disappeared, because relations among men and between men and nature have become "perfectly simple and intelligible."

Freedom from illusion about the relations of men in society is seen as a by-product of the classless society of the future. For Marx, knowledge of man and society remains ideological, an example of what he calls "false consciousness," as long as it is conditioned by the class struggle. No man is exempt from this conditioning by the class struggle. In this context, Marx posits a nexus between existing social relations and the ordinary man's ability to comprehend them. His repeated references to the simplicity and intelligibility of social relations suggest that these relations are more intelligible in some social structures than in others. "Intelligibility" refers to the understanding of ordinary men. A kind of prudence uncontaminated by ideology will become possible once class struggles have ceased and men make full use of their rational and creative faculties.

But Marx also contrasts his own scientific analysis with the ideological interpretations of classical economists, utopian socialists, and others.[37] He likes to compare his approach with that characteristic of the physical and biological sciences.[38] In this way, scientific knowledge of society—implicitly distinguished from the ordinary man's understanding of social relations—appears possible under capitalism. Ideological distortion is not therefore an inevitable by-product of a society rent by class conflict. Despite his distrust of prudence and reason, Marx clings to the eighteenth-century belief that scientific knowledge of society is attainable and will play an important historical role.

> In times when the class struggle nears the decisive hour, the process of dissolution going on within the ruling class—in fact, within the whole range of an old society—assumes such a violent, glaring character that a small section of the ruling class cuts itself adrift and joins the revolutionary class, the class that

holds the future in its hands. Just as, therefore, at an earlier period, a section of the nobility went over to the bourgeoisie, so now a portion of the bourgeoisie goes over to the proletariat, and in particular, a portion of the *bourgeois ideologists, who have raised themselves to the level of comprehending theoretically the historical movements as a whole.*[39]

In this view, the workers will provide the political momentum for the great historical change to come. They will cause a revolutionary upheaval against the material and psychological inhumanities to which they have been subjected, but they do not possess the intellectual tools to direct the upheaval. This direction will be provided by bourgeois ideologists who respond to the dissolution of their own class, the miseries of the proletariat, and the historical opportunities arising from the intensified class struggle and the underutilization of man's productive potential.

Accordingly, Marx clings to both horns of the ideological dilemma. He insists on the reductionist analysis of ideas as emanations of the class struggle. Illusion will vanish from our understanding of society only when freely associated men regulate society in accordance with a settled plan.[40] But social knowledge would have no constructive role now, if truth will be attained only in the society of the future. Marx does not accept this implication, which would cut the ground from under his own claim as a scientist and political leader. His work is a life-long insistence upon man's capacity to forge the intellectual instruments for the reorganization of society. Accordingly, he shifts back and forth between reductionism and the belief in the constructive role of ideas. Under capitalism the working class provides the lever for the reorganization of society (reductionist analysis), but the labor movement cannot be successful unless guided by the results of scientific inquiry (belief in reason). In responding to the contradictions of capitalist society (reductionist analysis), bourgeois ideologists "raise themselves" to an understanding of the historical movement (belief in reason).

Marx believes in the historically constructive role of human intelligence but his inquiries undermine that belief. By treating all knowledge as a distorting reflex of the real world, he casts doubt upon the ends and uses of knowledge and of all human activities. Since, under capitalism, men pervert rather than enhance the "benefit of life," all positive use of intelligence is precarious. Subsequent history and the vulgarizations of his followers have obscured the fundamental tragedy of Marx as a man of knowledge. He wants to know—accurately and dispassionately—but he also wants to make sure that the knowledge gained will play a constructive role in human affairs. Yet his theory casts doubt upon the belief in reason to which his life's work is dedicated. Perhaps these contradictions explain the passion of Marx, the wild polemics against his opponents, the Promethean hope, and the undercurrent of despair. Consideration of a near contemporary, Alexis de Tocqueville, will reveal the work of a man who grappled with similar problems but did not conceal from himself the tragedy of a man of knowledge who seeks to enhance the role of prudence in human affairs.

Alexis de Tocqueville (1805-1859). Tocqueville is a seeker after truth, he believes in reason, and he wants to enhance the "benefit and use of life"—quite as much as Marx. But while Marx is an heir of the Enlightenment, Tocqueville is an heir of its critics. Where Marx carries forward the eighteenth-century belief in science and develops particularly the "science of ideas," Tocqueville makes no reference to the scientific approach and, if anything, opposes the reductionist analysis of ideas, as Burke had done. Where Marx follows the model of the natural sciences and insists upon the objectivity of his materialistic approach despite the manifest passion of his writings, Tocqueville patterns himself after writers like Montesquieu and avows his passionate concern with moral problems.

Yet Tocqueville knows that the pursuit of knowledge must be guarded against the passions of partisanship aroused in the wake of the French Revolution. It is characteristic of the man that his discussions of method and his claims to objectivity appear not in his published writings but in his correspondence with friends. Tocqueville does not claim to be a scientist and does not publicize his procedures and erudition so that his objectivity may be checked by others, as in the natural sciences. Yet inquiry free of bias is indispensable to sound judgment, and Tocqueville states the reasons why he believes himself to be dispassionate.

> They ascribe to me alternately aristocratic and democratic prejudices. If I had been born in another period, or in another country, I might have had either the one or the other. But my birth, as it happened, made it easy for me to guard against both. I came into the world at the end of a long revolution, which after destroying ancient institutions, had created none that could last. When I entered life, aristocracy was dead and democracy as yet unborn. My instinct, therefore, could not lead me blindly either to the one or to the other. I lived in a country which for forty years had tried everything and settled nothing. I was on my guard, therefore, against political illusions. Myself belonging to the ancient aristocracy of my country, I had no natural hatred or jealousy of the aristocracy; nor could I have any natural affection for it, since that aristocracy had ceased to exist, and one can be strongly attached only to the living. I was near enough to know it thoroughly, and far enough to judge dispassionately. I may say as much for the democratic element. It had done me, as an individual, neither good nor harm. I had no personal motive, apart from my public convictions, to love or hate it. Balanced between the past and the future, with no natural instinctive attraction towards either, I could without an effort look quietly on each side of the question.[41]

Accidents of birth and historical circumstance are here advanced as the basis of objectivity. In reductionist analysis, the social conditioning of knowledge is ordinarily perceived as a source of error and bias, but Tocqueville attributes to that conditioning his own freedom from bias.[42] He readily acknowledges that other circumstances might have led him to adopt the aristocratic or democratic prejudices falsely attributed to him. That it did not happen is the result of attributes entirely unique to his personal situation. True to his aristocratic heritage, Tocqueville guards against bias in a manner that is incompatible with the equalitarian tenets of science. For in science, safeguards against error and bias are accepted only if they are open to public inspection and therefore in principle accessible to everyone who adopts the required procedures.

But if Tocqueville is aristocratic in his claim to objectivity, he also makes good his contention that he is dispassionate. In his view, the development of human societies toward greater equality is an established fact, decreed by providence. Unlike his fellow aristocrats, he dos not deny what he considers inevitable, quarrel with it or resist it to the last. He seeks to understand the conditions of equality in all their implications, as in his great work *Democracy in America*. He concludes, it is true, that under these conditions a government "cannot be maintained without certain conditions of intelligence, private morality, and of religious belief." But he believes that these conditions can be attained, since "after all it may be God's will to spread a moderate amount of happiness over all men, instead of heaping a large sum upon a few by allowing only a small minority to approach perfection."[43] Tocqueville thus accepts the goals of democracy but attempts to "diminish the ardor of the Republican party" by showing that democracy is not an easily realized dream and—while conferring benefits on the people—is not likely to develop the "noblest powers of the human mind." At the same time, he attempts to "abate the claims of the aristocrats" by showing that democracy is not synonymous with destruction and anarchy but compatible with order, liberty, and religion. Democracy of this kind, rather than an unspeakable tyranny, can be achieved if the aristocratic opponents will not resist what they lack the power to prevent. By making the "impulse in one quarter and resistance in the other . . . less violent" Tocqueville seeks to ensure a peaceable development of society.[44]

This balance in the political sphere is matched by Tocqueville's capacity for self-scrutiny, which helps him preserve the objectivity of his pursuit of knowledge. Aristocratic background and a realistic assessment of men lead to a somber view indeed. "I love mankind in general, but I constantly meet with individuals whose baseness revolts me."[45] Or, "If to console you for having been born, you must meet with men whose most secret motives are always actuated by fine and elevated feelings, you need not wait, you may go and drown yourself immediately."[46] But Tocqueville also reminds his friends and himself that in fact such high motives are predominant in a few men and that they occur even in a large majority of men from time to time. Consequently, one "need not make such faces at the human race." [47] Nor is it only a matter of general attitude. One should be aware that our estimate of men has unwitting effects upon human affairs and upon ourselves.

> Some persons try to be of use to men while they despise them, and others because they love them. In the services rendered by the first there is always something incomplete, rough, and contemptuous that inspires neither confidence nor gratitude. I should like to belong to the second class, but often I cannot. . . . I struggle daily against a universal contempt for my fellow-creatures. I sometimes succeed, at my own expense, by a minute uncompromising investigation into the motives of my own conduct. [48]

When Tocqueville tries to judge himself as if he were an indifferent spectator or opponent, he is more inclined to "drop a little in my own esteem" than to place too low an estimate on other men. And elsewhere he declares that "man with his vices, his weaknesses, and his virtues, strange combination though he be of good and evil, of grandeur and of baseness, is still, on the whole, the object most worthy of study, interest, pity, attachment, and admiration in the world, and since we have no angels, we cannot attach ourselves, or devote ourselves to anything greater or nobler than our fellow-creatures." [49]

Aristocrat though he was, Tocqueville put himself on a par with the masses of men, who were the objects of his most passionate concern. Considering the march toward greater equality inevitable, he devoted his life to the furtherance of men's understanding of the democratic societies that were emerging, so that they might be safeguarded against the dangers of despotism. He did not base his claim to be heard either on his background or on his standing as a scholar but solely on the strength of his concern, his personal detachment, and the persuasiveness of his reasoning. Tocqueville found a very direct relationship between his ideas and political action, even though he disclaimed not so much the ambitions, as the qualifications of great statesmanship.

> No! I certainly do not laugh at political convictions; I do not consider them as indifferent in themselves, and as mere instruments in the hands of men. I laugh bitterly at the monstrous abuse that is every day made of them, as I laugh when I see virtue and religion turned to dishonest uses, without losing any of my respect for virtue and religion. I struggle with all my might against the false wisdom, the fatal indifference, which in our day saps the energy of so many great minds. I try not to have two worlds: a moral one, where I still delight in all that is good and noble, and the other political, where I may lie with my face to the ground, enjoying the full benefit of the dirt which covers it. [50]

Here, then, is detachment in the pursuit of knowledge, a passionate concern for the "good of mankind" and a direct effort to use knowledge to this end.

For Tocqueville, politics is the natural arena in which that knowledge must be applied in order to affect the course of human affairs.[51]

Tocqueville's assessment of this task is strikingly different from that of Marx. Committed to the proletarian cause as the lever for the reorganization of society, Marx nevertheless distinguishes sharply between the untutored proletariat and the bourgeois ideologists who analyze the capitalist economy and understand history. Despite his populist stance and his insistence that ultimately proletarian class consciousness and the scientific understanding of capitalism develop in response to the class struggle, Marx makes clear that, for the time being, what workers *are* is far more important than what they *think*.

> It is not relevant what this or that worker or even what the whole proletariat *conceive* to be their aim, for the time being. It matters only *what* the proletariat *is* and that it will be forced to act historically in accordance with this *being*. The aim and the historical action of the proletariat are clearly and irrevocably outlined by its life situation as well as by the entire organization of present-day bourgeois society.[52]

Tocqueville, on the other hand, makes no distinction between men of knowledge and the masses of people—despite his aristocratic background. He is convinced, furthermore, that, to influence the course of events, it will not do to "cure all our ills" by institutional means, for institutions exert "only a secondary influence over the destinies of men." For him, the "excellence of political societies" depends upon the "sentiments, principles, and opinions, the moral and intellectual qualities given by nature and education to the men of whom they consist."[53]

Accordingly, Tocqueville believes that men will be able to avert the dangers of despotism implicit in democracy, if they develop the moral and intellectual qualities necessary to the task. His own inquiry into the natural tendencies of a democratic society seeks to point out these dangers so that by timely discovery and confrontation "we may look our enemies in the face and know against what we have to fight."[54] Tocqueville sees these "natural tendencies" in precarious balance with the forces opposing them.[55] It is not possible to predict the outcome. In the face of uncertainty he wishes society to behave "like a strong man who exposes himself to the danger before him as a necessary part of his undertaking and is alarmed only when he cannot see clearly what it is."[56] On another occasion, Tocqueville makes clear the significance of this position. The eighteenth century had "an exaggerated and somewhat childish trust in the control which men and peoples were supposed to have of their own destinies." That idea may have led to many follies, but it also produced great things. Since the revolution, however, so many generous ideas and great hopes have miscarried that men have been led to the opposite extreme.

> After having felt ourselves capable of transforming ourselves, we now feel incapable of reforming ourselves; after having had excessive pride, we have now fallen into excessive self-pity; we thought we could do everything, and now we think we can do nothing; we like to think that struggle and effort are henceforth useless and that our blood, muscles, and nerves will always be stronger than our will power and courage. This is really the great sickness of our age. . . .[57]

It is this sickness against which Tocqueville takes his stand, an heir of the Enlightenment in the tradition of Montesquieu.

Nevertheless, Tocqueville's life was marked by profound pessimism. At the age of thirty-one, he wrote to a friend of his desire to persuade men that respect for law and religion must be combined with freedom and that to grant freedom is the best way of preserving morality and religion. "You will tell me that this is impossible; I am inclined to the same opinion; but it is the truth, and I will speak it at all risks. . . ."[58] At the age of forty-three, at the time of the 1848 Revolution, he wrote to the same friend that, if he had children, he would warn them to be prepared for everything, for no one can count on the future.

> In France especially, men should rely on nothing that can be taken away; [they should] try to acquire those things which one can never lose till one ceases to exist: fortitude, energy, knowledge, and prudence. . . .[59]

And toward the end of his life, at the age of fifty-one, he wrote to Madame Swetchine:

> No tranquility and no material comfort can in my mind make up for the loss [of liberty]. And yet I see that most of the men of my time—of the most honest among them, for I care little about the others—think only of accommodating themselves to the new system and, what most of all disturbs and alarms me, turn a taste for slavery into a virtue. I could not think and feel as they do, if I tried: it is even more repugnant to my nature than to my will. . . . You can hardly imagine how painful, and often bitter, it is to me to live in this moral isolation; to feel myself shut out of the intellectual commonwealth of my age and country.[60]

We see that Tocqueville passionately believed in freedom and rejected the reductionist analysis as false wisdom tending toward "the unfair circumscription of human power." Yet throughout his life he was haunted by the impenetrability of the future and by the melancholy realization that the truths he had discovered were *not* being used for the "good of mankind." As a result, despite his relations, neighbors, and friends, his mind had "not a family or a country."[61] The contrast with Marx is startling, if we consider that this lifelong exile who had family but few friends and, one suspects, few neighbors, derived courage and confidence in his mission from the very determinism that Tocqueville rejected, from the conviction that he had "comprehended theoretically the historical movement as a whole.'' It is hard to resist the conclusion that the wish for power through knowledge was father to Marx's determinist and reductionist theories, while Tocqueville's quest for truth without the promise of power was linked with his willingness to face the tragedy of moral isolation.

Emile Durkheim (1858-1917). The experience of moral isolation is as central a problem for Durkheim as for Tocqueville. Writing some of his major works during the years of the Dreyfus Affair (1895-1906), Durkheim witnessed a threat to moral standards fully as great as did Tocqueville when he observed the consequences of the French Revolution and the failure of French society to achieve institutional stability. Like other critics of the Enlightenment, both men are preoccupied with questions of morality. Yet the two differ profoundly. For Tocqueville, moral isolation was an intense, personal experience, as well as an object of study. As a champion of liberty, he was conscious of the degree to which liberty is jeopardized by the moral weaknesses associated with the drive for equality. He believed that his contemporaries had abandoned the ideals of the eighteenth century, and he felt the loneliness of his position. For Durkheim moral isolation appears to have been a less personal experience than for Tocqueville. Belief in science furnishes the moral basis of Durkheim's approach. He is the champion of sociology, and he endeavors to introduce his chosen discipline into the scientific community. Durkheim states this purpose clearly:

> Our principal objective is to extend scientific rationalism to human behavior. It can be shown that behavior of the past, when analyzed, can be reduced to relationships of cause and effect. These relationships can then be transformed, by an equally logical operation, into rules of action for the future. . . . It therefore seems to us that in these times of renascent mysticism an undertaking such as ours should be regarded quite without apprehension and even with sympathy by all those who, while disagreeing with us on certain points, yet share our faith in the future of reason.[62]

We shall see that, in Durkheim's view, it is science and not—as with Tocqueville—liberty, morality, and religion that will reconstruct the moral order.

To establish sociology as a science is Durkheim's central concern. In his very first publication, his Latin thesis on *Montesquieu's Contribution to the Rise of Social Science*, Durkheim emphasizes the distinction between science and art.[63] Life goes on, decisions about what to do must be made quickly, and the reasons for our actions are hastily assembled. "We improvise a science as we go along," but such collected arguments, by which men of action support their opinions, "do not reflect phenomena . . . but merely states of mind."

Even in abstract questions, no doubt, our ideas spring from the heart, for the

> heart is the source of our entire life. But if our feelings are not to run away with us, they must be governed by reason. Reason must be set above the accidents and contingencies of life.[64]

Accordingly, science must be advanced in complete independence and "in utter disregard of utility." The more clear-cut the distinction between science and art, which Durkheim defines as decisions on what to do, the more useful science will be for art.

Durkheim proceeds to define "the conditions necessary for the establishment of social science." Each science must have its own specific object. The only objects that admit of scientific study are those that constitute a type, that share "features common to all individuals of the same type," that are finite in number and ascertainable. But description of types must be supplemented by interpretation, which presupposes stable relations between cause and effect, for without them everything is fortuitous and does not admit of interpretation.[65] No social science is possible if societies are not subject to laws. No one questions the possibility of natural science; the principal assumptions underlying these sciences have been tested and never found false; hence they are "also valid, in all likelihood, for human societies, which are part of nature."[66] Like Marx before him, Durkheim takes the established natural sciences for his model, and he is specific in his use of this model.

> So long as everything in human societies seemed so utterly fortuitous, no one could have thought of classifying them. There can be no types of things unless there are causes which, though operating in different places and at different times, always and everywhere produce the same effects. And where is the object of social science if the lawgiver can organize and direct social life as he pleases? The subject matter of science can consist only of things that have a stable nature of their own and are able to resist the human will.[67]

Even then a method of investigation is needed that does not exist ready-made but must be developed as social science grapples with the great complexities that confront it.

In his *Rules of Sociological Method*, Durkheim elaborates this point by stating the basic theoretical assumptions of his work.

1. Social phenomena are a reality *sui generis*, and they cannot be explained by reference to less complex or nonsocial phenomena—exactly as psychological phenomena can be understood only as such rather than by a reduction to physiological processes, for example.

2. Sociology is the study of social groups, albeit groups composed of individuals. The group, however, is a new, synthetic reality, arising from the *association* of individuals.

3. At its own level, society must be observed with regard to the consciousness a collectivity forms of itself, much as the individual is observed through

his consciousness. The collective thought embodied in language is an obvious example of such collective consciousness.

4. Language, moral rules, religious beliefs and practices, myth, folklore, proverbs, popular sayings, and other aspects of culture are *external* to the individual and exercise a *moral constraint* upon him. These collective "representations" exist when the individual comes into the world, and he acquires them unwittingly. That he is constrained to acquire them becomes apparent when his violation of cultural norms is censured.[68]

In later comments on his work, Durkheim seeks to correct the impression that his collectivist approach totally subordinates the individual. Society exists only in and through individuals; the collective derivation of their thought and feeling is as natural to them as the air they breathe.[69] Accordingly, "society" is immanent in the individual at the same time that it transcends him by virtue of its greater duration and power of constraint. Even Durkheim's efforts to qualify his emphasis on the collectivity re-emphasize how far he has carried the analytical reduction of individual consciousness.

Symptomatic in this respect are two explicit discussions of individualism. Durkheim considers the cult of the individual a great threat to social solidarity, especially in the context of economic competition. But he also appears to reconcile himself to this cult of the modern world by showing that individualism itself is a product of society.[70] Durkheim considers the problem again in his last writings, in which he discusses the frequent antagonism of social relations. Our bodily appetites are self-centered and therefore individualistic; our minds are preoccupied with ideas that are socially derived and therefore universal. Accordingly, *individuality* results from the biochemical nature of every person; it is a by-product of those purely physical attributes that make every man unique. *Personality*, on the other hand, has its source in the feelings and ideas that the members of a collectivity share. This conception is consistent with Durkheim's theory that the idea of the soul's independence from the finite body (immortality) is derived from the fact that society continues while individuals are born and die.[71] In this way, Durkheim rejects the earlier reductionism of the ideologues, which attributed all intellectual and moral activity to a substratum of bodily sensations. His own sociological reductionism cites man's biological attributes as the only source of individuality. Paradoxically, the individual is here located in what all men have in common, while his psychological and intellectual faculties become the locus of a common humanity, despite the fact that cultural differences rather than physical attributes have spread variety over the face of the earth.

This concluding paradox of Durkheim's work brings us back to the ideological dimensions of social theory. How does Durkheim's sociological theory affect his conception of the ends of knowledge and the uses of his ideas? He analyzes how European society is characterized increasingly by a moral decline attributable to the expanding division of labor. If modern society is to become "healthy" again, legal regulations are required that will encourage co-operation; and social solidarity must be fostered by voluntary associations of occupational groups.[72] To achieve these effects men must rely on knowledge, since traditional beliefs have lost their efficacy. Durkheim points out that:

> Man seeks to learn and man kills himself because of the loss of cohesion in his religious society; he does not kill himself because of his learning. It is certainly not the learning he acquires that disorganizes religion; but the desire for knowledge wakens because religion becomes disorganized. Knowledge is not sought as a means to destroy accepted opinions but because their destruction has commenced.[73]

Here and throughout Durkheim's work the basic cause of a declining morality is seen as a *loss of social cohesion* of which the decline of religion, the tendency to commit suicide, and the quest for knowledge are different symptoms or consequences. But if this view is valid, then why does Durkheim hope that knowledge, which is among these consequences, can construct a new and vigorous morality? His answer is:

> Far from knowledge being the source of the evil, it is its remedy, the only remedy we have. Once established beliefs have been carried away by the current of affairs, they cannot be artificially re-established; only reflection can guide us in life, after this. Once the social instinct is blunted, intelligence is the only guide left us and we have to reconstruct a conscience by its means. Dangerous as is the undertaking there can be no hesitation, for we have no choice. . . . [Science] has not the dissolvent effect ascribed to it, but is the only weapon for our battle against the dissolution which gives birth to science itself.[74]

Durkheim adds that one must not make a "self-sufficient end" out of science or education. They are only means or guides to aid us in our efforts to reconstruct a "social conscience."

But what can we hope from a science which tells us that moral standards remain intact only as long as sacred beliefs are shared by the members of a collectivity? Durkheim shows skepticism to a degree when he refers to intelligence and science as the *only guide or weapon left to us*. His work demonstrates that moral norms are viable if the social cohesion of groups is intact, but that this cohesion must decline as a result of the division of labor. At the end, Durkheim's subjective faith in reason remains, but intellectually it is undermined by the theory and evidence that he developed in order to sustain it.

Max Weber (1864-1920). Of the four theorists considered here, Max Weber concerns himself most directly with the problem of objectivity. He does not view scientific neutrality as a by-product of the historical process as does Marx, or circumstance and personal quality as does Tocqueville, or of the effort to establish sociology after the model of the natural sciences as does Durkheim. For Weber, objectivity results from the deliberate efforts of the scholar. While Tocqueville claims objectivity as a concomitant of personal experience, Weber seeks to achieve it through methodological clarification and self-restraint. But like Tocqueville, Weber emphasizes the importance of ideas and sentiments for an understanding of social life—in contrast to Marx and Durkheim, who continue the reductionist tradition of the ideologues. It is true that Weber, as well as Tocqueville, appreciates the insights of this tradition. Nevertheless, both consider ideas an irreducible factor in social life, and it is above all in his analysis of ideas that Weber's claim to scientific objectivity must be assessed.

The intellectual vantage point of these theorists is clearest perhaps in their treatment of religion. For Marx, the "religious reflex" provides a spurious gratification of human desires, a spiritual justification of the inhumanities of man's social condition. Now that technology can fulfill these desires, religion has become unnecessary and will disappear. Tocqueville considers religious faith among the highest manifestations of the human spirit and is aghast at the abuses and perversions to which it is subjected. To preserve liberty as relations among men become more equal, it is necessary to strengthen religion and morality. Toward the end of his life, Tocqueville became more religious though he recognized the growth of secularism among his contemporaries. For Durkheim, religion is an object of study, as enduring a phenomenon as Tocqueville believed it to be, but not a personal concern. Science cannot accept the literal truth of religious beliefs, but it recognizes and analyzes their symbolic truth. For Durkheim, religion arises from the reality of group life: "It is society which the faithful worship; the superiority of the gods over men is that of the group over its members."[75] Weber's approach to religion contains all these elements. Like Marx, he recognizes the material interests involved in religious beliefs and institutions, especially the economic interests of religious functionaries. Yet, like Tocqueville, he also considers religious ideas as an aspect of human creativity. Personally areligious, Weber takes as scientific an interest in religion as does Durkheim. But, while Durkheim focuses on primitive religion in order to understand its "essence," Weber concentrates on the age of religious creativity (Confucius, Buddha, Old Testament prophets) in order to understand the characteristics of Western civilization. This attempt to analyze the highest manifestations of human spirituality gives special point to Weber's concern with the problem of scientific objectivity.

All inquiry is initiated by the subjective orientation of the investigator. In the natural sciences, this orientation depends on the results previously obtained, the unresolved problems suggested by these results, and the ingenuity of the researcher. In the social sciences, cumulation is evident primarily in the collection of data. In the interpretation of these data, it is less evident and more difficult to sustain. The questions raised for investigation depend more upon considerations of cultural relevance (*Wertbezogenheit*) than upon previous findings. The different approaches to religion mentioned above exemplify the mutability of such considerations. But if the same questions are raised about the same data, then equally competent men will arrive at the same conclusions—provided that value-judgments (*Werturteile*) do not intrude. It is at this point that Weber sees the major obstacle to objectivity.

His most explicit statements in this respect are a criticism of professional malpractice. Nationalist professors in Imperial Germany were unable or unwilling to distinguish between their civic and academic responsibilities, and Weber attacked their propagation of political opinions under the guise of science. In many settings, it is relatively easy to meet this criticism. The speaker or writer himself declares what his values are and warns his listeners or readers that they must not mistake certain statements for judgments authenticated by scientific findings. Value-judgments must be assessed by each person in the light of his own evaluations. Weber insists passionately on the separation of value-judgments from scientific inquiry, for he is as deeply concerned with the one as with the other. Failure to observe this separation appears to him an abuse of science *and* a monstrous desecration of what men hold most dear—in contrast to Tocqueville who sees in that same separation a "false wisdom" and a "fatal indifference." At this point, the hiatus between the two men's ideas could not be greater—despite affinity in other respects.

Weber is directly concerned with the formulation of concepts for research; Tocqueville is not. For Weber, the exclusion of value-judgments is the precondition of scientific inquiry about man and society. Concepts must enable us to identify types of social phenomena unequivocally and without intrusion from "the will and the affections" (Bacon). Such classification and identification are elementary scientific procedure. The zoologist hardly requires a reminder that his own liking for fox terriers has no bearing on the classification of dogs. A social theorist like Weber, however, may wish to identify the magnetic appeal that commanding personalities have had for masses of people throughout history. Where the fact of this appeal is unquestioned, the concept "charisma" applies, whether the reference is to a holy man like St. Francis of Assisi or a "great bird of prey" like Alexander the Great.[76] Weber insists that the enormous ethical gulf between two such figures must be considered in its own moral terms, clearly separated from the finding that they have at least one trait in common.

The value-neutral formulation of concepts is as crucial for Weber as is the theoretical foundation of sociology for Durkheim. Both men are committed to the advancement of knowledge, but the difference between them is marked.

For Durkheim, social science becomes possible to the degree that "realities can be reduced to a type" consisting of "the features common to all individuals of the same type." A social science that characterizes a typical social phenomenon, "cannot fail to describe the normal form of social life...''; whatever pertains to the type is normal, and whatever is normal is healthy.[77] Durkheim subscribes to a philosophical realism that identifies the type with the prevailing characteristics of the phenomenon. Consequently, he considers it indispensable for social science

> to discover *in the data themselves* some definite indication enabling us to distinguish between sickness and health. If such a sign is lacking, we are driven to take refuge in deduction and move away from the concrete facts.[78]

This position Weber rejects *in toto*. Terms like "health" or "sickness" when applied to society are for him, criteria of moral worth by which men arrive at ethical judgments.[79] These criteria should not be confused with the normal or typical forms of social life. For Weber social phenomena exist in a continuity that allows no natural demarcation.[80] Instead of positing natural types with a more or less stable arrangement of their elements, as Durkheim would have it, Weber posits ideal types—benchmark concepts constructed out of a one-sided simplification and exaggeration of the evidence as it is found in society.

This basic difference in orientation has several consequences. For Durkheim, the purpose of ascertaining natural types is to understand the features common to all individuals of a given type. By recognizing the similar social constraints to which all these individuals are subject, we can explain their actions in terms of cause and effect. This knowledge enables us to understand what is normal and healthy in social life and to act accordingly. For Weber the purpose of constructing ideal types is to interpret the meaning of actions, to understand what sense it makes for men to act as they do.[81] The simplifications involved in this procedure give order to the multiplicity of phenomena. By referring to these artificial benchmarks, the analyst can assess the actions which are documented or observed.[82] An example is the ideal type of the charismatic leader and the routinization of his appeal. In Weber's view, the analyst can assess the degree to which a given action approaches the ideal type of a personal or institutionalized charisma without himself evaluating these approximations. The purpose of this procedure is not to achieve causal explanation, however. Weber makes quite clear that for him sociology is an auxiliary discipline, one that uses the comparative and classificatory procedure to distinguish between what is general and what is unique. In this way, sociology establishes what is recurrent in different societies, while history explains the unique event.[83]

It follows that Weber's conception of purpose is more cautious than that of

Durkheim. The idea that men pursue knowledge for its own sake or for intellectual clarity cannot be found in Durkheim, who puts major emphasis upon
enlarging man's control of human affairs. Weber subscribes to all three objectives. But he is circumspect with regard to the practical uses of social science in keeping with his emphasis on the hiatus between the detachment of the
scientist and the commitment essential to the man of action. Having once
taken the position that truth is not a by-product of history, and that types and
criteria of "social health" do not reside in the data themselves, Weber is consistent. The scientist can ascertain the facts, point out the assets and liabilities
of alternative actions, clarify value-positions in terms of their internal consistency and possible consequences. He can do no more; his role is that of ad-
viser, assistant, or expert if he is consulted. For Weber, there is no direct link
between knowledge and power in human affairs.[84]

Compared with the hopes of the Enlightenment this position is one of great
resignation. In contrast to Marx and Durkheim, Weber does not have a strong
faith in the power of knowledge in society. He shares Tocqueville's pessimism in this regard, though not his melancholy. In Weber's case, the hiatus
between fact and value, between the scholar and the man of action is not a
token of indifference, as Tocqueville sees it. It is evidence rather of Weber's
simultaneous commitment to scholarship and action. In his life-long effort to
achieve a creative relationship between these spheres, Weber put a premium
on preserving the integrity of both and thus exposed himself, as only Tocqueville had done before him, to tension and utter frustration. To assert and
search for the meaningfulness of the individual's life in a world without God,
to recognize the compulsions of human existence yet assert man's capacity to
act, to advance social science yet probe into the irrational foundations and
consequences of knowledge—this acceptance of tension left its mark on Weber's personal life. Like Tocqueville before him, he paid a price for tolerating
the ambiguities of reason in human affairs that Marx and Durkheim were less
willing to accept.

LEGACIES AND EMERGING PROBLEMS

Scientific inquiry presupposes a belief in science. Most people adhere to
this belief in the expectation that "knowledge is power." In the social sciences, confidence in this maxim has been undermined. Efforts to advance social knowledge have led unwittingly to changes in conceptions of human nature. Inquiry presupposes the control of bias. To control bias, we must understand its sources. In this respect, our understanding has advanced from Bacon's theory of idols to Nietzsche's and Freud's views of the organic conditioning of knowledge. The sciences of men have grown together with a skeptical view of human nature, and the latter raises questions about the utility of
social knowledge.

These questions have been evaded where belief in progress through science and distrust of common prudence have gone hand in hand. The view that the mass of humanity is subject to social laws has been linked—implicitly perhaps—with the assumption that an elite of social scientists can understand these laws and enhance knowledge, human utility, and power. But through the work they do, social scientists belie the assertion that *all* men are subject to social laws. This exception reveals an ''infusion of will and the affections'' against which Francis Bacon warned three centuries ago. But when everything is expected of science and nothing of man, we must take stock of our assumptions. Trust in science and distrust of prudence is a ''stage play'' that ''wonderfully obstructs the understanding,'' like Bacon's ''idols of the theatre.'' Emancipation from received opinion in this regard and repeated examination of the mental set with which we approach the study of society are indispensable methodological tools.

Such re-examination has been attempted in this discussion by reflection on the historical and theoretical dimensions of ideology. As we contrast the nonideological world view with the questioning of human knowledge and power that marks the ''Age of Ideology,'' we cannot conclude that the ''end of ideology'' is in sight.[85] Rather, the efforts to control bias and questions about the ends and uses of knowledge expose the action-involvement of all ideas. This involvement exists in all the sciences, but poses special problems in those fields in which every general statement applies to the man of knowledge as well as to the subject he investigates.

The paradox of the liar, as the ancient philosopher Zeno formulated it, is an integral part of theories about society. All social theorists are bound to begin with postulates on how they propose to investigate society dispassionately. For, in the ''Age of Ideology'' they seek truth through the quest for objectivity rather than praise God through discovery of His wisdom. This effort leads to two typical variants, at least. The reductionist approach seeks to control or exclude error by reference to an impersonal source or safeguard. Truth as a by-product of the class-struggle and of methods used in the natural sciences are the examples mentioned. The approach through self-knowledge seeks to ensure objectivity by cautions that the investigator applies to himself. Truth as a by-product of personal experience and opportunity and of methodological inquiry and self-discipline were our examples. Such approaches do not resolve the ambiguities of knowledge in human affairs; rather they accentuate these ambiguities through dogmatism or mitigate them even at the price of personal resignation. The belief in reason has been on trial ever since social philosophers began to employ the natural sciences as their model. Their hope was to discover universal principles of morality or regularities in the behavior of men and societies. This hope presupposed remnants of an earlier belief in man's God-given capacity to discover uniformities underneath the diversity of appearances. The resulting knowledge would enhance man's moral stature.

Eventually this view was superseded by the secular belief that knowledge would enhance man's "technical mastery of life" (Weber) and that such mastery is worthwhile. These latter assumptions are on trial today. We are learning that social theories are not alone in having failed to resolve the ambiguities inherent in the secularization of knowledge. The ambiguities of the nonideological world view had to be resolved by faith, but in the absence of faith we must live with the ambiguities of the human condition.

In his essay, "Science as a Vocation," Max Weber wrote near the end of his life (1920) that scientists are professionally dedicated to the advancement of knowledge. They do not ask what ends this knowledge will serve, because increased "technical mastery" is to them a self-evident good. When we observe the pain of those struck down by an incurable disease, we yearn for the day when these remaining scourges will have been eradicated. All of us are tender toward the sick, because the means to help them are or may be within reach; if we lacked that confidence, we could not permit ourselves to be so tender. There is a world-wide unanimity in favor of death control, and this unanimity is the spirit that has initiated and sustained the growth of medical knowledge. Yet, in the two centuries that have elapsed since the beginning of modern medicine, the *effect* of advancing knowledge has been equivocal. From ancient times until the end of the seventeenth century, the world population did not exceed 500 million people; by the 1920s, it had increased to more than two billion. A report from the United Nations predicts that, by the year 2000, it will exceed six billion. This twelvefold increase in world population over a period of 350 years occurred with the aid of medical knowledge. On humanitarian and political grounds, it is impossible to withhold such knowledge from countries whose productive capacity does not keep step with their reproductive capacity. Such countries face the Sisyphean task of narrowing a gap while it increases. A century after the *Communist Manifesto*, a specter *is* haunting the world: the age-old prospects of famine, epidemic, and political tyranny or chaos.

Most of us recoil at the suggestion that this prospect is also a product of knowledge. Most of us hope that advances of knowledge will enable men to banish this specter from the face of the earth. We know we must make the attempt, we want to advance our technical mastery for "the benefit and use of life." Bacon made that declaration when the population of Europe was only beginning to increase after centuries of stagnation or cyclical variation. We too support this declaration. The "inherent value" of knowledge is equivocal in a world in which medicine by its effects on population can foster starvation, albeit indirectly, and in which increasing "technical mastery" may lead to the annihilation of life. Yet who will abandon the benefits of science because men are unable to control the powers science has unleashed? No advocate of ending the nuclear arms race, no man who warns against the effects of nuclear testing has been heard to suggest that, along with these destructive uses of knowledge, we discard its constructive uses also. It is unusual to call the benefits of science into question, but today we are all aware that the "technical mastery of life" can lead to consequences beyond human control. So far, few men have grappled with the corollary that the advancement of knowledge may one day destroy man's "technical mastery of life."[86] The ends and uses of knowledge (and that means the ideological dimensions of intellectual effort) call for critical examination—more urgently than ever.

NOTES

1. An earlier version of this essay was published in David Apter, ed., *Ideology and Discontent* (Glencoe: The Free Press, 1964), pp. 294-327.
2. Francis Bacon, "Novum Organum," in E. A. Burtt, ed., *The English Philosophers from Bacon to Mill* (New York: The Modern Library, 1939), pp. 40-41.
3. See Daniel Bell, *The End of Ideology* (Glencoe: The Free Press, 1960), pp. 369 ff., passim. Cf. Seymour M. Lipset, *Political Man* (Garden City: Doubleday & Co., 1960), pp. 403 ff. The references in these and related writings are to the "end of ideology" in the West; it is acknowledged that there may have occurred a "rise of ideology" in Asia and Africa.
4. In principle there is also the possibility of a postideological epoch, but this eventuality lies in the future as long as we are witnessing the "end of some ideologies" rather than the "end of ideology." The more accurate phrase has less punch, however.
5. Carl Becker, *The Heavenly City of the Eighteenth Century Philosophers* (New Haven: Yale University Press, 1932), p. 47.
6. For a brilliant portrayal of this earlier world view with special reference to social and economic thought, see Otto Brunner, *Adeliges Landleben und Europäischer Geist* (Salzburg: Otto Müller Verlag, 1949), Chap. 2. In the field of literary history, parallel materials are found in Erich Auerbach, *Mimesis, The Representation of Reality in Western Literature* (Garden City: Doubleday & Co., 1957), passim. For a contrast between these premodern perspectives and the "Age of Ideology" I am indebted to Brunner, "Das Zeitalter der Ideologien," *Neue Wege der Sozialgeschichte* (Göttingen: Vandenhoeck & Ruprecht, 1956), pp. 194-219.
7. *American College Dictionary* (New York, 1947), p. 599.
8. Bacon, *op. cit.*, pp. 28, 62. The subtitle of the essay is "Aphorisms Concerning the Interpretation of Nature and the Kingdom of Man."
9. For an acute analysis of the modernity of Bacon's approach in relation to classical conceptions of knowledge and action, see Hans Jonas, "The Practical Uses of Theory," *Social Research*, XXVI (Summer 1959), pp. 127-50.
10. The quoted phrases are found in Bacon, *op. cit.*, p. 64.
11. Bacon, *op. cit.*, p. 65.
12. The fundamental commitment of scientists to a hedonistic and secular world view is examined in detail in the study by Lewis Feuer, *The Scientific Intellectual* (New York: Basic Books, 1963).
13. The most comprehensive treatment of this development is contained in Ernst Cassirer, *The Philosophy of the Enlightenment* (Boston: The Beacon Press, 1955).

Directly pertinent to the present discussion are Charles Van Duzer, *Contribution of the Ideologues to French Revolutionary Thought* (Baltimore: The Johns Hopkins Press, 1935); and Hans Barth, *Wahrheit und Ideologie* (Zürich: Manesse Verlag, 1945), pp. 54-70.

14. See J. W. Stein, *The Mind and the Sword* (New York: Twayne Publishers, Inc. 1961), p. 88, and passim. The term "ideology" was coined by Tracy in order to distinguish his "scientific" approach from conventional philosophy or metaphysics. See ibid., p. 186, n. 33.

15. Ibid., pp. 94, 107. Similarly, Cabanis—in his *Rapportis du physique et du moral* (1802)—sought to analyze morality by research in physiology, a method that would make progress in education and the social sciences as rapid as it had been in the natural sciences. See p. 82.

16. See Barth, *op. cit.*, pp. 15-35; and Stein, *op. cit.*, pp. 141-71 for accounts of this episode.

17. A given proposition might be true but impractical and politically beneficial (from some point of view); it might be true, practical, but politically dangerous (from some point of view); and so forth. Since truth, practicality, and political effect have been involved in the pejorative meaning of ideology ever since Napoleon, confusions abound, especially since utility or political effects have often been employed as tests of truth in order to strengthen or weaken the appeal of theories under the guise of the prestige of science. These confusions, however, are an important part of nineteenth-century intellectual history.

18. Edmund Burke, *Reflections on the Revolution in France* (Chicago: Henry Regnery Co., 1955), pp. 126-27.

19. In the passage preceding the one quoted, Burke polemicizes against Rousseau, Voltaire, and Helvétius: "We know that we have made no discoveries, and we think that no discoveries are to be made, in morality; nor many in the great principles of government, nor in the ideas of liberty, which were understood long before we were born, altogether as well as they will be after the grave has heaped its mould upon our presumption. . . . In England we have not yet been completely embowelled of our natural entrails; we still feel within us, and we cherish and cultivate, those inbred sentiments which are the faithful guardians, the active monitors of our duty, the true supporters of all liberal and manly morals. . . . We preserve the whole of our feelings still native and entire, unsophisticated by pedantry and infidelity. . . . We fear God; we look up with awe to kings. . . . Why? Because such ideas are brought before our minds, it is natural to be so affected; because all other feelings are false and spurious, and tend to corrupt our minds. . . ." Ibid., pp. 125-26.

20. Cf. Leo Strauss, *Natural Right and History* (Chicago: University of Chicago Press, 1953), pp. 307-11, for an extended statement of these contrasts derived from Burke's writings.

21. Cf. the detailed discussion of this point in ibid., pp. 294-323.

22. For this formulation of Weber's in his essay "Science as a Vocation," see H. H. Gerth and C. Wright Mills, eds., *From Max Weber: Essays in Sociology* (New York: Oxford University Press, 1946), pp. 150-51. It is a convenient summary of the assumptions underlying much social thought in the nineteenth century; its significance for Weber's approach is considered later.

23. Such reticence is not universal. Cf. George Lundberg, *Can Science Save Us?* (New York: Longman, Green & Co., 1961), passim.

24. Cf., for example, the telling arguments against premature consideration of these

questions of purpose in Robert K. Merton, "Social Conflict over Styles of Sociological Work," *Transactions of the Fourth World Congress of Sociology*, III (Louvain, 1961), pp. 21-44.

25. The paradox was first formulated by the Greek philosopher Zeno in the statement; "A Cretan says all Cretans are liars." Since the person making the statement is himself a member of the group of whom a lack of veracity is asserted, an infinite chain of mutually contradictory assertions follows. For our purposes the analogous statement would be: "Social scientists say that every man's knowledge of society is the product of that society," although this application lacks the simplicity of the classic model.

26. Quoted in Barth , *op. cit.*, p. 67.

27. Frank E. Manuel, *The New World of Henri Saint-Simon* (Cambridge: Harvard University Press, 1956), p. 134.

28. Quoted in ibid., p. 135.

29. Sigmund Freud, *The Future of an Illusion* (Garden City: Doubleday & Co., n. d.), p. 98. The numbered statements in the text are based on pp. 95-102.

30. Ibid., p. 99.

31. Ibid., p. 102.

32. Although the contrast between Saint-Simon and Freud suggests a diminution of hope concerning the benefits to be derived from knowledge, proof of this trend in the climate of opinion is a more complex affair and is not attempted here. Even in the eighteenth century there were great skeptics of the promise of science as applied to human affairs—men like Edmund Burke and Montesquieu—and this skepticism had numerous spokesmen throughout the nineteenth century along with the more dominant expressions of belief in progress. Hans Barth's *Wahrheit und Ideologie* contains a detailed philosophical analysis of changing conceptions of man and truth that supports the interpretations offered here.

33. Karl Marx, *Capital* (New York: The Modern Library, 1936), p. 89. The present discussion of Marx's view of knowledge may be compared with his analysis of social class and change, discussed in Chapter 12 below.

34. Ibid., p. 91.

35. Ibid., pp. 90-91.

36. Ibid., pp. 91-92.

37. See, for example, Karl Marx, *A Contribution to the Critique of Political Economy* (Chicago: Charles Kerr, 1904), p. 12.

38. See, for example, Marx, *Capital*, pp. 12-13, preface to the first edition.

39. Karl Marx and Friedrich Engels, *Manifesto of the Communist Party* (New York: International Publishers, 1939), p. 19. My italics.

40. See note 35 above for the source of this wording.

41. From Tocqueville's letter to Henry Reeve, dated March 22, 1837, in Tocqueville, *Memoir, Letters and Remains*, II (Boston: Ticknor & Fields, 1862), pp. 39-40. Tocqueville's work is analyzed further in chapter 5 with reference to comparative studies and in chapter 11 with reference to social change.

42. There is a similar argument in Marx, but it is very general and unclear, while Tocqueville is specific and lucid.

43. Tocqueville, *op.cit.*, I, p. 376. From a letter to M. Stoffels, February 21, 1835.

44. Quoted phrases are taken from the letter to Stoffels, ibid.

45. From a letter to M. de Kergorlay, November 13, 1833, ibid., I, p. 299.

46. From a letter to M. Stoffels, January 3, 1843, ibid., I, p. 392.

47. Ibid.

48. Ibid., I, pp. 299-300. From the letter to Kergorlay, already cited.
49. Ibid., I, p. 393. From the letter to Stoffels, January 3, 1843.
50. Ibid., I, pp. 374-75. From a letter to M. Stoffels, January 12, 1833.
51. See ibid., II, pp. 84-5, for a vigorous statement to this effect in a letter to M. de Corcelle, October 11, 1846.
52. See Karl Marx and Friedrich Engels, *Die Heilige Familie* (Berlin: Dietz Verlag, 1953), p. 138. Italics in the original; my translation. Marx constantly re-examined the labor movements in various countries for evidence of a rising class-consciousness in his sense of the word, but his judgments in this respect were notably unstable in terms of his own theoretical assumptions.
53. Tocqueville, *op. cit.*, II, p. 230. From a letter to M. de Corcelle, September 17, 1853.
54. Ibid., II, pp. 13-14. From a letter to M. de Corcelle, April 12, 1835.
55. Tocqueville, *Democracy in America* (New York: Vintage Books, 1954), II, p. 352.
56. Tocqueville, *Memoir*, I, pp. 13-14. From the letter to De Corcelle, April 12, 1835.
57. Tocqueville, *The European Revolution and Correspondence with Gobineau* (Garden City: Doubleday & Co., 1959), pp. 231-2. From letter to Gobineau, December 20, 1853.
58. Tocqueville, *Memoir*, I, p. 382. From the letter to M. Stoffels, July 24, 1836.
59. Ibid., I, p. 400. From the letter to M. Stoffels, July 21, 1848.
60. Ibid., II, pp. 305-6. From the letter dated January 7, 1856.
61. Ibid., II, p. 335. From the letter to Madame Swetchine, October 20, 1856.
62. Emile Durkheim, *The Rules of Sociological Method* (Chicago: University of Chicago Press, 1938), p. xi, from the author's preface to the first edition.
63. Emile Durkheim, *Montesquieu and Rousseau* (Ann Arbor: University of Michigan Press, 1960), pp. 3 ff.
64. Ibid., pp. 6-7.
65. Ibid., p. 10.
66. Ibid., pp. 10-11.
67. Ibid., p. 12.
68. My restatement here is brief in keeping with the purpose of the present discussion. Cf. the further discussion of Durkheim's work in a political context in chapter 11.
69. Cf. Durkheim's simultaneous insistence upon the collective origin and the individual manifestation of ideas and sentiments in *Rules, op. cit.*, pp. liv, n. 5, and lvi. n. 7. It may be added that Durkheim's strongly antipsychological argument, which is part of his case for sociology as an autonomous discipline, should be read in the context of nineteenth-century psychology with its emphasis on instincts and psychophysical parallelism.
70. These points are discussed in Durkheim, *The Division of Labor in Society* (New York: The Free Press, 1960), pp. 283 ff, and passim. Note also a later essay, published in 1898, discussed in Edward Tiryakian, *Sociologism and Existentialism* (Englewood Cliffs: Prentice-Hall, 1962), p. 57.
71. I am indebted to Tiryakian, *op.cit.*, for his analysis of this late phase of Durkheim's thought.
72. See his discussion of law and occupational groups in *The Division of Labor, op. cit.*, pp. 174 ff., and preface to the second edition. His efforts to clarify the concepts of normality or "social health" are contained in *Rules*, Chap. III.

73. Emile Durkheim, *Suicide* (London: Routledge & Kegan Paul, 1952), p. 169.
74. Ibid.
75. Tiryakian, *op. cit.*, p. 35.
76. The phrase is taken from Tocqueville's letter to Mrs. Grote, in *Memoirs*, II, p. 321.
77. Durkheim, *Montesquieu and Rousseau, op. cit.*, pp. 8-9.
78. Ibid., p. 55. My italics.
79. To consider these criteria a quality inherent in the phenomena is tantamount to the nonideological world-view discussed earlier or its organological legacy in a man like Durkheim. That is, facts and values are like emanations of the divine will just as body temperature and the limits of variation compatible with health are attributes of the biological organism. See chapter 5 below for further discussion of this approach.
80. "Denn gerade wegen der Unmöglichkeit, in der historischen Wirklichkeit scharfe Grenzen zu ziehen, können wir nur bei Untersuchung ihrer konsequentesten Formen hoffen, auf ihre spezifischen Wirkungen zu stossen." Max Weber, *Gesammelte Aufsätze zur Religionssoziologie* (Tübingen: J. C. B. Mohr [Paul Siebeck, 1947], I, p. 87.
81. I add this phrase because the term Weber employs is *Sinn* not *Bedeutung*, sense rather than meaning, although the latter word has been used in the translations.
82. Cf. Leo Strauss, *op. cit.*, for a comprehensive compilation of the evaluative terms that can be found in Weber's empirical works like his essays on the sociology of religion. Strauss criticizes Weber for his constant use of value judgments in his research, but he fails to note the basic difference between assessments based on ideal types and value judgments in the sense of personal evaluations.
83. Cf. Reinhard Bendix, "Max Weber's Interpretation of Conduct and History," *American Journal of Sociology*, LI (May 1946), pp. 518-26.
84. See Weber's discussion in "Science as a Vocation," in Gerth and Mills, *op. cit.*, passim.
85. This end has occurred, however, where a new orthodoxy has put a stop to the uncertainties endemic in the pursuit of knowledge—hardly the meaning that those who coined the phrase had in mind. One should note in this connection the pejorative use of "ideology" in Soviet terminology as a label by which Western thought is set off from the truth of Marxism-Leninism.
86. An example of such questioning, which goes beyond the fashionable cultural pessimism, is contained in the impressive work of Friedrich Wagner, *Die Wissenschaft und die gefährdete Welt* (München: C. H. Beck, 1969), passim.

3

SOCIOLOGY AND THE DISTRUST OF REASON

Introductory Note

In 1946 I was alarmed along with many by the greatly enlarged portents for good and ill brought on through the development of atomic energy. It was frightening to watch the disproportion between the "powers unleashed by science and man's impotence at controlling them"—frightening but not new. I went on to describe the ambiguous position of social scientists, who produced far less powerful results than their colleagues in physics, but faced moral dilemmas just the same. When social scientists become advisors or technicians for business or government, they are recognized for the work they do, but they lose the freedom which academic employment secures for them. Commonly education is not regarded as "social action," because its effects are long-run, diffuse, and difficult to pin down. When social scientists remain academics, they are free to formulate issues in terms of means, ends, and corollary consequences. This rational formulation of controversial issues appears to men of affairs in two ways. Either it does not fit in with their preconceptions and strategic considerations, in which case they disregard the studies they have ordered themselves. Alexander Leighton has mentioned the saying that a politician needs a social scientist the way a drunk needs a lamppost, for support not for illumination. Or social science findings enter the political arena, in which case opponents will label them as wrongheaded (impractical) or as dangerous (read: radical or subversive).[1]

Neither role is comfortable. Some academic social scientists try to boost their work by claims of practical importance, or by claims of hidden theoretical significance, which are hard to prove. On the other hand, applied social scientists feel ill at ease, because they are forced to slight their academic interests and also because they are uneasy about the use made of the work they have been hired to do.

By 1951 it was clear that I was launched on an academic career and I felt that, as a scholar and teacher, I must declare my professional commitment. That declaration should not be missing from this collection of selected essays:

> It is quite legitimate to conduct social science research which is useful in the short run. But it is both illegitimate and unwise to make claims for their long-run utility, especially since these claims are no longer sustained by a faith in prog-

61

ress or in the Divine order of things. At best such long-run claims are founded on spurious analogies from the natural sciences, and at worst they are self-serving. It would be far more *useful* in the long run to take our stand on the ground that our intellectual life is enriched by worthwhile research in the social sciences. Such research is [or can and should be, I would add today] a token of high civilization, worth preserving as an integral part of our quest for knowledge. And this quest manifests our abiding faith in the constructive and enriching *possibilities* of human reason. This is not a disinterested statement. In a world torn by wars of nerves, arms, and words the universities ought to be institutions of detachment, whose academic personnel have an important service to render in the community, for which they should claim recognition from the powers that be. It is the task of the social sciences to further the work of human enlightenment, not to claim a utility they frequently lack. Social scientists should have an abiding faith in human reason, even if they are often without the old religious foundations for such a faith. This is a more humane creed than a concern with improving the techniques of social manipulation. It is the only position worthy of the great intellectual traditions in which they stand. It is the baseline of the intellectual defense against the threat of totalitarianism.[2]

Some twenty years after this was written, it was my responsibility as President of that year, to give the Presidential address to the 1970 meeting of the American Sociological Association. Though peace negotiations were dragging on, the Vietnam War and student protests on university campuses continued. My son was writing a statement to his draft board as a conscientious objector. Even so, I felt I had to defend the institutional framework to which American soldiers would return, once the war ended. I knew I would be criticized by those who opposed not only the war but the "establishment," including the universities, which continued to operate during the war. This was the third time I had observed the Manichean division of the world into darkness and light. The Nazi movement had denounced all institutions of the Weimar Republic as *das System*. In the Red scare following World War II Senator McCarthy used the principle of "guilt by association" to divide the people into a majority of innocents and a minority of "the guilty." Now some opponents of the war were using the same method by denouncing not only weapons manufacturers as morally contaminated, but all institutions that continued to operate as implicated in the war, whether directly or indirectly.

I did not think it appropriate in a scholarly meeting to address this problem at a political level. My effort to do so at a scholarly level took the form of reminding my listeners that the critique of industrialism and of the wars and imperial expansions associated with it, had accompanied the development of modern society since the late eighteenth century. And paradoxically that critique, as Karl Mannheim's essay on conservative thought had shown more than a generation earlier, revealed a striking convergence between radical and conservative thought. To both camps the "industrial establishment" belonged to the children of darkness, though they differed greatly with regard to the children of light. The university as an institution, and social science scholarship in particular, has to take its stand somewhere between these stark alternatives, even in a period of political turmoil. This is why I spoke to that 1970 meeting of my professional association as I did.[3]

SCHOLARSHIP AND SOCIAL DESPAIR

Historical Perspectives and Sociological Inquiry as the theme of an American sociological convention would have been incongruous in the 1950s. It is not so in 1970. We meet amidst upheaval directly affecting the academic community. The social sciences and sociology in particular are at the center of the storm. The freedom to do scholarly work has been questioned when it is not directed to problems considered "relevant" by the critics. In this setting we must demonstrate to those willing to listen that great issues of the day can be examined with that combination of passionate concern and scholarly detachment which is the hallmark of reasoned inquiry in our field.

But there are those unwilling to listen. Detachment and analysis as hitherto practiced, and almost regardless of content, appear to them fatally impaired because they feel that even in the midst of great wealth they must live by an ethic of social despair. Here is one expression of this sentiment, taken from the privately circulated manuscript of a sociologist who is a respected member of a university faculty.

> Time is short; we cannot wait years for research to give us impregnable theses. America's academia fiddles while the fires are burning. Where are the studies of the new corporate power, of the Defense Department, of the military-industrial complex, of the new bureaucracies, of Vietnam? American academics are prisoners of liberal democratic ideology. Even as the chains rust, they do not move. A new current of reason and passion is arising in America—outside of its conventional institutions. The current of reason must flow faster to create an image of reality and hope for the future, for a ruling class in despair will soon reach for some other kind of ideology, and all that is left for the American establishment is "patriotism," that is fascism.

In this view the evils of the world loom so large that only those energies are employed legitimately which attack these evils head on. By that standard much or most scholarship fails.

You will say they are a minority. This is true. But the social despair that motivates this minority also moves larger numbers, perhaps at a distance but still significantly. Why do the few who feel moved by social despair evoke such resonance among the many?

In posing this question I am mindful of several contributions. The sharp rise in student unrest during recent years has been analyzed in terms of generational conflict. Lewis Feuer has amassed evidence on this theme from far and wide and on this basis delineated the symptoms of student protest. Bruno Bettelheim has provided us with "a psychograph of adolescent rebellion."

His emphasis, like that of Kenneth Keniston and Bennett Berger, is on an age-cohort of anxiety. In modern society there is a prolonged period of dependence between childhood and adult responsibility. In effect youths are permitted very early sexual experience. But when on that or other bases they claim or expect the independence of adults, education prolongs their dependence and an automated technology makes them feel obsolete. Edward Shils has analyzed the resulting protest in terms of a utopian fantasy of plentitude, a belief in the sacredness of immediate experience, and the consequent attack on all boundaries of discipline, institutions and authority.[4]

I have learned much from these and related analyses. But I also note that they end rather regularly with an appeal to the people over thirty. We are called upon to "stand firmly by the traditions of teaching, training, and research as the proper task of universities"; we should "not allow ourselves to be swept away by the desire to be 'with it,' to relive our lost youth or to prolong our fading youth."[5] I agree, but I ask myself whether this is enough. The literature on student protest often gives the impression of having been written by kindly uncles whose air of concern or sympathy and whose analytical stance give one no intimation of mortality. But we are mortal. When the value of scholarship is in question, an analysis confined to the protest of youth will appear patronizing. It will miss the fact that the protest expresses not only the disquiet of the children but also the growing uncertainty of their parents. In the midst of a crisis of legitimacy we must try once again to interpret the values we cherish and understand why our adherence to them has become ambivalent.

In addressing myself to this task I shall first characterize the belief in science that has become the central legitimation of universities. Second, I shall examine the attack on the value of academic scholarship which the great critics of modern civilization launched during the nineteenth century. Third, I want to show that, in the twentieth century, Western culture has been marked by a changed sensibility in the arts, which has increased the distrust of reason. Fourth, I will make reference to political aspects of this distrust of reason, especially by examining the rhetorical use of the term "fascism." Fifth, I shall note the greater institutional vulnerability of universities owing to the changed role of science since the Second World War. Finally, I shall offer an assessment of the problems facing sociology in a period when the belief in progress through knowledge has been impaired and the legitimacy of scholarship is in question.

THE BELIEF IN SCIENCE

The belief in science has remained remarkably consistent from the time of its first articulation in the seventeenth century to our own day. Francis Bacon wanted to inspire men with confidence that knowledge enhances human power. "Nature to be commanded must be obeyed; where the cause is not known the effect cannot be produced." He attacked the zealots who opposed science because they feared for religious faith and state authority.

> ... surely there is a great distinction between matters of state and the arts (science). . . . In matters of state a change even for the better is distrusted, because it unsettles what is established, these things resting on authority, consent, fame and opinion, not on demonstration. But arts and sciences should be like mines, where the noise of new works and further advances is heard on every side . . .[6]

By the mid-nineteenth century, the "noise of new works" was on all sides and scientists could speak with the confidence of great success.

For a representative statement we may turn to the physiologist Helmholtz who considered the purposes of the university in terms of the relation between the natural sciences and all other disciplines. In 1862, he noted the specialization and frequent incomprehension among the several disciplines and asked whether it made sense to have them continue in the same institution of learning. Helmholtz compared the disciplines in terms of the way in which they achieved their results and noted—as so many have since—the greater precision in the natural sciences and the greater richness and human interest in the *Geisteswissenschaften*. The latter have a higher and more difficult task and contribute to order and moral discipline. But in respect of method they can learn much from the sciences proper.

> Indeed I believe that our time has already learned a good many things from the natural sciences. The absolute, unconditional respect for facts and the fidelity with which they are collected, a certain distrust of appearances, the effort to detect in all cases relations of cause and effect, and the tendency to assume their existence—[all this] distinguishes our time from earlier ones and seems to indicate such an [exemplary] influence [of the natural sciences].[7]

The progress achieved through the advancement of science appeared to justify this position of the natural sciences as the model. Scientific knowledge is power and increases "the benefit and use of life." Helmholtz made two reservations only, as an aside. The scientist must become increasingly narrow in his specialization and "each student must be content to find his reward in rejoicing over new discoveries." Implicitly, all other qualities of the human mind were diminished.[8]

For a contemporary statement it is perhaps best to recall the thesis of C.P. Snow that "the intellectual life of the whole of Western society is increasingly being split into two polar groups."[9] World War II and the postwar years had been a period of unprecedented scientific advance and unprecedented public support of science. As a former research scientist Snow shared the resulting buoyancy of the scientific community. But as a writer sensitive to the critiques of science he put the case of science more perceptively than most. Everyone, he says, is aware of human tragedy at the individual level. Scientists certainly are. "But there is plenty in our condition which is not fate, and against which we are less than human unless we do struggle . . . . As a group, the scientists . . . are inclined to be impatient to see if something can be done: and inclined to think that it can be done, until it's proved otherwise. That is their real optimism, and it's an optimism that the rest of us badly need."[10] Snow contrasts this scientific creed with the cultural pessimism of literary intellectuals, whom he calls "natural Luddites." Ever since the industrial revolution men of letters have been critical witnesses of the tremendous advances of science and technology, unable or unwilling to see that the age-old scourges of hunger and poverty could be relieved only in this way.

The history of the belief in science still needs to be written, but the three examples I have cited are prominent enough. The commitment to scientific work makes sense if there is hope that in the long run the constructive uses of knowledge will prevail. Science presupposes a belief in the perfectibility of man; it does not flourish amidst preoccupation with its own potential evil. These are among the reasons why the scholar is freed of purposes extraneous to his inquiry, and why the institutional immunities of the university were considered legitimate.

THE ROMANTIC CRITIQUE

We accept these beliefs and institutional arrangements as long as we cherish the pursuit of knowledge. But during the last two centuries the legitimacy of this pursuit has been challenged repeatedly by appeals to the imagination and to authentic experience. Generational revolts have reflected this conflict of values between reason and the "poetry of life." Such revolts have erupted in movements of liberation during the nineteenth century and in radical movements at the end of World War I, during the Depression, and in the 1960's. Conflicts over the belief in reason are a major characteristic of Western civilization.

Schopenhauer, Kierkegaard, Nietzsche, Marx, and Freud are among the great iconoclasts of the last century. All of them questioned the autonomy of knowledge and asserted that knowledge is inseparable from its preconditions, whether these are called will, commitment, will to power, class situation, or libidinal sublimation. On this basis all five deny the possibility of scholarly detachment, and some deny that scientific knowledge is desirable at all.

Two distinct premises are involved. To Schopenhauer, Kierkegaard, and Nietzsche the search for knowledge appears as an arid suppression of life; they seek a true way to knowledge through Indian mysticism, or religious experiences, or a cultural regeneration by men larger than life. For these writers the sickness of our time is a deadened feeling and a mediocrity of spirit of which the universities are an especially glaring manifestation. Their attack on scholarship is part of a more general critique of culture.

By contrast, Marx and Freud believe in the pursuit of knowledge and its promise of emancipation, at the same time that they reject academic scholarship. According to Marx, universities are involved in the contentions of society and their claim to be above the battle is false. For him, true awareness of history requires a critique of the ideological foundation of scientific work. And this awareness is achieved through a unity of theory and practice only to be found in revolutionary movement, not in universities. By a similar reductionism Freud considers every intellectual position in terms of its function in the "psychic economy" of the individual. The quest for knowledge cannot escape this psychological process, just as for Marx it cannot escape the historical process. Hence the path to knowledge in psychology lies in a heightened awareness of self, induced by the analysis and control-analysis of psychoanalytic training. This extramural recruitment and training of psychoanalysis is as incompatible with academic psychology as Marx's unity of theory and practice is incompatible with academic sociology.

Whereas Marx and Freud believed in the pursuit of knowledge and its promise of emancipation, Schopenhauer or Kierkegaard, who revolted against the Enlightenment, believed in neither. Shelley's *Defence of Poetry* (1821) puts the case with great lucidity. Science and reason are distinguished from poetry and the imagination. The poets, says Shelley, "have been challenged to resign the civic crown to reasoners and mechanics" and he acknowledges that these have their utility. The banishment of want, the security of life, the dispersal of superstition, and the conciliation of interests are utilities promoted by the calculating faculty. This is of value as long as it remains confined to "the inferior powers of our nature." But poetry and imagination represent another, higher utility. "The great secret of morals is love; or a going out of our own nature, and an identification of ourselves with the beautiful which exists in thought, action, or person, not our own. A man, to be greatly good, must imagine intensely and comprehensively; he must put himself in the place of another and of many others; the pains and pleasures of his species must become his own."[11] The great difficulty is that in scientific and economic systems of thought "the poetry . . . is concealed by the accumulation of facts and calculating processes." Certainly, the sciences have enlarged our "empire over the external world." But in proportion as the poetical faculty is wanting, the sciences have also circumscribed the empire of the internal world.[12] Here is Shelley's own summation:

> We want the creative faculty to imagine that which we know; we want the

> generous impulse to act that which we imagine; we want the poetry of life: our calculations have outrun conception; we have eaten more than we can digest. . . . The cultivation of poetry is never more to be desired than at periods when, from an excess of the selfish and calculating principle, the accumulation of the materials of external life exceed the quantity of the power of assimilating them to the internal laws of human nature.[13]

It could not have been said more soberly.

But the romantic protest was not frequently sober. The praise of art was linked with a Promethean image of the poet as godlike, rising above mere humanity and achieving ends which nature is incapable of achieving by herself. These views from Shaftesbury and Goethe to Carlyle and Nietzsche meant, as Novalis put it, that "poets know nature better than scientists."[14] Such sentiments have a close kinship to attacks on the abstractions characteristic of all academic work. For Nietzsche all scientists were plebeian specialists and the worst enemies of art and artists. Kierkegaard made the central theme of his work the primacy of living over reflecting. Philosophy deals with man in general only and thus is a treason to life. What matters is man's personal situation and his vital relation to God.[15] In calling for more life and less thought, for more poetic imagination and less abstract reason, the romantics also attacked considerations of utility and the idea of material progress. Since the eighteenth century, scores of writers have elaborated the notion that the division of labor turns men into fragments, strangling their capacities and stultifying their emotions. This sentiment has implied an irrationalist, antiscientific stance so frequently since the industrial revolution that C.P. Snow is quite correct when he refers to literary intellectuals as "natural Luddites."

Yet the romantic protest of the nineteenth century was still bound up with the conventions of feeling and language that are the bases of discourse in ordinary life as well as in scholarship. By contrast, since before World War I a new sensibility in the arts has increasingly rejected that universe of discourse. The form and content of artistic expression have questioned the values of Western industrial civilization to such an extent that today the "Luddism" of literary intellectuals jeopardizes the legitimacy of academic pursuits and of much else besides. I can do little more here than sketch some tendencies that provide a ready arsenal for attacks upon universities and scholarship.

SUBJECTIVISM AND THE LOSS OF LANGUAGE

It is convenient to start with the generation of scholars and writers born in the 1850's and 1860's who were on the average a bit over forty around 1900. The classic writers of modern sociology belong to this generation. Beyond all the differences dividing them, men like Freud, Durkheim, Weber, Pareto, Park, Thomas, Cooley, and Mead are discernible as a group by their common concern with the subjective presuppositions of thought. This increased self-consciousness could easily become self-defeating. With Dilthey, for example, self-consciousness led to a skeptical relativism, while in the work of Sorel it produced a radical commitment in thought and action to overcome that relativism. Yet men like Freud, Durkheim, and Weber, while making room for this new awareness, fought "every step of the way to salvage as much as possible of the rationalist heritage."[16]

Max Weber's lecture "Science as a Vocation," delivered in 1919, is a document of this generation. It represents a careful blend of rationalist convictions and romantic sensibility. Like the great rationalists before him, but with none of their optimism, Weber commits himself to the scientist's calling. For him science is the affair of an intellectual aristocracy. It demands concentration, hard work, inspiration, and the passionate devotion to a task that can only be accomplished if all extraneous considerations are excluded. Increasing knowledge can enhance the "technical mastery of life." It helps us to perfect methods of thought and to achieve intellectual clarity about the relation of means and ends. Weber stated these goals with deliberate restraint. Like the great romantic iconoclasts before him, he viewed the ideal of progress through knowledge with profound skepticism. The very achievements of science have "chained [us] to the idea of progress." For every scientific achievement poses new questions and calls for investigations that will lead to the quick obsolescence of the scholar's contribution. Weber states: "It is not self-evident that something subordinate to such a law [of progress] is sensible and meaningful in itself. Why does one engage in doing something that in reality never comes, and never can come, to an end?"[17] Tolstoy attacked science because for men on this endless frontier death has no meaning; the logical goal of progress would be man's immortality. But in fact the scientific world view leaves the meaning of life and death undefined. Thus stating his case Weber deliberately rejected the idea that youth could find leadership and authentic experience in the universities.

Those academicians who want to assume the role of leader should engage in it where they can be challenged politically. Nor can the university teacher provide experience in the sense in which the churches offer it to the believer. Let those who search for authenticity learn that the individual who simply fulfills the exacting demands of the day, if he has found himself, expresses the creative spark that is within him. Weber addressed these remarks to a generation which rejected his own skeptical commitment to the Enlightenment tradition. The young men of the 1920's, like their age-mates in the years before World War I, demanded experience and action rather than words. Their drive had culminated in the enthusiasm with which they greeted the outbreak of war in 1914, and with which they were joining extremist movements of the Right or Left in 1918 to 1920.

But meanwhile imaginative writers had begun to explore the possibilities of relativism in a world without values, further helping to undermine the legacy of the Enlightenment still viable in men like Freud or Weber. The arts may have little direct bearing on science or scholarship, except where they destroy the notion of competence. However, their development in the twentieth century jeopardized the standards of discourse on which all academic work is based. The nature of this jeopardy is conveyed by two interrelated tendencies of modern art: the retreat from intelligibility and the emergence of a radical subjectivism. As Saul Bellow put it in *Mr. Sammler's Planet*: "When people are so desperately impotent, they play that instrument, the personality, louder and wilder."

Some nineteenth-century writers anticipated these developments. The German poet Novalis (1772-1801) wrote of poetry as a defense against ordinary life, a magical union of fantasy and thought, a productive language which like mathematics is a playful world of its own, intelligible only to a few.[18] Novalis was read in France. Many of these elements are elaborated by Baudelaire, whose poems are deliberately impersonal so that they can express every possible human emotion, preferably the most extreme. Baudelaire uses the term "modernity" to refer to the ugliness of large cities, their artificiality and sinfulness, their loneliness in large crowds, their technology and progress. He despised advertising, newspapers, the tide of a leveling democracy. But modernity also meant to him that these and other features of modern civilization result in a profusion of evil, decay, poverty, and artifice which fascinates the poetic imagination. Baudelaire and the many who followed him have had a desperate urge to escape this reality. Most of them were unbelievers with a religious longing. For them poetry became a magical incantation, designed to cast a spell rather than reveal a meaning. To this end fantasy decomposes the whole created world and by reordering the component parts out of the wellsprings of human experience fashions a new world of its own.[19]

A retreat from meaning and coherence is evident in this orientation. When the poet does not want to recognize the existing world, ordinary themes and objects lose their relevance. Instead, style and sound are the prevalent means of expression at the expense of meaning. The poet has no object, says one writer. Pure poetry must be devoid of content so that the creative movement of language can have free rein, says another. A third speaks of formal tricks maintaining the verve of style; nothing is interrelated either thematically or psychologically, everything is nailed up rather than developed. Writers like Rimbaud, Apollinaire, Saint-John Perse, Yeats, Benn, search for a "new language" which is tantamount to the destruction of grammatical rules and rhetorical order.[20] The spirit of this endeavor is beautifully expressed in T.S. Eliot's "East Coker." The poet is

> Trying to learn to use words, and every attempt
> Is a wholly new start, and a different kind of failure . . .
>   And so each venture
> Is a new beginning, a raid on the inarticulate . . .

And in "Burnt Norton" Eliot writes that "words strain, crack and sometimes break, under the burden, under the tension."

Where language thus loses its communicative power, a radical subjectivism comes into its own, much as in painting and sculpture a free experimentation with colors and forms followed the classical ideal of representation. In his study of poetry, Friedrich refers to this tendency as "dictatorial fantasy." Rimbaud had said that memory and the senses are only food for the creative impulse; the world which the poet leaves will no longer resemble its former appearance, because artistic fantasy has cruelly disfigured it.[21] Baudelaire, Mallarmé, Garcia Lorca, Proust, and Benn expressed similar ideas. In *The Counterfeiters* by André Gide, Edouard intends to write a novel which will be a sum of destructions, or a "rivalry between the real world and the representation of it which we make to ourselves. The manner in which the world of appearances imposes itself upon us, and the manner in which we try to impose on the outside world our own interpretation—this is the drama of our lives."[22]

In the main this drama has been "resolved" by a radical subjectivism of the artist. Not only language has been destroyed, but persons and objects as means and ends of creative activity. In the futurist manifesto of 1909, the rejection of language and of the human subject are directly linked. The author, Marinetti, argues for the destruction of syntax, the elimination of adverbs and adjectives, and the serial listing of nouns, in order among other things to destroy the ego in literature. "People are completely stupefied by libraries and museums, and they are subjected to a terrible logic and science. Man is no longer interesting. Therefore, one has to eliminate people from literature."[23] A parallel destruction of the object is evident in a comment of Picasso's. "I noticed that painting has a value of its own, independent of the factual depiction of things. I asked myself, whether one should not paint things the way one knows them rather than the way one sees them . . . . In my pictures I use the things I like. I do not care, how things fare in this regard—they will have to get used to it. Formerly, pictures approached their completion in stages . . . . A picture used to be a sum of completions. With me a picture is a sum of destructions."[24]

Here then is the paradox of the development I have sketched. Since the later nineteenth century modern art has been characterized increasingly by a retreat from meaning and coherence. That is to say, an ethics of social despair has led by circuitous routes to self-created, hermetic worlds of pure subjectivity in which neither the old romantic ideal of the human personality nor the objects and themes of ordinary experience have a recognized place or meaning. Thus, in the dominant culture of the West a type of sensibility has developed which reacts to the world as a provocation, and which is hostile to intellectual positions that retain a belief in the constructive possibilities of knowledge for all their questioning of fundamentals. In this way, the ground was prepared for protests which are based on

> the view that every human being simply by virtue of his humanity is an essence of unquestionable, undiscriminatable value with the fullest right to the realization of what is essential in him. What is essential is his sensibility, his experienced sensation, the contents of his imagination, and the gratification of his desires. Not only has man become the measure of all things; his sentiments have become the measure of man.[25]

Here is a statement which exemplifies this interpretation:

> We are fed reason in order to give an inferiority complex to the rest of our emotions and senses...
> We are trapped in a philosophical system of cause and effect. Rationality binds the mind and restricts the soul. It might even destroy the brain cells. We need to be liberated. We should be constrained no longer by possible rational consequences. We should begin to allow other emotions to dictate our actions.[26]

There is an "elective affinity" between a changed sensibility in the arts and the sectarian modes of protest which are inspired by a mystique of plenitude and subjectivism.

There is as well a political dimension to which brief reference must be made.

THE RHETORIC OF FASCISM

I emphasize the transformation of artistic sensibility for two reasons. The retreat from intelligibility and its radical subjectivism have long since prepared the ground for a distrust of reason among the educated middle class, including members of faculties as long as their own field is not in question. Also I emphasize the affinity between this changed sensibility and current student protests because I see little evidence that these protests have arisen from communist or fascist doctrines. To be sure, Bolshevism after the Russian Revolution of 1917 and the Nazi movement before and after 1933 launched a concerted attack upon the universities as bastions of false claims to scholarly objectivity. For example, A.A. Bogdanov declared in 1918 that with the exception of the social sciences transformed by Marxism "all the present sciences are bourgeois [though] not in the sense that they defend the interests of the bourgeoisie directly. [They are bourgeois] in that they have been worked out and presented from the bourgeois standpoint, in that they are suffused by the bourgeois Weltanschauung and as such have a bourgeoisifying influence. . . ." Bogdanov also added that all teaching and research must be transformed from the proletarian standpoint and based thenceforth on the "living, brotherly cooperation between teachers and students, rather than on authority and intellectual subjugation."[27] Overtones reminiscent of current protest themes will be noted, yet I believe that these are distinct.

The rhetorical use of the word "fascism" helps to characterize the situation in which we find ourselves. Students proclaim that the Establishment is fascist, and critics over thirty reciprocate by calling the protesters fascists, or as Jürgen Habermas had it, "left fascists." There is no clearer indication of mutual incomprehension. What does this mean? Let me take each side in turn, though of course, there is much diversity I must ignore.

Broadly speaking, "fascism" is for some students, some faculty members, and not a few writers an expressive term of utter derogation. It has a proven shock value for the older generation when applied to democratic institutions or indeed any aspect of industrial society. The term is also a potent weapon for a policy of escalation. Agitation may lead to police action, which proves that the regime is repressive like fascism. But if agitation does not lead to this result, then the question is raised: What did we do wrong? Since the regime is "objectively fascist" and the police was not called, the strategy of protest must have been at fault. There is no entry into this circle of a self-fulfilling prophecy.

Note the ethic of social despair that lies behind the provocation. Time has run out. No landing on the moon can assuage the prospect of a nuclear holocaust. The liberation movements around the world and the race problem at home have exposed the hypocrisy of the Western claim to liberty, justice, and equality. The invasion of Czechoslovakia and the manifest inequalities and repressions of Soviet society have exposed the hypocrisy of the Communist claim to represent the people and end the exploitation of man by man. Faced with ultimate horrors and proximate evils, protest draws once more on the arsenal of cultural pessimism with its total rejection of competition, efficiency, the division of labor, considerations of utility, and the whole world of technology. Last but not least is the visible tarnishing of the old promise of the Enlightenment, that knowledge is power for the benefit and use of life.

In the face of these massive evils, the first and sometimes the only response is to see everything as connected with everything else, and to call this web of iniquity fascism. Thus, universities, a central institution in a technological society, are a prime target. Their values of dispassionate inquiry and free discussion, of tolerance for ambiguity and diversity, presuppose an ethic of social hope, that means, a freedom to choose and to wait, to discuss and deliberate. To the protester this appears utterly incommensurate with the dire threats confronting us. An academia "which fiddles while the fires are burning" appears as actually engaged in an insidious "fascist repression," for discussion delays decision, and words are seen as a smoke screen for inaction. All the values of scholarship turn to dross: tolerance is repressive, objectivity or neutrality serve the "system," lectures become an abuse of authority, and indeed scholarship which uses abstract terms, as it must, "crumbles in the mouth like mouldy fungi,"[28] which phrase helped to initiate the change of sensibility I have traced. At one level or another, a good many people respond positively to these sentiments, faced as they are with a world of local wars and international stalemates in which the threat of nuclear destruction hangs over every move.

On the other hand there are the liberals, young or old, who are outraged by these attacks upon the values of civilization. To be sure, conservatives rather than liberals call for law and order. But as the legal system is dragged into the vortex of political polarization, "fascism" comes to be used by liberals as a term of alarm at the deliberate abandon with which standards of academic and democratic civility are flouted. It is a term of abuse against those who reject tolerance, discussion, and the rule of law—or in an academic setting against those who reject free inquiry, the quest for objectivity, and the civilities of academic deliberation. It refers as well to the all-or-nothing perspective which fails to distinguish between authority and oppression, normal national interest and violent aggression, political compromise and political corruption.

Liberals believe that the indiscriminate and immoderate attack upon all social and political conventions and upon traditional values is profoundly unpolitical. The liberals see protesters frequently attacking not only political abuses and empty pretensions, but the very institutions that protect their right to protest. To liberal critics it is clear that protesters are blind to the ways in which their activities consolidate opinion on the far right. But this characterization is answered by the protesters by saying that nothing else can be done, since ordinary politics have brought us to this impasse. Theirs is a sectarian mode of protest outside of time, of political calculation, and of technical efficiency.

Indeed, it is outside of ordinary communication when one considers how declamation has crowded out discussion. With or without drugs "the mystic finds himself exploring every negative experience in order to make possible his return to the world of a 'total' human being."[29] Meanwhile, his more activist brother develops a cult of distant savior-leaders like Mao or Che, identifies with populist causes everywhere, and unites with others in a desperate, if superficially euphoric, rejection of his own civilization.[30] In their indiscriminate attack upon social and political conventions the protesters begin to resemble intellectuals of the Weimar Republic, who were equally sweeping in their condemnations. Walter Laqueur has dubbed this the "Tucholsky Complaint" after the German satirist of the 1920's:

> Tucholsky and his friends thought that the German Judge of their day was the most evil person imaginable and that the German prisons were the most inhumane; later they got Freisler and Auschwitz. They imagined that Stresemann and the Social Democrats were the most reactionary politicians in the world; soon after they had to face Hitler, Goebbels, and Goering. They sincerely believed that fascism was already ruling Germany, until the horrors of the Third Reich overtook them.[31]

In a book entitled *Deutschland, Deutschland über Alles*, Tucholsky said "no" to everything except the landscape of Germany. But at least he despaired of a society without democratic traditions. Some recent critics like Herbert Marcuse simply despair of civilization altogether—without telling us how they would live without it.

Today, discussion within the academic community is gravely impaired by the distrust of reason of the present generation of dissenters. This rise of irrationalism in the cultural sphere is due in part to a failure of the national political community. In their relations with the young generation the universities cannot tackle issues like the Vietnam war, race relations, or the uses of technology which the political leadership has so far failed to resolve. The universities should not be asked to make the attempt. Nevertheless, protesters and politicians have misused the universities as a convenient battleground without immediate and obvious disadvantage to themselves. They have done so in part, because we are faced with a crisis of legitimacy within the walls of academe.

THE CHANGED ROLE OF SCIENCE

Agonizing questions are raised concerning the purposes to be served by a quest for knowledge wherever it may lead. When scientists help to create powers of destruction which threaten civilization, the authority of scholarship is placed in jeopardy, because the belief in progress through knowledge is impaired.

Strictly speaking, the uses of knowledge and the conditions that facilitate its pursuit are extraneous concerns. As Don Price has stated: "Science has achieved its great power by insisting on defining for itself the problems it proposes to solve, and by refusing to take on problems merely because some outside authority considers them important. But that power, and the precision of thought on which it depends, is purchased by a refusal to deal with many aspects of such problems."[32] The power referred to is the capacity to advance knowledge. But the capacity to define problems autonomously depends upon authority. And this autonomous authority has become more difficult to maintain in recent decades.

The role of science has changed. Scientific research in World War II and its culmination in the military and peaceful employment of atomic energy produced a marked rise in the authority of the scientific community. In his report to the president in 1945, Vannevar Bush spoke for that community when he argued strongly that basic scientific research is indispensable for the nation's welfare in war and peace.[33] Remember: only a year later Bernard Baruch declared that we tremble with fear as we think of the power science has put at our disposal, but science does *not* show us how we can control the dangers inherent in that power.[34] Nevertheless, for a time, the positive claims of science were accepted very generally. Between 1953 and 1966, gross national product in the United States doubled, but total funds for basic research increased more than six times. During the same period the federal government increased its support of basic research from one half to two thirds of the national total.[35] In the five-year period from 1959-60 to 1963-64, federal support of research in universities more than doubled.[36]

In the last twenty-five years science has become very prominent; even the social sciences have advanced, albeit at a great distance. Clark Kerr, in his Godkin lectures, has analyzed the resulting changes in academic decision-making. By offering projects, federal agencies exert a subtle but potent influence upon the directions which research at universities will take. They affect the allocation of funds and space and hence the establishment of priorities. As extramural research funds become a major portion of a university's research budget, many scholars are prompted to shift their identification and loyalty from their university to the grant-giving agency. Increased emphasis on research through extramural funds entails a shift of resources to graduate, at the expense of undergraduate, education, and to the employment of research personnel without faculty status. Projects, costly facilities, and program planning introduce a new managerial dimension. Scientists who launch a series of projects can become caught up in the apparatus they have helped to create, and may be deflected permanently from what they would prefer to do if they still had a free hand.[37] Thus the earlier autonomy of science and of universities is in doubt just at the time when the destructiveness of weapons and the dangerous side effects of modern technology have become urgent concerns.

In addition, the demands on the educational system have increased greatly. In 1939/40 50 percent of those aged 17 were high school graduates. By 1967/68 that percentage had risen to 74. During the same period college enrollments and the total number of college degrees increased by a factor of four and the number of higher degrees by a factor of seven. Nor is it a question of numbers alone. Increasingly, politicians, administrators, the general public, and not a few scientists, who should know better, have called upon the university to help solve the race problem, the urban crisis, generational conflict, pollution, the arms race. Scientists are called upon to be responsible for the application of their increasing knowledge at the same time that questions are raised whether the consequences of science are still beneficial. These and other demands subject the universities to a barrage of expectations which they cannot possibly fulfill. From being a method of inquiry to answer carefully delimited questions, science has been turned into a fetish with which to interpret the world, advise politicians, examine the future, provide an education, and entertain the public.

A crisis of legitimacy results whenever in critical periods the very claims of authority are used to question its justification. The claim is that "basic research performed without thought of practical ends" is indispensable for the nation's welfare.[38] But this claim has led to public support for science, which undermines the freedom of scientists from practical ends. The claim has also led to uses of knowledge which have a destructive potential that appears incompatible with welfare. In their eagerness to advance knowledge scientists have made claims for the unequivocal beneficence of their results. Inadvertently, they have contributed to the distrust of reason which is upon us.

THE PLACE OF SOCIOLOGY

Ordinarily we do not think of science and scholarship as bases of authority. But knowledge has an authority of its own, and I have tried to show why the legitimacy of that authority is now in question. Protest aimed at the foundations of academic institutions has found considerable resonance among people ostensibly committed to the life of the mind. What then of sociology?

Like all academic disciplines sociology depends on the existence of a scholarly community. A modern university comprises a congeries of such communities. Teachers and students in the different disciplines may communicate little or not at all. But while they live with their different interests and obligations, all of them can share an interest in the advance of knowledge—an advance facilitated by independent inquiry, free discussion, and academic self-government. When this shared interest is in doubt, more is at stake than spurious talk about an academic community. For when the legitimacy of the pursuit of knowledge is questioned, discourse itself is threatened by a withdrawal of affect. Let me spell this out in relation to sociology.

As in other disciplines, scholarship in sociology depends on communication concerning the findings and methods of study. In this context every statement made invites consent and helps to define the circle of those who agree, while to some extent marking off those who do not. We are all familiar with the feeling of dismay and anxiety, or with the displays of aggression, when such agreement is not achieved. We are also familiar with the school- or clique-building tendencies that arise from this desire for consensual validation. Accordingly, the twin principles of toleration and free discussion are more difficult to achieve within disciplines than in the university at large. Indeed, there is more to discuss within disciplines than between them, and withdrawal of affect within disciplines threatens discourse quite directly.

Many sociologists aspire to bring their field of study to the status of a science of society. To an extent this is salutary. The aspiration to engage in empirical inquiry is an indispensable bulwark against speculations which are complacent towards idiosyncrasies and take a lofty view of the merely factual. Yet today sociologists as scientists face a crisis of legitimacy. The destructive possibilities of knowledge and the diminished autonomy of science have prompted a questioning of premises which is bound to affect a discipline whose scientific aspirations are well ahead of its achievements. Moreover, sociologists of this persuasion should have noted the antihumanistic impulse of their model all along. It appears that the qualities of the scientific mind have been extolled at the expense of philosophical breadth and historical perspective, of literary distinction and aesthetic sensibility, of moral imagination and the cultivation of judgment. To be sure, much has been gained in the process. But a sociology that takes the natural sciences as its model also falls heir to a tradition in which these other qualities are at a discount.

At the same time we are all aware that in our discipline there have always been those who thought science not enough, who believed that the cultivation of judgment and moral sensibility was indispensable for sociology as a scholarly discipline. Such cultivation provides a bulwark against the dangers of scientism, against the preoccupation with techniques for their own sake, and against the unthinking denigration of contextual understanding. At the same time, sociologists of this persuasion are committed to empirical inquiry, broadly conceived. But today they, also, face a crisis of legitimacy. For the destructive possibilities of the distrust of reason, with its craving for authenticity and relevance, are evident once again. Hence the plea for more cultivation of judgment and sensibility in sociology should be made with care. A humanistic sociology which takes the distrust of reason as its model thereby undermines its own existence.

To me the tensions and debates between the scientific and the humanistic impulses appear as the foundation of modern sociology. Twenty years ago I wrote an essay on social science and the distrust of reason. My purpose then was to contrast an unreflective faith in science with the tradition of critical self-scrutiny reaching from Francis Bacon to Sigmund Freud. I wanted to warn that methodological preoccupations not be permitted to encroach on substantive concerns, lest we do harm to our discipline.[39] In the meantime there have been notable attempts to redirect our efforts, to which I have tried to contribute. Hence today I would emphasize that the distrust of reason is not furthered by scientism alone. It consists also in a consciousness of crisis, an ethic of despair, and a call for action which do away with learning and deliberation altogether. I think sociology is as endangered by this retreat from meaning and coherence as it was by spurious analogies from the natural sciences.

Still, we are also enriched by the creative interplay of the traditions that have formed us. Their constructive use depends upon faith in the possibilities of human reason. Those who would destroy that use and that faith would not long survive in a world in which the ideals of reasoned inquiry have been abandoned. As long as we do not go back to the caves in anticipation of holocausts to come, learning has a creative role to play in the human community. It can do so only in universities which exist in the society and for it, and which provide institutional protection for learning in order to perform their mission.

NOTES

1. Reinhard Bendix, "Social Science and Social Action in Historical Perspective," *Ethics*, LVI (April, 1946), 217-18. I have paraphrased my earlier wording, but retained the content.
2. Reinhard Bendix, *Social Science and the Distrust of Reason* (Berkeley: University of California Press, 1951), 42.
3. Reinhard Bendix, from *American Sociological Review*, 35:5, Oct. 1970, 831-43; prepared as Presidential Address, 65th Annual Meetings of the American Sociological Association, Washington, D.C., Sept. 1970.
4. See Lewis Feuer, *The Conflict of Generations* (New York: Basic Books, 1969), esp. chs. I and X; Bruno Bettelheim, "Obsolete Youth," *Encounter*, XXXIII, Sept. 1969, 29-42; Kenneth Keniston, *Young Radicals* (New York: Harcourt, 1968), 257ff. and *passim*; Bennett Berger, "The New Stage of American Man—Almost Endless Adolescence," *New York Times Magazine* (Nov. 2, 1969); and Edward Shils, "Plenitude and Scarcity," *Encounter*, XXXII, May 1969, 37-57.
5. Shils, *op. cit.*, 56.
6. Francis Bacon, "Novum Organum," in E.A. Burtt, ed., *The English Philosophers from Bacon to Mill* (New York: Modern Library, 1939), 64.
7. Hermann Helmholtz, "Über das Verhältniss der Naturwissenschaften zur Gesamtheit der Wissenschaft," *Populäre Wissenschaftliche Vorträge* (Brunswick: Friedrich Vieweg, 1865), I, 23. The lecture was delivered in 1862.
8. The second point is noted in ibid., 27; the first point is found in "Über das Ziel und die Fortschritte der Naturwissenschaft," *Populäre Wissenschaftliche Vorträge* (Brunswick: Friedrich Vieweg, 1876), II, 186. This lecture was delivered in 1869.
9. C.P. Snow, *The Two Cultures and a Second Look* (New York: Mentor Books, New American Library, 1964), 11. Originally formulated in 1956, these lectures were given and published in 1959; the addendum dates from 1963.
10. Ibid., 13-14.

11. P.B. Shelley, "A Defence of Poetry," in R.J. White, ed., *Political Tracts of Wordsworth, Coleridge and Shelley* (Cambridge: Cambridge University Press, 1953), 202.
12. Ibid., 205.
13. Ibid., 205-206.
14. See Judith Shklar, *After Utopia* (Princeton: Princeton University Press, 1969), 44-45, 54-57 and *passim*, for documentation of this point.
15. See the cultural critique based on these convictions in Sören Kierkegaard, *The Present Age* (New York: Harper Torchbooks, Harper and Row, 1962), *passim*. On this basis Kierkegaard directed a virulent polemic against scholars and universities.
16. H. Stuart Hughes, *Consciousness and Society* (New York: Knopf, 1958), 17.
17. Max Weber, *Essays in Sociology*, tr. and ed. by H.H. Gerth and C.W. Mills (New York: Oxford, 1946), 138.
18. These paraphrases are taken from the profound book by Hugo Friedrich, *Die Struktur der Modernen Lyrik* (Hamburg: Rowohlt, 1967), 28-29.
19. See ibid., 35-58, for an analysis of Baudelaire on which this statement is based.
20. Ibid., 149-52.
21. Ibid., 81-83, 136-38, 202-203.
22. Quoted in Wylie Sypher, *From Rococo to Cubism* (New York: Random House, 1960), 300-301.
23. Quoted from Walter Höllerer, ed., *Theorie der modernen Lyrik* (Hamburg: Rowohlt, 1965), 138.
24. Quoted from Walter Hess, ed., *Dokumente zum Verständnis der Modernen Malerei* (Hamburg: Rowohlt, 1956), 53.
25. Shils, *op. cit.*, 44. See the related comments by George Steiner, "The Language Animal," and by David Martin, "Visit to Inner Space," *Encounter*, XXXIII, Aug. 1969, 23, 71-73. Robert Nisbet's argument in "Who Killed the Student Revolution?" *Encounter*, XXXIV, Feb. 1970, 10-18 that the protest aimed at the society rather than the university, misses the amorphous quality of these sentiments. The "web of iniquity" critique does not allow for institutional distinctions.
26. Richard Hyland in *The Harvard Crimson* (Oct. 22, 1969) quoted in *Encounter*, XXXIV, April 1970, 30.
27. Quoted in Richard Lorenz, ed., *Proletarische Kulturrevolution in Sowjet-Russland (1917-1921)* (Munich: Deutscher Taschenbuchverlag, 1969), 218f. Analogous declarations, but with the accent on blood and soil, race purity, and the rest can be cited from the Nazi period. See the documentation in Hans Peter Bleuel and Ernst Klinnert, *Deutsche Studenten auf dem Weg ins Dritte Reich* (Gütersloh: Sigbert Mohn, 1967), 237f. and *passim*.
28. This phrase is taken from Hugo von Hofmannsthal, "The Letter of Lord Chandos," in *Selected Prose* (New York: Bollingen Series XXXII, Pantheon Books, 1952), 134; originally published in 1902.
29. David Martin, *op. cit.*, 73.
30. The two modes are well described by Shils, *op. cit.*, 43-46, and Richard Lowenthal, "Unreason and Revolution," *Encounter*, XXXIII, Nov. 1969, 28-32.
31. Walter Laqueur, "The Tucholsky Complaint," *Encounter*, XXXIII, Oct. 1969, 78.
32. Don K. Price, *The Scientific Estate* (Cambridge: Harvard University Press, 1967), 105.

33. Vannevar Bush, *Endless Horizons* (Washington: Public Affairs Press, 1946), 39-81. Progress in the social sciences and humanities is "likewise important," Bush said then, but that appears to be the only reference of this kind in the report.

34. See Bernard Baruch, The United States Proposals for the International Control of Atomic Energy, presented to the U.N. Atomic Energy Commission (June 14, 1946) in U.S. State Department, *The International Control of Atomic Energy, Growth of a Policy* (Washington D.C.: U.S. Government Printing Office, 1946), 138.

35. U.S. Department of Health, Education, and Welfare, *Digest of Education Statistics, 1968 Edition* (Washington, D.C.: U.S. Government Printing Office, 1968), 128 (Table 160).

36. Ibid., 95 (Table 115). It should perhaps be added that the total of $3.2 billion spent for basic research in 1966 compared with $18.9 billion spent for applied research and development.

37. Clark Kerr, *The Uses of the University* (New York: Harper Torchbooks, Harper and Row, 1966), 57-69. This summary selects the aspects most directly related to the autonomy of decision-making by scholars and universities. It should be noted that Kerr concentrates on the "federal grant university," but that analogous considerations apply to research funds from private foundations.

38. Bush, *op. cit.*, 52.

39. Reinhard Bendix, *Social Science and the Distrust of Reason* (Berkeley: University of California Press, 1951), *passim*.

4

SCIENCE AND THE PURPOSES OF KNOWLEDGE

Introductory Note

There is no last word in this debate about the hopes and fears associated with the quest for knowledge. In giving the preceding address to my socio-logical colleagues, I felt strongly that our problems as social science profes-sionals were not the real problems. Whatever effects and utilities the social sciences might have, they are not comparable in the foreseeable future with the world-wide impact of atomic energy, micro-chips, and computers. Therefore I participated for some years during the 1970s on the Berkeley campus in monthly discussions of science policy with colleagues from the natural and the social sciences, certainly an unusual opportunity for me. I learned a great deal about the policy choices physicists, chemists, geologists and engineers confront. I also learned a good bit about the frustra-tions they encountered in dealing with administrators and political decision-makers. But learning about these experiences and reading the related literature left a strong impression of the marked separation between the pursuit of knowledge and political decision-making. In the councils of government even the capacity of scientists to advise on questions of science policy is in doubt. What is more, I gained the impression that science advisors and practicing scientists are willy-nilly engaged in a quasi-political struggle with decision-makers over the distribution of scarce funds among competing lines of re-search. In this way I began a project on knowledge and action in the physical sciences, which I cannot complete. The following essay developed out of the discussions I have mentioned. It may be a first step in the right direction.

PURPOSES OF KNOWLEDGE

Until recently, nearly everyone wanted the benefits bestowed by science. Nearly everyone assumed that there are some scientists who understand or could analyze natural phenomena which are puzzling or unintelligible to us. But today these desires and assumptions have become troublesome. We have come to weigh the benefits of science against its destructive potential. And the questions arising from that comparison are casting a shadow of doubt over the quest for knowledge itself. In the light of these apprehensions I want to explore what scientists have said about the purpose of their work and what light these statements shed on the relations between scientists and the community at large. As a background for this discussion, I find it useful to review some of the different purposes which men have pursued in their search for knowledge.

Such a review must employ the term "knowledge" in the broad sense of man's cognitive faculties. Even as we confine ourselves to Western history, knowledge has been sought for many reasons and men have had different kinds of knowledge in mind. Indeed, the types and the purposes of knowledge are not easily distinguished. The classical Greek historians like Herodotus or Polybius witnessed the rise and fall of empires in quick succession. They were heirs to a view of the world which saw human affairs subject to the will and whim of the gods. By combining these two themes, they conceived of the mutability of fortunes as a general law. The future can be foreseen since good and ill fortune are as recurrent as the seasons. And because this is so, knowledge has the purpose of fortifying the soul and assuaging the envy of the gods. For in periods of the greatest triumph or the greatest calamity, the wise man bears in mind the opposite extremity of fortune. Knowledge is virtue where it helps men attain inner peace in the midst of the vicissitudes that are their lot.

In the eyes of Christian believers, this classical doctrine of eternal recurrence was profoundly impious. Only God can foresee the future, for the existence of the world depends upon His will and man is the purpose of God's creation. Holy Scripture contains God's word, which is vouchsafed to us through faith. Scripture teaches us that God made the world, that in the beginning man committed original sin, that Christ has suffered for our sins, and that at the end of time there will be a day of judgment. In contrast to the classical view, Christianity projects the image of a created world in which God's designs—however dimly understood—are fulfilled and in which for all their sins men can hope for a future different from the past. In the classical view, knowledge involves contemplation of the visible world. But in the Christian view, knowledge—based on faith—involves contemplation of what is invisible: God's providence behind the world of appearances and hope for redemption in a world to come.

In his systemization of these Christian views, Thomas Aquinas distinguished between speculative and practical reason. The first concerns things that are unchangeable and eternal, like God's act of creation and the "fulness of Being which all things seek after and desire."[1] These are objects of contemplation only. By contrast, practical reason involves knowledge that springs from experience and concerns that which is changeable. There is a connection between these two kinds of reason. Speculative reason or contemplation of truth, goodness, and beauty can have an enlightening effect on the whole person and hence lead to wisdom in our use of knowledge provided by practical reason. But such theory in the classical sense is an end in itself. It is not a means used to improve scientific methods or promote the invention of new knowledge. In this view, practical reason is always second best, a response to man's necessities. The best is speculative reason, contemplation for its own sake, where man is most free. This view presupposes the belief in a hierarchy of being. Beyond necessity, apart from the spell of common things, a realm of perfection is believed to exist. Contemplation of that realm is the kind of knowledge which alone can create happiness in the soul of the knower.

Modern science originated when this Christian interpretation was rejected. For Francis Bacon, science is man's way of conquering the necessities and miseries of mankind. He was right to insist that these worldly concerns had been neglected by speculative reason, which, he says, is barren of results. Indeed, as long as theory consists in contemplating what is eternal, it cannot be used for the "invention of knowledge." In his famous advocacy of science, Bacon proposes that men seek knowledge of nature through observation and experiment, "by commanding nature in action." In this way, knowledge of nature's laws of action is achieved, because the scientist himself engages nature in action. As Professor Jonas points out, nature here consists only of common things. All dignity belongs to man the knower, who studies necessities in order to achieve delivery from the yoke of necessity. In Bacon's view, knowledge is "for the benefit and use of life," the "kingdom of man" consists in his mastery over nature. In taking this position,

> be it remembered then that I am far from wishing to interfere with the philosophy which now flourishes. . . . I do not object to [its] use . . . for supplying matter for disputations or ornaments for discourse—for the professor's lecture and for the business of life. Nay, more, I declare openly that for these uses the philosophy which I bring forward will not be much available. . . . It does not flatter the understanding by conformity with preconceived notions. Nor will it come down to the apprehension of the vulgar except by its utility and effects.
> Let there be therefore (and may it be for the benefit of both) two streams and two dispensations of knowledge; and in like manner two tribes or kindreds of students in philosophy. . . . Let there in short be *one method for the cultivation, another for the invention, of knowledge.*[2]

Bacon knew that he faced opposition on two fronts. To the clergy he said in effect that science is concerned with nature rather than questions of faith and morals. He prayed that "things human may not interfere with things divine." He urged upon all right-thinking men that increased knowledge of nature would fortify faith and that those who doubted this gave little evidence of their religious conviction. To men of affairs his argument was that there is as great a distinction between science and matters of state as there is between science and faith. In the sciences, "the noise of new works is (and should be) heard on every side," because this is evidence of "*new* light" on questions of nature.

But "in matters of state a change even for the better is distrusted, because it unsettles what is established; these things resting on authority, consent, fame and opinion, *not on demonstration*."[3] Thus politics is as excluded from the concern of the scientist as is religion.

Still, Bacon made a significant distinction between the clergy and men of affairs. With regard to the former, he only pleaded for toleration of this new learning. With regard to the latter, he noted that whereas the growth of knowledge comes from "great wits," the prizes and rewards for "new works" are in the hands of "great persons, who are but in very few cases even moderately learned." And even "great persons" despair and think things impossible, so that Bacon's task is to inspire hope. Since cautions and doubts will seem plausible even to

> grave men and of great judgment, we must take good heed that we not be led away by our love for a most fair and excellent object to relax or diminish the severity of our judgment; we must observe diligently what encouragement dawns upon us and from what quarter; and putting aside the lighter breeze of hope, we must thoroughly sift and examine those which promise greater steadiness and constancy. Nay, and we must take state-prudence too into our counsels, whose rule it is to distrust, and to take the less favorable view of human affairs.[4]

It seems, then, that Bacon thought he could leave questions of faith to one side, but that the advocacy of science had to concern itself with things "resting on authority, consent, fame and opinion, not on demonstration."

Ever since Bacon, scientists have stated the purpose of knowledge and justified their own efforts in much the same terms. Of course, they have differed from Bacon in specifics, as their understanding of science has advanced beyond his. Nor have they observed his cautionary comments on affairs of state. Rather, under the profound impression of Newton's work, scientists enlarged the domain of nature to include man and society. As Fontenelle put it in the eighteenth century: "A work on ethics, politics, criticism, or even eloquence, other things being equal, is merely so much more beautiful and perfect if it is written in the geometric spirit."[5] Still, in basic terms scientists have agreed with Bacon that their purpose is to advance knowledge "for the benefit and use of life." With Bacon, they have assumed that all knowledge is conducive to that end. Hence, the defense of science partly takes the form of describing what is proper to the pursuit of scientific knowledge.

THE IDEOLOGY OF SCIENCE

What do modern scientists say concerning the purpose of knowledge? To answer this question properly would require a representative survey of opinion which cannot be attempted here. Instead, an effort is made to portray the *range of opinion* that has been expressed without assessing which views are indeed prevalent. The point is that practicing scientists strike certain characteristic attitudes, and a review of these is sufficient to raise the further question concerning relations between scientists and the community at large.

Since the Baconian tradition identifies the progress of knowledge with "the benefit and use of life," scientists often see little difference between a description of scientific knowledge and a statement of its purpose. Broadly speaking, one can distinguish two positions, each subject to considerable elaborations with consequent overlaps between the two. One position starts from the *utility* of science and elaborates on the causes and consequences of that utility. The other starts from the *community* of scientists (presupposing utility) and elaborates on the causes and consequences of the scientific community. I shall discuss these in turn.

Bacon's justification of science was that it is conducive to the "benefit and use of life." From the seventeenth century to the present, this hope and expectation has had pervasive influence.

> Nobody nowadays any longer reproaches Newton with having ravished the rainbow of its beauty. Scientific knowledge has, it is true, killed many legends; but has it not also been a source of enthusiasm, of self-dedication and self-sacrifice and, indeed, of poetry? The earth of the astronomers . . . is not less moving, no less exciting for a poet, a psychologist or a religious mind than the earth-at-the-centre-of-the-world which the ancients and the Middle Ages extolled. Man has adapted himself to the progress of science, and the life of the mind has lost nothing in the process.

The author of this passage then lists the ways in which applied science has benefited man. Labor output ceases to be the product of toil alone. Technical innovations like the car or the airplane have "multiplied all the emotions of speed, thrilling and enriching the lives of millions of men." Synthetic products are often an aesthetic as well as utilitarian improvement over natural products. In sum, the history of scientific discoveries and technical innovations is a great human epic, their future progress is inevitable, and the task is to overcome the dissociation between technology and the life of the mind.[6] Not that this appeal elaborates upon what "utility" means. References to the reduction of labor and the usefulness of synthetic products blend with appeals to the aesthetic improvement of new products, the emotional excitation of new knowledge and new techniques, and the poetry, enthusiasm, and self-sacrifice involved in scientific discovery.

There are many elaborations upon the "beauty" of scientific work, but the bedrock of utility should be noted. Scientists are clearly aware that public confidence in the promise of science has weakened and they respond by emphasizing its indispensability. As Victor Weisskopf has noted:

> Despite the loss of public confidence, the fact remains that society is more dependent on science today than ever before in history. . . . The new knowledge which results from basic science is crucial to the development of practical solutions and to the improvement of human welfare.[7]

Much of the same sentiment is expressed by Gerald Holton, who buttresses the argument further by raising the specter of ignorance and appealing to man's (God-given?) capacities:

> In order to survive and to progress, mankind surely cannot ever know too much. Salvation can hardly be thought of as the reward of ignorance. Man has been given his mind in order that he may find out where he is, what he is, who he is, and how he may assume the responsibility for himself which is the only obligation incurred in gaining knowledge. . . .

Holton's is perhaps the most comprehensive defense of science on utilitarian grounds. He expresses particular alarm at the recurrent call for a moratorium on research. He explicitly rejects the idea that we should wait until humanity will develop the "spiritual and social resources for coping with the inhumane uses of modern technical results." In taking this position, he seems to subscribe to the view that science alone must and can discover answers to the problems which science and technology create. But he also seems to imply that even in the absence of such answers we must still move forward in research while hoping for a change in human attitudes.[8]

It seems, however, that scientists are never entirely comfortable with the appeal to utility. They will be the first to emphasize that a search for knowledge solely concerned with producing directly usable results will have little importance. Basic research without thought of where it might lead is their watchword, and they have much evidence to back them up. As a result, the utilitarian argument has a fallback position in terms of the psychology of scientific work. Weisskopf refers to "the intrinsic value of basic science and the constructive spirit it engenders." He writes:

> This passionate search for greater insight is a powerful force in today's world. . . . The scientific state of mind leads to . . . an awareness of laws and principles. . . . These concepts have created a scientific community with a unique character—a community rooted in a common aim, a common approach, a common set of values, a common satisfaction in new advances and discoveries.

Gerald Holton puts the same idea even more strongly:

> Science is not an occupation, such as working in a store or on an assembly line, that one may pursue or abandon at will. For a creative scientist, it is not a matter of free choice what he shall do. Indeed, it is erroneous to think of him as advancing towards knowledge; it is, rather, knowledge which advances towards him, grasps him, and overwhelms him. . . . It would be well if in his education each person were shown by example that the driving power of creativity is as strong and as sacred for the scientist as for the artist.[9]

Writings of this type come in fragments, but they have certain pervasive themes. The thrill of discovery is noted. Understanding and control of nature is counted among the great successes of mankind, along with the great religious insights and the enrichment of life by the arts. The qualities of scientists are extolled: the aesthetic experience of discovery, the striving for truth as a principle of conduct and a ground for morality. The division between science and the humanities is deplored as artificial; education in science should be part of general education. Public distrust of the sciences is deplored, and it is hoped that enlightened public relations will set these matters to rights.[10]

Accordingly, the transition from a utilitarian to a communitarian perspective is inevitable. Scientists quite appreciate the utility of their work, but those who emphasize utility will be quick to add that scientists are something more than tinkerers or empty empiricists and that random collections of facts will not satisfy them. Scientists are as unanimous as men are likely to get that the single-minded pursuit of knowledge and the "need to communicate one's findings and to make them acceptable to other people" are foundations of the scientific enterprise. Conceptual rigor and creative imagination are alike indispensable to productive research. But once these qualities of mind are stated clearly, it becomes important to emphasize the type of community in which they can thrive. Both single-minded concentration and effective communication require that scientists confine themselves to carefully selected and clearly defined problems. As Don Price put it:

> Science has achieved its great power by insisting on defining for itself the problems it proposed to solve, and by refusing to take on problems merely because some outside authority considers them important. . . . The demand of each scientific discipline for the right to choose its own problems, and fit them to its concepts and techniques and instruments, suggests that science is not eager to undertake to solve the problems as society would define them . . .[11]

Thus the very functions of the scientific community depend upon its relative isolation from the problems of society and so, it seems, do the ethics of searching for truth in general. Of course, those who emphasize this autonomy will be quick to add that only in this way can the pursuit of knowledge be effective. And from there it is a short step to the claim that such effective pursuit must be allowed, for in the long run it is indispensable for human welfare. In a sense, the two positions are interchangeable. Scientists cannot make claims for the long-run utility of knowledge without some reference to the conditions that facilitate scientific inquiry. And they cannot well lay claim to the privileges of the scientific community at work without some reference to the benefits to be derived from knowledge.

In a defensive posture it is difficult to maintain a balance between such related but conflicting imperatives. It is not surprising, therefore, that exaggerations abound. Some scientists question appeals to utility altogether. At least one professor of chemistry is reported to have said that he who works on the body of nature with diligence and care is exempted from the question of whether his activity makes sense.[12] Few scientists would accept this statement, but many would agree that the search for knowledge must be valued for itself. Not the use of knowledge, but the search for truth is the central value of the scientific enterprise. Bronowski has formulated a categorical imperative for such a scientific community: "We *ought* to act in such a way that what is true can be verified to be so." Scientists, he elaborates,

> do not make wild claims, they do not cheat, they do not try to persuade at any cost, they appeal neither to prejudice nor to authority, they are often frank about their ignorance, their disputes are fairly decorous, they do not confuse what is being argued with race, politics, sex or age. . . . These are the general virtues of scholarship, and they are peculiarly the virtues of science (75). . . .
>
> Science is not a mechanism but a human progress . . . Human search and research is a learning by steps of which none is final, and the mistakes of one generation are rungs in the ladder, no less than their corrections by the next (82). . . . As a set of discoveries and devices, science has mastered nature; but it has been able to do so only because its values, which derive from its method, have formed those who practice it, into a living, stable and incorruptible society (86). . . .
>
> The society of scientists is simple because it has a directing purpose: to explore the truth. Nevertheless, it has to solve the problem of every society, which is to find a compromise between man and men. It must encourage the single scientist to be independent, and the body of scientists to be tolerant. From these basic conditions, which form the prime values, there follows step by step the spectrum of values: dissent, freedom of thought and speech, justice, honor, human dignity and self-respect (87-88). . . .
>
> The society of scientists must be a democracy. It can keep alive and grow only by a constant tension between dissent and respect, between independence from the views of others and tolerance for them (80). . . .

But this idealized community of knowledge seekers is perhaps as questionable as the utilitarian model. For the ethics of the community are also confined to that community and have not entered our conduct of public affairs. "Science," says Bronowski,

> has nothing to be ashamed of even in the ruins of Nagasaki. The shame is theirs who appeal to other values than the human imaginative values which science has evolved. The shame is ours, if we do not make science part of our world, intellectually as much as physically, so that we may at last hold these halves of the world together by the same values (93-94). . . .[13]

Here the purpose of knowledge is said to be that *scientists* practice the virtues *all of us* cherish. And we end in the *imperative* mode, that one day these values of the scientific community must become universal, the values of the human community at large.

These exaggerations of utility and community probably result from the passionate commitment without which scientific work cannot be done. But there are good reasons why even the more moderate statements of purpose blend the utilitarian with the communitarian position. Once the Baconian position is assumed, descriptions of scientific knowledge will include statements of purpose, tacitly or otherwise. Hence, when scientists describe the methods of inquiry required for constructive work, such description characterizes the scientific community as well. The point becomes clear in a discussion by von Weizsäcker, who deals explicitly with the "crisis of science." Weizsäcker sums up the characteristic methods of science as a striving for objectivity, if this phrase is taken to mean that scientific work is factual, detailed, causal, radical, public, and free of extrascientific purposes. It will suffice to concentrate here on the last three points, which are especially germane to an understanding of scientific communities at work.[14]

The objectivity of scientific work in terms of its factual, detailed, and causal bent is generally familiar. But in what sense is that work *radical*? Every discovery leads to further questions, and as long as this is the case knowledge remains incomplete. Radical questioning is what drives this quest forward and has led to the augmentation of verified knowledge in such fields as astronomy, physics, and biochemistry. In other fields, such intensity of questioning is less practicable, because the phenomena are more complex and hence the analytic decomposition needed to reach clear-cut results is more difficult to achieve. Accordingly, scholarly disciplines may be distinguished by their degree of "radicalism," and physicists are wont to look at some disciplines as flabby because they do not carry their questioning very far. At the same time we should distinguish clearly between *theoretical* and *technical* radicalism, between the desire to enhance knowledge and the drive to construct whatever we are technically capable of constructing. Weizsäcker notes a dangerous affinity between these two types of radicalism, especially in a phase of scientific development in which the manipulation of technical instruments itself has become an integral part of scientific research.

The *public disclosure of research results* is another paradoxical aspect of modern science. Science may be esoteric but it is not secret. Its success depends on institutions which train and recruit new scientists, whose capacity for radical inquiry will set them apart from the public. Within the circle of specialists, complete and rapid communication is demanded. No contribution to science is recognized as such until it has been published, although in some fields claims to priority are recognized if they are based on mimeographed and dated papers that have been circulated. Specialized publications are indispensable to scientific progress but addressed to a very circumscribed audience. In this way, freedom of expression is confined to a circle of specialists and intensifies their cultural isolation. The purpose of freedom is an exchange of views and the establishment of consensus among specialists. When that freedom is used to alter consensus by new theories and discoveries, it is only the community of specialists which can assess the new ideas. But the repercussions of such altered consensus may reach far beyond that community.

The *exclusion of purposes extraneous to science* can only be justified by a belief in the *value* of knowledge and of the methods appropriate to advance knowledge. Thus research should not be contaminated by what we would like to be true; it should be capable of an empirical validation by those competent to judge, regardless of personal preferences. This simple injunction solves no methodological or philosophical problems. It describes the attitude of the average scientist as Francis Bacon did three centuries ago:

> The human understanding is no dry light, but receives an infusion from the will and affections; whence proceed sciences which may be called "science as one would." For what a man had rather were true he more readily believes. Therefore he rejects difficult things from impatience of research; sober things, because they narrow hope; the deeper things of nature, from superstition; the light of experience, from arrogance and pride, lest his mind should seem to be occupied with things mean and transitory; things not commonly believed, out of deference to the opinion of the vulgar. Numberless in short are the ways, and sometimes imperceptible, in which the affections color and infect the understanding.[15]

Thus the scientist should beware of credulity, faintheartedness, and superstition as well as of pride or an undue deference to the opinions of others. Any of these impulses might prompt men to pronounce judgment, when it would be more honest for them to withhold it. But once all such extraneous emotions or forces are excluded, one should state one's opinion forcefully when one thinks it justified on scientific grounds, and clearly reject opinions which are false. This code of conduct may appear simple, but it was developed with considerable difficulty and in disciplines without rigorous criteria of validation it is difficult to follow to this day.

THE CIVIC PROBLEM OF SCIENCE

These different statements of purpose add up to a characterization of the scientific community as an elite. To be sure, scientists do not put the purpose of knowledge that way. But they say that their aim is to make a contribution to knowledge which will be recognized by the community of their peers, that is, those competent to judge in a given specialty. Hence the purpose of training is to enable the scientist to so conduct his research that he can convince others of his findings. The purpose of scientific methods is, then, not only to increase knowledge but also (through publications) to obtain and even to compel consent.[16] There is some danger that we define scientific "communities" in terms of a membership which already subscribes to the consensus it is supposed to establish by critical evaluations arrived at independently. But in practice the danger is averted because consensus among scientists always remains provisional and extends only to the accumulated knowledge which scientists teach their beginning students. On the frontiers of exploration, new questions are raised and may challenge previously accepted conclusions so that much remains uncertain and controversial.[17] Neither a lawyer nor a doctor could make the case for his profession in the same terms. These professions are also communities based on a common training and esoteric knowledge which sets them apart from the public. But lawyers and doctors make their living by providing their esoteric services to clients, who have encountered problems which they cannot handle by themselves. By contrast, scientists engaged in basic research choose their own problems. Their solutions do not render a personal service at all.[18]

The contrast may be exemplified further. To scientists, a moratorium on research amounts to a preference for ignorance.[19] Yet in a profession like medicine the concept of a moratorium is more acceptable because the purpose of healing is more specific than that of acquiring knowledge. A clinical moratorium refers, for example, to a suspension of certain surgical techniques when the fatality rate is considered too high.[20] By contrast, a moratorium on research would have to be quite general, just because increases of knowledge, its uses and misuses, are unpredictable. Thus the difference between science and the professions is related to the difference between general and specific purposes. Such differences are found within science itself: many scientists provide services like professionals. Their work in "applied fields" is expected to suit the purposes of their clients or employers. For that reason the scientific community of basic researchers usually does not include them. Underlying this distinction is a different conception of purpose. As a research

director of the Atomic Energy Commission pointed out: "The more specifically one tries to define the practical purpose of a research, the more indefinite
becomes its bearing on the important questions of science and the less reason a
scientist can find for doing it."[21] Accordingly, those scientists whose only
purpose is the search for knowledge put a barrier between themselves and all
those who are naturally interested in specific accomplishments.

Scientists have no choice in the matter. They *are* engaged in an endless
quest for knowledge in which direct utility must remain a secondary consideration and in which questions of purpose can only be answered by reference
to the excitement of exploration and discovery. Their endeavor is regarded by
the ability to obtain, even to compel, consensus by men of critical acumen,
trained to subject all findings to ruthless examination, but trained also to give
their emphatic consent once the work has passed muster. In such a scientific
community, questions about what progress means, or challenges posed by the
destructive potential of knowledge, are found disquieting or even alarming.

In his essay "Science as a Vocation," Max Weber pointed out that the sciences have three basic aims: they develop methods of research; they advance
our technical mastery of nature; and they clarify how events are, or can be,
brought about. Weber spoke of scholarship in the broad sense of *Wissenschaft*
rather than of science only, and he commented on the spiritual uncertainty at
the core of all scholarly endeavor. Every achievement in research calls for investigations that will supersede it. The individual scientist who hopes for advances in his field must welcome such evidence of progress. His own contribution can only be part of a collective undertaking. He is caught up in a demanding task, for which no end is in view. He is trapped by progress for its
own sake, by that "most fatal of human follies—[not knowing] when to
stop," as Henry James put it. Nor can the sciences relieve men of the need to
make moral and political decisions. The scientific world view leaves open the
meaning of life and death, and scientists should not pretend otherwise. Men
who cannot find peace in a world bereft of such meaning should go to their
church, not to the university. Thus, for all of his appreciation of scientific
achievements, Weber expressed a bleak view of the scientific enterprise as a
whole: "It is not self evident that something subordinate to such a law [of
progress] is sensible and meaningful in itself. Why does one engage in doing
something that in reality never comes, and never can come, to an end?"[22]

Until recently, scientists themselves have not shared these misgivings.
Their work commits them to an ethic of social hope which has little room for
Weber's demand that the mounting problems of scientific progress be faced
squarely. As Ziman pointed out:

> The scientific community is not nearly so troubled about its own well-being as
> some of the sociologists of science seem to think. It is not a tribe, or an indus-
> trial corporation, trying to maintain its own stability and continuance as a social

entity; it is a voluntary association of individuals dedicated to a transcendental aim—the advancement of knowledge.[23]

There are, indeed, sociological reasons why scientists thus neglect the negative repercussions of scientific progress. It is still debated in what sense scientific inquiry is limited at any given time by the questions and methods which scientists in a given field consider plausible or promising. But a degree of consensus results from the academic socialization of young scientists as well as from the peer-group orientation of accomplished scientists. And such consensus is more easily maintained where the value of the enterprise itself is not in question.[24]

But while scientists have not shared Weber's misgivings, they have taken much the same view of the restrictions under which they work. They are indeed an intellectual elite who select and train aspiring scientists in esoteric skills and who claim sole competence to evaluate the results of research. Certainly there is keen competition among scientists, especially on the frontiers of research. The acknowledged contribution of the pioneer is highly prized. But such competition occurs within a cooperative framework which alone can provide the required standards of validation. Scientists are necessarily distinguished from laymen. They need not, and mostly do not, question the value of knowledge which gives them this privileged position, for their "privilege" is one of achievement. It is open to any aspirant with the requisite talent and willingness to learn. As an individual, the scientist thus tends to have a good conscience, even with reference to the elitism from which he benefits.

However, collectively scientists are in a much weaker position. Their civic problem consists in their need for support from the society. Laymen are called upon to provide resources for scientific research. Yet laymen are aware, if they are not reminded, that they do not understand what they support. They are baffled by the methods through which scientific results are achieved. Scientists achieve their results without power in the ordinary sense. As men, scientists are weak. They lack the accoutrements of strength like wealth, public position, or military force upon which other groups base their exclusive rights or special authority. Instead, scientists use skills to acquire knowledge and the power which knowledge provides. To laymen, these skills seem a "mystery" and hence vaguely dangerous. Moreover, secularism makes it impossible for scientists to acquire that purity in the eyes of the laity which in other civilizations has accrued to the religious guardians of mysteries. Unlike these guardians, scientists cannot readily assure the public that forces not commonly understood (like those associated with knowledge) are in safe hands.[25]

Collectively, scientists possess a latent power which neither their personal probity nor their professions of good intent can legitimate before the public. In the absence of accountability, either symbolically through ritual purification or through secular control, scientists depend on the trust which their work has inspired in the past. That trust has been considerable, but today it is beset by doubts. Scientists push for increased support and become restless when it is denied. But the public, when it grants more resources, also has occasion for the renewal of anxiety. In this setting, declarations on behalf of science are made and an ideology of science develops.

Like everyone else, scientists want to be appreciated, and not only by their own kind. While they know that the beauty and subtlety of their work is understood only by their peers, they are quite willing to explain that work to a broader public. Some of the best scientists are also very gifted popular expositors, and it is standard practice for eminent men to take their turn at such popularization. But as these activities proliferate, they encroach on the scientist's time. In the long run, scientific work and activities in its behalf are barely compatible activities. For such activities exact their toll in time and in a diminution of scientific acumen, especially as work in a given specialty advances. Thus a dilemma is built into the role of the scientific specialist. Preoccupation with research is inversely proportional with attempts to manage the civic problems of science, or very nearly so.

But the civic problems must be handled, lest their neglect harm the scientific enterprise. Younger scientists are often reluctant to undertake the task. On the other hand, there are many others who become active on behalf of science. Some older, established scientists welcome these less demanding activities. Among the younger scientists, not all come up to the mark in their own eyes or those of their peers. Still other scientists with the requisite training prefer not to become research scientists themselves. Thus in this penumbra of science, a good many persons fill in for those whose research leaves them no time to handle the civic problems of science. But this obvious division of labor between researchers and scientific spokesmen may be strained. For the criteria of excellence within the scientific community are frequently at odds with the symbolic representations made to the public at large.

Moreover, science has a special audience within this larger public. Laymen in high political, civilian, or military positions make decisions affecting science. Large numbers of service personnel make up the "infantry" of the scientific enterprise, people who aid in research and the transmission of knowledge without being engaged in its creation. And many people within the general public have become aware, in one degree or another, that their daily lives are bound up with the results of scientific work. These are among the constituencies whose understanding of science depends upon popularization and ideological appeals. The legitimacy of science is based upon the trust of these constituencies. It may be that since Hiroshima and Nagasaki scientists have entered an era when that trust can no longer be taken for granted.

SCIENCE AND CULTURE

The elitism of scientists is an attribute of modern culture that poses special problems when the legitimacy of science is questioned. In this concluding section, I want to discuss this general cultural problem and the challenges to science which have been raised over the years.

All major civilizations face a split between the great and the little traditions, as Robert Redfield has suggested. The great tradition includes the arts and sciences, the esoteric preoccupations of a cultural elite. The little tradition includes the way of life of the people, the artifacts of daily life, and the conventions transmitted from one generation to another. There are scientific theories which explain how our science-based technology works. These theories are part of the great tradition. But science also touches our daily lives through the technical application of its principles. Wherever it does, it becomes part of the little tradition, and so does the ideology of science, the promise that "science works" which is accepted by large numbers. The daily use of a science-based technology and the public's failure to understand how "it works" are part of the little tradition.

Scientific spokesmen have been able to count on a general approbation of their belief in progress through science. More knowledge is always demanded to help solve problems that have arisen, even problems that are repercussions of increased knowledge itself. Indeed, the mass media use science as a magic incantation, much as sorcerers employ certain ritual formulae. There seems good reason to hope for miracles where such marvels have been accomplished already. And where such hope prevails and is deliberately encouraged, the public is unrestrained by any knowledge of the difficulties that scientists face. Accordingly, scientists encounter little comprehension when they refuse to attack certain problems altogether. They will insist that they can hope to solve only problems they have formulated themselves. But this insistence necessarily disappoints the rising expectations of what science can do. In this popular perspective, scientists seem to hold back on the very promise of knowledge that has been widely accepted. Thus the layman is divided from the scientist by a great cultural distance much as the average believer was divided from the theologian. And scientists face the same problem theologians faced: how to relate the abstract preoccupations of a cultural elite to the daily conduct of ordinary men.[26]

Religion and science have interesting similarities and differences. Some aspects of religion also belong to the great tradition. Among these are theology, ecclesiastical organization, and the inspiration of religious teachers and prophets. But these religious concerns of an elite must involve the feelings and thoughts of large numbers. Indeed, religions that go beyond the confines of small sects obviously transcend the gulf dividing the great from the little tradition. Ritual observances make people aware of transcendental doctrines, if only inchoately. The churches concern themselves with how the religious awareness of the people can be enhanced. In this respect, science differs from religion. Scientists are sufficient unto themselves as far as the pursuit of knowledge is concerned. But for the salvation of souls it will not do, if theologians only speak to one another. The purposes of the two enterprises differ fundamentally, although both science and religion may look for support from public faith and both may point to the benefits they bestow.

Religious and scientific leaders of the great tradition also attempt to maintain the cohesion of the cultural elite. Thus churches must cope with schismatic tensions within their hierarchies. Similarly, there are both substantive disputes and many degrees of intellectualization within the culture of science. Hence, while small groups of specialists are continually engaged in sorting out the controversies endemic in the scientific enterprise itself, spokesmen of science are concerned with cohesion in the scientific community as a whole and in the wider public as well. In the early period of the scientific revolution, this task of persuasion was eased by a euphoric belief in the promise of science. This euphoria has remained a widespread sentiment to this day. But ever since Bacon's time, the championship of science has also met with disbelief, and in recent years this disbelief has grown rapidly. I began the discussion with a review of attacks upon the Baconian belief in progress through science. This challenge of science has been formulated in three different modes, which I call the imaginative, the conventional, and the dialectical ideas of reason.

Imaginative reason is concerned with forms of cognition other than those encompassed by scientific methods. As early as 1735, Voltaire expressed apprehension that science might become "a tyrant that excludes all the rest." He could not see "why the study of physics should crush the flowers of poetry," but he feared for "sentiment, imagination, and the finer arts" all the same.[27] Some three generations later, P.B. Shelley expressed the same concerns in his *Defence of Poetry* (1821). Science, says Shelley, deals with the enumeration of quantities that can be ascertained, whereas only imagination can perceive the value of those quantities. True, the sciences have "enlarged the limits of the empire of man over the external world." But the mechanical arts have been cultivated out of all proportion to the creative faculty. "Our calculations have outrun conception; we have eaten more than we can digest."[28] And more than a century and a half after Shelley, the case for imagination and the affections is made in much the same terms. In 1961, the literary critic Erich Heller speaks of objectivity as the chosen virtue of science which bars the affections from interfering with "the advance or direction of discovery." Scientists, says Heller, trust in objectivity because they believe that the advance of knowledge will be "not only of use, but of true value," if not immediately then in the long run. But scientists ban values from their methods of inquiry; they have set up a kind of truth that leaves the human affections "unemployed.'' Yet these affections are our only way of responding to values. ''The workshops in which our truths are manufactured are surrounded by swarms of unemployed affections,'' which are a danger to science and the social order.[29] These views can be summed up by saying that the purpose of imaginative reason is the creation and appreciation of values.

Conventional reason may be considered a specific response to the idea that science be applied to man and society. We saw that in the eighteenth century scholars ignored Bacon's statement that affairs of state were outside the scientific domain. But as they applied reason to public affairs and developed a science of man, they introduced a rationalist bias which is best conveyed in a statement by Saint-Simon. The eighteenth century witnessed a number of attempts to found a science of man upon some more basic discipline. Locke, Condillac, and others looked to sense impressions, Montesquieu to climate, and Saint-Simon to physiology. Morals and politics would be made into a ''positive science of man.''

> When those who cultivate this important branch of human knowledge will have learned physiology during the course of their education, they will no longer consider the problems which they have to solve as anything but questions of hygiene.[30]

The argument for conventional reason was a protest against this reductionist approach to human affairs.

Edmund Burke was its foremost spokesman. Since French rationalism had been advanced as an attack upon prejudice and vested interests, Burke made his polemic a defense of prejudice and established privilege. He declared that ''we are generally men of untaught feeling,'' cherish our prejudices, and are afraid to depend on man's reason because we suspect that each man's ''private stock of reason'' is small. In Burke's view, there was much to be said for ''prejudice'' or preconceived opinion because the practical man required it to be ready with a decision when needed. The theory of the French rationalists was defective as a guide to practice because it was concerned with the universal, disrespectful of precedent, idealistic, detached, oblivious to time and circumstance. Thus theory was blind to that slow cumulation of reason which derived from the conventional wisdom of practical men who judged the here and now in terms exactly suited to their interests and circumstances. But when Burke advanced this argument in 1790, he could still draw upon existing traditions that lent some plausibility to his views. Since then, the conservative argument against the use of science in affairs of state has remained much the same despite the erosion of the traditions to which Burke could refer. At any rate, in the view of Burke and of those who followed him the purpose of knowledge is to guide the cautious adaptation to circumstance in the interest of preserving the existing institutional framework.[31]

Dialectical reason opposes the Baconian tradition in a different manner, though it has complicated affinities not only with imaginative and conventional reason but also with the older theological tradition. For our purposes, the main dialectical point is that men act without knowing what will come of their action. As Marx put it, "Men make their own history, but they do not make it just as they please . . . [they make it] under circumstances directly found, given and transmitted from the past." The pursuit of knowledge is a special type of action. Men engage in scientific work in the mistaken belief that all they do is to advance our understanding of nature. But the pursuit of knowledge is not that unencumbered. It takes place in a context carried over from the past which includes not only past scientific achievements but the whole institutional complex on which those achievements depend and to which they have contributed. Likewise, contemporary scientists contribute not only to knowledge but to the institutional complex of science and more indirectly to the technology using that science and to the institutions engendered by the consequences of science and technology. Thus scientific work is embedded in a nonscientific context carried over from the past and in turn contributes to such a context.

Yet typically scientists ignore the bearing of the past on their own unwitting contribution to that context in the future. In their view, the pursuit of knowledge must be freed from all consideration of contingency, if it is to fulfill its proper role in the advancement of learning. Accordingly, they tend to endow that pursuit with a character of its own, so much so that one philosopher of science has argued for a view of science independent of scientists themselves, "a world of articulated knowledge . . . independent of knowing subjects." [32] Whatever its merits on theoretical grounds, such a view is itself a consequence of earlier and a progenitor of future contexts. It encourages the social isolation of the scientific enterprise and identifies that isolation with rationality itself. In the dialectic view, such fetishism of science actually militates against rationality both in the pursuit and in the utilization of knowledge. Fetishism divorces science from all inquiry into contexts and a proper assessment of priorities. And without such assessment science becomes an end in itself rather than a means to the achievement of ends. For dialectical reason, the proper purpose of knowledge lies in the elucidation of contexts and priorities so as to preserve the rational core that is embodied in science itself. [33]

MORAL CHOICES

Considered together, these challenges to science do more than raise questions of priorities. Or to put it another way, the culture of science is changed when such questions are raised. For the pursuit of science in the name of progress has had this much in common with nineteenth-century liberalism and materialism—that major advances of indeterminate quantity and quality were expected from the unfettered pursuit of private interests. Only Marxism had raised questions concerning the fetishism of private gain and individual freedom and projected a future society (however vaguely) in which priorities would be planned for the society as a whole. But even Marxism assumed that abundance was the necessary precondition of a successful socialism just as liberalism assumed that it was the by-product of successful capitalism. Thus the common assumption of scientism, liberalism, and Marxism was that the intractable problems of today would be resolved by the increased productivity (or knowledge) of tomorrow.

In an era of potential abundance, this assumption made sense. Private vices like the pursuit of gain and private virtues like the pursuit of knowledge could yield public benefits, to adapt the old saying of Bernard de Mandeville. Even the monopolistic appropriation of opportunities in the pursuit of gain or knowledge could be tolerated—up to a point.

> But there comes a moment when the atmosphere changes. The significance of the unreflectively utilized viewpoints becomes uncertain and the road is lost in the twilight. The light of the great cultural problems moves on. Then science too prepares to change its standpoint and its analytical apparatus. . . .[34]

In an era of mounting scarcities (or what comes to the same, our awareness of mounting scarcities), the old assumptions become less and less serviceable. As long as the private pursuit of knowledge yielded public benefits, the question of priorities could be ignored and the pluralism of seeking knowledge wherever it might lead enjoyed. But when priorities become pressing, choices must be made and these encroach sooner or later upon the bastions of academic freedom. The old equation of progress and knowledge is in jeopardy and the road ahead is lost in the twilight.

There is mounting evidence that scientists are concerned with these issues. In applied fields like medicine, that concern is direct because the application of knowledge impinges upon the lives of individuals. In fields bearing on health and welfare more generally (like genetics and demography), the concern with the moral implications of knowledge is an immediate challenge as well. In one notable instance that challenge has led recently to the termination of genetic research projects because further inquiry "could cause epidemics, or resist control by antibiotics, or increase the incidence of cancer." The potential misuse of knowledge in biological warfare could not be ignored.[35] Related questions concerning knowledge and technology used *against* the "benefit and use of life" are raised in fields like computer technology, radiation, nuclear wastes and older concerns like the environmental impact of freeways, deforestation, pollution, and others. In this context the conventional argument has always been that knowledge itself is neutral, that abuses arise from inappropriate applications, and that we must not cut off the potential good arising from the unfettered pursuit of truth. But today our collective bafflement seems to indicate that this argument no longer provides satisfactory guidelines for action, and one wonders when it ceased to do so. Every genuine pursuit of knowledge does not know the answers in advance. And today scientists of moral sensibility find that in a number of fields they confront decisions concerning their work which must be made *without* the earlier confidence that the knowledge to be obtained will be beneficial.[36]

NOTES

1. Quoted in Hans Jonas, "The Practical Uses of Theory," *Social Research*, XXVI (Summer 1959), 127. I am greatly indebted to this interpretation of the contrast between the medieval and the Baconian conceptions of knowledge. See also R.G. Collingwood, *The Idea of History* (New York: Oxford University Press, 1956) and Karl Löwith, *Meaning in History* (Chicago: University of Chicago Press, 1949).

2. Francis Bacon, "Novum Organum," in E.A. Burtt,ed., *The English Philosophers from Bacon to Mill* (New York: The Modern Library, 1939), p. 26; my italics.

3. Ibid., p. 64; my italics. The earlier reference to religion is found in "The Great Instauration," in ibid., pp. 12-13.

4. Ibid., p. 65.

5. Quoted in Ernest Cassirer, *The Philosophy of the Enlightenment* (Boston: Beacon Press, 1955), p. 16.

6. This paragraph summarizes the position expounded by Louis Armand, "Machines, Technology and the Life of the Mind," in Paul C. Obler and Herman A. Estrin, eds., *The New Scientist: Essays on the Methods and Values of Modern Science* (Garden City: Doubleday & Co., 1962), esp. pp. 40, 42-43, 46-48, 51.

7. Victor Weisskopf, "Why Basic Science?", *Bulletin of the American Academy of Arts and Sciences*, XXIV (October 1970), 3-4 and *passim*.

8. Gerald Holton, "Modern Science and the Intellectual Tradition," in Obler and Estrin, *The New Scientist*, pp. 28-29. Originally published in *Science* (April 1960), the article contains a comprehensive defense of the scientific community. In the text, Holton expresses confidence in science with particular reference to the "causes and prevention of aggression among nations," but this appears to be a special application of the still larger claim made at the end of the quotation cited in the text. The dilemma which Holton fails to resolve is pointed up by an exchange among Peter Medawar, Paul Ehrlich, and "R" in *Encounter*, XXXV (December 1970), 90-91.

9. Cf. Weisskopf, "Why Basic Science?", pp. 3-4 and Holton, "Modern Science and the Intellectual Tradition," pp. 28-29.

10. The points noted here are expressed by various writers in Obler and Estrin, *The New Scientist*, pp. 81, 96-97, 127-40, 143-47, 215-36, 117-26. The respective authors are Francis Bello, Warren Weaver, C.P. Snow, J. Bronowski, Eugene Rabinowitch, George Boas, Bentley Glass, and Dael Wolfle.

11. Don K. Price, *The Scientific Estate* (Cambridge: Harvard University Press, 1967), p. 105. The sentence in quotation marks in the preceding paragraph is taken from John Ziman, *Public Knowledge* (London: Cambridge University Press, 1968), p. 144.

12. Quoted in Helmut Krauch, *Die Organisierte Forschung* (Neuwied: Luchterhand Verlag, 1970), p. 7.

13. The quotations in this paragraph are taken from J. Bronowski, *Science and Human Values* (Harmondsworth: Penguin Books, 1964), pp. 75-86, 93-94. The sequence of statements has been rearranged.

14. For the following discussion cf. Carl Friedrich von Weizsäcker, *Kritik der Wissenschaft* (Tonbandnachschrift der Vorlesungen, Wintersemester 1968/69, University of Hamburg; Hamburg, 1968), pp. 71ff.

15. Bacon, "Novum Organum," p. 37.

16. As Ziman points out in *Public Knowledge*, this emphasis is widely shared by other writers on the sociology of science. Note, for example, the importance of communication in Hagstrom's analysis of social control in science. See Warren Hagstrom, *The Scientific Community* (New York: Basic Books, 1965), chap. 1 and *passim*. Emphasis on communication can also inform a more methodological approach to what scientists do, e.g., by attention to the ways in which agreement can be reached through discussion. For a lucid example of this approach, cf. Gerhard Frey, *Philosophie und Wissenschaft* (Stuttgart: Verlag W. Kohlhammer, 1970), pp. 32-76.

17. Cf. Ziman, *Public Knowledge* p. 63. The term "community" is as awkward as it is convenient, for it implies a level of agreement which is plainly absent from the collegial groups of working scientists. Where the term is used in the following discussion it should be understood that consensus and conflict coexist, that "scientific community" is an instance of what Kant called asocial sociability.

18. See Everett C. Hughes, *Men and Their Work* (Glencoe: The Free Press, 1958), pp. 139-144.

19. Cf. the variety of reactions to the idea of a moratorium in Anthony Michaelis and Hugh Harvey, eds., *Scientists in Search of their Conscience* (Berlin: Springer Verlag, 1973).

20. Cf. Judith P. Swazey and Renee G. Fox, "The Clinical Moratorium: A Case Study of Mitral Valve Surgery," in Paul A. Freund, ed., *Experimentation with Human Subjects* (New York: George Braziller, Inc. 1970), pp. 315-57.

21. Quoted in Francis Bello, "The Young Scientists," in Obler and Estrin, *The New Scientist*, p. 73. This article also contains evidence of the low standing of "applied science" in relation to the scientific community.

22. Max Weber, "Science as a Vocation," in H.H. Gerth and C. Wright Mills, eds., *From Max Weber: Essays in Sociology* (New York: Oxford University Press, 1947), p. 138 and *passim*.

23. Ziman, *Public Knowledge*, p. 96.

24. Cf. Randall Collins, "Competition and Social Control in Science," *Sociology of Education*, XLI (Spring 1968), 123-40, in which the author summarizes and systematizes the contributions by Kuhn, Hagstrom, Storer, and others.

25. The ramifications of this idea are examined in Mary Douglas, *Purity and Danger* (Baltimore: Penguin Books, 1970).

26. Cf. the discussion of the Weberian problem of "doctrine and conduct" in Reinhard Bendix, *Embattled Reason* (New York: Oxford University Press, 1970), pp. 141-50. See below pp. 154-62.

27. Cf. the two letters by Voltaire quoted in Gerd Buchdahl, *The Image of Newton and Locke in the Age of Reason* (New York: Sheed & Ward, 1961), pp. 63-64.

28. P. B. Shelley, "A Defence of Poetry" in R. J. White, ed., *Political Tracts of Wordsworth, Coleridge and Shelley* (London: Cambridge University Press, 1953), pp. 111, 125. I have reordered Shelley's phrasing in the interest of continuity.

29. Erich Heller, *The Disinherited Mind* (Harmondsworth: Penguin Books, 1961), pp. 235-36.
30. Quoted in Frank E. Manuel, *The New World of Henri Saint-Simon* (Cambridge: Harvard University Press, 1956), p. 135.
31. The main source of Burke's views is his *Reflections on the Revolution in France* (1790), available in many editions. A useful analysis of Burke's views on prejudice is contained in Leo Strauss, *Natural Right and History* (Chicago: University of Chicago Press, 1953), esp. pp. 301 ff. Michael Oakeshott is a modern representative of the Burkean tradition. For a lucid critical appraisal of his work, cf. Hanna Pitkin, "The Roots of Conservatism: Oakeshott and the Denial of Politics," *Dissent*, XX (Fall 1973), 496-525.
32. Imre Lakatos, "Falsification and the Methodology of Scientific Research Programmes," in Imre Lakatos and Alan Musgrave, eds., *Criticism and the Growth of Knowledge* (London: Cambridge University Press, 1970), p. 180.
33. There are, of course, other uses of dialectical reasoning, but the one referred to is most germane to the present discussion. The brief reference to the "fetishism of science" is modeled after Marx's analysis of the "fetishism of commodities." Cf. Karl Marx, *Capital* (New York: The Modern Library, 1936), pp. 81-96.
34. Max Weber, " 'Objectivity' in Social Science and Social Policy," *The Methodology of the Social Sciences*, translated and edited by E. A. Shils and Henry Finch (Glencoe: The Free Press, 1949), p. 112.
35. Cf. the report in *Time Magazine* (July 29, 1974), p. 59 concerning the termination of research on fertilizer-implantation techniques and experiments in the genetic manipulation of bacteria. A philosophical exploration of these questions is contained in Hans Jonas, "Technology and Responsibility," *Social Research*, XL (Spring 1973), 31-54. With regard to organ transplants, these issues are examined in detail in Renee Fox and Judith Swazey, *The Courage to Fail* (Chicago: University of Chicago Press, 1973). A comprehensive bibliography of the growing literature in this field is available through the newsletters of the Program on Public Conceptions of Science, Department of Physics, Harvard University.
36. An earlier version of this study was facilitated by Grant GS-31730X of the National Science Foundation at the Institute for Advanced Study, Princeton, N.J. The article is part of an unfinished study for which support was received in 1970-71 from the Program on Technology and Society, Harvard University. Later revisions have profited greatly from discussions of the Science Policy Colloquium, Institute of International Studies, University of California, Berkeley. See also Chapters 12 and 13 in *Embattled Reason*, vol. 2, for a more detailed analysis of the early advocacy of science.

PART II
Theoretical Perspectives

Introduction to Part II

We want to understand society and cannot do so without assumptions about the future. Our hopes and fears concern the capacities and limitations of "man." The view we take of the human prospect is linked closely with the conditions of knowledge. Some think of advances in knowledge with the expectation that the endless quest is worth the risk, because we cannot know what cannot be known, and we look forward to the benefits of new discoveries. Others consider the human prospect with more trepidation. They see the constructive possibilities of increased knowledge, but are also concerned with the problems facing us, including those created by increased knowledge.

In his methodological writings, Max Weber argued that all the sciences aim at causal explanations. These comprise the cumulative understanding achieved through the quest for knowledge. Nevertheless, there is a basic difference between an interest in what phenomena have in common and what makes them singular, between their repeatable and their nonrepeatable aspects. In his time Weber wanted to vindicate the scientific status of history and the cultural sciences. The principal objective of these disciplines is the discovery of how particular concrete events or patterns come about rather than the discovery of laws or rules, under which observations can be subsumed.

To understand this distinction it is helpful to remember that Weber was trained as a lawyer. His writings on social action and causal explanation were influenced (among others) by Gustav Radbruch, a prominent legal theorist. Distinctions like those between premeditated murder and involuntary manslaughter make sense only if we study the circumstances of a case, the testimony of witnesses, and the statements of the accused. We do that from the standpoint of the likelihood of events (general rules of experience), the plausibility of motives, and so on. Such a study does not involve the distinction between natural and social sciences at all. Both would be needed. Ballistics experts are interested in the physical evidence of the weapon and the bullets used, in the likely trajectory of the bullet judged in terms of the angle of impact, the force of penetration, etc. Only after they have established these facts will they turn to the witness and check their testimony in terms of its compatibility with the physical evidence. Psychiatric experts will take that evidence into account in order to avoid manifest contradictions with it. But their main interest is in the personal history of the accused, his or her state of mind just before the deed was done, particularly the likelihood of subjective premeditation. Note that both experts are concerned with the causal explanation of whether, and if so how, the action occurred. Both will apply rules of experience to the case. But the laws of motion are different from the rules derived from clinical evidence, and these again are different from the framework of legal rules, within which lawyers and judges operate.

There is, then, a nomological side to the search for knowledge, the discovery of laws or rules of experience, and an ideographic side, the interest in explaining a particular concrete event. Weber thought both sides important in the natural and social sciences, but with one notable difference. Theoretically oriented natural scientists are primarily interested in the discovery of laws, leaving the explanation of particular concrete events to their colleagues in the applied fields. For social scientists the relation between these two sides of scientific inquiry is more complex.[1] Here Weber emphasizes two aspects. History and the cultural sciences are primarily interested in explaining particular concrete events or patterns. For these disciplines the discovery of rules of experience (laws would be the wrong word) is an auxiliary enterprise, since their purpose is to facilitate ideographic explanations. At the same time, these explanations are enriched by the fact that the concrete events in which historians and social scientists are interested involve human actions that make sense to the individuals concerned. This subjective meaning of human experience is the distinguishing characteristic of the socio-cultural sciences. There is little argument, so far as I can see, that purposes, attitudes and beliefs play a role in human affairs, but have no direct bearing on the course of natural events. These preliminary comments provide the context in which my own theoretical perspectives developed.

Social scientists are people acting in society before they become scholars studying the actions of others. A hidden theoretical agenda arises from this condition, a set of intellectual priorities. My own set was shaped by the Hitler experience from 1933 to 1938. I witnessed how a new dictatorship took over control by placing party-activists inside each unit of a functioning society to spy and report on ordinary citizens. The incentive for the activists was to advance in the party-hierarchy, or at least play it safe by demonstrating their loyalty. The reason for conformity by ordinary people was fear of the consequences of non-compliance mixed with hopes for benefits accruing from the party's apparent success. The justification was to protect a racially defined folk community as represented by the commands of a leader and his close associates. Later study revealed the same operation at work in Communist regimes and other types of one-party dictatorships, all of them inspired by some appeal to total authentication.[2] These takeover operations demonstrated to me with singular impact the contrast between the pluralism of societies, however differing in structure, and the totalism of an ideologically guided state apparatus, regardless of the kind of ideology at work.[3]

Theories "explaining everything" are in the last analysis mono-causal, seeking to account for all there is by some creation-myth or other ultimate principle. Such total explanations existed long before the era of modern dictatorship, when I encountered them personally. One need only think of the several world religions which developed cosmologies based on analogies derived from the human body or various elements of nature. Then again, modern theory-constructions have often used biological (organismic) or mechanical (feedback mechanisms) analogies. Within specified limits such modern analogies, or even ancient myths, can be useful analytically, but without such specification they tend to dominate thought rather than serve it.

At any rate, ever since my experience under Hitler I have taken a stand against theories claiming to explain everything. In my view the quest for total explanations is not compatible with the quest for knowledge. The reason is simple: principles of total explanation have the answer before they have examined the evidence. The facts they take into account merely exemplify the basic principle. Or, in more modern language, theories explaining everything are not falsifiable. By contrast, theories of more modest scope—including those embedded in terms like *bureaucracy, authority,* or *popular mandate*—can be verified or refuted.

NOTES

1. A lucid exposition of this issue will be found in Lelan McLemore, "Max Weber's Defense of Historical Inquiry," *History and Theory*, XXIII (1984), 277-95.
2. For an extended treatment of this point cf. Martin Jay, *Marxism and Totality* (Berkeley: University of California Press, 1985), passim.
3. It may be the absence of a functioning state-apparatus which has led in several Latin American countries to one-party regimes or military dictatorships which are marked by seemingly random killings of opponents and civilians. Much organizational efficiency is required to mount takeover operations of the kind described. If that efficiency is unavailable, then the precautionary murder of potential opponents becomes a plausible alternative.

5

IMAGES OF SOCIETY AND PROBLEMS OF CONCEPT FORMATION IN SOCIOLOGY[1]

Introductory Note

As a graduate student of sociology and during my first years of teaching I had to come to terms with the multiplicity of social theories. At the University of Chicago courses on the subject consisted of so many weeks devoted to the study of Simmel, Durkheim, Weber and Pareto as well as lesser classics like Tönnies, Le Bon, Mosca and near contemporaries like Veblen, Park, Dewey and Mead. Occasional efforts were made to have these "Greats" or "Near Greats " engage in imaginary dialogues, but the results were inconclusive. The efforts were soon abandoned. The student was left with many theories to learn and little guidance how he might choose among them. Ultimately it seemed a matter of preference for one style of sociological inquiry rather than another. For each theory pointed to some aspect of social experience. Parts of Simmel suggested patterns of social interaction, Durkheim was concerned with moral integration, Weber with comparative world religions, Dewey and Mead with the development of the self, and so on. These crude distinctions did not do justice to any writer, but they helped students pass their examinations. It is hardly surprising that neither the faculty nor the brighter students were satisfied with this hodge-podge, a dissatisfaction which helps explain the impact of Talcott Parsons' *Structure of Social Action* (1937) and its attempted integration of several major theorists.

On the other hand, the multiplicity of theories had its rewards, because it provided a quasi-theoretical underpinning for the diversity of interests which any groups of students will display, whatever "orthodoxies " their teachers might propound. More to the point, the multiplicity of approaches has its own rationale. Theory construction in sociology proceeds from a condition of knowledge. A rudimentary image of what is important in society seems to be a basic impulse of each theorist and such impulses should not be discarded lightly. They were, and are, major reasons for theorizing about society. Hence the diversity of views should be respected. The following essay accepts this rationale and yet attempts to perceive common themes in the diversity of theories. Only a sampling of theories is offered. My emphasis is on another image of society, an impulse of viewing the social world which facilitates the perception of common themes in many theories without attempting to replace that multiplicity by one unified theory.

111

DEFINITIONS OF THE "SOCIAL FACT"

Sociologists frequently modify old concepts, or offer new ones, because the standard concepts neglect or omit some range of facts now considered important. To remedy this deficiency, a new formulation is offered though in due time it may be challenged in turn. This conceptual instability is attributable to the youth of the discipline, its want of rigor, the emergence of new problems. It is also due to certain metatheoretical views which influence social theory, but often without the explicit consideration they deserve. These views are expressed in divergent images or interpretations of what is significant or "real" in society, leading to conflicting definitions of the "social fact."

Georg Simmel, for one, was explicitly concerned with delimiting the subject matter of sociology as an independent discipline. He identified it as the process of interaction among individuals. Accordingly he criticized conventional concepts like the state, administration, the church, and others as lacking "real" social content. For these official "social formations" take on meaning only when they are studied in terms of interactions among individuals.[2] On these grounds Simmel argues for interaction as the proper focus of sociological inquiry. At the same time he argues against the familiar assumption that society is an abstraction, but the individual is "real." In his view every abstraction simplifies and exaggerates "the facts" in order to formulate concepts of analytic utility. In this respect the "individual" is as much of an abstraction as society. Yet "interaction" is an abstraction as well. And Simmel considers it the object of sociological inquiry because it represents a realistic approach to the study of society.

Simmel's problem is not fortuitous. All concepts are based on *some* evidence, arranged to facilitate understanding. In that sense all concepts are realistic and abstract. To argue nonetheless that the interaction approach is more realistic than more traditional concepts, suggests other than logical considerations. Definitions of man and society are also social acts. Just as research is initiated by some sense of what is significant, so sociological theorizing is guided by a strong sense of what is "real" in society. Each theorist's definition of the "social fact" is a clue to his image of society.[3]

Emile Durkheim was concerned with the individual's group affiliation as the foundation of morality. For Durkheim the central fact is that a society's beliefs and practices are imposed on the individual. Certainly he recognizes that beliefs are internalized and conformity is limited by individuation. But the reconstruction of social morality is Durkheim's overriding concern, and with it the question how we can find or reestablish social norms which provide firm guidelines of conduct. This concern differs sharply from the impulse behind the work of Max Weber, and accordingly the two scholars offer divergent definitions of the "social fact." For Weber the central fact is the meaning which individuals in society attach to their own actions and those of others. In the course of Western civilization that meaning has changed as magic has disappeared and rationalism has risen in many spheres of life. A major aspect of rationalism is the coexistence in modern Western society of several antagonistic values or world views. Weber's fundamental respect for the individual and his relative autonomy requires that the scholar withhold his value judgment in the interest of fully understanding the meaning of actions, of conflicting norms and "many Gods" as individuals experience them. What for Durkheim was a decline of social morality demanding constructive action, was for Weber a fact of modern society to be analyzed in its own right—apart from the problem of what policies and what findings of social science might help to alter that fact.

Men like Simmel, Durkheim, and Weber define the "social fact" in accord with their orientation to substantive problems. Such definitions generate pseudo-controversies, when differences among theorists are discussed without regard for their different *purposes* of cognition. There is no single sociological theory. There are only schools of sociological theory because the most eminent scholars in the field choose their theoretical orientation in accord with substantive concerns and with their sense of what is real or significant in society.[4]

In his *Structure of Social Action* (1937) Talcott Parsons undertook to terminate this "war of schools." He sought to show that Pareto, Durkheim, Marshall, and Weber agree on certain ideas in their analyses of social action. More recently, Parsons endeavored to establish a common theory of action among outstanding representatives of anthropology, sociology, and psychology. The resulting "action-frame-of-reference" has been linked in turn with a theory of society as a system. But this work of integration is based on yet another interpretation of society. In this case the definition of the "social fact" is derived from the belief that the concept "system" is indispensable for a scientific theory of society.[5]

The approaches reviewed here exemplify a common tendency of social theorists. Starting from divergent and specific purposes of cognition, they develop theoretical categories basic to the whole discipline. This practice is of doubtful value. One alternative is to approach theories of man and society from the universalist standpoint discussed below. This approach is not new. The perspective we make explicit is familiar to every major sociological theorist.

THE PERSPECTIVE OF DUAL TENDENCIES

The task of sociological theory is to attend to the social and individual aspects of human behavior. To say that behavior is socially conditioned means that the individual takes his cues on how to act from the expectations of others. But these cues are not determinants. He may comply with, evade, or resist the expectations of others and this room for maneuver is an aspect of his independence. Attention to both the restrictive and the permissive aspects of culture and society also involves a definition of the "social fact." Man and society are not finite systems. Rather they are capable of indefinite (though not infinite) elaboration through tendencies or forces which are linked and opposite at the same time.

This insight has a venerable intellectual history. It has been expressed in Empedokles's view of a world divided by love and hate and in Freud's theory of death and eros, in the medieval idea of a universal determinism coupled with individual freedom and in Marx's view of men as partly free and partly involuntary actors under given historical conditions, in the Confucian concepts of Yin and Yang and in Kant's idea of "unsocial sociability." The variations increase but the theme remains.[6] At the end of his analysis of freedom and equality in American society Alexis de Tocqueville formulated this theme as his own basic creed:

> I am aware that many of my contemporaries maintain that nations are never their own masters here below, and that they necessarily obey some insurmountable and unintelligent power. . . . Such principles are false and cowardly. . . . Providence has not created mankind entirely dependent or entirely free. It is true that around every man a fatal circle is traced beyond which he cannot pass; but within the wide verge of that circle he is powerful and free; as it is with man, so with communities.[7]

The same theme has been reflected in sociological theory. Simmel emphasizes the double effect of multiple group-affiliations. In modern society such affiliations strengthen an individual personality and give it the capacity to sustain great internal tensions. But these affiliations can also threaten the personality far more than in a society with less group-differentiation.[8] Robert Park combined this idea of his teacher Simmel with the related concepts of Ferdinand Tönnies. In studies of the city, of newspapers, and of race relations Park distinguishes between individuating and socializing aspects of interactions.

> Competition and communication, although they perform different and uncoordinated social functions, nevertheless in the actual life of society supplement and complete each other. . . . Competition seems to be the principle of individuation in the life of the person and of society. . . . Communication, on the other hand, operates primarily as an integrating and socializing principle.[9]

In social psychology George H. Mead makes a similar distinction between the organic actions of the individual (the "I") and the orientation towards a "generalized other," which the individual has internalized through interactions (the "Me").

The same perspective is found in Max Weber's work. In emphasizing the subjective meaning of action Weber distinguishes two aspects. The individual makes sense of his actions, and he responds to the expectations of others. In practice these two aspects of meaning may be inseparable, but analytically they are distinct.[10] The distinction is reflected in Weber's substantive work. His study of the Protestant Ethic emphasized the autonomy of ideas. The Great Reformers as well as "the [common] people of that period had very specific ideas of what awaited them in the life after death, of the means by which they could improve their chances in this respect, and they adjusted their conduct in accordance with these ideas."[11] In other respects Weber emphasized the influence of social structures on the development of ideas. He showed, for example, that the political and military autonomy of Occidental cities was an important precondition of bourgeois class consciousness and prepared the way for the ideas of Puritanism.[12]

The perspective of dual tendencies can be exemplified from the work of sociologists but on the whole it runs counter to major trends in the field. Contemporary sociology accounts for the conduct of individuals in terms of their group membership and cultural participation. Concepts like culture pattern, subculture, social role, reciprocal expectations, social class, status group, communication, human relations, and many others make it appear that individuals act as group-influences dictate. This interpretation likens the individual to the actor on the medieval stage who read his text from the rolled script in his hands.[13]

A case in point is Ralph Linton's influential attempt to formulate the relation between the individual and his culture. Culture is described as "the way of life of any society." It consists of "the normal anticipated response of *any* of the society's members to a particular situation." Culture provides these members with "an indispensable guide in *all* the affairs of life." Linton continues:

> I realize that in the foregoing discussion of society and culture emphasis has been laid mainly upon the passive role of the individual and upon the way in which he is shaped by culture and social factors. It is time now to present the other side of the picture. No matter how carefully the individual has been trained or how successful his conditioning has been, he remains a distinct organism with his own needs and with capacities for independent thought, feeling and action. Moreover, he retains a considerable degree of individuality. His integration into society and culture goes no deeper than his learned responses, and although in the adult these include the greater part of what we call the personality, *there is still a good deal of the individual left over.*[14]

In this way culture and society determine and, therefore, explain the normal responses of all individuals. What they fail to explain is left over as residue. This is indeed a "good deal," since Linton himself emphasizes that no two individuals in a culture are exactly alike. Such residues are unavoidable where we deal with the formulation of hypotheses in particular inquiries. But they are not admissible at the most abstract level where sociology focuses attention on the universals of man's social condition. The *basic* concepts of sociological theory should be applicable to all societies.

PAIRED CONCEPTS

Concepts of such comprehensiveness will be empty. They cannot encompass the full range of social experience by singling out some dominant feature while leaving others aside. Indeed, any single concept necessarily excludes as well as includes. Yet the paired concepts of sociological theory achieve what single concepts cannot. Paired concepts so conceptualize what we know about the variability of social phenomena that they encompass social and individual aspects of interactions and institutions. Examples are: socialization and individualization, primary and secondary relations, status and contract, symbiosis and cooperation, etc. Concepts of this kind have been developed without analysis in depth. At least three difficulties have stood in the way.

Paired concepts invite dichotomous classifications. Interactions are either intimate or impersonal, organizations either formal or informal, social strata either ascriptive or oriented towards achievement, societies either folk or urban. Social actions or relationships approximate one or another of these reference points and various factors may be related to the degree of approximation observed. At the end of such investigations the concepts appear less serviceable than at the beginning. "Urban" elements are found in folk societies, informal relations are present in formally rational bureaucracies, and so forth. Since this use of dichotomous classifications is misleading, a number of sociologists wish to discard paired concepts altogether.

A second difficulty arises from the failure to distinguish between paired concepts and the formulation of hypotheses. Communities may be distinguished by their degree of isolation, heterogeneity, literacy, and so forth. But in using the terms "folk" and "urban" society Robert Redfield indicated that these traits tended to vary together. As isolation increases, so does homogeneity for example. The extent to which this occurs is an empirical question which paired concepts cannot answer. To explain correlation, or its absence, we would need hypotheses concerning the social and psychological links between isolation, heterogeneity, and the other attributes of community life.[15] In this respect paired concepts provide only a preliminary mapping of areas of social life in which analysis may be productive.

Thirdly, many paired concepts have not been fully analyzed. New paired concepts frequently overlap with, but also differ from, past formulations. Sir Henry Maine's distinction between status and contract has much in common with Durkheim's contrast between organic and mechanical solidarity, Tönnies's contrast between *Gemeinschaft* and *Gesellschaft*, MacIver's contrast between culture and civilization, and Redfield's contrast between folk and urban societies.[16] Admittedly these broad contrasts have many drawbacks. But their universal applicability makes them potentially useful. Where such universalism is intended, it is a good rule of thumb to search for missing opposites, when single concepts are proposed.[17]

Related to this is the logical distinction between dichotomous (contradictory) and contrary incompatibilities. Dichotomous contrasts refer to two mutually exclusive attributes, such that the existence of one is incompatible with the existence of the other. Contraries refer to proximate contrasts such that the existence of one attribute militates against, but does not preclude, the existence of one or several others. Although paired concepts are formulated in dichotomous terms they are likely to involve such proximate contrasts rather than logical incompatibilities.

Dichotomous contrasts abound only in normative contexts; they are rarely, if ever found in social action. The reason is that all rule making must distinguish between conformity and deviance and classify actions accordingly. However, the ease of formulating norms of right and wrong stands in sharp contrast to the difficulty of fitting any particular action into this preconceived scheme. For empirically, social actions show continuous gradations and human relationships are marked by much ambiguity and ambivalence. Mankind is neither entirely dependent nor entirely free; social interaction is partly communicative and partly asocial; both the "I" and the "Me" are involved in social action. The paired concepts of sociology do not, therefore, formulate dichotomous choices; they express the perspective of dual tendencies with its emphasis upon links between proximate contrasts. How do we deal with this insight conceptually and in the formulation of hypotheses?

PAIRED CONCEPTS OF INTERACTION

Primary relations may be defined as personal and intimate. They involve "responses to whole persons rather than to segments," "communication [that] is deep and extensive," as well as a primacy of personal satisfactions.[18] These formulations refer to a universal: it is difficult to think of societies in which relations of this kind are entirely absent. Scholarly analysis will focus on the degree and kind of primary relations in different social contexts. It will also safeguard its detachment by avoiding the tacit implication that intimate relations are necessarily benign.

The definition of a universal can only be an element in a proposition. Take the assertion that the family is the major locus of primary relations, and assume a definition of the family that is clearly separated from this proposition. Such facts as formal property settlements in a family, or a materialistic attitude towards the choice of marriage-partners would be neglected by the statement. Such secondary relations are impersonal and instrumental by definition, whatever personal and emotional qualities may be imparted to them. These two concepts may be formulated as a universal proposition: all relations between men in society are both intimate and impersonal.[19] Such a proposition has a double utility.[20]

A. *It is based on generalized, inductive knowledge and points to a problem with which men in all societies deal.* In this sense it is a guide to relevant questions.[21] For example, romantics would say that two people genuinely in love have a relationship entirely free of impersonal elements. This idea would be contradicted by the asserted universality of impersonal relations. And primary relationships from which such impersonal elements are indeed absent, can then be expected to create special social and psychological problems. One might generalize and say that love relationships tend to be fragile unless buttressed by suitable formal arrangements, or that the survivor of a love relation faces special burdens if he must cope with his loss without meaningful rites of burial and mourning. Yet primary relations militate against such impersonal considerations. Married couples often neglect the legal settlement of their mutual obligations, which suggests either a lack of trust or the inability to tolerate an impersonal consideration of death.

Related questions arise when elements of intimacy intrude in secondary relationships. Such intrusion is often faked for personal advantage, as in the "folksy" approach of radio advertisers. But intimacy can also imply conventional obligations and serve as a bar against exploitation. In the United States such uses of intimacy pose special problems in hierarchical organizations. Equalitarianism and the human relations approach have led to personalized work relations, but without personal and social distance it is often difficult to apply criteria of efficiency. Yet if intimacy in secondary relations is minimized, as in German managerial practice, other social problems and psychological burdens arise. The two conditions produce very different dilemmas of action.[22]

B. *Universal propositions reveal the limitations of the concepts we use.* If all social relations are both intimate and impersonal, we may examine a primary relationship for its frequently hidden, secondary attributes and vice versa. The paired concepts may be conceived also as two ends of a scale on which social relations may be ranked in terms of relative intimacy and impersonality. For example, the relative isolation of a community can be ranked in terms of the number of communications with the world outside. Yet two communities with the same number of communications may possess different kinds of contact.[23] No measure of a community's isolation is meaningful without analysis of the contacts involved, just as a primary relation is understood best in relation to its more impersonal attributes.[24]

The paired concepts of sociological theory thus serve as the basis for formulating hypotheses. A classic example of such preparatory or preliminary analysis is contained in Max Weber's discussion of class and status. In his last formulation of these concepts Weber defines the two terms as follows:

> "Class" means all the persons in the same class situation. "Class situation" means the typical probability of 1) procuring goods, 2) gaining a position in life and 3) finding inner satisfactions,—a probability which derives from the relative control over goods and skills and from their income-producing uses within a given economic order. . . .
>
> "Status" (*ständische Lage*) shall mean an effective claim to social esteem in terms of positive or negative privileges; it is typically founded on 1) style of life, hence 2) formal education, which may be (a) empirical training, or (b) rational instruction, and the corresponding forms of behavior, 3) hereditary or occupational prestige.[25]

In these definitions Weber uses two conditions of collective action as ideal-typical antitheses. The market knows of no personal distinctions. Transactions on the stock exchange are reduced to a few standardized phrases or gestures. Distinctions among brokers are factual and impersonal, depending on their respective credit rating. "The factor that creates 'Class' is unambiguously economic interest, and indeed, only those interests involved in the existence of the market."[26] At the same level of abstraction exactly the reverse is true of the status order, in which men are grouped in terms of their prestige and style of life. To safeguard their status such men will reject all claims to "status honor" based on economic acquisition and power alone. Stratification based on the status order would be undermined quickly, if a wealthy man could claim more "honor" than those whose status rests on family lineage and style of life.

Thus, economic interests militate against the dominance of status-distinctions, especially in periods of rapid economic change. Considerations of status "hinder the strict carrying through of the sheer market principle," especially in periods of relative economic stability.[27] But these antithetical tendencies are also linked. Actions based on economic interests frequently aim at the preservation or acquisition of "honor." Weber points to the example of English stock brokers who safeguard fair dealing on the market by excluding "unreliable" elements from membership in their voluntary and exclusive associations. In turn status-groups use their social prestige to monopolize economic opportunities. Thus, the East German landowners (*Junkers*) exploited their aristocratic status to maximize their economic interests as landowners. To understand the linkages and antitheses between class and status it is necessary to define each unambiguously, i.e. *as if* they were mutually exclusive and *as if* each of them were governed by a principle of internal consistency.[28]

PAIRED CONCEPTS OF INSTITUTIONS

Many sociological concepts refer, not to social action or relations, but to more or less enduring institutions like bureaucracy, types of urban society, specific status-groups like aristocracies, etc. The sociologist can only observe actions, but is bound to use concepts of institutions or social aggregates when he analyzes the conditions of action, or their enduring results.[29] Paired concepts can be applied at this institutional level of analysis as well.

A case in point is Weber's analysis of bureaucracy. The elements of his definition are generally familiar and are repeated here in abbreviated form. A bureaucracy tends to be characterized by:

1. Defined rights and duties, which are prescribed in written regulations;
2. Authority relations between positions which are ordered systematically and hierarchically;
3. Appointment and promotion which are regulated in accordance with contractual agreement;
4. Technical training or equivalent experience as a formal condition of employment;
5. Fixed monetary salaries;
6. A strict separation of office and incumbent in the sense that the employee does not own the "means of administration" and cannot appropriate the position;
7. Administrative work as a full-time occupation.[30]

These conditions of public (and private) employment have been instituted only gradually in the course of Western civilization. To understand "bureaucracy" fully it is necessary to contrast these conditions with those prevailing under traditional authority.

a. "In place of a well-defined functional jurisdiction, there is a conflicting series of tasks and powers which at first are assigned at the master's discretion. However, they tend to become permanent and are often traditionally stereotyped."

b. "The question of who shall decide a matter or deal with appeals—whether an agent shall be in charge of this, and which one, or whether the master reserves decision for himself—is treated either traditionally, at times by considering the provenience of certain legal norms and precedents taken over from the outside; or entirely on the basis of the master's discretion..."

c. "The household officials and favorites are often recruited in a purely patrimonial fashion: they are slaves or dependents (*ministeriales*) of the master. If recruitment has been extra-patrimonial, they have tended to be benefice-holders whom he can freely remove."

d. "Rational technical training as a basic qualification for office is scarcely to be found among household officials and favorites."

e. "Household officials and favorites are usually supported and equipped in the master's household. Generally their dissociation from the lord's own table means the creation of benefices. . . . It is easy for these to become traditionally stereotyped in amount and kind."[31] These contrasting conditions of employment under legal-bureaucratic and traditional authority also involve linked and opposite tendencies of action. But this level of abstraction refers to a contrast derived from historical experience, not to the universals of man's social condition.[32]

Paired concepts of institutions serve only as benchmarks that can facilitate detailed analysis. The correlations to which they refer are proximate and unstable. The attributes of bureaucratic or of traditional authority need not occur together. Even when the rights and duties of officials are defined clearly, appointments and promotions may be handled arbitrarily. Even when a ruler assigns different tasks arbitrarily, he may be legalistic in delegating authority. Therefore, institutional complexes are relatively unstable. Written regulations may be altered through personal influence, though the intent is to preclude such influence. Tasks can be assigned arbitrarily to curtail the independent power of subordinates, but officials may still succeed in limiting the discretionary authority of their ruler. To a degree these dissociations and instabilities may be overcome by secular tendencies which favor several of the attributes of the bureaucratic or of the traditional type.

Statements of such tendencies are descriptive, not definitional. They make no assumption of logical consistency like the statement that the market knows no personal distinctions if purely economic considerations predominate. Yet statements of secular tendencies also go beyond description. They combine observed attributes into a model or pattern which may be contrasted with one or more alternate patterns.

Keeping contrasting patterns in mind may be considered the analyst's equivalent of always remembering the mutability of historical constellations. For example, the salary scales of officials are readily fixed and administered under modern conditions. Yet, fringe benefits, promotions, and job classifications are subject to bargaining or personal influence; their cumulative effect could nullify the basic salary scale. Much will depend upon the efforts of those who administer the scale. If they were completely successful, fringe benefits, promotions and job classifications would be codified so minutely that bargaining would have little influence. Much will depend also on those who bar gain over the rules and their implementation. If they were completely successful, a condition of traditional authority might be reestablished with remunerations dependent upon arbitrary judgments. In this sense institutions represent the more or less enduring balance of social relations which are the result of past contentions. Institutions are never complete or permanent and analysis must take account of the forces which circumscribe them.[33]

THE STRUCTURE OF CULTURE AND SOCIETY

What are the implications of paired concepts for an understanding of culture and social structure? From the perspective of "dual tendencies" the integration of culture and society is a matter for investigation.[34] A holistic approach discourages such investigation. Durkheim's work provides a striking example. In his *Rules of Sociological Method* Durkheim makes crime a "normal" aspect of culture. Without crime there would be insufficient awareness and enforcement of social norms. How much crime is "needed" to help maintain the norms of society? To answer this question Durkheim distinguishes between normal and pathological degrees of crime, between social health and disease. Yet he fails to establish criteria which would allow us to make that distinction.[35]

The perspective of "dual tendencies" suggests a different approach. Crime is always both: an opportunity for the maintenance of social norms and a hazard to their integrity. Nothing more can be said of *all* societies. Every society faces the problem of achieving a balance between reaffirmation and hazard. This achievement is the work of men who make history but under conditions not of their own choosing—to cite the still telling phrase of Marx's *18th Brumaire of Louis Bonaparte*. The maintenance of morals is not due to a "normal degree" of crime. Rather, the violations of norms result in interaction in which the balance between denial and affirmation is once more at issue. Not only criminals and deviants, but judges and policemen vary in the degree to which they contribute to the integrity of social norms, or detract from it. As the history of school-desegregation has made all too clear, failure of the authorities to enforce the law undermines confidence in its efficacy, but vigorous enforcement of a law that remains controversial all too easily casts doubt upon the legitimacy of the law itself. As we thread our way between that Scylla and Charybdis, the integrity of norms and with it the unity of culture hang in the balance—hardly a view that is compatible with Durkheim's approach.

This reference to "balance" may suggest the idea of a social system in equilibrium mentioned earlier. This idea differs from Durkheim's moral concerns. He reacted to the social disorganization of France with a passionate desire to reconstitute the normative order. His theories of religion, of suicide, and of education are only intelligible in that context. Nothing like this moral preoccupation is evident in systems theories which derive their models from biology and from self-regulating mechanisms. Against this background, Max Weber's work takes on added significance, because it is informed by a conception of "balance" which is incompatible with Durkheim's approach as well as with the image of society as a "system." [36]

Instead of the word "culture" Max Weber uses such terms as *mores* (ethics), *convention*, or *style of life*. [37] These terms are general designations of different ways of life. Each man's participation in his society involves a personal commitment to the behavior-patterns, ideas, and interests of a particular status group. By virtue of their styles of life, such groups "are the specific bearers of all conventions. In whatever way it may be manifest, all stylization of life either originates in status groups or is at least conserved by them." [38] Such styles of life may become representative for a whole society. The domineering and paternalistic manner of the *Junkers* influenced many aspects of German society. Certain ideas of ascetic Protestantism gained widespread influence in modern capitalism; they "prowl about in our lives like the ghost of dead religious beliefs." [39] Weber summarized one aspect of his sociology of religion by designating the status groups which were the principal exponents of the several world religions. [40] But the influence of ideas and behavior patterns can reach far beyond the status group with which they originated. Weber construes culture as an outgrowth of group power and group conflict in their historical development, and hence relates a given style of life to the group from which it has spread. The culture of a society is interpreted as a more or less enduring result of past conflicts among status groups. [41]

This formulation also implies a conception of the individual's relation to his culture. Individuals always engage in attempts to redefine their roles. Social roles limit the alternatives available to the individual, but they also provide opportunities for maneuvering and initiative. Through their social roles individuals participate in the interactions among dominant, symbiotic, and subordinate status groups, each with vested interests in its style of life. As individuals and groups seek to enhance their interests, they also reformulate and institutionalize their position in society. Sometimes this is deliberate. Negro protest movements in the United States seek to alter the Negros' collective position vis-à-vis the white majority. When Negro spokesmen use the nationalist movements of colored peoples around the world, they want to enhance their own dignity as well as change their status as a lower caste. Sometimes the relation between action and status is quite indirect. Officially, government administrators in the United States implement legislative policy. Yet their status and role is characterized better by the continual pulling and hauling among prominent administrators, Congressional committees, and organized interests. This interplay of many groups continually redefines the role of administrators in the making of public policy and thereby gives them a place in the American social structure. Thus, culture can be related to society and power by an analysis of the strategies of argument and action which individuals and groups use to define their respective roles as advantageously as possible.

The inequality of status groups is found in all societies. Frequently a particular status group and its style of life is dominant for prolonged periods and the pattern it imprints on the culture may endure long after that dominance has passed. This is one reason for the coherence of societies, though the dominance of such groups is often partial and subordinate groups exert cultural influences of their own. To characterize the structure of a society it is necessary to consider the changing interactions among dominant and subordinate groups, and this depends, as Weber's work did, on a wide-ranging use of the comparative method. As suggested below, the perspective of "dual tendencies" is the theoretical foundation of this method.

IMPLICATIONS FOR COMPARATIVE ANALYSIS

The perspective of "dual tendencies" contrasts with theories of evolution, although the familiar dichotomies of social theory have often been an aspect of evolutionism. Concepts like status and contract or pattern variables like ascription and achievement always refer to differences between social structures, and hence to changes over time. By contrast, the perspective of "dual tendencies" uncovers the element of uncertainty in all societies. Kenneth Burke calls attention to this approach with his phrase "perspective by incongruity."

> Any performance is discussible either from the standpoint of what it *attains* or what it *misses*. Comprehensiveness can be discussed as superficiality, intensiveness as stricture, tolerance as uncertainty—and the poor pedestrian abilities of the fish are clearly explainable in terms of his excellence as a swimmer. A way of seeing is also a way of not seeing. . . .[42]

This is a conceptual strategy, but it is also a social scientist's critique of utopian thought. It asks us to consider *every* social phenomenon as transient. Social action evokes or provokes reactions; it has intended and unintended, valued and devalued consequences. It follows that sociological inquiry should search each fact for what it may become as much as for what it is, for what it hides as much as for what it reveals. In this sense paired concepts and the perspective of "dual tendencies" are a theoretical adaptation to the Janus-faced quality of social life, as the concept of "systemic equilibrium" is not.

This consideration casts doubts upon analyses which assess facts in terms of their contribution to the adaptation (function) or impairment (dysfunction) of a society. Take the statement that frequent industrial strikes prevent maximum production. To turn this descriptive statement into a generalization, we would have to demonstrate that at certain levels strikes are quite compatible with the successful adaptation of the society, but at other higher levels they are not. However, we do not have a criterion of "successful adaptation" that is free of wishful thinking. Strikes may interfere with maximum production in the short run, whereas in the long run they may help accelerate capital investment and increase overall productivity. Also, strikes may increase cooperation by providing an outlet for accumulated grievances and establishing a new plateau for labor-management relations. The long-run balance between negative and positive effects on production, capital investment, and cooperation is uncertain. And in the face of that uncertainty the temptation is great to advance judgments with an air of assurance: e.g. strikes jeopardize the consensus required for social integration.[43] From a scholarly standpoint such judgments are ideological shortcuts of doubtful value.

In the absence of unequivocal criteria of social health or societal survival it is best to accept uncertainty. The strains and conflicts of society account for the uncertainty of social change, because the same facts may help to maintain or impair the social structure. Party activity, agitation for civil rights, the representation of organized interests are ways by which pressure for (or resistance to) change is exerted. Such pressure (or resistance) is an opportunity for the accommodation of grievances or conflicts and/or a hazard to the institutions by which accommodations have been achieved in the past. Both accommodation and impairment of an institutional framework are possible. In this sense social facts are seen as points of transition to the adaptation, or the impairment, of a social structure.

Probably there are limits to what is possible in any one society, but it is difficult to specify them in advance or even with the wisdom of hindsight. While comparative analysis suggests that the actions of individuals fall within a range of tolerance, the limits of this range are in a continual process of redefinition. Men in society repeatedly define what individuals are prohibited to do; yet people often fail to comply with what is expected of them. Sociological theory should comprehend both tendencies by focusing on the boundary-extending as well as the boundary-maintaining activities of individuals. Culture and society enable individuals to experiment with what is possible, but social controls also limit the range of tolerated behavior without defining that range clearly.[44]

This image of society is the theoretical counterpart of comparative analysis. The link between the two is exemplified by the work of Alexis de Tocqueville and it is worthwhile to make this explicit. In the first volume of his *Democracy in America* Tocqueville had dealt with the institutions of a democratic society, principally in a descriptive manner. But in the second volume he had used the ideas derived from American and French democracy only as data, . . . [in order] to paint the general features of democratic societies; no complete specimen of which can yet be said to exist. This is what an ordinary reader fails to appreciate. Only those who are much accustomed to searching for abstract and speculative truths, care to follow me in such an inquiry.[45]

To know how men will act tomorrow and how they will deal with coming events, one must be in a position to see continually what they are doing and thinking. At the same time one must take a bird's-eye view of affairs in order to understand the "sentiments, principles, and opinions, the moral and intellectual qualities" which are given by nature and by an education that has lasted for centuries.[46]

In his second volume on America Tocqueville was concerned with this truth for the long run. The progressive development of democracy appeared to him inevitable, and he favored it. But he was concerned to show that it was not a brilliant and easily realized ideal, that such a government was not viable, "without certain conditions of intelligence, of private morality, and of religious belief."[47] As a nation France had not yet attained these conditions. Indeed, in France the democratic revolution had gone astray, uncertainly alternating between despotism and anarchy, with no signs at all as to when and how a stable social order might be re-established. But while he was extremely pessimistic about the prospects of his own country, Tocqueville derived a more hopeful outlook from his studies of America.

Indeed, his insights into American democracy arose in part from contrasting her institutions with those of France.

> In my work on America . . . though I seldom mentioned France, I did not write a page without thinking of her and placing her as it were before me. And what I specifically tried to draw out, and to explain in the United States, was not the whole condition of that foreign society, but the points in which it differs from our own, or resembles us. . . . I believe that this perpetual silent reference to France was a principal cause of the book's success.[48]

American conditions provided Tocqueville with a picture of the "sentiments, principles, and opinions, the moral and intellectual qualities," which could sustain democratic institutions. By contrast French society exemplified the qualities which *might lead* to a "species of oppression unlike anything that ever before existed in the world."[49] And by superimposing French portents on American actualities Tocqueville projected his picture of the despotic possibilities inherent in democratic institutions generally.

His analysis of American society contains comparisons with analogous conditions in another country and "speculative truths" concerning possible developments in the future. In his view such speculation cannot be more than a judgment of limits and possibilities.

> I own, that this old world, beyond which we neither of us can see, appears to me to be almost worn out; the vast and venerable machine seems more out of gear every day; and although I cannot look forward, my faith in the continuance of the present is shaken. I learn from history, that not one of the men who witnessed the downfall of the religious and social organizations that have passed away, was able to guess or even to imagine what would ensue. Yet this did not prevent Christianity from succeeding to idolatry, servitude to slavery, the barbarians from taking the place of Roman civilization, and feudalism in turn ejecting the barbarians. Each of these changes occurred without having been anticipated by any of the writers in the time immediately preceding these total revolutions. Who, then, can affirm that any one social system is essential and that another is impossible? [50]

This reasoned conviction holds a precarious balance between hope and despair. Tocqueville did not think it possible to predict the future of society. It depends upon men and nations whether their drift towards equality leads to servitude or freedom.[51] Yet he also believed the possible directions of social change to be limited in number. By means of "speculative truths" one can extrapolate observed tendencies. It is fictitious to assume that nothing would interfere with their ultimate realization. But extrapolation is useful as a means of mapping out possibilities of thought and action, however proximately. Tocqueville's approach fits in well with a view of culture and social structure as more or less enduring results of past conflicts, and with a definition of the "social fact" as a point of transition to a provisional adaptation, or impairment.

The approach to social theory presented in this chapter is also an approach to the role of knowledge in society. We adopt an attitude of hope *and* uncertainty concerning the constructive potentialities of social knowledge. We do not know enough to be sure of what cannot be known. We stand between the pessimists who think sociology as a science impossible and the optimists who think it is a science already. But we do not believe that man must only know enough in order to solve pressing social problems.

The approach presented here is obviously tentative, requires considerable elaboration, and does not stand or fall on superseding all other approaches. We candidly regard it as experimental and would like to have it read in the same spirit. As stated at the beginning, it is related to an intellectual tradition which views men and society in terms of tendencies or forces which are linked and opposite at the same time. This tradition has special relevance for contemporary sociological theories which have generally sided with the conservative tradition of the nineteenth century. The task is to emancipate sociological theory from the limitations of this intellectual heritage. But the import of these concluding remarks is not to label given theories or thinkers as conservative, liberal or anything else. It is to make plain that the definition of the "social fact" embodies each theorist's image of society which has its distinct utility and unique blindness.

NOTES

1. Written together with Bennett Berger and originally published in Llewellyn Gross, ed., *Symposium on Sociological Theory* Copyright (c) 1959 by Harper & Row, Publishers, Inc., pp. 92-118. My colleague Bennett Berger has given his permission to this republication of our joint essay in the present revised form. Aside from stylistic changes and some necessary amplifications two changes have been made. I have adapted the essay to the context of this volume, and the last two sections have been rewritten with a clearer emphasis on comparative studies. Some pages on Max Weber's work have been deleted also, because their content overlapped with other essays in this volume. The responsibility for this revision is mine alone.
2. "To confine ourselves to the large social formations resembles the older science of anatomy with its limitation to the major, definitely circumscribed organs such as heart, liver, lungs, and stomach, and with its neglect of the innumerable, popularly unnamed or unknown tissues. Yet without these, the more obvious organs could never constitute a living organism. On the basis of the major social formations, the traditional subject of social science, it would be similarly impossible to piece together the real life of society as we encounter it in our experience." K. Wolff, ed., *The Sociology of Georg Simmel* (Glencoe: The Free Press, 1950), p. 9. See also pp. 10-13, and 187-88.
3. By the phrase "sense of the 'real'" we refer not to formally stipulated assumptions, but to the intuitive feeling for what is significant in society and basic for a scientific theory of society. The multiplicity of social theories is in part attributable to this psychological involvement of social theorists. Yet, the assessment of theories should be independent of this consideration, for the criteria by which a theorist defines "the social fact" must be abstract themselves as well as explicit, so that they may be judged by others. This theoretical level must be maintained, else theorists would merely argue about why they make statements, rather than about what they say. Nonetheless, this psychological precondition helps explain, and also takes into account, the peculiar perspectivism of theorizing about society.
4. This tendency creates controversies due to the attempt to impose a theoretical perspective, developed on the basis of *certain* substantive interests, on *all* substantive interests. It is partly for this reason too, perhaps, that so much criticism of sociological theories has an emotional undertone.
5. See Talcott Parsons, *The Social System* (Glencoe: The Free Press, 1951), vii, p. 38. "The title, *The Social System*, goes back, more than to any other source, to the insistence of the late Professor L. J. Henderson on the extreme importance of the concept of system in scientific theory. . . . 'The fundamental starting point is the concept of social systems of action. The *inter*action of individual actors, that is, takes place under such conditions that it is possible to treat such a process of interaction as a system in the scientific sense and subject it to the same order of theoretical analysis which has been successfully applied to other types of systems in other sciences.'"
6. Cf. the related discussion of the "principle of polarity" in Morris Cohen, *Reason and Nature* (Glencoe: The Free Press, 1953), passim.
7. Alexis de Tocqueville, *Democracy in America* (New York: Random House, 1945), II, p. 352.
8. Georg Simmel, *Conflict and the Web of Group Affiliations* (Glencoe: The Free Press, 1955), 140-141.

9. Robert E. Park, *Race and Culture* (Glencoe: The Free Press, 1950), p. 42. See also Robert E. Park, *Human Communities* (Glencoe: The Free Press, 1952), pp. 258-9 and passim.

10. Max Weber, *Economy and Society*, ed. and trans. by Guenther Roth and Claus Wittich (New York: The Bedminster Press, 1968), I, p. 4.

11. Max Weber, "Kritische Bemerkungen zu den vorstehenden 'Kritischen Beiträgen'," *Archiv für Sozialwissenschaft* XXV (1907), p. 248.

12. Max Weber, *Economy and Society, op. cit.*, III, esp. pp. 1260 ff., 1322 ff.

13. The term "role" was originally derived from this reference to the "roll" in the hands of the actor. Its modern usage together with the term "status" go back to Ralph Linton, *The Study of Man* (New York: D. Appleton-Century Co., 1936). Cf. David Bidney, *Theoretical Anthropology* (New York: Columbia University Press, 1953) for an illuminating exception to the foregoing characterization.

14. Ralph Linton, *The Cultural Background of Personality* (New York: D. Appleton-Century Co., 1945), pp. 19, 22, and passim. Italics added.

15. Within this conceptual framework it is quite feasible to handle the fact that a relatively isolated community is found which is individualistic, lacking in solidarity, and secularized, for such a finding does not disprove the utility of the variables which are subsumed under the concept "folk society." Cf. the questionable criticism of Redfield in Oscar Lewis, *Life in a Mexican Village* (Urbana: University of Illinois Press, 1951), pp. 427-40. Much the same criticism has been leveled at Weber's concept of "bureaucracy," because administrators were found to engage in actions which are out of keeping with the formally stipulated conditions of their work. Cf. Alvin Gouldner, "On Weber's Analysis of Bureaucratic Rules," in R. K. Merton, et al., eds., *Reader in Bureaucracy* (Glencoe: The Free Press, 1952), pp. 48-51; and Peter Blau, *Bureaucracy in Modern Society* (New York: Random House, 1956), pp. 35-36. The trouble with these critiques is that they do not distinguish between concept formation and the formulation and testing of hypotheses. In cases where such critiques are justified, it would be necessary to replace the discarded with a new concept, which is more serviceable. As it is, a concept is criticized and then used anyway.

16. As Redfield has shown in his *Folkculture of Yucatan*, these comprehensive terms are in fact composites of many paired concepts. To subsume a number of these (like isolation, homogeneity, predominance of the sacred) under one ideal type like "folk society" may suggest a closer degree of association than is useful. But not to do that also raises problems, for a concept like "competition" has many usable opposites like "communication," "cooperation," "solidarity," and others, which are in fact interrelated. Cf. also the analysis of pattern variables in Talcott Parsons, *The Social System, op. cit.*, pp. 46-51, 58-67, 101-12 which represents a systematic decomposition of *Gemeinschaft* and *Gesellschaft*.

17. An example may make this clearer. Robert Bierstedt has noted that Weber's concepts of traditional and rational authority differ from his concept of charisma in the sense that the latter refers to leadership, not to authority. Implicitly Weber appears to have acknowledged this point since he referred to charismatic leaders under conditions of traditional and of rational authority. But then the question may be asked what concept we should use for leadership which is noncharismatic, an eventuality for which Weber employed the phrase "routinization of charisma" though he did not explicitly formulate this idea as a contrast conception. Cf. Robert Bierstedt, "The Problem of Authority," in Morroe Berger, Theodore

Abel, and Charles Page, eds., *Freedom and Control in Modern Society* (New York: Van Nostrand Co., 1954), pp. 67-81. It may be added that the absence of an opposite term is often due to the linguistic difficulty of finding an equally appropriate word for both concepts. "Routinization of charisma" is not as neat nor as positive as "charisma."

18. Leonard Broom and Philip Selznick, *Sociology* (Evanston: Row, Peterson & Co., 1955), pp. 124-26.

19. This formulation is identical with Redfield's statement: "In every primitive band or tribe there is civilization, in every city there is the folk-society." See Robert Redfield, "The Natural History of a Folk Society," *Social Forces*, XXXI (March 1953), p. 225.

20. In addition, such universal propositions can also reveal the limitations of sociological analysis. That is, their claim to universality can be refuted, when instances are found in which, for example, no impersonal qualities enter into a primary relationship.

21. Functionalists would say here that societies must find some balance between intimacy and impersonality in human relationships, if man's basic needs are to be satisfied sufficiently for societies to survive. This formulation attributes the results of man's problem-solving activities to "the society" which is said to have properties of its own that are in some sense independent of these activities. And one of these properties is thought to consist of some given, but unknown degree of satisfaction which is indispensable for the survival of society. Thus, functional propositions will refer given attributes to "society," while propositions using paired concepts would refer such attributes to social actions with their anticipated and unanticipated consequences.

22. Cf. the related comments on the "dialectic of opposites" in Robert Redfield, *The Little Community* (Chicago: University of Chicago Press, 1955), Chap. IX.

23. Karl Deutsch has suggested such a measure in his calculation of "input-output" ratios of foreign mail, showing among other things that in 1928-38 Germany and the United Kingdom had a similar excess of foreign mail sent out over foreign mail received (.65 for Germany and .70 for the U.K.). But the U.K. was the center of an empire with no restrictions on international communications, while for half this period Germany was a dictatorship whose censorship isolated the country culturally and politically, even if the volume of foreign mail remained unaffected. Cf. Karl Deutsch, "Shifts in the Balance of Communication Flows," *Public Opinion Quarterly*, XX (1956), pp. 147-48. Some logical techniques for handling the problems of typology which are involved here, are discussed in Paul F. Lazarsfeld and Allen H. Barton, "Qualitative Measurement in the Social Sciences: Classification, Typologies, and Indices," in Daniel Lerner, ed., *The Policy Sciences* (Stanford: Stanford University Press, 1951), pp. 155-92.

24. A telling illustration of the problem involved is the agonized appraisal of primitive societies in the context of Western expansion and destruction by Claude Lévi-Strauss in *Tristes Tropiques* (New York: Atheneum, Publishers, 1967), pp. 44-45, 118-30.

25. Weber, *Economy and Society, op. cit.*, I, pp. 302, 305-6. I have re-ordered the wording of this passage slightly. The editors rightly emphasize the difference between this later formulation and the earlier one, which appears in vol. II. pp. 926 ff. However, aside from the greater conciseness and clarity of the later formulation, both passages show Weber's technique of contrasting ideal-typical formulations with the fluidity and interpenetration of contrasting conditions like class and status in social relations.

26. Ibid., II, p. 928.
27. Ibid., II, p. 938.
28. In this connection Parsons and Shils have stated that goal-directed actions must be analyzed by establishing "primacies among types of interest" so that "the ... ambiguities intrinsic to the world of social objects" can be resolved. The authors accomplish this resolution of ambiguities by stipulating that the actions of the individual must be examined and classified when he makes his choice, on the knife edge of the present as it were. The discussion of pattern variables appears to be based on the assumption that all choices are dichotomous *in fact* if analyzed minutely enough, whereas for Weber the internal consistency of any action was a *logical* construction. See Talcott Parsons, E. A. Shils, et al., *Towards a General Theory of Action* (Cambridge: Harvard University Press, 1951), p. 91. Our view is that choices are provisional and interests ambivalent. Accordingly, Weber's "as if" construction appears to us less rationalistic than the assumption made by Parsons and Shils.
29. Swanson has pointed out that Parsons and Shils have failed to derive the classic concepts of collectivities from the "action frame of reference" which they have developed. See Guy E. Swanson, "The Approach to a General Theory of Action by Parsons and Shils," *American Sociological Review*, XVIII (1953), pp. 132-33.
30. Weber, *Economy and Society, op. cit.*, I, pp. 217-20.
31. Ibid., I, pp. 229-30. In this passage Weber did not explicitly contrast the last two conditions of employment. It may be added, however, that under traditional authority the chief's arbitrary decisions frequently identify an office with the household official or favorite who occupies it, and the holders of benefices frequently attempt and succeed in appropriating the position. The term "full-time occupation" is not applicable to an administrative staff under traditional authority either. Cf. also Max Weber, *Religion of China* (Glencoe: The Free Press, 1951), pp. 33-104, for an analysis of patrimonial government which shows close approximations to this concept of traditional authority.
32. Since the first publication of this essay I have elaborated this contrast between employment under legal and traditional authority in my book *Nation-Building and Citizenship* (Berkeley: University of California Press, 1977), pp. 129-39.
33. This perspective is a corollary of Georg Simmel's emphasis on the reciprocity of all social relations. But attention is focused here on collective actions and institutions rather than upon interactions among individuals.
34. References to sub-culture emphasize an important aspect of culture, but this terminology also has peculiar disadvantages. Cf. Robert Bierstedt, "The Limitations of Anthropological Methods in Sociology," *American Journal of Sociology*, LIV (July, 1948), pp. 22-30.
35. Emile Durkheim, *The Rules of Sociological Method* (Chicago: University of Chicago Press, 1938), Chap. 3.
36. The detailed exposition of Weber's views and their implication is left to chapters 6 and 8 of vol. 2.
37. Though the term *Kultur* appears occasionally in Weber's text, there is no sustained discussion of it. Probably he wanted to avoid the ethical connotations the term has in German as well as its amorphous quality. Terms like *ethics, convention,* and *style of life* can be made group-specific, as *Kultur* cannot. These terminological choices can now be checked easily with the aid of the index of the English edition of *Economy and Society*.
38. Weber, *Economy and Society, op. cit.*, II, p. 936.
39. Weber, *The Protestant Ethic, op. cit.*, p. 182.

40. Thus, Confucianism is the work of the world-ordering bureaucrats, Hinduism of the world-ordering magicians, Buddhism of wandering mendicant monks, Islam of world-conquering warriors, Judaism of itinerant traders, Christianity of itinerant craftsmen. See Weber, *op. cit., Economy and Society*, II, p. 512, and the detailed discussion of this theme in ibid., pp. 468-517.
41. See Edmund R. Leach, *Political Systems of Highland Burma* (Cambridge: Cambridge University Press, 1954), esp. pp. 1-17 for an anthropological field study which illustrates the usefulness of this perspective. Leach's theoretical position is quite similar to the one discussed in this paper.
42. Kenneth Burke, *Permanence and Change* (New York: New Republic, 1936), p. 70.
43. Every social theorist recognizes the deficiencies of this procedure. The practice persists, nevertheless, presumably because sociologists are not satisfied with the unscientific character of political judgments. Yet, in the absence of agreed-on criteria of "social health" it remains a political judgment whether or not a given number of strikes impairs the desired cooperation or cohesion in society. As Merton has stated, "Embedded in every functional analysis is some conception, tacit or expressed, of functional requirements of the system under observation. . . . This remains one of the cloudiest, and empirically most debatable concepts of functional theory." See Robert K. Merton, *Social Theory and Social Structure* (Glencoe: The Free Press, 1949), p. 52.
44. This experimentation with what is possible can be identified in the boundary-extending activities of individuals, whether these consist of criminal activity and all other forms of deviance or of scientific research and all other forms of creative work. But this identification does not preclude the search for "hidden" results (say, the boundary-extending implications of boundary-maintaining actions, or vice versa), which our paired concepts suggest. Cf. Talcott Parsons, *The Social System, op. cit.*, for a different view of "boundary maintenance" in a social system.
45. Letter to John Stuart Mill of December 18, 1840 in *Memoirs, Letters and Remains of Alexis de Tocqueville* (Boston: Ticknor and Fields, 1862), II, p. 68. Some of these letters were referred to in Chapter 2 above, where they were related to Tocqueville's concept of knowledge. In the present context they are related to his approach to comparative analysis. See also chapter 5 in vol. 2.
46. Ibid., II, pp. 230-31, 237, 272.
47. Letter to Stoffels, dated February 21, 1835, in ibid., I, p. 376.
48. Letter to Louis de Kergorlay, October 19, 1843, in ibid., I, p. 342.
49. Alexis de Tocqueville, *Democracy in America* (New York: Random House, 1954), II, p. 336.
50. Letter to Mrs. Grote, July 24, 1850, in *Memoirs, op. cit.*, II, pp. 104-5.
51. Letter to M. de Corcelle, April 12, 1835, in ibid., II, pp. 13-14: "You suppose my view of the prospects of democracy to be more gloomy than it is. . . . I have endeavored, it is true, to describe the natural tendency of opinions and institutions in a democratic society. I have pointed out the dangers to which it exposes men. But I have never said that these tendencies, if discovered in time, might not be resisted, and these dangers, if foreseen, averted. It struck me that the republicans saw neither the good nor the evil of the condition into which they wished to bring society. . . ."

6

SOCIAL THEORY AND THE BREAK
WITH TRADITION

Introductory Note

Thirteen years elapsed between "Images of Society" and a major critique of my work, which Talcott Parsons published in 1972. In the meantime I had published *Max Weber, An Intellectual Portrait* (1960) and *Nation-Building and Citizenship* (1964) and other books and articles. Then, in 1971, Guenther Roth and I published *Scholarship and Partisanship*, a collection of our essays on Max Weber, which was the occasion of Parsons' review article. At the time I jotted down my response to this review but put it aside, because I was at work on a major substantive study. *Kings or People, Power and the Mandate to Rule* was published in 1978. After completing this book, it occurred to me to add a substantive section on the antecedents of the French Revolution to my response to Parsons. I wanted to give some empirical grounding to the reservations I had expressed about system, function, and evolution as concepts suitable for the analysis of social change. Eventually, this article was published in 1983 in a *Festschrift* for my colleague and friend, Henry Ehrmann.

This publication record shows that theorizing holds but second place in my work. Nevertheless, I have my reasons for the cautionary and tentative position outlined in Parts One and Two of this volume.

SYSTEM AND FUNCTION

In a review of my work, Talcott Parsons states that I reject the three basic concepts of sociological theory: system, function, and evolution.[1] It will focus my discussion if I indicate why I regard these terms with some skepticism. Concepts should serve our thinking about society, not dominate it. We adopt them because they fit in with how we look upon the world and because we find them useful. We reject them because they conflict with basic assumptions and because they obstruct our view of what we want to investigate. I shall confine myself to elementary considerations. If simple notions present great difficulties, then one has grounds for skepticism towards a more recondite use of such abstractions.

Following this theoretical review, I shall turn to the prerevolutionary situation in eighteenth-century France, which has been a point of departure for the modernization of countries around the world. At an ideological level, later transformations like the Industrial Revolution, the Bolshevik revolution, and the process of decolonization can be understood with reference to that precedent. But my main concern is to show that the transformation of eighteenth-century France is worth exploring as a prototype of societal transitions from tradition to modernity.

At a minimum the term "system" implies a high degree of interdependence. Changes in one part are inevitably followed by changes in other parts. Second, system implies that this interdependence is regulated internally. Specific variables may change only within specifiable limits. Third, systems are marked off by boundaries. The inside is clearly separated from the outside. We are in no doubt when we attribute features or parts to a system. Examples from biology provide some sociologists with their favorite model. Increases in heartbeat when running, the lower and upper limits of body temperature, attributes of the body as distinguished from attributes of the world outside of the body: these illustrate the systemic dimensions I have in mind.

To me the difficulties of the term "system" loom large. The *interdependence* of whole societies varies with their degree of integration. In complex social structures this integration is seldom high. It is easier to think of aspects like the stock market or medical care in systemic terms than of the entire society. The reason is that it is difficult to foresee the repercussions that follow an action in different parts of society. Societies do not have an equilibrium in the way the body has a normal temperature. In all complex societies there is much uncertainty. The actions of individuals fall within a range of tolerance. But the limits of this range are difficult to specify, because people redefine what individuals may or may not do. Emile Durkheim made crime a normal aspect of culture without which the awareness and enforcement of norms would be insufficient; but he did not say how much crime is needed to help maintain the norms of society. Similarly, Talcott Parsons has found it difficult to state what he means by a sufficient degree of motivation and satisfaction. Robert Merton has called the idea of social health (which I take to be a synonym for equilibrium) one of the cloudiest and empirically most debatable concepts of functional theory. Finally, societies do not have *boundaries*, in contrast to bodies that are clearly defined organisms or nation-states that are politically defined units. Perhaps the idea of boundaries suggests itself because we live in a world of nation-states. Often we use "society" and "nation" interchangeably. Yet generally accepted frontiers around a contiguous territory are a historical phenomenon. Primordial ties like those of race, kinship, language, or religion cut across national boundaries. So do secondary ties like those of intellectual or organizational affiliation. Ideas and techniques cross frontiers with special ease. And the center of cultural activities has shifted frequently. During the last century France was the center of culture for Russia and Latin America.

England, France, and Germany were the center for the United States, in about that sequence. The former colonial power continues to be the center for many of the new nations. And the United States itself has moved from the periphery as a cultural dependent to the center of cultural diffusion.

Since I do not accept the assumption of society as a system, I am in trouble with the term "function" also. We would all be functionalists if we meant no more than our common interest in causal relations. The terms "function" and "cause" are easily interchanged, but "function" implies purpose while "cause" does not. When you say that fighting against a common enemy has the function of increasing group solidarity, you are close to a statement of purpose. Conservatives defend war in these terms. You can say just as easily that fighting against a common enemy increases group solidarity—a causal statement. The functional approach fuses fact and purpose; the causal approach separates them. Some sociologists see in the persistence of group structures the main object of their analysis. For them it makes sense to ask what specific social facts contribute to the functioning (or the dysfunctioning) of a social system. No doubt, functionalists would be surprised to learn that they are beholden to a belief in providence; they are secularists who do not hold theological views. But language can betray intellectual influences of which we are not aware. Causal inquiry emancipates us from an earlier world view in which purpose was inherent in nature as part of a providential design. Functional analysis has not cut this umbilical cord.

I have stated an alternative approach in the preceding chapter 5.[2] Group structures persist while individuals come and go, but they do not persist unchanged. Sociological analysis should move back and forth between the social structure and the action and subjective awareness of individuals. My main objection to system and function is that these concepts obstruct the second part of the analysis. As long as our understanding of what people do depends in part on how they see their own world, we should not move to a level of abstraction that makes the individual a mere function of the social structure. Also, sociological theory should focus attention on the boundary-extending as well as the boundary-maintaining activities of individuals. This conceptual strategy is one social scientist's critique of utopian thought, which asks us to search each fact for its intended and unintended, its valued and devalued, consequences. In this perspective the term "function" is too undirectional to be useful.

In addition, I try to keep in mind that the concepts we use are not free inventions. Sociologists are like the people they observe. After all, even scholars interact with others in an effort to make sense of the world and attain some mastery over it. In what historical setting did the view emerge that society is a self-sufficient system in which individuals interact so as to achieve a sufficient degree of pattern maintenance, integration, goal attainment, and adaptation, to employ Parson's terminology? Of course, his particular formulation is indebted to recent technological developments like cybernetics. But the biological mode of functional differentiation and integration has older intellectual roots, going back to classical antiquity as Robert Nisbet has shown. In modern times, the idea that society is a self-sufficient, functioning system came into its own during the eighteenth century, following two centuries of European expansion overseas. In the U.S. this approach has been revived following the United States' ascendance to the position of a world power. Obviously other factors are at work as well. Newtonian cosmology and biological models have been used as successive analogues appropriate to the study of society. But I believe it would be difficult to view society in these terms if you see the world from India, the USSR, or modern Japan rather than from France, England or the United States.

Thus, there are reasons for skepticism when sociologists use their terms "system" and "function." Apparently societies retain their identity while encompassing many apparent incompatibilities and conflicts of interest. Evidence for this view is on all sides. Consider the primordial ties that divide us along religious, ethnic, racial, and familial lines. Add to these our innumerable secondary affiliations through formal organizations. The people in this country are divided, yet they are all recognizably American in speech, behavior, and ways of thought. Some unity is achieved through the medium of culture. A certain degree of comprehensive decision making is achieved through the political process. But these are proximate and often precarious achievements. Perhaps the most serious objection to the terms "system" and "function" is that they take as given what is problematic, namely, the degree of interdependence and of unity that characterizes societies. And it is at this point that an evolutionary approach to social and political change is especially questionable.

SOCIAL CHANGE AND THE CONCEPT OF "EVOLUTION"

Social change refers to the differences we observe in a society before and after a given interval of time. The later social structure may show point-for-point contrasts with the earlier one; the literature is filled with contrasts of this kind. Since this proliferation of terms is bad, Parsons has provided us with a comprehensive set of categories at a higher level of abstraction. Yet the application of his categories is no simple matter, because neither the earlier nor the later social structure possesses a consistent set of attributes.

To perceive a society as a consistent whole is easiest for a foreign visitor. De Tocqueville said that he did not write a page of his book on America without thinking about France. The things he noted most were those that differed from what he knew of France. Similarly, comparisons between traditional and modern societies tend to bring out the distinctions between them in more or less dichotomous fashion. But these distinctions are the starting point of analysis, not its end product. There are no completely modern societies: think of the role kinship and status play in our own experience. There are no completely traditional societies: think of the role contract and religious universalism played in medieval Europe. Only mixed types exist that should be understood in their own right. U.S. society is surely modern. On the whole people in this country are oriented toward achievement. But the achievement of one generation becomes the ascriptive status of the next. And during the last few years many children of well-to-do parents have rejected achievement *and* ascription by opting for a life of affluent poverty. Let me use this most recent and familiar experience to make a more general point. If we knew as much about other societies as we do about the 1960s, we would recognize our experience as quite typical. Complex social structures are never true to type; societies are always in transition from past to future. We should try to develop categories for coping with this phenomenon intellectually.

Since I discuss these antievolutionist views in chapter 12 below, I can summarize them here. There is much continuity between traditional and modern societies. It is appropriate to think of a build-up of modernization over many centuries. Even major disruptions like the French Revolution or the Industrial Revolution in England have been traced to much earlier antecedents. But once such revolutions have occurred, they may represent breakthroughs that have repercussions around the world. It is in this sense that democratization or industrialization cannot occur in the same way twice. For such breakthroughs provide an incentive for other countries to do likewise. Social change is always a combination of extrinsic and intrinsic stimuli. This is true of the many societies that have been transformed in conscious adaptation of the changes they have witnessed from afar. But it is just as true of the interaction between England, France, and the United States in the eighteenth century. In this process of adaptation intellectuals and governments have played a major role. With the model of another, pioneering country before them, they see their own country as politically and socially backward, and they seek to overcome this backwardness. By adapting items from the arsenal of foreign ideas and practices they hope to create a better society. (In principle this includes the opposite reaction, namely, a society that uses foreign models to reaffirm its traditional structure, but I exclude this consideration for the present.) I want to explore the prerevolutionary situation in France in order to understand the social structure of transition. I am less concerned with the revolutionary outcome as a unique event than with the preceding period as a prototype of transition from tradition to modernity. My warrant for this exploration is that in eighteenth-century France we can witness the process of modernization that influences us still.

EIGHTEENTH-CENTURY FRANCE AND MODERNIZATION

Reference Societies

Eighteenth-century France was the major European power, both politically and culturally. Its population increased from 18 to 25 million people. In Europe only Russia was close to the latter figure by the end of the century. In contrast to Germany and Italy, France had been a unified state for a long time. For much of the century the country was prosperous though this economic position grew worse. Politically and militarily the country suffered major setbacks. But these economic and political ups and downs did not jeopardize France's cultural preeminence. French had superseded Latin as the international language. Prussia's Frederick II observed that he who knew French could travel throughout Europe without an interpreter. In fashion, France and specifically the court at Versailles set the tone for the continent.

But while France was the cosmopolis of other countries, in France itself England was the fashion. Following the death of Louis XIV in 1715, the French aristocracy sought to reverse a century of autocratic rule. French aristocrats looked with envy on the political power of the English aristocracy in the provinces and in Parliament. Montesquieu's interpretation of English government (1748) in terms of checks and balances among its three branches enjoyed wide influence. To scientists and men of letters England was the home of Newton and Locke. Voltaire made invidious contrasts between Descartes, who had to leave France to philosophize in liberty, and Newton, who lived his whole life in a free country where he was entirely tranquil, happy, and honored. Leading strata of French society suffered from Anglomania, as it was called derisively. English ideas were encouraged further when Scotch refugees established Masonic lodges in France. Freemasonry provided an organizational setting for the growing communication between discontented aristocrats and men of letters.

The Seven-Year War (1756-1763) ended with the defeat of France, and the idea of England as a model did not survive intact. But meanwhile the idea of America had increased in importance. Earlier in the century some note had been taken of the British colonies, both favorable and unfavorable. America was a new and primitive land, with the Indians being considered good savages by some and an inferior breed by others. The American climate was believed unfavorable to human life. Attractive only to settlers motivated by avarice, the country was thought incapable of producing any notable cultural achievement.

A Dutch writer, publishing in French in 1768, considered the discovery of America the most important and disastrous event in the history of civilization; he believed a second such catastrophe would bring the extinction of mankind. One should add, of course, that he was influenced by his sojourn at the Prussian court, which actively discouraged emigration, and that he opposed the evils of colonialism and the myth of the good savage. The counterarguments went back to the end of the seventeenth century when some French writers noted the accomplishment of the Quakers in Pennsylvania. Another writer remarked that in New Jersey there were neither lawyers, doctors, nor theologians, which to the French of the period seemed a very good thing. These pamphlets were addressed to French Huguenots in order to encourage their immigration. Similar ideas were broadcast by Locke, Montesquieu, Voltaire, and the writers of the *Encyclopédie*, who noted the principles of religious toleration and enlightened government in several colonies. Following the Treaty of Paris in 1763, interest in America gradually increased. A number of American artists and scientists visited France. Prime Minister Choiseul prepared to redress French reverses by exploiting the troubles in England's American colonies. When Benjamin Franklin came on the scene as the American colonists' representative in London (1767), his scientific and political reputation won him ready acclaim, which he proceeded to exploit in a propaganda campaign favorable to the American cause.[3]

I shall return to France presently, but I want to illustrate my theme of reference societies by a brief glance at this side of the Atlantic. Among the cumulative grievances against England the American fear of standing armies loomed large. In the pamphlets of the period that fear was elaborated by telling references to despotic countries overseas. Turkey headed the list because the power of her despotic rulers rested on the swords of the janissaries. Next came the French kings who had used force against the liberties of their subjects and reduced to nothing the puny privileges of the parliaments. Poland, Spain, Russia and Egypt were other despotisms mentioned. A still more forceful warning was given by reference to Venice, Sweden, and above all Denmark, countries that had enjoyed liberties at one time but were now the victims of autocratic rule. On the other side were the countries like Switzerland and Holland that had struggled successfully against the abuse of power by the few. Above all, there was England. Her glorious history of constitutional government was cited in evidence against current English abuses of authority in the colonies. Indeed, the colonists built their case for independence by developing a theory of government based on English precedents while English practice was likened to the despotic states of Africa and the notorious cases of European autocracy. Thus, the transition from tradition to modernity involves an intense awareness of positive and negative reference societies in the process of defining new national goals.[4]

Men of Letters

This process depends on a group of men sensitive to the fate of their nation, aware of what goes on elsewhere, and capable of formulating ideas. In eighteenth-century France such men called themselves *gens des lettres*. These were men well versed in many fields rather than specialists in any one field. Voltaire pointed out that their philosophical spirit, their searching and purified reason, had greatly contributed to instructing and refining the nation.[5] That partisan description is peculiar to its country and period; elsewhere other characteristics would be more appropriate, such as the term ''intelligentsia'' and its connotations in nineteenth-century Russia. It may be futile to search for a uniform terminology when dealing with men of ideas whose sense of identity depends upon *their* definition of the situation. But diverse as they are, such men have a certain family resemblance.

They depend upon a reading public because they do not want to write only for each other. In France such a public developed with the proportion of literates doubling between 1700 and 1786-1790.[6] They depend as well upon social recognition from the leading strata of society. In 1726 Voltaire was beaten up by hired thugs because he had offended the Chevalier Rohan-Chabot and was sent to the Bastille for daring to seek revenge. By 1778 he returned to Paris in triumph, being treated with adulation at the Academy, the Comédie Française, and in the streets. Related to social recognition is the development of a sense of importance among literati. In 1734 Voltaire had noted how much consideration was accorded to men of letters in England, in pointed contrast to their lowly position in France. By the 1770s an English observer noted that French men of letters had considerable influence on the manners and sentiments of people of rank and of the public in general and consequently were not without effect on the measures of government.[7] As a result the closer relation between men of letters and the leaders of high society became a favorite theme of philosophical writing.

Yet this new sense of importance was never untroubled. At one point Diderot speaks of philosophy as the opium of the passions, suggesting a painful awareness of the discrepancy between theory and practice. Among the contributors to the *Encyclopédie* a certain tension developed between activists and literati over the relative emphasis upon propaganda and style. Because he rejected the neglect of literary quality Voltaire voiced his skepticism to the two editors, Diderot and d'Alembert. He addressed them occasionally as Atlas and Hercules who carry the world on their shoulders, the department for the instruction of mankind.[8] As Robert Darnton has shown, the familiar figures of the Enlightenment were an elite.

> In their view taste belonged to a very small number of privileged souls. . . . It is unknown in bourgeois families, where one is constantly occupied with the case of one's fortunes. Yet in the wake of these famous men a host of lesser writers

flocked to Paris. Intent on making their fortune they were often condemned for prolonged periods to eke out their existence by hack work. These declasse men of letters were instrumental in turning the main ideas of the Enlightenment into a revolutionary ideology.[9]

It may be a distinguishing characteristic of eighteenth-century France that up to a point the ancien regime allowed the expression of such ideas—owing in part to the considerable number of prominent aristocrats who embraced and protected the philosophy of humanity.

Revolutionary Ideology

It is somewhat daunting to say anything in brief compass about this philosophy. The shortcut I choose depends upon my belief that in breaking away from tradition men of letters coalesce as a class and status group of their own. Dependent upon the new way of life made possible by a growing reading public, they are animated by certain archetypical ideas that give them a new sense of identity. I shall presuppose the existence of a hateful regime that in France had governed the country autocratically since the early seventeenth century. The medieval assembly, the so-called estates-general, had last met in 1614. The country had witnessed famines, epidemics, and wars for over a century. Religious persecution was rife. And a centralized police regime had preempted the quasiautonomous, governmental functions of municipalities and the land-owning aristocracy.

> The spectacle of so many wrongful and absurd privileges, of which the weight was felt more and more, and the cause was less and less understood . . . seeing so many irregular and bizarre institutions . . . which no one had attempted to harmonize with each other . . . they readily conceived a loathing for things ancient and for tradition.[10]

Faced with this system of iniquity men of letters and their friends wished to rebuild society . . . by the sole light of reason, as de Tocqueville put it. Long before the revolution occurred, the old regime had become unacceptable in many, very influential strata of the population.

The starting point was the attack upon privilege—even among the privileged. The breakup of tradition depends upon some such black-and-white contrast between the hateful present and the ideal future. In eighteenth-century France the old, religious conception of a transcendental order embodying truth and justice was rejected in favor of the sovereign national will as the ultimate source of law. Yet this populist appeal to the intrinsic goodness of human nature was expressed by men of letters proudly conscious of having acquired social recognition for themselves. The Freemasons are an instructive, organizational example of this combination of populism and elitism.

Between 1772 and 1789 the number of Masonic lodges increased from 104 to over 600, with 65 of the most prominent in Paris alone. There was nothing suspicious about an organization engaged in drinking, singing, philanthropy, religion without orthodoxy, vague mysticism, and fake chivalry, all combined with a belief in progress and the value of science. The order made much of its secret rituals. Each member pledged himself to guard them or undergo penalties that would obliterate his memory from the minds of men and Masons. Each member obliged himself to be a religious believer and a peaceable subject—no further questions asked. Religious and political controversy were excluded from all Masonic meetings. The order as a whole declared time and again that it had no interest in affairs of church or state. It was nondenominational and nonpolitical in its endorsement of religious tolerance and civic probity. But where a humanitarian appeal is combined with a great secret, a new and better and as yet unknown life seems promised. Eventually the initiate can discover that life. Meanwhile he joins all other Masons as equal sharers in a promised revelation. The rest of the world is foreign territory where caution or distrust is indicated and the danger of treason lurks. Toward the outside all masons are equal. But internally the order is divided into a multitude of hierarchic ranks, with each rank harboring an arcanum of its own. At the highest rank a Mason could hope to learn the innermost secret and thus partake of a final enlightenment. On the long road to that rank he must give willing obedience to the brothers who are entitled to judge whether he is worthy of promotion. This multiplication of ranks increased the incentives of those below while also increasing the attraction of the order for the nobility.

Separation from organized religion and political activity was indispensable for achieving external acceptance and internal harmony. Free from the bonds of the outside world, the Mason is a man among men, engaged jointly with them in the cultivation of morality. Here is a poetic description of the Masonic spirit:

> The cry of nature, friend, is Liberty;
> This right so dear to man is here respected.
> Equality without anarchy, liberty without license,
> In obedience to our laws lies our freedom.[11]

By separating the order from all narrowly religious or political preoccupations and by their secrets the Masons institutionalized an independent realm of morality. Nonpolitical as they were, the Freemasons vindicated to this realm the capacity of sitting in judgment over the outside world, of being the conscience of humanity. Within the order and guarded by its secrecy the brotherhood of man had been realized. By comparison, churches and states appeared as necessary evils.

To be sure, Freemasonry was only one facet of the break with tradition. Its importance for the revolution should not be exaggerated. But the order exemplifies two aspects of the revolutionary ideology that I would like to emphasize. The order was elitist in terms of the social composition of its members and the emphasis on hierarchy. But the order was also populist by resolutely denying religious and social differences among the members, by emphasizing fraternity, and by virtue of its appeal to a philosophy of humanity. Secondly, the well-guarded secret of the order implicitly linked virtue and ideas with power. Where esoteric knowledge is guarded by secrecy, there is an intimation of power. For where secrets are kept, men must have something to hide. The more is made of secrecy, the greater the power that it is designed to hide. In *The Magic Flute* the wisdom and majesty of Sarastro appears indeed larger than life, and Mozart based his treatment of that figure upon the master of his own Masonic lodge. Only a few are permitted to learn the secret of the order. When they do they discover that the cultivation of virtue establishes both the brotherhood of man and the moral ability to judge the affairs of the world.

Ambivalence between elitism and populism, tacit assumptions about the relation between virtue and power, between ideas and power: these are archetypical ingredients of an ideology that breaks away from tradition. Men of letters cannot pursue ideas without implying or affirming their own preoccupation with ideas. That preoccupation sets them apart from ordinary folk. But these men of letters also seek a responsive audience in their own society. And as they sense their isolation while seeking a response they realize the backwardness of their country in comparison with others. This situation creates ambivalence enough, but it is compounded further by a sense of impotence. Typically, men of letters do not have access to positions of power, and just as typically they are highly sensitive about the fate of their country. Thus, powerlessness is experienced most acutely just when men of letters develop a group consciousness of their own. They are confronted with the tragic discrepancy between what is and what ought to be, with their political impotence and the significance of ideas in their own lives. In this setting it is a great temptation to implicitly attribute to theory, to principle, and to ideas a potential impact, a power to move men. For men will seek mastery where they can find it, and when ideas are their only weapons they will attribute power to ideas.

POPULAR SOVEREIGNTY, EQUALITY, REPRESENTATION, AND PROPERTY

Now we must turn from the social context to the content of ideas. To do this succinctly I confine myself to the concepts of popular sovereignty, equality, representation, and property. This is an arbitrary selection, but it allows me to focus attention upon problems of government. Once again I am concerned with the archetypical patterns that emerge when the leading strata in a society undertake to break with the continuity of its tradition.

Popular Sovereignty

In the Western setting appeals to popular sovereignty were associated with the concept of lawful rule. Monarchical government is absolute and yet subject to God's law. However vague and disputed, this limitation meant that when a king's rule became tyrannical the people had a right to resist his unlawful acts. For the people, like the king, owed their first allegiance to God, and unlawful acts were a violation of divine justice. I mention this traditional view in order to note that the eighteenth-century appeal to popular sovereignty became absolute. As the Abbé Sieyès put it: "The nation is prior to everything. It is the source of everything. Its will is always legal; indeed it is the law itself . . . the source of all legality."[12] The law under God was limited in principle by a higher law; the law that a nation gives to itself has no limit. This absolute consisted in the will of the people. A government based on that will would be founded on ethical principles. It is in virtue and the sovereignty of the people that one must search for the guarantee against the vices and the despotism of government, as Robespierre put it.[13] If one comes to this literature afresh one is struck by the degree to which the *philosophes* of the eighteenth century were made comfortable by a proliferation of synonyms. The people and the nation, virtue or ethical principles and the general will, fraternity and equality and freedom of men as citizens and as participants in the sovereign power: these and related terms were used interchangeably.

In practice the matter was more complex. Popular sovereignty became a historical reality when on June 17, 1789, the Third Estate—having been convoked under rules that had been in abeyance for 175 years—rejected these rules and arrogated to itself the title of National Assembly. Until 1614 the three estates had met and voted separately; their charge was to petition the king under an imperative mandate of their respective electorates. Now the National Assembly constituted itself as an extraordinary, collective representative of the nation. When the assembly was joined by the clergy and nobility on orders from the king, it proceeded to formulate a new constitution of fundamental laws. (The French used philosophical principles in contrast to the Americans who used an idealized version of the English constitution; one result was that the Bill of Rights precedes the French Constitution but was added in amendment to the U.S. one.) The basic problems facing the assembly can be seen in its statement of principles, the famous *Declaration of the Rights of Man and Citizen*. There it is stated that the aim of every political association is the preservation of the natural and inalienable rights of man and that all men are equal in their rights of liberty, property, security and resistance to oppression. All citizens have the right to concur personally or through their representatives in the formation of the law as the expression of the general will. Also, all citizens, being equal before the law, are equally admissible to all public offices, positions, and employments, according to their capacity and without other distinction. These familiar phrases from the 1789 declaration were omitted from, or reformulated in, the subsequent declarations. This suggests that fundamental issues were in dispute. I shall discuss three of these issues.

Equality

The ideal of equality in the declaration referred to natural or moral equality, not to an absolute or literal equality. Time and again the *philosophes* asserted that they were well aware of the necessity of different ranks, honors, and prerogatives, that in all government subordination must prevail. In their gifts and possessions men are unequal, but let the state not add an unjust inequality of rights alongside this actual inequality of means, as the Abbé Sieyès put it.[14] The impulse behind this ideal was generous and humane. Let men value and treat each other as natural equals. Let those who rise above others avoid insults to their inferiors, demand nothing beyond what is required, and be humane in demanding what is their due. Certain universal rights to justice should be enjoyed equally by all or enjoyed in some distributive manner that removes all suspicion of contempt or partiality.[15] The accent upon opposition against privilege is apparent in this interpretation.

The practical realization of equality was something else again. The disputes that followed the *Declaration* of 1789 make clear that no one quarreled with the idea of a *passive equality* before the law. This meant that the law itself should not be discriminatory, in contrast to the old law, which had protected many special privileges. Under these circumstances little attention was paid to the many privileges of the rich that would survive, even where formal equality was assured. But the *Declaration* also referred to the *active rights* of citizenship, the right of each to concur in the formation of laws and to be considered for public office or employment. This active right was much disputed. As a practical matter the idea of representation and special qualifications for public office won out over the idea of a plebiscitary democracy and equal access to public positions. But both standpoints were aired in debate and mark a recurring issue of democratic rule to this day.

Representation

It is difficult to think of equality and representation as mutually compatible. Logical consistency was clearly on the side of Robespierre and his friends. They argued strongly for equality of direct participation in the expression of the sovereign will, which was to them the same basic idea. By contrast, every representative agency would give disproportionate weight to special interests. The defeat of special privilege had been the main purpose of the revolution. The Jacobin wing could not see the logic of reinstituting under a democratic veneer what had finally been eliminated in its aristocratic guise. This logically consistent position did not prevail. Robespierre had no answer to the practical question of how direct democracy was to be implemented without representation and still remain compatible with orderly government.[16]

Today we know also that the Bolshevik extension of the Jacobin principle led necessarily to a further development of representation. To be sure, the Bolshevik attack on bourgeois capitalism was made again in the name of the people. The argument for the working masses as the true source of sovereignty is very similar to the argument by Sieyès that the 25 million members of the Third Estate represented the nation while the two hundred thousand clergymen and nobles were merely trivial. In the constitutional thought of the French Revolution the rights of the minority were no more protected than in that of the Bolshevik revolution, though the two revolutions differ in other respects. In practice, the Bolshevik leaders were as inconsistent as the leaders of the French Revolution. They favored direct democracy as a revolutionary weapon. But once in power they interpreted this to mean the sovereign power of workers and peasants as represented by the Communist party.

Eighteenth-century France witnessed an analogous reinterpretation. For decades the ancien regime had been attacked in the name of popular sovereignty. Diderot's article on political authority opposed authority based on conquest with the ideal of authority based on consent ten years before Rousseau's *Social Contract* (1762). Now, during the first months of the revolution, the Abbé Sieyès distinguished between the great mass of the population who enjoy the passive equality of the law and those members of the Third Estate who have an active right of citizenship. The former make no economic contribution to the state; hence, like women, children, and foreigners, they should be excluded from active influence upon public affairs. On the other hand, there are

> *available* classes in the Third Estate; and like everyone else I call "available" those classes where some sort of affluence enables men to receive a liberal education, to train their minds and to take an interest in public affairs. Such classes have no interest other than that of the rest of the People.[17]

In structure this argument is no different from the contention that the members of the Communist party represent the interests of the people. However, in this case political loyalty and a party career are substituted for education and income as the qualification required for active citizenship. Elsewhere, Sieyès states that all can enjoy the advantages of society; but only those who contribute to the public establishment are like true shareholders in the great social enterprise. Only they are active citizens, properly speaking, and hence true members of the political association.[18]

In France neither direct nor representative democracy came to prevail, but rather a mixture of the two. The franchise embodied the ideal of popular consent to the fundamental laws, by voting for a constitutional assembly, and to the policy decisions of representatives, by voting in elections that provide a choice of candidates. The principle of representation without imperative mandate embodied the ideal that elected deputies would speak on behalf of national rather than local partisan interests. In practice, democratic institutions can only approximate these ideals. Their viability depends, I believe, upon conditions that allow the meaningful coexistence of both the plebiscitary and the representative principle.

Finally, I turn to the question of property.

Property

It is difficult to think of equality and property as mutually compatible. Logical consistency was again on the side of the Jacobin party. They argued strongly for equality and hence against the distinction between a passive enjoyment of rights and active citizenship. Robespierre and his friends opposed a franchise limited by property qualifications. They questioned whether probity, talent, or patriotism depended upon ownership. In their view the rights of active citizenship belonged to all adult males who would constitute the general will. The rich merely represented a special interest. The Jacobins distrusted the rich and had little regard for their property rights. But they also wanted to make sure that everyone had an equal opportunity to acquire property. Clearly, it was difficult to square a policy of redistributing wealth with the theory of a natural right of property that was a basic tenet of the French Revolution. Yet in 1793 Robespierre asked whether the legal safeguards provided for property had not in fact been made for the rich, for monopolists, for speculators, and for tyrants. He wanted the assembly to consider the nature and legitimacy of property. To this end he proposed that the right of property cannot prejudice the security or the liberty or the existence or the property of our fellow creatures. Consistent to the last, he also proposed that the state assume the duty of providing work or relief for everyone and that the relief of poverty is a debt, owed by the rich to the poor.[19] But France was a nation of small property owners. They did not feel reassured by an approach that considered their property sacred but not that of the rich.

With the defeat of the Jacobin party the original position was reaffirmed. The declaration of 1795 reiterated that property is the right to enjoy and dispose of one's property, one's income, and the product of one's labor and industry. The inequality of means was not considered. In the words of the Abbé Sieyès:

> Political rights derive from a person's capacity as a citizen. These legal rights are identical for every person, whether his property happens to be great or small. Any citizen who satisfies all the formal requirements for an elector has the right to be represented. . . .[20]

The conditions of the franchise included minimum age, residence, and tax payments equivalent to the earnings of a certain number of working days. It was assumed that such a property qualification would go together with a certain level of education, interest, and judgment on the part of the qualified voter.

In conclusion, I want to raise a question that will lead me back to the theoretical problems with which I began. How could the men who endorsed a limited franchise still claim that they believed in equality? The answer is, I think, that they only believed in an equality of legal rights. The law does not evaluate. Since all men have the right to develop their capacities, the law must protect the whole range of moral and esthetic values. To ensure that all men possess the same legal rights, the law asks only whether or not this man's acting as he does prevents another from developing to the full his own natural capacities. The law does not even facilitate equality. It only seeks to ensure that each man can do what he will with his person and property without thereby curtailing the freedom of another. This highly abstract idea considers men only in their capacity as legal agents and stipulates their equality in this respect. As such, legal equality has proved to be an instrument not for combating inequality but for ignoring all the distinctions dividing men except those bearing on their formal legal capacity.

In the eighteenth century these views were formulated on the assumption that the rights of property owners required legal protection. The spokesmen of natural rights were combating a social order in which special privileges enjoyed the protection of the law. Hence the idea that a man's rights to his property are equal to the rights of every other was a revolutionary, not a conservative, doctrine. And in that context it was quite plausible to maintain that property and equality were compatible. Commenting on Rousseau's *Social Contract*, G.H. Mead has stated that "the citizen can give laws only to the extent that his volitions are an expression of the rights which he recognizes in others . . . [and] which the others recognize in him." Mead points out further that such consent upon the terms of interaction presupposed the institution of property. For "the individual wills his control over his property only in so far as he wills the same sort of control for everyone else over property."[21] I see in this approach an early antecedent of the sociologist's analysis of interaction. This analysis is as abstract as the economist's classic definition of the

Homo economicus interacting with others like himself on a free market. The actual inequalities dividing men do not come into the picture in either case. For when it is said that the social system is made up of the interaction of individuals who are in each case both actors and objects of orientation, the actors concerned are treated implicitly as equals in just the way that property owners may treat each other as equals.[22]

To me, this assumption seems unwarranted. I see men interacting in society in a manner that combines three aspects. Their actions make sense to themselves, they are oriented towards the reactions of significant others, and through ideas and interactions they seek to attain increments of mastery. This last element is missing from theories that seek to explain social structures from interactions among equals. There is no consensus on the terms of interaction between property owners and those without property. There may be a formal agreement, of course, but that presupposes the presence of authority. I see a basic flaw in social theories that seek to account for social structures without focusing attention on the role of authority.

NOTES

1. In an untitled review article dealing with Bendix and Guenther Roth's *Scholarship and Partisanship* (Berkeley: Unversity of California Press, 1971), in *Contemporary Sociology*, I (1972), pp. 200-203.
2. See especially pp. 113-17.
3. Cf. Durand Echeverria, *Mirage in the West* (Princeton, N.J.: Princeton University Press, 1957), ch. 1.
4. For a discussion of the American case see Bernard Bailyn, *The Ideological Origins of the American Revolution* (Cambridge, Mass.: Harvard University Press, 1967), pp. 63ff., 79, and passim.
5. Voltaire, "Men of Letters," in Stephen J. Gendzier, ed., *Denis Diderot's The Encyclopedia* (New York: Harper and Row, Harper Torchbooks, 1967), p. 167.
6. This estimate is based on the proportion of men and women who could sign their names on the marriage registers. Cf. John Lough, *An Introduction to Eighteenth Century France* (New York: David McKay Co., 1960), pp. 235-236. The author documents the rising economic position of writers during the eighteenth century.
7. Quoted in ibid., pp. 266-267. In addition to Lough's chapter, "The Writer and his Public," cf. Fritz Schalk, "Die Entstehung des schriftstellerischen Selbstbewusstseins in Frankreich," in *Einleitung in die Encyclopaedie der Französischen Aufklärung* (Heft VI of Münchner Romanistische Arbeiten; München: Max Hueber Verlag, 1936), pp. 45-65.
8. Quoted in Schalk, *op. cit.*, pp. 61-62.
9. Robert Darnton, "The High Enlightenment and the Low-Life of Literature in Pre-revolutionary France," *Past and Present*, no. 51 (May 1971), pp. 81-115. The quoted sentence is taken from Voltaire's article on taste in the *Encyclopédie*.
10. Alexis de Tocqueville, *L'Ancien Regime* (Oxford: Basil Blackwell, 1947), p. 149.

11. Quoted in Paul Hazard, *European Thought in the Eighteenth Century* (Harmondsworth: Penguin Books, 1965), p. 291.
12. Emmanuel Joseph Sieyès, *What is the Third Estate?* (New York: Frederick A. Praeger, 1963), pp. 124, 126.
13. Quoted in Alfred Cobban, ''The Fundamental Ideas of Robespierre,'' in *Aspects of the French Revolution* (London: Paladin, 1971), p. 139.
14. Quoted from a statement of 1789 in G. G. van Deusen, *E. J. Sieyès: His Life and His Nationalism* (New York: Columbia University Press, 1932), p. 82, n. 27.
15. This is the interpretation of the Chevalier de Jaucourt in his article on natural law in the *Encyclopédie*.
16. An instructive analysis of Robespierre's changing views as he moved from the opposition into a position of authority is contained in Alfred Cobban, ''The Political Ideas of Maximilien Robespierre during the period of the Convention,'' in *Aspects of the French Revolution, op. cit.*, pp. 159-191.
17. Sieyès, in van Deusen, *op. cit.*, p. 78.
18. Quoted in Heinz Klay, *Zensuswahlrecht und Gleichheitsprinzip* (Heft 19 of Berner Untersuchungen zur Allgemeinen Geschichte; Aarau: Verlag H.R. Sauerländer, 1956), p. 107.
19. Quoted from Robespierre's speech of April 24, 1793, in Richard Schlatter, *Private Property* (London: George Allen & Unwin, 1951), pp. 229-230.
20. In van Deusen, op. cit., pp. 79-80.
21. G. H. Mead, *Movements of Thought in the Nineteenth Century* (Chicago: University of Chicago Press, 1936), pp. 21, 17.
22. The formulation but not the inference is that of Talcott Parsons, *Societies, Evolutionary and Comparative Perspectives* (Englewood Cliffs, N.J.: Prentice-Hall Inc., 1966), p. 8.

7

CULTURE, SOCIAL STRUCTURE, AND CHANGE

Introductory Note

Parsons' critique of my work was published in 1972, but I published my answer to it (see chapter 6 above) only in 1983. The reason for this delay was not only preoccupation with other work, but the feeling that I had already dealt with these matters. Part of my difference with Parsons' systemic approach had been formulated in "Images of Society" (1959), but that formulation was still exploratory. It was not sufficient to show that the structural-functional approach was not the only way to go; it was necessary to formulate an alternative. To an extent, I had done this in the essay "Culture, Social Structure and Change" which I wrote for the first edition of collected articles that appeared under the title *Embattled Reason* in 1970. Since by then ten years had passed since the first publication of *Max Weber, An Intellectual Portrait* (1960), I knew that one day I wanted to write a piece in which Weber's emphasis on action that made sense to the individual was related to the collective constraints which we have in mind when using the term "social structure."

Behind this idea, and the following chapter which tries to spell it out, lies the sense that Weber, who has inspired my work throughout, was not always the best expositor of his own standpoint. This was not just a matter of his involuted style of writing, or the unfinished condition of much of his work. It was above all the obvious fact that he had responded to the intellectual challenges of his time, which differed from the challenges we faced. Parsons had seen that and used Weber's work together with that of Marshall's and Durkheim's as introductions to a theoretical synthesis of his own. I was simply troubled by the way in which Parsons' initial emphasis on voluntary action seemed to stand side by side in his later work with the idea of a social system. As I see it still, the latter term makes of social constraints so compelling a structure that voluntary action seems to become an epiphenomenon—if not impossible altogether. That did not appear to me a step forward. Hence my question whether Weber's own work did not contain in rudimentary form a more balanced approach to both sides of what we observe, the actions which make sense to us as individuals and the ways in which time and again we orient ourselves by what significant others expect of us. After all, these were the two sides which Weber had emphasized in his basic definition of sociology on the first page of his *Economy and Society*. The following essay should be read, therefore, as an attempt to show that Weber's analysis of meaningful action, preeminently exemplified by his *Protestant Ethic*, was linked (however implicitly in his own writings) with his analysis of social structure arising from patterns of interaction and types of authority. By achieving this linkage, Weber provided an even-handed approach to individual and society, to the possibility of innovation and the great pressures of social constraint, to the often baffling coexistence between the static and dynamic aspects of social structure.

IDEAS, BELIEFS, AND ACTIONS

The history of sociology is marked by a basic controversy between those "who stress conflict and change . . . and those who stress integration and stability." The first group ranges from Marx to Dahrendorf and "tends to rely more on the 'person' or 'group' perspective." The second ranges from Durkheim to Parsons and "tends to rely more on the 'social-structural' or 'cultural' framework." The task is to develop "a more profitable synthesis of these two perspectives than we have been able to effect in the past."[1]

Each set of theories leaves as a residue what the other considers its main focus of attention. Weber belongs to the first set rather than the second. But in his day the bifurcation of schools was not as clearly marked as it is in ours. And while his studies do not contain a theoretical synthesis, they do move in that direction. Neither the "person" or "group" nor the "social structural framework" are left as unexplained residues. The following discussion attempts a systematization of Weber's approach which reflects much of my own image of society.

To a foreign visitor a culture appears unified at first; then, gradually, this impression weakens or disappears. The longer he stays, the more he learns to distinguish the diversities previously obscured by a uniform strangeness. Eventually he recognizes diversity in the great and the little tradition, as Redfield has phrased it. In the great tradition of the arts and sciences, styles and conflicting schools of thought abound. There is a disjunction between the cultural elite and the large number of those who are more or less passive participants in the great tradition. In the little tradition of popular culture, language, and convention there is much diversity in every-day behavior, grouped by class or region or ethnic origin. These and other diversities become apparent even to the casual observer. Others are more difficult to discern. Our beliefs are often hard to reconcile with one another and may be at odds with our actions as well. Such incongruities arise in part because cultural patterns are a patchwork of legacies and contemporary adaptations. They arise also because each of us plays many roles, leading to incompatibilities between our self-perceptions and the expectations of others.[2]

These diversities and incompatibilities are glossed over by the assumption of an underlying consensus. It has been argued that all social behavior depends upon common understandings. Two speakers using the same language communicate because they share an understanding of words and syntax. But where communications are marked by hostility and incomprehension, it is misleading to speak of consensus. The term suggests shared understandings which go beyond the elements of language, a minimal degree of mutual comprehension and shared belief. These phrases should not be used as synonyms of culture. Rather, analysis must show how a degree of unity coexists with the diversities characteristic of complex cultures.

Weber's studies of religion make a contribution in this respect. In this section I deal with *The Protestant Ethic* as a study of cultural change, with the distinction between cultural elites and the people at large, and with the question of how new ideas can influence the latter. Each of these themes bears on the meaning of "shared beliefs" as an object of study.

A PARADIGM OF CULTURAL CHANGE

The theme of *The Protestant Ethic and the Spirit of Capitalism* is familiar. By their development of theological ideas Luther and Calvin espoused an innerworldly asceticism. Men were enjoined to seek the salvation of their souls by diligently serving God in their worldly callings. Having analyzed this meaning of certain theological doctrines, Weber proceeded to show its inadvertent affinity with the "capitalist spirit." Secondly, he examined the pastoral admonitions of English divines in the seventeenth century. These encouraged conduct in keeping with the Reformed doctrine and favorable to a methodical, self-denying maximization of gain. Eventually, religiosity declined, but the pattern of conduct remained.

Several levels of analysis may be distinguished. Weber examines the theological doctrines of the Reformers in terms of the ideas and actions which they encourage in the ordinary believer. He focuses attention on the innovative contribution of religious leaders and on the formation of religious movements among the people at large. In a religious civilization changes may be induced by external conditions, but

> the most important source of innovation has been the influence of individuals who have experienced certain "abnormal" states . . . and hence have been capable of exerting a special influence on others. These influences . . . overcome the inertia of the customary. . . . Very often a collective action is induced, which is oriented toward the influencing person and his experience and from which, in turn, certain kinds of consensus with corresponding contents may be developed.[3]

In time such consensus may be institutionalized in religion or law, leading to a feeling of obligation among members of the community and joint action against nonconformists.

The Reformers had been followed by disciples who proselytized the religious truth revealed to them. Proselytizing implies a distinction between religious disciples, who preach the new truth, and the people at large who are set in the old ways. How can abstract, theological ideas influence the beliefs and actions of ordinary people? And if they do, what is the intensity and duration of that influence? In attempting to answer these questions Weber develops an analytic paradigm which may be summarized as follows:

1. Cultural innovation is the result of extraordinary individuals like Luther or Calvin who were religious virtuosi.

2. Their virtuosity consisted in the first place in the expression of their extraordinary personal qualities through the development of theological doctrines.

3. Analysis at the level of meaning can be pursued in many ways. Weber singles out the explicit and implicit incentives of Reformed doctrine for the conduct of the believer.

4. The Reformers together with their disciples and followers constitute an elite of articulate spokesmen intent upon spreading the message.

5. Pastoral sermons by ministers of the church are the most direct vehicle of communicating the new religious ideas to the people at large.

6. Weber attributes the influence of doctrine upon conduct to the intense concern with salvation characteristic of the seventeenth century. Once that intense concern waned, implications of Reformed doctrine remained influential in secular guise.

ELITES AND MASSES

Emphasis on elites has major significance for Weber's approach to the study of culture. In *The Protestant Ethic*, but still more in his comparative studies of China, India, and ancient Israel, Weber analyzes eras of religious creativity. Confucius, Lao Tse, Buddha, the Old Testament prophets, and others express the divergent world views of the great civilizations. At the same time, Weber begins his most systematic discussion of religion with an explicit refusal to define it. Not religion, but religious behavior as a type of social action is his major concern.

The most elementary forms of behavior motivated by religious or magical factors are oriented to this world. "That it may go well with thee . . . and that thou mayest prolong thy days upon the earth'' (Deut. 4:40) expresses the reason for the performance of actions enjoined by religion or magic. Furthermore, religiously or magically motivated behavior is relatively rational behavior, especially in its early manifestations. It follows rules of experience, though it is not necessarily action in accordance with a means-end schema. Rubbing will elicit sparks from pieces of wood, and in like fashion the mimetical actions of a magician will evoke rain from the heavens. . . . Thus, religious or magical behavior or thinking must not be set apart from the range of everyday purposive conduct, particularly since even the ends of the religious and magical actions are predominantly economic.[4]

Thus, religious behavior has a mundane meaning for the ordinary person. Nor is religious experience a thing apart, since ''the notion of 'supersensual' forces that may intervene in the destiny of people'' is seen ''in the same way that a man may influence the course of the world about him.''[5]

To understand religion and magic from their own standpoint we must enter into the mind of the believer and religious functionary. The person performing a magical act will distinguish ''between the greater or lesser ordinariness of the phenomena in question.''[6] Not every object can serve as a source of special powers. Nor does every person have the capacity to achieve the ecstatic states which in primitive experience are the condition for achieving certain effects. The believer can hope for comfort and benefits only from the particular object or person which possesses charisma. The sense of religious awe and reverence is due to the hopes and fears with which he regards that object or person. Weber focuses attention on religious elites because believers single out the power to assist them in their need, not only because innovation and leadership are the work of individuals.

The idea that such power exists is associated with ''the notion that certain beings are concealed 'behind,' and are responsible for, the activity of the charismatically endowed natural objects, artifacts, animals, or persons.''[7] But the beings or spirits which are the source of charisma are also at the command of those endowed with charisma. Thus, the necromancer turns ecstasy into an enterprise, because in the eyes of the layman ecstasy ''represents or mediates charisma'' and thus authenticates his special powers over the spirits. In their afflictions or their everyday affairs men seek assistance from the spirits. Consequently they go for help to those who can communicate with spirits and demons.

Where such beliefs prevail, elites form easily. The charisma of an object or person may be seen as a natural endowment that cannot be acquired. In that case it is a question of the criteria by which its presence may be recognized. To know these criteria is a special art which is readily monopolized. But charisma may also be produced artificially. Objects or persons are assumed to possess a dormant propensity which can be awakened by special rites or ascetic practices. In that case it is a question of performing these rites or practices in an authentic manner. Again, this puts a premium on knowing what is authentic, and such knowledge is a secret power that cannot be widely shared.

The formation of elites lies at the root of religious experience, because the believers are convinced that the good things in life can be attained only with the aid of higher powers. Subjective convictions of this kind must be understood in their own terms. In Weber's view critics of his *Protestant Ethic* had neglected that

> people in the past had after all very concrete ideas of what awaited them after death and of the means by which they could improve their chances in this respect. They adapted their behavior accordingly. For the development of culture it became important, in what forms this adaptation occurred depending upon the various views on the preconditions which—if fulfilled—would guarantee their salvation. For us moderns it is exceedingly difficult to put ourselves in their place and appreciate the agonizing power of these metaphysical conceptions.[8]

Thus, maxims concerning time, work effort, and the sense of duty in one's calling had been at one time a matter of religious devotion among the Puritan faithful. These maxims are still current, but are largely devoid of religious significance today. At the end of his essay Weber refers to them as the "ghost of dead religious beliefs." Between then and now one can suppose that intense religious beliefs have gradually given way to a process of secularization, though Weber's studies did not extend this far.[9]

Part of this transition must be a declining belief that the good things in life are affected by higher powers. With this decline the difference diminishes between the popular regard for religion and for other realms of high culture. All works of high culture involve arcane knowledge. Therefore, a presumption of some mysterious power is associated also with the painter, the concert artist, the writer, and others creatively engaged. But ordinary men are not intensely concerned with these realms of high culture. Since they do not expect benefits to accrue to them from knowledge or skill in the arts, they have no sense of that power which they believe manifest in the magician or prophet or priest.

Perhaps this explains the popular attitude towards the artist. People are at once slightly apprehensive and belittling. By virtue of his skill the artist possesses mysteries which make him somewhat formidable. But this skill does not give him power in the religious sense. This makes him appear quaint or even suspect, because mysteries without power are a form of charlatanism. In the eyes of the public the modern scientist may be closer to that of the magician, because his knowledge is mysterious *and* powerful, but the quasi-religious significance of this attitude still needs to be explored.

Weber's approach to religion highlights the fundamental difference between cultural elites marked by arcane knowledge and the masses who lack such knowledge. In the case of religion, people look with much fervor and concern for themselves upon the promises and guidelines held out to them. Weber does not deal with the difference between elites and masses where people have a "take it or leave it" attitude towards the activities of the cultural elite.

The hiatus between high culture and everyday experience is probably much greater in periods of secular culture than in periods of intense religiosity. In the former there is little cultural integration in the sense that arts and sciences are apart from everyday experience despite popularization and an equalitarian credo. In the latter there is considerable integration in the sense that religious symbols provide a universal language for high and low alike. The study of such periods can advance our understanding of cultural integration by analyzing how aspects of high culture, like new theological doctrines, can affect the daily experience of the ordinary believer.

DOCTRINE AND CONDUCT

It makes sense to ask how cultural creations are transmitted to the masses, if there is a proselytizing impulse on one hand and an audience eager for the message on the other. But the influence of doctrine on conduct is not a simple process even in periods of intense religiosity. In *The Protestant Ethic* Weber approached this problem in a deliberately limited way. The existing literature warranted the assumption that religious dissent and successful entrepreneurship were somehow linked.[10] He assumed further that religious doctrines made a *prima facie* difference to the people of the seventeenth century, concerned as they were with the salvation of their immortal souls.

On the basis of these assumptions Weber pursued three lines of inquiry. First, what incentives to daily conduct were implicit in the Reformed doctrine of Luther, Calvin, and their followers? Here analysis spelled out what these doctrines would mean to a true believer. Second, how did the Puritan divines of the seventeenth century translate these doctrines in their sermons and pastoral counselling? Here analysis moved away from theology in order to examine how religious doctrines were presented to the congregations. Third, how did the communities of the faithful respond? Here analysis moved still closer to the study of behavior by examining how the congregations censored or commended the conduct of their members. Weber believed that only letters and diaries would contain more direct evidence on the nexus between doctrine and conduct, but he did not undertake that task.[11]

Weber's problem is of general interest for the study of culture. An element of unity arises where the gulf between high culture and everyday behavior is bridged by doctrinal influence on behavior. Weber's essay demonstrates such influence, but only generally. His assumption that all people in the seventeenth century cared deeply for the salvation of their souls is too undifferentiated to carry conviction. It is more promising analytically to differentiate degrees of religiosity even in a universally religious population. This was apparent to the Puritan divines of the seventeenth century who were concerned with the quality of religious belief and attacked the spiritual slumber of their flocks. As William Haller has put it on the basis of an extensive study of seventeenth-century sermons: "The endeavor of the preachers was . . . to arouse men out of their indifference by warning them of the wrath to come. After that they were engrossed with two supreme dangers to morale, the failure of confidence and the excess of confidence."[12] What follows is an analytic commentary on this quotation.

1. In Weber's view Catholicism had provided people with a safety valve through the confessional. The religious views of the Church were accepted as a matter of course. People would engage in their daily rounds of virtues and vices, knowing that at regular intervals moral accounts could be balanced and forgiveness obtained, for the most part without hazard to their eternal souls. "The agonizing power of metaphysical conceptions" had to be brought home to such people, before their fate in the hereafter became a matter of urgent concern. Periods of universal religiosity are not necessarily periods of uniform religious intensity. It is more plausible to assume that few people were indifferent and a considerable minority was truly faithful, while the majority was moderately, one might say conventionally, concerned. What the Puritan divines probably did was to move this majority towards a greater religious concern, and specifically those who were anti-Papist on various secular grounds.

2. How could they do that? The success of the preachers becomes puzzling, once we abandon the notion that a period of universal religiosity is also one in which all people are moved by intense religious concerns. Ordinarily, preaching by itself does not move people out of their customary ways. In *Ancient Judaism* Weber himself analyzed a comparable intensification of belief. He showed the conjunction between prophecy and the historical experience of the Jewish people. The prophetic message of impending doom received its frightful poignancy by the savage military destruction which followed. The events of the English Reformation were entirely dissimilar, but the historical experience of the English people also led to an intensification of belief. The Reformation of the sixteenth century was initiated by political considerations without religious ethos. For three decades, politically inspired church policies succeeded one another without a definite stand on the part of the government itself. Competing doctrinal systems created a welter of conflicting opinions in the absence of genuine religious leadership. As a result, a mounting desire for certainty went together with widespread religious anxiety, as Herbert Schoef-

fler puts it. In this setting various groups of believers came to hold fast to different sets of beliefs and practices, once they had chosen them as their religious sheet anchor in the midst of change. Thus, propitious circumstances helped to arouse people out of their religious slumber.[13]

3. The preachers had to deal with the spiritual consequences of this development. Now that conventional piety was no longer enough, a large number of believers had become anxious. Some became genuinely frightened and lost confidence. Others tried to maintain their customary stance and became confident of their virtue under a veneer of piety. Accordingly, Haller's statement describes a threefold preoccupation of the preachers. They would arouse the people's religious concern repeatedly, or people would slide back into conventional religiosity. The preachers would give confidence to those who lost heart. And they would attack others who arrogantly believed that their good fortune was evidence of virtue.

In this way we get a differentiated view of the relation between doctrine and conduct. *The Protestant Ethic* demonstrates the direction of doctrinal influence. But it assumes rather than demonstrates an intense religious concern among the faithful. As Schoeffler suggests, the history of the English Reformation provides circumstantial evidence for an intensification of religious concern among large numbers. Where such intensification occurs, people reorient their beliefs and actions in response to new ideas.

The preceding discussion has used Weber's *Protestant Ethic* as a paradigm of cultural change, rather than for its intrinsic interest. A new set of ideas is first articulated by a cultural elite and eventually influences large numbers of people. Through diffusion and the decline of religiosity these ideas lose their original force, though in secular form their influence continues. This pattern probably recurs in other spheres of high culture, though with less widespread influence upon people and with less difference between periods of intense concern and of secularization.

At any one time a culture represents a congeries of beliefs and actions that originated at different times and with different cultural elites. Complex cultures lack integration because the most antagonistic world views and personalities exist side by side in the same society.[14] This condition accounts for the continuing efforts to achieve greater integration, for example through the articulation of a common tradition. Like consensus, integration is a matter of degree.

In secular societies not much integration is likely in view of the gulf between cultural elites and the masses. But while a great deal of high culture develops with little or no influence upon the people, it is otherwise with the structure of authority and the system of stratification. People subject to authority or of low status tend to accept "the ruling ideas of the ruling class," to use a phrase of Marx. And unlike the cultural elite, holders of authority and persons of high status tend to back their claims to allegiance by an implied threat of force. The following section continues the analysis of shared understandings as an attribute of social structure.

MODELS OF SOCIAL STRUCTURE

At different levels of a society there are likely to be varying degrees of integration. These can be analyzed, once the conceptual problems are resolved. But at the level of society as a whole the meaning of integration or coherence is questionable. Societies can resemble the living people in Hofmannsthal's trenchant epigram: "The main difference between living people and fictitious characters is that the writer takes great pains to give the characters coherence and inner unity, whereas the living people may go to extremes of incoherence because their physical existence holds them together."[15] Likewise, geographic contiguity, conventions and institutions hold societies together, even as they go to extremes of incoherence.

Social scientists have developed three models which seek to account for the coherence of social structures: the interdependence model, the exchange model, and the coercion model. These three are not mutually exclusive, nor are they as simple as I shall present them here.[16] Following this discussion I turn to an analysis of authority and of stratification.

The first model is based on the reciprocity of expectations among individuals. Individuals learn their roles in society by conforming to what others expect of them. As they mature, they will use the expectations of others partly as cues for further action; this greatly facilitates interaction and mutual comprehension even where it does not lead to conformity. Both role learning and shared understandings are frequently attributed to the values learned by the individual and incorporated in social institutions.[17] In this way, society's capacity to function as an interdependent system is greatly facilitated. Critics of the interdependence model have pointed out that reciprocity of expectations is not synonymous with agreement. There is much indifference or absence of contact which makes the simple idea of reciprocity problematic. Nor is the interdependence of society a product of reciprocal expectations alone. The division of labor creates complementary roles in the absence of direct interaction. Still other types of interdependence are the result of environment, demographic patterns, institutional and intellectual legacies. In addition, we are often affected by the interactions of others without being aware that they have occurred and impinge on our lives. Accordingly, the interdependence model, important as it is, has limited applicability.

The exchange or market model is a special case of the interdependence model. As developed by classical economists and liberal social theorists, the exchange model posits interactions among equals as the basis of the social structure. The classic case is Rousseau's theory of the general will which implicitly presupposes the equality of property owners. The man of property who maintains that all men of property should have their rights of property defended, has the best of both worlds. He can be egoistic and altruistic at the same time. But this benign condition changes the moment the man of property interacts with someone who owns nothing. Both are free to acquire property, but only one actually enjoys the rights of ownership. In this way equality in one respect is accompanied by inequalities in many others. The resulting cleavages may be handled by negotiation, as in labor-management relations. But such negotiations depend upon accepted rules of the game, and these are not derived from interactions in the market. Accordingly the market model can account for the coherence of societies only to a limited extent.

The coercion model proceeds in an opposite direction. It emphasizes the inequalities which make for a cumulation of benefits on one side and deprivations on the other. Where interactions are marked by such inequalities, reciprocal expectations foster conservative and radical postures. The few want to buttress their good fortune and the many strive for equality and justice. Between men divided by good and ill fortune, even accommodations are colored by tension so that the social structure appears to be dichotomous.[18] But in fact there are many ties between them. Authority wants to be considered legitimate and considers the reactions of those it can command; the subordinate temper their resistance by the degree to which they accept dominant values. While the possibilities of coercion and revolt remain in the background, the coercion model is weakest where societies are marked by accommodation.

The choice among these models often depends on the purpose of inquiry. The economist will find the exchange model suitable for his purpose. The child psychologist or the sociolinguist will probably opt for the interdependence model. Students of war or international relations may choose the coercion model. The three models may serve their purpose as long as they account for shared beliefs which have a specifiable meaning. But they are inadequate as general theories of social structure.

At this level, Weber borrowed from all three models but with a logic of his own. Interdependence, exchange, and coercion are for him aspects of social action. They may lead to constellations of interests and levels of agreement among individuals or groups. The shared understandings existing in a society vary widely in intensity and generality; except for rare occasions they are probably least intense where they are most general. As a rule social actions do not occur at the level of society as a whole, though Weber does not make this point explicit. Rather, he contrasts the shared understandings of society with the shared understandings of authority. Two attributes distinguish the latter:

administration and a belief in the legitimacy which makes that administration valid for the polity. Weber's theory of social structure focuses attention on social actions at the two levels of society and authority.

The belief in legitimacy plays a role at both levels. Divisions among individuals or groups of unequal social, economic, and political position are a prime characteristic of societies. Authority and stratification involve institutionalized ways of resolving or at least managing tensions arising from that inequality. A general theory of social structure should interpret the ties of feeling or sentiment among people divided by cleavages of legal position, status, and interest.

AUTHORITY AND LEGITIMATION

References to a belief in legitimacy are always suspect. They are difficult to separate from self-serving apologetics because persons in authority are *prima facie* evidence of power and inequality. Still rulers and ruled demand a rationale, and the cynics are wrong who would have us think that explanations and symbolic acts are automatically discounted. Rulers want to exercise authority with a good conscience; indeed many of them want to be loved. The ruled want to have some sense of equity and compassion in high places, a proximate, if tacit, *quid pro quo* for the act of obedience. Even democratic governments are surrounded by pomp and circumstance. These along with statements to the press, gala receptions, official hearings, and many other manifestations of authority are ways of meeting the desires of both groups. But it is true that modern forms of publicity easily jeopardize the credibility of justifications in high places. And modern forms of government with their massive bureaucracy certainly emasculate the sense of give and take between the authorities and the public. Accordingly, the belief in legitimacy fluctuates, and evidence for its importance is most telling when that belief has vanished and institutions crumble.[19]

The concept of legitimacy refers to shared beliefs of rulers and ruled, and such beliefs tend to be ambiguous. Weber defines the term tautologically. "Social action may be guided by a belief in the existence of a legitimate order." Such an order exists when "conduct is oriented towards determinable maxims." He acknowledges that much of the time a people's regard for their institutional order will be based on expediency or habit. But the viability of a legitimate order will be enhanced if the people consider those maxims "as in some way obligatory or exemplary" for themselves.[20] Since an institutional order is legitimate only to a degree, there is no clear distinction between legitimacy and illegitimacy in contrast to the law with its dichotomy between valid and invalid rules.[21] Therefore, the legitimacy of an institutional order fluctuates with the sense of civic obligation in contrast to a merely customary or expediential compliance.[22]

Beliefs in legitimacy appear tenuous, since they wax and wane as different groups respond to the public issues before them. Nevertheless, an institutional order remains intact to the extent that a belief in certain maxims for the long run is shared by office holders and the public, notwithstanding the great social and political distance dividing them. When this belief contains an element of shared hope or trust, people will get along with the tensions of authority and to this extent help maintain the social structure. Weber's discussion of charismatic and legal authority exemplifies the tenuous quality and the importance of beliefs in legitimacy.

CHARISMATIC AUTHORITY

Genuine charisma makes its appearance when a leader and the people at large become convinced that the accommodations of everyday politics will no longer do. Then consummate belief on one side, and the promptings of enthusiasm, hope, or despair on the other, call imperatively for unconditional commands and obedience.

> The term "charisma" will be applied to a certain quality of an individual personality by virtue of which he is considered extraordinary and treated as endowed with supernatural, superhuman or at least specifically exceptional powers or qualities. These are such as are not accessible to the ordinary person, but are regarded as of divine origin or as exemplary, and on the basis of them the individual concerned is treated as a "leader."[23]

But charisma is not a supernatural, superhuman, or exceptional quality of an individual. It is rather a quality which he claims and others attribute to him.

Charismatic authority depends upon a shared understanding between leaders and followers.

> It is recognition on the part of those subject to authority which is decisive for the validity of charisma. This recognition is freely given and guaranteed by what is held to be a proof, originally always a miracle, and consisting in devotion to the corresponding revelation, hero worship, or absolute trust in the leader. But where charisma is genuine, it is not this which is the basis of the claim to legitimacy. This basis lies rather in the conception that it is the duty of those subject to charismatic authority to recognize its genuineness and to act accordingly. Psychologically this recognition is a matter of complete personal devotion to the possessor of the quality, arising out of enthusiasm, or of despair and hope.

> No prophet has ever regarded his quality as dependent on the attitudes of the masses toward him. No elective king or military leader has ever treated those who have resisted him or tried to ignore him otherwise than as delinquent in

duty. Failure to take part in a military expedition under such a leader, even though the recruitment was formally voluntary, has universally met with disdain.

If proof and success elude the leader for long, if he appears deserted by his god or his magical or heroic powers, above all if his leadership fails to benefit his followers, it is likely that his charismatic authority will disappear. This is the genuine meaning of the divine right of kings (*Gottesgnadentum*).[24]

This passage might suggest that followers recognize a leader as charismatic, because they see "powerful results achieved in the absence of power."[25] But recognition by the followers and the leader's own claims and actions are in fact ambivalent.

To recognize the charisma of a leader is the duty of his followers. But the desire for a sign confirming the existence of charisma easily contaminates a personal devotion born of enthusiasm, despair, or hope. In turn, the leader demands unconditional devotion from his followers. He will construe any demand for a sign of his gift of grace as lack of faith and a dereliction of duty. Yet his "charismatic authority will disappear... if proof or success eludes him for long."

Charismatic authority is thus not a label to be applied, but a problematic relationship to be studied. A leader may feel the call, or people at large search for someone to satisfy their longing for a miracle. Such a search for charisma may prove of no avail. Moreover, the followers' desire for a sign and the leader's demand of unconditional faith may jeopardize the reciprocal expectations on which authority is based. Genuine charisma appears only when one man feels possessed by a mysterious gift, and his belief in that gift is shared by those who follow him.[26]

Charismatic authority exemplifies the meaning of legitimacy at its most tenuous. Weber emphasized that it becomes more enduring only when the gift of grace and the devotion to duty become institutionalized, as in the apostolic succession of the Papacy and the ritualized piety of Catholic believers. In addition, charismatic authority occurs more or less frequently as a sudden intrusion into stable political structures, as when a charismatically gifted king appears in a traditional monarchy, or an exceptionally gifted political leader appears in a constitutional system.

Weber did not anticipate, however, that under modern conditions belief in charisma could be combined with secular bureaucratic structures, leading to a terrifying corruption of both. A charismatic leader will claim unquestioned validity for his every utterance. At the same time he avoids all tests of his authority by making the agencies of government responsible for every implementation. In the eyes of his followers the leader's claim is unimpaired. All failures are attributed to subordinates who violated the leader's trust. But these subordinates also try to evade responsibility by reference to the absolute commands they are obliged to obey. For a time the day of reckoning may be put off. The claim to authority is divorced from all tests of its validity. And the responsibility of subordinates is obscured by the omnipotence attributed to the leader. In this way the dangers inherent in charismatic authority are compounded by those inherent in bureaucratic administration, leading to a reciprocal escalation of abuses for which Hitler's regime is the most striking modern instance.

In all these instances authority is sustained by shared beliefs in the special powers of an individual, though these beliefs weaken where charisma is institutionalized, or become perverted where charisma is corrupted. I turn now to the beliefs in legitimacy which sustain the legal order.

LEGAL AUTHORITY

The authority of the law is an example of a relatively stable structure. It rests on several interdependent ideas. Law is embodied in a consistent system of abstract rules. Any legal norm may be established by agreement or imposition. The result is an impersonal order of rules which are binding on the persons in authority as well as on those subject to it. The obligation to obey is limited in each case to the relevant jurisdiction.[27] The persistence of legal authority is due to three factors: its rules are implemented by administrators; officials and citizens are subject to the same rules; and the rulers and ruled share a belief in the legitimacy of the legal order.

Weber states that the law rests "on a belief in the legality of enacted rules and the right of those elevated to authority under such rules to issue commands."[28] These highly abstract maxims become meaningful only through a general belief in the "rules of the game." In practice that involves trust in the fairness with which conflicting legal claims are adjudicated. To a certain extent this fairness is institutionalized, as in the respective functions of judge and defense attorney under the same body of laws. The judge sees to the maintenance of the law and of procedural rules in reaching a verdict. The defense attorney has the special task of protecting the substantive rights of his client to the full extent of the law. Thus, the maintenance of laws and rules as well as the defense of individual rights are principles built into the rules governing the conduct of trials.

These principles involve conflicting imperatives. For example, legal enactments are administered by an administrative staff, defined by such formal characteristics as delimited spheres of competence and personnel selection based on tested qualifications. At the same time there is "the tendency of officials to treat their official function from . . . a utilitarian point of view in the interest of the welfare of those under their authority. . . . This tendency to substantive rationality is supported by all those subject to authority."[29] Thus, administrators are bound by rules and obliged to uphold them in their own decisions and procedures. On the other hand, they adjudicate disputes or implement policies in keeping with substantive goals like justice or equity or maximum benefit. Consequently administrators, like judges and others in legal authority, are pulled in divergent directions as they seek to reconcile the attributes of formal and substantive rationality.

Laws or rules are formal to the extent that in all procedural or substantive issues "only unambiguous general characteristics of the facts of the case are taken into account." This can mean that only tangible characteristics are considered legally relevant, like the utterance of certain words or the execution of a signature. Or it can mean that a logical analysis of meaning discloses those characteristics of the facts which are legally relevant, thus leading to highly abstract legal concepts. These formal aspects of laws or rules stand in sharp contrast to all substantive decision making, based on ethical imperatives or on considerations of expediency.[30]

The viability of a legal order depends upon the success with which these opposing principles are reconciled in practice. According to the decision of the U.S. Supreme Court, Negro children have the formal right to attend integrated schools. In Little Rock, Arkansas, segments of the white population opposed integration, despite the law decreeing it. Not to call out the troops would have violated the government's formal obligation to enforce the law; but to have done so frequently would reveal the persistent discrepancy between the law and important segments of public sentiment. Both strategies undermine respect for the law. In practice the formal rights of Negro children have been promoted by many expedients short of enforcement by troops or police, apparently in the hope that gradually the gulf between law and public sentiment would diminish.

Thus, legal enactments formulate normative aspirations for the community as a whole. Together with the procedures regulating adjudication and enforcement they constitute the law's system of abstract rules. Action in conformity with these norms and procedures preserves the integrity of the rules and represents the law's formal rationality. At the same time, there is a hiatus between these abstract rules and the world in which Negro children have a claim that is denied by others. This hiatus is not a recognized part of the law. But since it exists, enforcement practices are adapted to effect some workable or manageable relationship between legal norms, procedures, and the conflicting claims in the public arena. This balancing of conflicting claims with the rules as a constant point of reference is the practical reconciliation between the law's formal and substantive rationality. The task of the legal order is to preserve the system of legal norms while managing and adjudicating substantive conflicts of rights and interests.[31]

The development of formal rationality in law, administration, economic enterprises, the sciences, and other spheres is one meaning of the term "rationalization." Throughout his work Weber points out that by promoting formal rationality lawyers, officials, entrepreneurs, scientists, and others also protect and advance their own position and function. In this sense rationalization is inseparable from the self-interest of specialists and their struggle for power. On the other hand, there are many who believe their interests diminished by formally rational action. Those subject to an impersonal implementation of rules will demand a personal consideration of the particular case, regardless of the effect this might have on equity or the calculability and consistency of rules. Sometimes men in high places are sensitive to the ideas and interests left out by adherence to formal criteria, and become champions of ethical or political imperatives. Accordingly, under legal authority tensions recur between the requirements of formal rationality and the concern with achieving certain ethical or social goals.

DUAL TENDENCIES REVISITED

Weber endowed concepts like charismatic or legal authority with a "not only but also" quality for which it is difficult to find an unequivocal designation. Such concepts do not refer to a specific set of attributes. Instead they refer to patterns of action and reaction which have an unstable "feed back" mechanism as their common denominator. The claims of charismatic leaders and the expectations of their followers affect each other, and in a different way so do the body of formal laws and the ways in which people regard the rules of the game in relation to their conflicting interests. Charismatic or legal authority are legitimate as long as the conflicting claims of authority and of those subject to authority are accommodated.

Since these concepts refer to characteristics of a social structure, they are also relatively empty. The legitimacy of legal authority may fluctuate as various accommodations are achieved between formal and substantive rationality. But legal authority as a structure remains intact as long as a tension is maintained between the integrity of the law and the substantive claims of individuals or groups. That structure will be destroyed only when the formal rationality of the law is made so paramount as to deny all substantive claims, or when these claims are made so paramount as to destroy the system of rules. This is the sense in which Weber's concepts of social structure encompass tendencies or forces which are linked and opposite at the same time.

So far social structure has been discussed in terms of the ties of feeling and sentiment between the few in positions of authority and the many who are subordinate to them. Social stratification likewise involves great differences of status and also poses problems of legitimation.

STRATIFICATION AND LEGITIMATION

Authority and stratification may converge or diverge, but their problems of legitimation are analytically distinct. Whereas public authority must act for the whole community, social and economic privileges are *prima facie* evidence of narrow self-interest. Yet those who enjoy such privileges also want to make it believable that they deserve their good fortune.

For long periods, religious beliefs legitimated inequality. To the happy few good fortune seemed evidence of divine blessing, while the sufferer was hated by the gods. This interpretation satisfied a general craving.

> Strata with high social and economic privilege will . . . assign to religion the primary function of *legitimizing* their own life pattern and situation in the world. This universal phenomenon is rooted in certain basic psychological patterns. When a man who is happy compares his position with that of one who is unhappy, he is not content with the fact of his happiness, but desires something more, namely the right to his happiness, the consciousness that he has earned his good fortune, in contrast to the unfortunate one who must equally have earned his misfortune.[32]

Yet religious beliefs could also give satisfaction to the lowly. While rulers and owners would see suffering as evidence of a secret guilt, the poor could look upon it as a promise of salvation. The poor were the pure in spirit to whom the good fortune of others appeared as the sure road to damnation. Obviously the lot of the common people was often extremely hard to bear, and to the secular mind the consolations of religion appear threadbare. But religion provided a universe of discourse from which people of good and ill fortune could derive diametrically opposed conclusions. In periods when religion provided a universal symbolic language, people sharply divided by status and learning were yet part of the same cultural milieu.

Religion was not alone in providing a common language. Secular powers like kingship and a landowning aristocracy were considered legitimate in their own right. The capacity to decide and command was frequently combined with a ceremonious display and a distinguished bearing which overawed and inspired the populace. A medieval lord's "profession"

> not only qualified him admirably for the defense of his own class interest—he was not only able to fight for it physically—but it also cast a halo around him and made him a ruler of men. The first was important, but more so were the mystic glamour and the lordly attitude—the prestige with all classes of society and in every walk of life. That prestige was so great and that attitude so useful that the class position outlived the social and technological conditions which had given rise to it and proved adaptable, by means of a transformation of the class function, to quite different social and economic conditions. With the utmost ease and grace the lords and knights metamorphosed themselves into courtiers,

administrators, diplomats, politicians and into military officers of a type that had nothing whatever to do with that of the medieval knight. . . .[33]

This aristocratic capacity to rule could flourish where kings and nobles combined social and economic privileges with a consecrated right to rule. Here authority and high social class reinforced each other. Subsequently the two diverged as the aristocratic capacity to rule came to be considered an attribute of family tradition, maintained and enhanced by education. The old consecrated order lost its legitimacy as aristocratic conduct became an aspect of social privilege, and eventually even the utility of an aristocratic bearing declined.

In a secular period neither religious imagery nor aristocratic culture can legitimate inequality. Good fortune has no transcendent sanction in the eyes of the many who carry the burdens of the world.

> There is surely no trace of mystic glamour about [the industrialist and merchant] which is what counts in the ruling of men. The stock exchange is a poor substitute for the Holy Grail . . . the industrialist and merchant, as far as they are entrepreneurs, also fill a function of leadership. But economic leadership of this type does not readily expand, like the medieval lord's military leadership, into the leadership of nations.
>
> I have called the bourgeois rationalist and unheroic. He can only use rationalist and unheroic means to defend his position or to bend a nation to his will. He can impress by what people may expect from his economic performance, he can argue his case, he can promise to pay out money or threaten to withhold it, he can hire the treacherous services of a *condottiere* or politician or journalist. But that is all and all of it is greatly overrated as to its political value. Nor are his experiences and habits of life of the kind that develop personal fascination. . . .[34]

In the political field this argument is persuasive. With the decline of kingship and aristocracy, public authority has become divorced from wealth. The industrialist as a type enjoys great influence due to economic success. He does not enjoy the prestige of authority.

But high social and economic status still has much prestige. As before, the happy few want to be entitled to their good fortune, while the many want to reverse their lot, or at least compensate for their ill fortune. A secular language of legitimation has replaced the earlier religious and political one. In the early period of industrialization entrepreneurial ideologies of deserved success on one side of the class structure were matched by panegyrics to labor's right to the whole product on the other. Conflicting claims were put in a language of material gain, with each group rewarded for its contribution. This was not a stable legitimation of the social order, but its influence continues to the present day.[35]

The apotheosis of the self-made man idealized personal qualities like diligence and frugality, and above all the value of material advance. This materialist appeal was successful, however much the secular version of the Protestant Ethic came to be discounted. Here is the root of the worker's quest for citizenship and of the intellectual's alienation from the industrial society. Here also is the source of recurrent tensions between them.

As Western societies industrialized and the welfare state emerged, workers gradually accepted the legitimacy of stratification. They adopted as their own the consumption ideals of the upper strata. Here again no more is meant by acceptance than that they contrived to get along with the tensions engendered by the class structure. On the other hand, intellectuals have challenged those ideals throughout, even though they enjoyed high levels of consumption. Cultural standards conflict with the prevailing materialism. Thus, the stratification of industrial societies is legitimate at one level, but lacks a corresponding intellectual and cultural justification. And this discrepancy accounts for the paradox that economically successful societies tend to have adversary high cultures.[36]

MODELS OF SOCIAL CHANGE

The culture of complex societies as well as their systems of authority and stratification are marked by cleavages so great that the degree of unity achieved becomes a prime object of study. Our discussion suggests that the coherence or integration of societies is a precarious achievement since geographic contiguity, conventions, and institutions may hold societies together without unifying them. Thus the sources of change are ever present, though any particular change is neither necessary nor continuous.

A generation ago theories of evolution and the work of Herbert Spencer were out of fashion in American social theory. By the late 1960s evolutionist theories were a major preoccupation once again.[37] The scholarly concern with economic and political development, rather than the earlier idea of progress through competition, probably accounts for this revival.[38] Max Weber's work contains contributions to the analysis of social change which have not received the attention they deserve. One can be described as "breakthrough and routinization." The other concerns the direction in Western history which he called "rationalization." I shall comment on each theme in turn, and then relate Weber's approach to the perspective of dual tendencies discussed above.

BREAKTHROUGH AND ROUTINIZATION

Societies are characterized by continuity and the prevalence of conventional behavior. Daily activities are marked by much routine even in the midst of change. Yet at times there are extraordinary needs or situations which jeopardize complacency and convention. It is then that a person endowed with charisma may appear, or may be found by the people searching for a solution. Weber focuses attention on those historical instances that seem to exemplify the contrast between charismatic breakthroughs and the prevalent continuity of social life. He emphasizes the instability of charismatic domination and its tendency to be transformed into more stable structures.

> Charismatic rulership in the typical sense . . . always results from unusual, especially political or economic situations, or from extraordinary psychic, particularly religious states, or from both together. It arises from collective excitement produced by extraordinary events and from surrender to heroism of any kind. This alone is sufficient to warrant the conclusion that the faith of the leader himself and of his disciples in his charisma—be it of a prophetic or any other kind—is undiminished, consistent and effective only in *statu nascendi*, just as is true of the faithful devotion to him and his mission on the part of those to whom he considers himself sent. When the tide that lifted a charismatically led group out of everyday life flows back into the channels of workaday routines, at least the "pure" form of charismatic domination will wane and turn into an "institution". . . .[39]

The prototype for this pattern of change was the charismatic figure of Jesus, the small band of his apostles, the role of charismatic beliefs in the conventicles of early Christianity, and the later institutions of Catholicism.

The concept of "charismatic leadership" appears equally applicable to other founders of the great world religions, like Buddha, Confucius, Moses, and Mohammed, though the religiosity of each is distinctive. At the beginning a great religious innovator achieves a high point of inspiration. Later on, an eager band of disciples seeks to preserve that inspiration beyond the lifetime of the founder. The institutions set up to accomplish such preservation necessarily substitute office for person, ritual for inspired words or actions. Training in doctrine and conduct develops, and rites of initiation become regular means to achieve the desired commitment and solve the problem of succession. In the Catholic church exceptional qualities become embodied in offices and functionaries, in the sacred service and the thoughts and acts of ordinary believers (*Veralltäglichung*). Such routinization weakens the extraordinary power of charisma. Those who seek its spiritual and material benefits may, therefore, challenge conventional teaching and the institutions of the church by appeals to the original source of religious inspiration.

The pattern here described is familiar in a number of non-religious contexts as well. Lenin was a charismatic leader. He possessed exceptional qualities and the Bolshevik revolution was a high point of ideological commitment. Major changes in the political and economic organization of Russian society were initiated. But in the course of time routinization set in. The charisma of

Lenin faded into the background despite the verbal adulation of decades and the physical preservation of his body. The original communist tenets have been undermined by monotonous recapitulation and by the abuses of bureaucratic and dictatorial rule. However, massive industrialization and Russian nationalism may have taken the place of Marxist-Leninist legitimation, at least in part.

Still other examples come to mind. In his theory of economic development under capitalism Schumpeter has attributed exceptional qualities to entrepreneurs who break through "business as usual" by developing new methods of production and distribution. Yet each innovation is a starting point of a new "business as usual." Vested interests cumulate once more and resist the further changes needed to initiate new economic developments. Something like this has also been suggested in the case of science, as in Thomas Kuhn's distinction between normal science and scientific revolutions. The first involves a paradigm of theory and method which has been accepted by a scientific community at work. The second involves a breakthrough of new theory and method achieved by some pioneer who takes as his point of departure the difficulties and unexplained residues left out of account by normal science.

Jacob Burckhardt did not use the term "charisma." But he would have considered instances of such pioneering leadership as moments in which history breaks free of the encrustations of the past. And he emphasized as Weber did that the men who accomplish such breaks may be great birds of prey as well as saints and heroes.[40] Charisma can be the grace of divine inspiration or the terror of self-deification; it may liberate pent-up forces for good or unleash frenzies of destruction. Similarly, the routinization of charisma may embody the original message or ossify into a monopolistic organization of self-serving votaries. But I write "or" without conviction. The human condition is so beset by motivational ambivalence and situational ambiguity that these antitheses exist side by side, even in the same person.

Weber had as acute a sense of this condition as did Freud, but his concern was the fate of reason in society, not the cure of souls. He certainly accepted the idea that in human affairs reason can advance through revolutionary change and its subsequent transformations. But social change, and specifically the advance of reason, can also occur through cumulative innovation. The latter is the pattern of change suggested by Weber's concept of rationalization.

RATIONALIZATION

The term has many meanings whose most common denominator is probably the idea of systematization. Men behave rationally, when they take into account and weigh the end, the means, and the secondary results of their actions. Weber contrasts this instrumental rationality with a rationality of ultimate values. The latter consists of actions governed by commitment to an ultimate end and by plans of action consistent with that end.[41] Therefore, one aspect of rationalization "is the substitution for the unthinking acceptance of ancient custom, of deliberate adaptation to situations in terms of self-interest." Another is the substitution of "a deliberate formulation of ultimate values (*Wertrationalisierung*)" for "every sort of unthinking acquiescence in customary ways."[42]

In his use of "rationalization" Weber went far beyond these rudimentary meanings. His critique of the idea of progress restricts the term to technology and makes it a synonym of increasing differentiation.[43] His introduction to the sociology of religion suggests links between rationalization in Western science, music, architecture, law, administration, and economic enterprises.[44] Elsewhere, he pursues the possible meanings of this process in economic and political institutions, in the law, and in religion. In all these spheres it is possible to substitute deliberation for unthinking acceptance and thus systematize not only very mundane pursuits but also the most otherworldly orientations of mind and spirit. All types of rationalization are specific historical developments rather than aspects of an evolutionary scheme.

The difference appears clearly in Weber's sociology of law. The general development of law from charismatic legal revelation by law prophets to the systematic elaboration of law and the professional administration of justice is a succession of stages superficially similar to the evolutionary models put forward in the nineteenth century. But this line of development appears only as a convenient summary towards the end of the volume. In Weber's view such schemes explain nothing. Rather, the development of law has been affected by power struggles between the *imperium* on one hand, and kinship groups, folk communities, and status groups on the other; by struggles between theocratic and secular powers; and thirdly by differences among the strata of legal notables which have become significant for the legal development of different societies.[45]

Rationalization, then, is not a uniform developmental process. Its various forms contribute to the persistence and change of societies. In Weber's view social structures are marked by the continuity of conventional behavior. Probably legal norms arise when habits of conduct are experienced as binding and when conventions are turned into rules and acquire the back-up of coercive enforcement. Here rationalization acts as a conservative force. But this hypothetical view of social continuity does not answer "the question of how anything could ever change this inert mass of canonized custom which, just because it is considered binding, seems as though it could never give birth to anything new."[46] New lines of conduct including new legal norms may arise unconsciously. Either actual changes of meaning are not perceived or an old law is applied to a new situation in the belief that this was always done. Also, external changes may lead to new rules. But the decisive cause of legal innovation has always been "a new line of conduct which then results either in a change of the meaning of the existing rules of law or in the creation of new rules of law."[47]

Here is a pattern of innovation through "formally elaborated law constituting a complex of maxims consciously applied in decisions." Such elaboration "has never come into existence without the decisive cooperation of trained specialists."[48] These specialists are of many kinds: officials, legal notables, elected or appointed judges, occasionally priests, private attorneys, and others. All of them contrast sharply with the role of the law prophet in various types of folk justice. In the early development of law the judge sees to the adherence of certain procedures, but only the law prophet is believed to possess the wisdom required for rendering a verdict. At the conclusion of the trial he answers the decisive question of guilt or innocence through charismatic inspiration.[49] Such law finding is an essential part of justice where adjudication is considered a matter of magical revelation which alone can preserve the integrity of custom and belief. Here charisma is not an innovative break with tradition. In the development of law, it is rather the trained specialist who innovates through rationalization, while the charismatic interpreter guards the tradition through inspiration and extraordinary powers. Thus, according to Weber, bureaucratic or legal rationalization as well as charismatic leadership can become revolutionary forces, but bureaucracy, law, and charisma may also be bulwarks of tradition.[50]

CHANGE AND HISTORY

Weber's two models of change have an "open-ended" quality in common. Charisma may be a source of innovation, but priests or kings may also use their exceptional gifts to maintain the social order. Also, rationalization may involve cumulative innovations as legal specialists substitute formal rules for the unthinking acceptance of social norms. Yet such substitution may be a means of preserving the status quo as well. Thus, both models can be patterns of change as well as conservation. At the same time they remain distinct in their emphasis on inspiration or systematization. It is doubtful that Weber would have attempted to integrate these dual tendencies. He used them as guide lines for research, not as models to be elaborated deductively.

Weber's approach is incompatible with evolutionist theories of change. As Robert Nisbet has shown, the latter assume change to be natural, directional, immanent, continuous, necessary, and proceeding from uniform causes.[51] None of these attributes fit Weber's approach. The two models briefly described above start with the view that the persistence of custom is the prevailing condition. Where change occurs, Weber studies it as a charismatic break with tradition or as the rationalizing work of notables. In neither case is change immanent, continuous, necessary, or the result of uniform causes. In addition, Weber emphasizes that the direction of change is reversible. Thus, charismatic breaks with tradition lead to an institutionalization which begins a new tradition. Also, his sociology of law is preoccupied with the process of rationalization, but ends with an analysis of "anti-formalistic tendencies" in modern law.[52]

The rationale of Weber's approach is akin to the classic idea of a mutability of fortunes. To the ancients day and night, the seasons of the year, the passage from childhood to senescence and death were instances of an eternal recurrence which characterizes the universe. In the face of such forces human action is basically presumptuous, a challenge to the gods, and hence a danger to man. Yet men must act, withdrawal is cowardly, and anxiety unmanly. In a universe indifferent to human kind, man's virtue consists in fortitude and his wisdom in equanimity. Men and nations should always remember the opposite extremity of fortune, for those of good fortune must still meet their end and the lowly may one day be victorious.[53]

Where the classics sought equanimity in the face of mortal hazards, Weber formulates concepts to find landmarks in the flux of events. But facts are ascertained at the price of a world of facts neglected. And every pattern the scholar can discern in the course of history must take account of chances missed, opportunities forgone, and aspirations unfulfilled. Weber endeavors to formulate his concepts rigorously enough to be useful tools of analysis, but flexibly enough to allow for corrections of their necessary arbitrariness. His principal aim is scholarly. But his effort is animated by the conviction that every fact or pattern ascertained must be seen against a background which gives it meaning. It must be seen also in the light of the questions asked and the concepts employed.[54]

Multiple, but finite, interpretability lies at the core of an empirical world possessed of continuous gradations and hence lacking natural benchmarks or distinctions. In such a world the scholar is obliged to imprint distinctions of his own devising which have nothing to commend them but a scholarly productivity for which we possess only proximate criteria. In the classical view man's actions disturb the "seamless web" governed by an infinite number of determinants. The scholar who would comprehend that world must impose his abstractions, well knowing that they are indispensable and arbitrary.

NOTES

1. Cf. Neil Smelser, "The Optimum Scope of Sociology," in Robert Bierstedt, ed., *A Design for Sociology*, Monograph N. 9 (Philadelphia: American Academy of Political and Social Science, 1969), pp. 8-9.

2. The perspective here emphasized was formulated by Georg Simmel, *Conflict and the Web of Group Affiliations* (Glencoe: The Free Press, 1955). For modern developments of this position see Ralph Turner, "Role-Taking: Process versus Conformity," in Arnold Rose, ed., *Human Behavior and Social Processes* (Boston: Houghton Mifflin Company, 1962), Chap. 2; and William J. Goode, "A Theory of Role Strain," *American Sociological Review*, XXV (1960), pp. 483-96.
3. Max Weber, *Economy and Society*, trans. and ed. by Guenther Roth and Claus Wittich (New York: The Bedminster Press, 1968), I, pp. 321-22.
4. Weber, *op. cit.*, II, pp. 399-400.
5. Ibid., p. 402.
6. Ibid., p. 400.
7. Ibid., p. 408.
8. Max Weber, "Kritische Bemerkungen zu den vorstehenden 'Kritischen Beiträgen,'" *Archiv für Sozialwissenschaft*, XXV (1907), p. 248. I have simplified the sentence structure in this translation to ensure intelligibility.
9. A brilliant analysis of the first phase of that process is now available in Clifford Geertz, *Islam Observed* (New Haven: Yale University Press, 1968), passim.
10. Cf. on this point Reinhard Bendix, "The Protestant Ethic Revisited," *Comparative Studies in Society and History*, IX (1967), pp. 266-73.
11. Points one and two are covered in the essay itself. Point three was examined in Weber's supplementary essay on the Protestant Sects. The assumptions as well as Weber's defense are contained in a number of answers to critics which are now published in Max Weber, *Die Protestantische Ethik, Kritiken und Antikritiken*, ed. by Johannes Winckelmann (München: Siebenstern Taschenbuch Verlag, 1968), passim.
12. William Haller, *The Rise of Puritanism* (New York: Harper and Row, 1957), p. 154.
13. For details see the striking interpretation of Herbert Schoeffler, *Auswirkungen der Reformation* (Frankfurt: Vittorio Klostermann, 1960), pp. 189-324. I have used this analysis in a comparative study of Japan. See Reinhard Bendix, "A Case Study of Cultural and Educational Mobility: Japan and the Protestant Ethic," in Neil J. Smelser and Seymour M. Lipset, eds., *Social Structure and Mobility in Economic Development* (Chicago: Aldine Publishing Co., 1966), pp. 262-79.
14. Accordingly Weber calls references to "national character" a confession of ignorance, as well as historically inaccurate. "Cavaliers" and "Roundheads" in seventeenth-century England were not only two parties, but radically different human types, whereas English and Hanseatic merchant adventurers were quite similar in outlook and behavior despite their different cultural and national backgrounds. See *The Protestant Ethic, op. cit.*, pp. 91-92.
15. Hugo v. Hofmannsthal, *Selected Prose*, Bollingen Series XXXIII (New York: Pantheon Books, 1952), p. 370.
16. A more exhaustive and systematic discussion at least of the first two models is contained in Walter Buckley, *Sociology and the Modern Systems Theory* (Englewood Cliffs: Prentice-Hall, 1967).
17. See Talcott Parsons, Edward Shils, et.al., *Towards a General Theory of Action* (Cambridge: Harvard University Press, 1951), p. 107; and Talcott Parsons, *The Social System* (New York: The Free Press, 1951), pp. 204-5. In sociology this perspective goes back to Durkheim and Spencer, though on other grounds Durkheim was a severe critic of Spencer.

18. Perhaps it should be called the coercion-and-revolt model. It is related to the dichotomic conception of social classes which has a long intellectual history. For a perceptive analysis, cf. Stanislaw Ossowski, *Class Structure in the Social Consciousness* (London: Routledge and Kegan Paul, 1963).
19. See Samuel P. Huntington, *Political Order in Changing Societies* (New Haven: Yale University Press, 1968), esp. Chaps. 1 and 4.
20. Weber, *Economy and Society, op. cit.*, I, p. 31. Weber refers to a legitimate order as possessing validity (*Geltung*), but this is not easily understood. Viability appears to convey the same meaning.
21. Ibid, I, pp. 31-32.
22. Accordingly, the empirical difficulties in studying legitimacy are formidable. The study by Gabriel Almond and Sidney Verba, *The Civic Culture* (Princeton: Princeton University Press, 1963) is an important attempt in this respect.
23. Weber, *Economy and Society, op. cit.*, I, p. 241.
24. Ibid., I, p. 242.
25. I am indebted for this phrase to Dankwart Rustow, *A World of Nations* (Washington: The Brookings Institution, 1967), p. 165.
26. The preceding two paragraphs paraphrase an earlier discussion. See Reinhard Bendix, "Reflections on Charismatic Leadership," in R. Bendix et. al., eds. *State and Society* (Boston: Little, Brown and Co., 1968), p. 620.
27. Weber, *Economy and Society, op. cit.*, I, pp. 217-18.
28. Ibid., I, p. 215.
29. Ibid., I, p. 226.
30. Ibid., II, pp. 655-57. The distinction of formal and substantive rationality applies to Weber's concepts of instrumentally rational and value-rational action. Cf. *op. cit.*, I, pp. 24ff. for an analysis of the conceptual ramifications of that division.
31. Cf. Gerhard Leibholz, *Strukturprobleme der modernen Demokratie* (Karlsruhe: F. Müller Verlag, 1958), pp. 280-81.
32. Weber, *Economy and Society, op. cit.*, II, p. 491.
33. Joseph Schumpeter, *Capitalism, Socialism and Democracy*, 3rd ed. (New York: Harper and Bros., 1950), p. 137. Cf. also the summary of Weber's analysis of feudal and patrimonial ideologies in R. Bendix, *Max Weber, An Intellectual Portrait* (Garden City: Doubleday & Co., 1962), pp. 361-69.
34. Schumpeter, *op. cit.*, pp. 137-38.
35. For details see Reinhard Bendix, *Work and Authority in Industry* (New York: Harper and Row, 1962), passim.
36. This point is elaborated in Chapter 14 below.
37. These shifts can be followed in the work of Talcott Parsons. His *The Structure of Social Action* (1937) began with the verdict that "Spencer is dead." By contrast his book *Societies, Evolutionary and Comparative Perspectives* (Englewood Cliffs: Prentice-Hall, 1966) is explicitly evolutionist, and not only Spencer but also Max Weber are interpreted in this framework. Cf. Parson's introduction to Max Weber, *Sociology of Religion* (Boston: The Beacon Press, 1963). For the intellectual background of evolutionism cf. Robert A. Nisbet, *Social Change and History* (New York: Oxford University Press, 1969).
38. In passing I note that since World War II, twentieth-century Marxism appears to go through its anti-evolutionist phase, as did "bourgeois" social theory in the heyday of pragmatism some fifty years ago. See, for example, the review by Norman Birnbaum, "The Crisis in Marxist Sociology," *Social Research*, XXXV (Summer 1968), pp. 348-80, which documents the decline of the evolutionist

element in Marxism, but does not focus on its implications.

39. Max Weber, *Economy and Society, op.cit.*, III, p. 1121.
40. Jacob Burckhardt, *Force and Freedom* (New York: Pantheon Books, 1943), pp. 255-92, 301-46.
41. Weber, *Economy and Society, op. cit.*, I, pp. 25-26.
42. Ibid., I, p. 30. I have reordered Weber's phrasing in the interest of brevity.
43. Max Weber, *The Methodology of the Social Sciences* (Glencoe: The Free Press, 1949), pp. 27 ff.
44. Cf. Max Weber, *The Protestant Ethic and the Spirit of Capitalism* (New York: Charles Scribner's Sons, 1958), pp. 13-27.
45. Weber, *Economy and Society, op. cit.*, II, pp. 882-83.
46. Ibid., II, p. 754.
47. Ibid., II, p. 755.
48. Ibid., II, p. 775.
49. Ibid., II, pp. 768-69 ff.
50. Ibid., III, p. 1116.
51. Robert Nisbet, *op. cit.*, pp. 166-88.
52. Weber, *Economy and Society, op. cit.*, II, pp. 882-89.
53. Cf. Karl Löwith, *Meaning in History* (Chicago: University of Chicago Press, 1949), pp. 8-10, and passim. The belief in eternal recurrence is found in India and China as well as in classical antiquity. Its significance as a prelude to theories of evolution is analyzed in Nisbet, *op. cit.*, pp. 29-61.
54. Cf. here R.G. Collingwood's spirited attack upon the propositional calculus of his philosophical colleagues in *An Autobiography* (London: Oxford University Press, 1939), Chap. 5. He asserts that the same proposition may have several meanings, depending upon the questions to which it may be an answer. Hence, a logic of propositions without inquiry into these prior questions is a futile undertaking. Similarly, Weber's compendium of sociological concepts seeks to separate the formulation of concepts from the questioning process of scholarly inquiry.

8

REFLECTIONS ON MODERN WESTERN
STATES AND CIVIL SOCIETIES[1]

Introductory Note

Countries in their entirety are distinguished from one another by their political attributes. For example, individuals as elected or appointed representatives act for their country as a corporate body by voting on laws valid throughout that country's jurisdiction, by diplomatic negotiations with the representatives of other countries, by their presence on ceremonial occasions, and so on. The capacity to vote on laws, engage in diplomatic relations, or represent the country endures over time regardless of the particular government in office. The term *state* refers to this capacity to act as (and for) the country as a corporate whole.

The inhabitants of countries also possess social attributes like language, a cultural heritage, and a common history. They share these attributes most often by virtue of their birth. Each attribute changes over time and at different rates. But even if one could take all the shared attributes together, they would still not constitute a whole. Unlike a country's political structure, the common attributes of *society* do not possess any representative agency which speaks for the whole. One can only think of such attributes as a whole by contrasting them with comparable attributes of other societies.

We do not usually think of this elementary distinction between state and society when we refer to countries as wholes. Instead, we refer to them by name and rely on subsequent contexts to make the intended meaning clear. Scholarly language, especially when it relies on ordinary rather than technical terms, cannot let it go at that, in particular when superficially simple terms like "state" and "society" evoke connotations from ordinary usage which cannot be exorcised at will.

Discussions of the state as distinct from society began with the economists. As recently as 1980, Kenneth Dyson was explaining why in France and Germany the state possessed "an immanent intelligence, directing social change," because it was endowed with sovereignty. By contrast, society was an area of "particularity" like the market that "provides self-regulating mechanisms for the satisfaction of material needs." Dyson pointed out that "such a perspective avoids the character of the idea embedded in institutions and their influence on conduct, for the state is identified with a regulating and

179

powerful intelligence and society is identified as an arena of conflicting material interests.[2]

Since Dyson's book we have had calls for "Bringing the State Back In"—with conferences held and a volume by that title. It is true that society-centered models have prevailed recently, partly due to an unwitting legacy of the Marxist tradition which relegated governments to the superstructure of society and hence to the status of an epiphenomenon. From our point of view, the "new" emphasis on the state is a step forward, if a more balanced approach is the result. But unless the basic terms "state" and "society" are defined and the limits of their applicability established, this will be a difficult enterprise. Theda Skocpol refers to administrative and coercive organizations as forming the "core of the modern state" and "as the likely generators of autonomous state activities," but the studies she cites on that occasion deal with advanced industrial states (Peru excepted) and we should be sure we know what we mean by this "autonomous actor."[3] Unfortunately, recent discussions make clear just how uncertain our usage of the term is—hardly surprising if "the state" has been treated as an epiphenomenon. In one case, Weber's definition of the *modern* state is applied to all regimes in all historical periods.[4] In another, it is said that "a state exists if the basic decisions in the polity are made independently of civil society."[5]

If confusion reigns with regard to "the state," "civil society" has fared even less well. The editors of the *International Encyclopedia of the Social Sciences* (1968) did not think the concept important enough to warrant inclusion. The following essay attempts to explicate what is too often implicit. We recognize that terms like *state* and *society* are not standardized and various usages are reasonable, as long as their intended meanings are consistent and explicit. Still, clarification seems to be needed, when it can be regarded as "new" that states can act autonomously, and when social scientists long familiar with "society" become uncertain what is meant when the adjective "civil" is added.[6]

The level of analysis attempted is ideal-typical, which means that it tries to provide a framework for causal analysis with appropriate illustrations, but should not be mistaken for causal analysis itself. The concepts used simplify and exaggerate (to cite Weber), so that we can think about the phenomena dealt with in an orderly fashion. But clarification is not our main or only purpose. Rather, the discussion will reach into comparative political and intellectual history, the study of "modernization," as well as touch on vital political issues of our day. Even so, our starting-point should be kept in mind. These reflections on modern Western states and civil societies propose a dualistic approach to the body politic as a whole.

In the sixteenth century, Jean Bodin saw the need of protecting the king as head of state from the encroachments of society. By contrast, the welfare states of today, whatever their approach or philosophy, do much to bring state-directed benefits to many of the most passive members of civil society, as well as to middle-class strata who articulate their demands forcefully enough. Naturally, such a contrast is only the first step towards a more detailed analysis of the relations between states and societies. But before such an analysis becomes feasible, one ought to be clear that the distinction of state and society, ideal-typical though it is, raises again the fundamental question of the "general will" or the will of all, which Rousseau posed more than two centuries ago.

Our contention is that without the distinction between state and society, economic growth and political institutions will be difficult to preserve (or achieve), either in Western states or in the Third World. Demands arising within society can impede, and even prevent, the development of profitable enterprises and of an efficient government administration. On the other hand, the dictatorships of the twentieth century have demonstrated that modern governments are technically capable of intervening in every aspect of civil society, even the most private. Both eventualities, the hypertrophy of society or of the state, the phenomenon of "failed modernization" and the phenomenon of totalitarianism, suggest that the distinction of state and civil society (and hence the countervailing forces of both) must be preserved, if the existence of civil societies with their economic development and freedom of association are to be ensured in the future.

Within this framework our discussion will turn first to Max Weber's and Ernest Barker's definitions of the state in an effort to distinguish between the modern and the medieval political organizations of Western Europe. (Further remarks on this distinction are contained in chapter 11 below.) Next, following the lead of Albert Hirschman, we discuss civil society in the simplified sense of the market "as the self-regulating mechanism for the satisfaction of material needs" (Dyson). The market, as Hirschman recognizes without much elaboration, is too simplified a model for a conceptualization of civil society, because it remains restricted to short-run individual choices and organizational responses. Nevertheless, Hirschman's analysis can be used to encompass long-run individual and collective participation in civil society without losing sight of the short-run market behavior which is also part of civil society. In the process, we review the anti-associational theory of the liberal tradition which stands in marked contrast to the actual proliferation of associations in Western civil societies. We also offer a typology of socio-political participation in civil society, as a first step towards developing a model for the sequence of West-European political structures (formulated below in chapter 9), which has been compatible with the definitions of state and civil society presented here.

DEFINITION OF THE MODERN WESTERN STATE

In his discussion of ruling organizations (*Herrschaftsverbände*) Max Weber writes that "the concept of the state has only in modern times reached its full development." This qualification has two implications. The *concept* of the state can be traced back to the sixteenth and seventeenth centuries; the *institutions* of the state, such as formal legal dispute settlement or impersonal administration, can be traced back either much farther or to a more recent date, depending on how one uses the adjectives "modern" and "full." One can speak broadly of the concept "state" in the writings of Machiavelli, Bodin and Hobbes as referring to the institutions of royal absolutism in the 16th and 17th centuries. But the claims of absolutist rule were not realized in Italy as a whole, were hardly approximated in England during the Tudor revolution in government, and came close to realization in France only after 1661 under Louis XIV. Weber writes of the institutions of the modern state in the following terms:

> It possesses an administrative and legal order subject to change by legislation, to which the organized activities of the administrative staff, which are also controlled by regulations, are oriented. This system of order claims binding authority, not only over the members of the state, the citizens, most of whom have obtained membership by birth, but also to a very large extent over all action taking place in the area of its jurisdiction. It is thus a compulsory organization with a territorial base.[7]

This definition refers to political institutions of the nineteenth and twentieth centuries in the countries of Western Europe and in the Western European settlements abroad. In Weber's usage, it is clear that past regimes of feudal or patrimonial rule, the Chinese or Roman empires, Greek city-states and even the absolutist states of Western Europe were not *modern* states.

Such a specification raises problems. One may want to add other countries to the list, point out the partial institutionalization of Western European administrative forms in other parts of the world, or specifically exclude the countries governed by one-party rule. We believe that one reason for confining the "state" to the countries in which the *modern* state developed is the lack of a civil society in other countries. We also believe that there is a connection between modern states and the rule of law, the absence of which is one characteristic of one-party states. Finally, there is the issue of the historical transition of countries to a condition of statehood.

Loose applications of the term *state* to all kinds of rule (or the substitution of the term "regime" to fudge the issue) has two consequences. One is that the terms of Weber's specification are used too broadly to remain meaningful.

The other is that, by relaxing the definition, we tacitly ignore the fact that the state as here defined developed out of many antecedents into *a new historical configuration*. One would not discard the terms Christianity or Confucianism because there has been a long history of disputes over the meaning of their basic beliefs. Similarly, one should not discard the term *state* because it applies to a select number of countries for a limited period, involves continuous disputes over its purpose and range, and is only approximately valid even where, as an ideal type, it is useful to employ it.[8]

But just what are the "organized activities" of a "compulsory organization"? Even an abbreviated list must include the following functions with regard to which *the legitimate use of force over a territory* is monopolized today by a legal and administrative order:

1. Lawmaking (legislative and administrative enactments);
2. Maintenance of public order (police);
3. Defense (military command hierarchy, procurement of ordnance, recruitment, secret service);
4. Control of currency (coinage, printing of money, control of banking and the amount of circulating money);
5. Dispute settlement (judiciary, administrative tribunals, arbitration or mediation, special prosecutors);
6. Public revenue (tax assessment and collection);
7. Public works (provision of public necessities—disaster relief, road building, harbor construction and maintenance—which are beyond the financial capacity of individuals or private organizations); and
8. Social services (basic educational facilities, unemployment insurance, social security).

The items in parentheses are merely illustrative. We accept Weber's reason that one cannot define any ruling organization in terms of the ends they have pursued, but only in terms of the means they have employed. In the case of modern Western states a monopoly of the legitimate use of force (or, more accurately, the threat implied by that monopoly) has underlain the implementation of the public functions we have enumerated.

The state is only one kind of ruling organization, and all such organizations use (or threaten to use) force. It is not force as such, but *the legal monopoly of its legitimate use over a territory*, which is the distinguishing attribute of the state. An administrative staff is required to implement the directives of many ruling organizations. Yet in a modern Western state, the staff itself is subject to legal regulations as much as are the enactments which the staff is charged to put into effect.

Ultimately, as previously noted, the rule of law is the distinguishing mark of modern Western states. In all other types of ruling organizations, rulers themselves are not subject to the law, nor are they bound to their own previous enactments. But it is also true that the rule of law is defined quite differently at different times and places. One finds modern states only in cases in which a citizen can obtain redress against another (including officers of the state) for breaches of law, and where such redress is constitutionally guaranteed. In other words, in modern Western states the legal monopoly of the use of force can be checked by a rule of law, permitting redress by the citizens and by legislation, which may curb the effects of monopoly. This in turn suggests that a more detailed examination of the terms *monopoly*, *legitimacy* and *force* is in order.

To arrive at his definition of the state, Weber had to arrest the flow of history. This is one meaning of his formula that ideal types "simplify and exaggerate" the evidence. For none of the functions we have listed, like lawmaking or social services, nor any of the instrumentalities of the state, like policing or tax collecting, nor yet the attributes of legitimacy, force, or territory have a static, once-and-for-all meaning. That is the reason why the defining characteristics of the state and its various functions are grasped most easily as contrast-conceptions. Ernest Barker has suggested that before the obviously arbitrary date of 1660 the state was identified with family, property, and society. Affairs of state were the exclusive concern of a ruling elite, consisting typically of the king or queen, members of the royal family, principal advisors, and leading members of the clergy, nobility, and the urban patriciate. To this elite it appeared a matter of course that family ties colored all handling of the affairs of the country. No distinction existed between household staff and royal officials, family income and revenue due to the crown, family councils and royal councils. Offices of royal government were treated as private property, not a farfetched idea when the King of Prussia (in 1740) derived as much income from his royal domains as he did from the general revenue, or when in France public offices were acquired by purchase and treated as inheritable property. Royal government and high society were so closely intertwined as to be indistinguishable. It was not so much a confusion of state and society, as Barker would have it, as an inability to see that there was a difference. If the king and the "upper class" had a special position in society, it followed that they must also have a special position in the affairs of the country.[9]

After 1660, by a very gradual process, these "public" affairs were disentangled from private, hereditary claims to administrative and judicial preferment. Neither Weber nor, as far as we know, anyone else argues that in the modern Western state family influence, property, and society play no role in the recruitment of civil servants, the adjudication of disputes, tax assessments, or the letting of government contracts. Distinctions between historical configurations are never that neat. We can only say that intimate relations between "high society" and affairs of state have been diminished substantially in comparison with the earlier condition. Efforts to keep family, property, and "high society" out of public affairs continue, which implies of course that efforts to bring these influences to bear continue as well.

The institutions and functions which define the modern state are at the same time issues in contention. Ruling organizations remain modern states, as long as the efforts to decrease the influence of family, property and society prevail over efforts to increase that influence. Note that this is a matter of definition. Individuals and organized groups interact with some branch or agency of the state at many points, in order to manage or manipulate family, property and society. Witness the care of the elderly, control over inheritance, or bestowal of rank as in the army, to mention three items at random. But note also that interaction implies the relative autonomy of both state and society, as well as the relative influence of both on each other. This interaction does not alter the appropriateness of defining the modern state in terms of its authoritative subordination of family, property and society in the appointment of public office, the collection of revenue, and other functions mentioned earlier. Exceptions to this definition such as the Grimaldi family's control of Monaco, the Saudi's control of Saudi Arabia, or even the Nehru-Gandhi succession in the Indian government are only reminders that ideal types "simplify and exaggerate" the evidence.

The nominalism of our definitions should not be misinterpreted, and here we come to the explication of monopoly, force, and legitimacy.

How can one speak of *monopolization*, when all the functions of the modern Western state are debated continuously and frequently become the focus of major disputes? The answer is that the state, or rather the agents and agencies of modern Western states considered collectively, have an ultimate decision-making authority on questions of public policy. The monopolization of ultimate authority in principle often coexists with divided institutionalization in practice, which means that this "authority" may be both questioned and difficult to locate.

The monopolization of legitimate force on the part of the state is clearest when its present-day functions are contrasted with their earlier analogues. At one time, the control of the currency, military recruitment and organization, the settlement of disputes, tax collection and lawmaking were in many private hands and there was little pressure to coordinate them. Each function consisted of separate transactions between the individuals concerned and the local authority, with a fee paid for the "public service" to be rendered.

Today, all these functions are the exclusive prerogative of the modern Western state which possesses the authority to set public policy. We cannot now turn to another authority when we dispute a given policy, unlike what Pierre Goubert has described for eighteenth-century monarchical France. The French monarchy rested on a series of contracts made

> with the different units of which France was composed: provinces, cities, ecclesiastical foundations, social classes and even economic groups such as the trade guilds. All these contracts left to each group its own liberties and privi-leges and no one saw anything out of the way in their existence side by side with submission to the king. Provinces, cities, foundations, groups, orders and es-tates were all faithful subjects of the king, but with their own privileges.[10]

Under these conditions, the ruling organization of France was not a state pos-sessing a monopoly of the legitimate use of force over a territory.

Our remarks on *force* can be briefer. Weber writes that "the use of physical force is neither the sole, nor even the most usual, method of administration of political organizations."[11] On the contrary, public officials in leading posi-tions tend to use every conceivable means short of force to bring about an im-plementation of policy, although the threat of force is in the background and at their disposal, if need be. This threat is central to Weber's definition of the state, but not the use of force. His thoughts on the subject may be summarized by two imperatives and a set of conclusions: When analyzing states, always attend to the threat of force and the available means of compulsion while also attending to the consent or acquiescence of the people. Weber's whole discus-sion suggests that compulsion without some consent erodes the efficacy of rule, even if force prevails for a long time. Conversely, consent without some threat of force lacks institutional stability. Weber's discussion also suggests that consent as the sole bond of organization removes that organization from the political realm. This applies, for example, to organizations without au-thority like the free schools analyzed by Ann Swidler (1979).

These remarks suggest the importance of *legitimacy* as the counterpart of compulsion or the threat of force. In other words, to the extent that institutions of the state are trusted, the importance of the threat of force diminishes. Al-though legitimacy has a "now you see it, now you don't" quality, the idea is as real and important for the state as trust and confidence are in personal rela-tions.[12] Banks rely on the confidence of their depositors, even though they keep only a small fraction of their assets on hand in order to meet the expected rate of withdrawal. Most of their assets are invested in order to produce in-come, and these assets are unavailable to meet spot-demands for cash. Most bank customers do not reflect on this condition. The bank has a kind of legiti-macy in their eyes, because they believe the bank will cash their checks on demand. Part of that confidence depends on a vague knowledge of business standards, periodic inspection of bookkeeping procedures, federal insurance schemes, or occasional court cases in which a bank official is convicted for having made off with other people's assets. Of course, experience with getting their checks cashed on demand strongly reinforces these general impressions. Runs on banks thus indicate a loss of trust in the institution.

The bank is only one institution, whereas the state comprises many, so that trust in a bank is easier to achieve than the legitimacy of the state. Still, the state's threat of force is held in abeyance and actual force is used rarely, as long as a majority of citizens believes that the government has been installed properly (entrance legitimacy), shows competence in handling public affairs and delivers on its important promises to a sufficient extent (performance legitimacy). There is always some discrepancy between promise and performance. Where dissatisfactions rise, the legitimacy of government comes into question. By holding periodic elections, democratic governments allow for the venting of dissatisfactions and hence re-establish their formal legitimacy. Even then, in countries with a free press, incumbent governments are subjected to a barrage of verbal assaults from the day they are elected to office. Dissatisfactions with particular actions and public criticisms are not, however, synonymous with a belief in the illegitimacy of an incumbent government.

Obviously, there are regimes or ruling organizations which monopolize the use of force over a territory, but do so illegitimately. Weber approached this question, but did not deal with it fully. He emphasized that mere conformity with government orders or reliance on customary routines are not sufficient evidence of legitimacy. An additional element is needed for a government to be considered legitimate, namely that the citizens of the state regard the prevailing order "as in some way obligatory or exemplary" for themselves.[13] Legitimacy emphasizes positive assent rather than mere acquiescence or passive consent. Since December 1981 we have witnessed in Poland a manifest example of an illegitimate monopolization of force through martial law. The Solidarity trade union has been outlawed, demonstrations prohibited, opposition leaders jailed. But the Poles with their candles in windows, pilgrimages to national and religious shrines as well as the symbolic use of Catholic observances have demonstrated for us that they do not consider the prevailing military rule, let alone the Communist party, legitimate, even though that ruling organization retains many other attributes of the modern state. Though comments on current events in a theoretical article are hazardous—we cannot know what the effects of countermeasures by the incumbent government may be—the Polish example makes evident that the outlawing of protest from the public arena can divert the expression of political sentiment into other, still legitimate channels such as the Catholic church or various forms of literature.

DEFINITION OF A CIVIL SOCIETY

Before turning to the discussion of civil society, we need to disaggregate the term itself.[14] Generally, "civil" is a synonym of polite (as in civility), whereas "civic" goes together with public affairs (as in civic duty). But we also speak of civil rights or civil defense,thereby referring to public affairs. Several dictionary definitions highlight a central ambiguity of the adjective "civil." Civil, in the sense of citizens living together in a community, suggests a formal equality. But civil, in the sense of organization and internal affairs of the body politic, suggests the authority of officials directly in charge of public affairs. The people's participation is indirect, confined to the election of representatives or, say, demonstrations seeking to influence the actions of officials. The common usage of *civil* or *civic* seems to imply both the formal equality under the law and the real inequalities of legal authority which can be a byproduct of formal procedures.[15]

Prior to the French Revolution, the term *civil society* was another word for high society, a synonym of inequality. For the French statesman, the Duc du Rohan (1647), civil society meant the ruling groups concerned with the interests of king and country, touching on matters of law, religion and territorial boundaries.[16] A century later, in 1765, the English lawyer William Blackstone wrote that "the civil state consists of the nobility and the clergy." Both men described and represented the ruling class of their day and country. Both considered the population at large only insofar as it entered into the political calculations of ruling a country in competition with other countries.

For Rousseau the state was an aggregate of individuals and the embodiment of the general will. According to *The Social Contract* (1762), that will would result if the people are sufficiently informed and individuals would deliberate by themselves but *not* communicate with each other. In the absence of such communication only trifling differences would exist among them.

> But when cabals and partial associations are formed at the expense of the great association, the will of each such association, though general with regard to its members, is private with regard to the State: it can then be said no longer that there are as many voters as men, but only as many as there are associations.... It is therefore of the utmost importance for obtaining the expression of the general will, that no partial society should be formed in the State, and that every citizen should speak his opinion entirely from himself.... When there are partial societies, it is politic to multiply their number, that they may all be kept at an equality.[17]

The logic of this position is that the belief in the "general will" makes all "specific will " appear suspect. The individual was lifted to prominence as a means of curbing the influence of nobility and the church, but without providing a framework of intermediate organizations for individuals to articulate their interests. Whatever Rousseau's intentions may have been, he became the progenitor of an anti-associational tendency which has had repercussions in France and elsewhere to this day.

In the thirty years after *The Social Contract*, various groups in French society came under attack. La Chalotais (1763) criticized the control of education by the Society of Jesus, arguing that "the children of the State should be educated by members of the State."[18] In 1764, the Jesuits were banned in France as well as in other European countries. Jews, the delegate Clermont-Tonnere declared in the National Assembly of 1789, should not be allowed self-governing rights in such matters as religious education, the settlement of disputes, or the management of buildings and cemeteries. For in that case their communities would constitute a "nation within a nation. Everything should be denied to the Jews as a nation; everything should be granted to them as individuals."[19] Two years later, mutual aid societies to protect workers against sickness or unemployment seemed a threat to the general will at least as great as religion:

> It is for the nation and the public officials . . . to supply work to those who need it for their livelihood. . . . It should not be permissible for citizens in certain occupations to meet together in defense of their pretended common interests. There must be no more guilds in the State, but only the individual interest of each citizen and the general interest. No one shall be allowed to arouse in any citizen any kind of intermediate interest and to separate him from the public weal through the medium of corporate interests.[20]

Such sentiments led to the outlawing of mutual-aid societies through the eponymously named *Loi Le Chapelier* (1791), not repealed until the 1880s. This is of particular interest with respect to the proliferation of voluntary organizations which seems to indicate that the current situation is diametrically opposed to that of 200 years ago.

Suspicion towards associations was not confined to France or to revolutionary thought. Adam Smith's *Wealth of Nations* (1776) developed a whole theory of classes based on the connection between group interest and public welfare. Those who "naturally" received the rent of land and the wages of labor, while lacking in intelligence, had a self-interest which coincided with the general interest. Those who lived by profit had an interest that was

> never exactly the same as that of the public. [They] have generally an interest to deceive and even to oppress the public, and [they] accordingly have, upon many occasions, both deceived and oppressed it.[21]

None of this was lost on the Americans. President Washington, in his farewell address (1796), warned against the "baneful effects of the spirit of party." The most enduring expression of this sentiment was given by James Madison in *The Federalist* (1787: No. 10):

> By a faction, I understand a number of citizens, whether amounting to a majority or minority of the whole, who are united and actuated by some common im-

pulse or passion, or of interest, adverse to the rights of other citizens, or to the permanent and aggregate interests of the community.[22]

To the generation influenced by Rousseau and Adam Smith, political parties suggested conspiracies against the general will of the nation. The current written constitutions of the Western democracies—with the notable exception of the German Basic Law of 1949—fail to provide for the existence of political parties, even though the basic rights of assembly, speech, petition and voting would seem to suggest it. There also appears to be a paradox here, for to the extent that there is *not* a deliberate effort to capture the "general will" in centralized political institutions, parties become weakened.

This apparent paradox is closely related to two situations in which we feel civil societies do not exist: under one-party dictatorships and during civil war. The crucial limiting factor is the *prohibition of associations to freely pursue limited interests*—every "private" organization is under surveillance under a dictatorship. There is an intellectual affinity here with those leaders of the French revolution who sought to protect the general will by prohibiting the relative independence of private associations; we therefore suggest that the independence of private associations is a synonym for civil society.

Perhaps the most important "association" to which the individual belongs is the family. The family is often the primary unit which defends the interests of its members: it is often so strong a center of concern that it militates against larger social considerations. Freud expressed this latent antagonism between family and society when he wrote that

society must defend itself against the danger that the interests which it needs for the establishment of higher social units may be swallowed up by the family.[23]

Freud wrote this sentence before the advent of totalitarian regimes in which political authorities became the aggressor against the family, forcing children to report on the loyalty of their parents, or using family members as hostages to ensure conformity. The fact that one-party dictatorships feel compelled to reach into the family sphere suggests that families are one cornerstone of civil society.

In countries which possess civil societies by allowing private associations, families are at the farthest remove from the state. This is not to say that the *welfare* of the family or its members is a matter of indifference to the state. Education and social services are offered in the modern Western state to assist the family and are evidence to the contrary. But families do not (and perhaps cannot) represent themselves effectively. As a practical political matter, heads of households join together in organizations in order to represent their common interests and those of their families. It is also more practicable for the state to deal with such organizations than with millions of individual families. Accordingly, civil society manifests a functional differentiation between the private affairs of individuals or families, and the public affairs of the state. Private associations may thus "put into effect certain rules of particular interest to them in some special area of social and political life, *albeit without seeking direct responsibility in public affairs.*"[24] Such autonomy is impossible under constant state surveillance. While the contrast between private and public affairs is formal and there are many overlaps, the activities of associations are nonetheless distinct from the affairs of state.

The lack of civil society under conditions of civil war is simpler to describe, as civil war violates the various notions of "civil" mentioned earlier. The consensus required between state and society is lacking when internal dissent leads to war, and there are many modern examples. Lebanon is perhaps one of the clearest, for each faction in the area has its own private army such that the state, rather than monopolizing legitimate force, becomes merely another faction.

From this survey of definitions and situational contexts in which the two terms "state" and "civil society" arise and are useful, we now turn to a closer examination of civil society. We begin with a discussion of civil society and the market, and then turn to issues of individual and collective participation.

CIVIL SOCIETY AND THE MARKET

If civil society is defined by "citizens dwelling together in a community," then it is easier to say when that society lapses, when its citizens quarrel or leave, than what "dwelling together" means. It is impossible, as indicated above, to speak of a whole society or of all citizens except in formal political terms. Accordingly, we will begin this substantive discussion of civil society in the simplified terms suggested by Albert Hirschman. The individual economic actor is a part of every citizen, the economy is a part of every civil society, and it is easier to tell when things go wrong (changes of consumer taste, business failures) than when citizens "dwell together" in mutual satisfaction.

> Under any economic, social or political system, individuals, business firms, and organizations in general are subject to lapses from efficient, rational, law-abiding, virtuous, or otherwise functional behavior. . . . Each society learns to live with a certain amount of such dysfunctional or mis-behavior; but lest misbehavior feed on itself and lead to general decay, society must be able to marshal from within itself forces which will make as many of the faltering actors as possible revert to the behavior required to its proper functioning.[25]

The self-correcting behavior of organizations occurs ideally in response to the "lapses" of customers or members which are noted because they lead to a decline of revenue or membership. Hirschman defines his two basic terms of *exit* and *voice* accordingly:

1. Some customers stop buying the firm's products or some members leave the organization: this is the exit option. As a result, revenues drop, membership declines, and management is impelled to search for ways and means to correct whatever faults have led to exit.
2. The firm's customers or the organization's members express their dissatisfaction directly to management or to some other authority to which management is subordinate or through general protest addressed to anyone who cares to listen; this is the *voice* option. As a result, management once again engages in a search for the causes and possible cures of customers' and members' dissatisfactions.[26]

For Hirschman, the unit of analysis is the individual actor on the market or the individual member of an organization, deciding on his next step (purchase, non-purchase, voice, acquiescence) at a given moment in time.

To this scheme Hirschman adds the concept of "loyalty" which can limit the individual's inclination to exit, or to voice protest. At its simplest the buyer is disinclined to change the brand he has always bought (from breakfast cereals to automobiles), even though the quality has declined and his dissatisfaction increased. In the same way, the voter is disinclined to change his party, because people in his family have always voted Republican (or Democratic), even though he is thoroughly disgusted with current party policies. In either case, a temporary or short-run choice has inadvertently become habit-forming. Even then, the loyalty shown to a commodity or a party can be changed at will, when the occasion arises. Hirschman has rung the changes on exit, voice and loyalty in exemplary fashion and in doing so he has analyzed that aspect of civil society which depends upon the economic or political behavior of the individual actor, when he buys or votes at one moment in time. Even when he exits to another commodity, or changes his mind about voting, it is still a single act which—except for what loyalties he feels—does not commit him in the future.

But such individual choices at one point in time are not a suitable model of civil society, and Hirschman himself notes this fact when he distinguishes the market or ordinary political action from such "primordial human groupings as family, tribe, church, and state." He marks this distinction when he notes that certain organizations are able to exact *a high price for exit*.

> Such a price can range from loss of life-long associations to loss of life, with such intermediate penalties as excommunication, defamation, and deprivation of livelihood. Organizations able to exact these high penalties for exit are the most traditional human groups, such as the family, the tribe, the religious community, and the nation.[27]

But are family members, the faithful of a religious community, and the citizens of a nation distinguished from Hirschman's economic and political man only by the high price of exit?

We think not. Hirschman's bridge-building between economic and political behavior makes two assumptions which are unsatisfactory for an understanding of civil society. The only persons he and other economists consider are functioning adults, i.e., persons capable of acting in the market or the political arena. The approach presupposes a whole infrastructure of children born and grown to maturity so that they can function as adults. And once we consider children, we start with entry rather than exit, we deal with persons born into communities not of their own choosing, who have to live in the long term (see below), not from one short-term decision to the next.

Hirschman's bridge-building is also premised on the response of organizations to the clues and threats of decline. But this very premise assumes the functioning of organizations prior to the onset of serious deterioration, which leads to exit and/or voice and hence to organizational efforts to improve performance. The capacity for remedial action (short-term) exists within a framework of long-term operations, just as the short-term decisions of persons in the market or the polity are part of their long-term commitments to family, church, and nation.

"Civil society" cannot be understood in terms of short-term decision-making alone. Citizens who dwell together in a community, and the many communities which constitute a society, encompass persons throughout their life-cycle. In addition to growth (infancy, childhood, adolescence, phases of adult life), life-cycles consist of periodic commitments (schooling, first job(s), career choices, location, status attributes) with long-term consequences. These commitments are cumulative and increasingly irreversible, a mix of choice and subsequent compulsion. One can think of the time and effort spent in these periodic commitments as analogues of capital investment.

Yet while both involve the expenditures of resources as well as risk, there are differences. The assets of capital investment can be sold again, at a profit or loss, indicating that the process of investment is reversible. By contrast, the time and effort spent in building up a career involve a permanent commitment. It is not only that the transaction costs of life-cycle commitments are higher than many capital investments, they are also virtually impossible to transfer or sell. One can think of life-careers as the totality of voluntary and involuntary commitments and the consequences following therefrom. Each choice along the way adds increments of training or experience, and increases the person's interest in preserving the value of the time and effort spent and of the skills acquired in the process. It is very costly and often impossible to recapture or reemploy such commitments in an entirely different line of endeavor. Capital investment, by contrast, may be recaptured and the assets reinvested. The interest in preserving and enhancing the value of acquired skills, we believe, is the basic reason for the proliferation of associations. When individuals protect and promote their interests and activities collectively, they can do so more effectively than they can individually, despite the anti-associational ideology of the early modern period.

INDIVIDUAL AND COLLECTIVE PARTICIPATION

In substituting the life-cycle of individuals for Hirschman's momentary decision-making in the market (or in periodic elections), we have moved analysis to another level of abstraction. From birth, the individual becomes involved in long-term commitments. Once he is a functional adult, each commitment—voluntary as it may be at its inception—turns into the assets and liabilities which make up his competence as well as his identity. The organizations he joins can enhance by collective strength his own efforts at safeguarding or enhancing his interests. One building block of civil society thus consists of a person's (and/or a family's) cumulative commitments. The other consists in the organizational safeguards which help protect an individual's (and/or a family's) interests in the cumulative life-chances he has (or they have) obtained. The organizations which provide individuals and families with opportunities and perchance protect them, form an aggregate framework that represents the collective side of civil society and can be considered at its own level.

The individual and collective approaches to the analysis of civil society complement each other. Civil society is the principal arena in which the individual can make choices, limited as these are by the conditions of his being and the consequences of his own earlier commitments. Analysis in this field should not remain confined to the monetary decision-making of *homo œconomicus*, though the market in which such decision-making occurs is part of civil society. But civil society consists of organizations and institutions in which decisions tend to be for the long term. Although Edmund Burke's emotive language sounds suspect today, he makes a valid contrast between society and the market.

> Society is indeed a contract. Subordinate contracts for objects of mere occasional interest may be dissolved at pleasure—but the state [and, we would add, civil society] ought not to be considered as nothing better than a partnership agreement in a trade of pepper and coffee, calico or tobacco, or some other such low concern, to be taken up for a little temporary interest, and to be dissolved by the fancy of the parties. It is to be looked on with other reverence, for it is not a partnership in things subservient only to the gross animal existence of a temporary or perishable nature. It is a partnership in all science; a partnership in all art; a partnership in every virtue, and in all perfection. As the ends of such a partnership cannot be obtained in many generations, it becomes a partnership not only between those who are living, but between those who are living, those who are dead, and those who are to be born.[28]

Our mundane age takes account of this view to the extent that it protects the environment or struggles not to burden the next generation with the financial consequences of current debts. Still, the modern observer must add that the partnership between the dead, the living, and those to be born is *not* all science, art, virtue and perfection, but likewise superstition, vice, and long-standing liabilities. Burke failed to see the weakness that can be part of a tradition.

An individual becomes a building block of civil society through an irreversible birth, tied in a web of involuntary relations to adults, country and culture that precedes all subsequent commitments. Education and socialization bring the child to functional and independent adulthood, whereby both state and societal relations exert their influence in molding each citizen, with family influence diminishing over time. The nature of commitment to family differs from that to country or culture, however, for while the former may retain a psychological hold and is irreversible, it is possible to reverse the commitment to country and culture through emigration and change of citizenship.

FIGURE 1
Entry and Exit of Association Membership

| | EXIT | |
	Low Cost	High Cost
Voluntary	Trade unions (currently) Trade associations Political parties *Benefits paramount*	Monastic Orders Terrorist groups French Foreign Legion *Commitment and service paramount*
Involuntary	????	National citizenship *Rights and duties paramount* Family *Love and hate paramount*

ENTRY (row label, between the two rows)

Note: The italicized paramount motivation of individual participants is discussed in the text.

When we consider a functional adult's commitment of time and effort to an organization, we enter the more amorphous area of collective aspects of civil society. To join an organization the individual pays membership fees, meets conditions of entry, adheres to rules and, if it comes to that, pays penalties for exit. The motive for this commitment is the expectation that membership will help him increase his skills, make a living or pursue his interests and thus enhance his life-chances as well as afford him protection beyond what he could obtain by his solitary efforts. Of course, organizations also pay a price by the bureaucracies they construct and the means they use to perform their functions. The critical question of civil societies consists in the adequacy with which the organizations existing between the individual and the state (Montesquieu's *pouvoirs intermédiares*) reconcile the satisfaction of individual needs and of organized group interests with the competing individual and group interests of other organizations in the public arena. At this point, the momentary decision-making of a person on the market is left behind, and his membership and participation in an organization makes him (or her) at least an indirect participant in the interaction between civil society and the state.

We can summarize the categories of voluntary or involuntary entry and low or high cost exit in the following fourfold figure. But we place little confidence in it, because the categories used are not in practice dichotomous (see Figure 1).

Nevertheless, by commenting on the overall distinctions in conjunction with the organizations or affiliations listed in each quadrant, and by characterizing some motivational correlates of individual participation, we can describe different degrees of commitment and kinds of satisfaction experienced by *homo sociologicus*, to use Dahrendorf's phrase. A complete listing is not attempted and may well be impossible. But the sketch provided gives meaning to the idea of "civil society in action."

We start with voluntary organizations which may be entered and left easily at low cost, usually in the form of membership dues (and their termination). People (or organizations) joining trade unions, trade associations and political parties usually do so because of the benefits expected from having joined. Even here there are complexities, because the benefits may not be large and quick enough, leading to exit sooner or later. Some organizations react to this fluidity of membership. Voluntary entry may be modified by provisions for probationary candidacy or other half-way houses of tentative participation, which allow for termination of candidacy by the organization or the individual. In this way, entry is made conditional upon some degree of commitment which makes exit less likely and the organization stronger.

From here one may go on to other organizations in which voluntary entry becomes a figure of speech. For example, family tradition may make membership in a political party an automatic corollary of birth so that membership only becomes voluntary in later life when a person *decides* to remain in, or to break with, the family tradition. In such cases entry is involuntary, whereas exit becomes possible, while there are others in which entry is indeed voluntary, but exit is impeded. Some trade associations make the cost of exit financially prohibitive, an example which moves us closer to the next alternative of voluntary entry but a high cost of exit.

This second alternative is typical of organizations which require of their voluntary members a very high degree of commitment. We have listed monastic orders, terrorist groups, and the French Foreign Legion precisely because of the diversity of their goals. Nevertheless, they have in common not only the requirement of a total commitment by the applicants for membership but also a rigorous training and indoctrination, which make even the thought of exit a wrenching personal experience. Moreover, in particular cases, organizations use countermeasures to keep members in line and defections to a minimum. Such measures range from various penalties to social ostracism, and from excommunication to physical liquidation. The cost of joining can be high or even prohibitive. In these cases commitment and service are paramount, the first as evidence that training and repeated testing have been completed successfully, the second as evidence that the commitment remains as total as it was upon full admission to the organization.

Next we move to an "empty box," because cases of involuntary entry with low cost of exit require substantial qualifications, even if approximations exist. One can construct an example to fit the criteria. Say parents force an unwanted marriage on a young couple with independent means, an involuntary entry which can be terminated by a quick divorce at low cost. This contrived example fits the criteria, but it is hardly representative of many cases. Somewhat more common may be involuntary membership in a church or fundamentalist sect, where exit becomes an easy option in later life (as in some cases of party membership). But in modern Western societies such cases of involuntary entry that still allow low cost exit occur typically where an unimpaired tradition exists in juxtaposition with conditions facilitating choice. Although such juxtapositions occur and may continue, they are sources of friction for the individuals involved and for the society at large.

National citizenship is a major example of involuntary entry. Citizenship is the corollary of being the child of our parents, who already possess citizenship and bequeath it to us. (We disregard the complications of parents who are citizens of two different countries, or cases in which the location of the birthplace determines citizenship.) The infant is born into a set of rights, a birth certificate and passport may be issued soon after birth, and the child immediately benefits from whatever rights of protection the citizenship of his or her country bestows. The duties of school attendance, the rights and duties of legal majority, the eligibility to various benefits, the duties of tax-payment and compulsory service in emergencies: all these come later. It is an open question among modern states, what other "human rights" go with citizenship. The Bill of Rights of several Western constitutions include human rights such as free speech and assembly, the rights against self-incrimination, the right to legal defense, and others. In recent years, Soviet propaganda has claimed that rights to full employment (including the duties to work assignments) or full health care and nursing facilities (again based on assignments) are equal or superior to "merely formal" legal rights. However, the evidence of emigration and options for another citizenship reveal a preference for countries in which civil society is allowed some degree of autonomy.

Finally, there is involuntary participation in our families and their wider kinship networks. Since we are born into a family, the word *involuntary* is unambiguous, but the high cost of exit is not. The ties between children and parents have an "emotional logic" of their own, which we try to suggest by the terms *love* and *hate*. Actually, it is misleading to classify families under entry and exit as mutually exclusive categories, when children grow to an independence as adults which is by no means synonymous with exit. But while the entry-exit alternative cannot be applied in this case, families are a vital ingredient of civil society nonetheless. They provide the socialization through which infants become adults capable of participating in the society of which they are a part. And where families fail to do so, civil society and the state must cope with the consequences.

Two caveats are in order to round out this attempt to convey even an approximate sense of "Western civil society in action." One concerns the consequences of the individual's various kinds of commitments and participation. Our guess is that in Western civil societies associations with voluntary entry and low exit-cost are the most numerous, though as we have noted, the term "voluntary" often requires qualifications and the low degree of internal constraint makes many organizations relatively ineffective. Such loosely formed organizations have two quite divergent effects. On one hand, they allow for an ease of entry and exit which probably facilitates the social life of Western civil societies by promoting the contacts leading to superficial or enduring relationships among people. But on the other, this very ease of entry and exit also engenders a lack of personal fulfillment or satisfaction (Durkheim's anomie) that may be the price of freedom and the cause of a widespread malaise in these same societies.

The second caveat concerns the limits of this discussion of civil society. Categories like family, organizations and the state suggest the existence of functioning institutions and imply a population encompassed by them, however passive an individual's involvement or participation may be. But children abandoned at birth have no family to which they below. Rules pertaining to school attendance do not encompass children who escape enrollment. Market relations do not involve the derelicts who sleep on the streets and pick over the garbage. Illegal immigrants slip through the border controls of the state. Trade unions do not represent the unorganized—if we disregard the curious anomaly of the French "Union of the Unemployed," which to our knowledge is unique in Western industrial societies. Examples could be multiplied. In other words, civil society comprises only a segment of the population. And even if the "excluded" are disregarded, it still remains true that civil society "includes" a large number of individuals who are members by birth but in name only. Through lack of education, handicaps or perpetual dependency they do not participate "sufficiently" to be more than passive recipients of services. Any use of the term "civil society" should be cognizant of all the people to whom the terms "civil" and "society" do not apply in the ordinary way.[29]

Both of these caveats not only concern the limits of the preceding discussion. They are at the same time a reason why these reflections are continued in the following essay with a consideration of the developing interrelations between state-institutions and the institutions of civil society. These institutional structures cannot stay put as long as the problems with which they deal remain unresolved. We do not assume that they can be resolved. We do assume that they can be alleviated.

CONCLUSION

In the context of the modern Western world the state has been defined as a country's capacity to act as a corporate whole, based on the monopolization of the legitimate use of force over a territory with clearly defined boundaries. The corresponding civil societies do not constitute corporate wholes in the same way. They consist rather of aggregates of families and private associations which "put into effect certain rules of particular interest to them in some special area of social and political life, albeit without seeking direct responsibility in public affairs," to use the definition cited above (p. 191). Modern western states are distinctive in that they incorporate civil societies in contrast to one-party dictatorships and many Third World countries, which do not. Within these limits it is analytically useful to consider the interaction between "states" and "civil societies," which do not constitute independent empirical domains.

To this summary we want to add one final theoretical reflection. In our discussion of civil society we shifted the emphasis from the short-term, individual decision-making of *homo œconomicus* to the long-term commitments of *homo sociologicus*. We argued that the individual's commitment to the phases of his life-cycle lays the foundation of civil society. Long-term commitments represent identity-forming investments of time and effort which entail a strong interest in safeguarding the value of these irreversible assets. We saw that such an interest prompts individuals to participate in organizations that can enhance the security of that value. At a more abstract level that interest also prompts an individual's identification with a constitutional order within which the safeguarding of life-time commitments is made legally secure. Such commitments are a strong inducement to look beyond immediate self-interest to the institutional safeguards which protect us against any sudden devaluation of those commitments. Early on, all this came under the umbrella of securing property ownership. More recently, the development of the state's regulatory functions have made it clear that states and civil societies together can provide a broad, collective foundation for the security of life-cycle commitments.

NOTES

1. Written together with John Bendix. A larger version of this essay appears in Reinhard Bendix, John Bendix and Normal Furniss, "Reflections on Modern Western States and Civil Societies," Richard G. Braungart (ed.), *Research in Political Sociology*. Volume 3. Greenwich, CT: JAI Press, Inc., 1987. Copyright 1987 by JAI Press, Inc. Reprinted by permission.
2. Kenneth Dyson, *The State Tradition in Western Europe* (New York: Oxford University Press, 1980), 228-30.
3. Theda Skocpol, "Bringing the State Back In," *Items* (Social Science Research Council), vol. 36, Nos. 1/2 (June 1982), 1-2.
4. Michael Mann, "The Autonomous Power of the State," *European Journal of Sociology*, XXV (1984), 185-213. There can be no mistake that this is the author's meaning, since he has published "State and Society, 1130-1815: An Analysis of English State Finance," in Maurice Zeitlin (ed.), *Political Power and Social Theory* (A Research Annual), Vol. 1 (Greenwich, Conn.: JAI Press, 1980), 165-208. The author, the editor and Professor Skocpol omit mention of the fact that reputable scholars question the suitability of applying the concept "state" to medieval society. Cf. the various contributions in Ernst-Wolfgang Böckenförde, ed., *Staat und Gesellschaft* (Darmstadt: Wissenschaftliche Buchgesellschaft, 1976), passim.
5. The sentence quoted is found in Metin Heper, "The State and Public Bureaucracies: A Comparative and Historical Perspective," *Comparative Studies in Society and History*, Vol. 27 (January 1985), 96.
6. Skocpol emphasizes the novelty of the idea of state autonomy in her book *States and Social Revolutions* (New York: Cambridge University Press, 1979), 24-33. Her sense of novelty was evidently shared by the officers of the Social Science Research Council, who sponsored a conference on the State and published the report on it, as quoted in footnote 3, without reference to their own previous publication by Hugh Aitken, ed., *The State and Economic Growth* (New York: Social Science Research Council, 1952). On the many meanings of the word "civil" see the relevant articles in the various Oxford dictionaries.
7. Max Weber, *Economy and Society* (tr. and ed. by Guenther Roth and Claus Wittich; New York: The Bedminster Press, 1968), I, 56.
8. Like other key terms, the word state is not free of partisanship, unless special care is taken. Because it is part of common speech, its technical use must be defined, before it can be freed of conflicting political aspirations. These aspirations are due to such features of the modern Western state as orderly and regular procedures governing the succession to office, lawmaking and adjudication, more or less impersonal and efficient administration, and others. Any student of Western civilization knows that such institutions were created over long periods and that even today they fall short of their highest potential. Outside the countries of Western civilization, its history and cultural presuppositions are ignored, while certain outward features like constitutions, legal codes, administrative structures and, of course, much technical hardware are adopted more or less piecemeal. The conse-

quences of such adoption are frequently contrary to the hopes associated with it. In that context the term "state" is replete with frustrated aspirations, while "*civil society*" has no clear meaning. For a related analysis of "modernization without achieving modernity," cf. Reinhard Bendix, "Tradition and Modernity Reconsidered," reprinted as Chapter 12 in this volume.

9. Ernest Barker, *The Development of Public Services in Western Europe* (New York: Oxford University Press, 1944), 4-5.
10. Pierre Goubert, *Louis XIV and Twenty Million Frenchmen* (New York: Random House, Vintage Books, 1970), 52.
11. Weber, op. cit., I, 54.
12. Alessandro Passerin d'Entreves, *The Notion of the State* (London: Oxford University Press, 1967).
13. Weber, *op. cit.*, I, 31.
14. We prefer the older term "civil society" to the more familiar Marxist term "bourgeois society," though in his early writings Marx still used that earlier term, as Hegel had done. It is an open question whether the groups involved are bourgeois, whenever a Western society impinges on the state, and even if they are bourgeois, what that reference to social class implies. The impact of society on the state is the problem and the answer to a question should not be prejudged by the term employed.
15. *Oxford English Dictionary* (1933), II, 446 for the source of the preceding definitions and the quotation from Blackstone cited in the text below.
16. Quoted in Reinhart Koselleck, "Interesse," in Otto Brunner, Werner Conze, Reinhart Koselleck, eds., *Geschichtliche Grundbegriffe* (Stuttgart: Klett-Cotta, 1982), III, 346.
17. Jean-Jacques Rousseau, *The Social Contract* (New York: Hafner Publishing Company, 1957), 26-27. A defense of Rousseau against the opposition to associations which his disciples attributed to him, is contained in Maure L. Goldschmidt, "Rousseau on Intermediate Associations," in Roland Pennock and John Chapman, eds., *Voluntary Associations* (Nomos XI; New York: Atherton Press, 1960), 119-37.
18. La Chalotais as quoted in Reinhard Bendix, *Nation-Building and Citizenship* (2nd ed.; Berkeley, University of California Press, 1977), 110.
19. Clermont-Tonnere as quoted in Jacob Katz, "A State Within a State," *Emancipation and Assimilation* (Westmead: Gregg International Publishers, 1972), 67.
20. Le Chapelier as quoted in Bendix, *op. cit.*, 101-102.
21. Adam Smith, *The Wealth of Nations* (Everyman's Library; New York: Dutton, 1964), II, 230-32.
22. *The Federalist* (New York: The Modern Library, 1937), 54.
23. Sigmund Freud, *Three Essays on the Theory of Sexuality* (London: Imago Publishing Co. Ltd., 1949), 103.
24. See Hans-Josef Varain, "Verbände," in Hermann Kunst and Siegfried Grundmann, eds., *Evangelisches Staatslexikon* (Stuttgart: Kreuz Verlag, 1966), p. 2322. Examples of the violation of the private/public distinction become notorious from time to time, because they violate basic norms. In the late 1970s the Council of the City of Berkeley, California, undertook to formulate a public policy position towards China, nominally on behalf of the United States. On the other hand, in the early 1980s the French-Canadian separatist leader of Quebec, J. Levecque, paid an "official" visit to the Jura Canton of Switzerland, which is predominantly French and which had recently won separate cantonal status within

Switzerland. Neither case was more than a curious episode; both illustrate, albeit indirectly, the monopolization of legitimate force by the state, and its occasional disregard by subnational representatives.

25. Albert O. Hirschman, *Exit, Voice and Loyalty: Responses to Decline in Firms, Organizations and States* (Cambridge: Harvard University Press, 1970), 1.
26. Ibid., Chapter 7.
27. Ibid., 96. In this passage Hirschman adds, ''as well as such more modern inventions as the gang and the totalitarian party; but this seems a lapse on his part since these latter are not ''traditional'' by his own admission. Hence the high price for exit they exact should be treated separately.
28. Edmund Burke, *Reflections on the Revolution in France* (Gateway editions; Chicago: Henry Regnery, 1955), 139-40. Originally published in 1790.
29. For an illustration of what happens with some of these people, see Ken Auletta, *The Underclass* (New York: Random House, 1982), xvi.

9

CHANGING PATTERNS OF AUTHORITY IN RELATION TO INDUSTRIALIZATION AND SOCIAL PROTEST

Introductory Note

The following essay originates in an introduction to the second edition of my book *Work and Authority in Industry* (1974), published initially in 1956. I recounted how I had come to conceive of this comparative, socio-historical study, and went on to relate *Work and Authority* to materials covered in *Nation-Building and Citizenship* (1964). Both studies could be integrated in a framework of changing relations between state and civil society since the French Revolution, though I did not use the terms at the time. Adapting these materials for present purposes, I have highlighted how Weber's types of domination and the social protest incident to Western European industrialization fit in with changing relations between modern Western states and their civil societies. Since this essay concludes Parts One and Two, I recapitulate briefly the rationale of the sequence of essays presented here. Though these essays were written on different occasions in response to one concern or another, I think they do add up in a reasonably coherent way.

All my theoretical explorations have begun with an attempt to "position myself" in the world in which I live. Every social scientist is first of all a person living in a society which sustains his desire to understand that society. From this I derive my sense of obligation to account, to myself and to my readers, for the vantage point from which I start.

I am *not* suggesting that the conditions of my knowledge, or the conditions of anyone else's knowledge, either validate or invalidate what is being stated, theoretically or empirically. I *am* saying that social knowledge is impermanent and many-sided. Our interest in what is worth knowing changes. Past findings, even if true, lose their relevance or pertinence for later generations; and in complex societies we find a plurality of images at any one time, not only as time passes. Theorizing about man and society proceeds along different tracks, guided by different senses of "the real." My sense of "the real" has led me to distrust unitary or systemic views of man and society for the reasons I have indicated in the preceding essays. These reasons must commend themselves on their own ground. How I have come to see our social world in this way is not germane to an assessment of their merit and validity, though I examine this biographical dimension elsewhere.[1]

Instead of a systemic view of man and society I have proposed a dualistic one, though there is nothing unique or sacrosanct about the number two. Dualistic views are found in many civilizations, not only in the Western tradition. Also, classifications of more than two elements may be found convenient, as for example in Max Weber's tripartite division of domination or the psychologist's distinction among man's cognitive, evaluative and emotive faculties. Fourfold distinctions are also common as in our distinction between conditions of entry and exit in voluntary associations. Other multiples of two recur as well. The preceding essays have employed many dualistic distinctions, as in elites and masses, interdependence through exchange or association or through the exercise of authority which comes down to state vs. civil society, doctrine as contrasted with conduct, or routinization (convention) vs. breakthrough.[2] The utility of such contrasts needs to be tested in each case and depends in good part on the purpose of inquiry. In the present case it is appropriate to conclude these theoretical explorations with an attempt to get a bit closer to the evidence which has been of primary interest to me, namely the study of social change and in particular the transformation of Western societies in the course of industrialization.

TYPES OF AUTHORITY

This discussion of the transformation of Western societies starts from the common observation that modern states are distinguished from civil societies by their enduring capacity to act for the polity as a whole. But although this capacity has endured at least since the French revolution, its formal organization has changed. To study these changes I have found it useful to elaborate upon Max Weber's analysis of *Herrschaft*, or domination, while bearing in mind the "quid-pro-quo" basis of his three types to which I referred in chapter seven.

Weber related authority or "the probability that commands will be obeyed by a given group of persons" to administrators, the people, types of legitimation and the limitations implicit in each type of rule. All the elements tabulated in Table 1 are found in some part of his discussion, but it is helpful to set them out in a more schematic form than he did. Weber emphasized that his three types of charismatic, traditional, and legal domination are "ultimate principles" in the sense that all empirical variations can be reduced to these three types. On the other hand, specific historical cases are bound to be admixtures, often combining elements from each of the three types.[4] In practice it is difficult to keep the general and the specific in proper balance and Weber is not always helpful on this point. For example, by including administrative structures, he moves his general types of domination close to historical configurations like feudalism, even though the discussion of legitimation remains at a very abstract level. It is more useful to consider this abstract level first by concentrating on the meaning of legitimation (Columns 1, 4, and 5) and then attempt an historical typology proper (see Section III).[5]

Reading from left to right, I have chosen the phrase "personal authority" to designate the first type. This is an all-encompassing term which includes personal leadership as well as the special case of a leader with charismatic appeal. Both ordinary and charismatic leaders typically assemble confidants or disciples around them who will assist them in their mission. The main point here is that these assistants are tied to their leader by a shared belief in his mission as well as by personal loyalty. In addition, leaders have a following of true believers and echoes of that commitment reverberate at least to some extent among the population at large. This much is straightforward. The legitimation of authority and its related limits are more complex. Legitimation is always based upon a belief shared by rulers, their "staff" and the people subject to authority. An order founded upon personal authority involves the conviction that a leader possesses

> a certain quality . . . by virtue of which he is set apart from ordinary men and treated as endowed with supernatural, superhuman, or at least specifically exceptional powers or qualities. These [powers or qualities] . . . are regarded as of divine origin or as exemplary, and on the basis of them the individual concerned is treated as a 'leader.'[6]

The circularity of this definition is related to the interaction between the leader and his confidants and followers. For the leader's claim to exceptional powers or qualities is inevitably modified in practice, however unconditionally he construes the claim in theory. Similarly, the followers are ever seeking for some sign or symbol of those special qualities, however unconditionally they have committed themselves to a duty of obedience in theory. Personal authority emerges through the problematic relations between leaders and followers, which are marked by such opposite and ambivalent imperatives of theory and practice. Joseph Schumpeter's analysis of entrepreneurial leadership makes plain that the concept has its place in studies of economic development.

Traditional authority is more directly relevant to an understanding of two centuries of industrialization. Weber's concept was formulated largely from the standpoint of the ruling strata in medieval European society. There, authority was believed in "by virtue of the sanctity of age-old rules" *and* by virtue of the master's traditional status-prerogative which enjoined personal obedience on his subjects and allowed him to use his discretion (to act at pleasure, to bestow his grace). Such authority was exercised directly through household servants and retainers (patrimonialism, family enterprises) and indirectly through vassals who might emerge from the ranks of personal retain-

TABLE 1
Types of Domination

	1 Authority	2 Staff	3 People	4 Legitimation*	5 Limitation
I	Personal (including charismatic)	Confidants, Disciples	Followers	Personal gift (inc. Divine inspiration, destiny, etc.)	Followers demand proof of gift (e.g. miracles)
II	Traditional	Household servants, retainers, vassals, etc.	Subjects	Custom sanctioning (a) ancient usage (b) ruler's perogative	Traditional rights associated with an established rank-order of society
III	Legal	Bureaucrats	Citizens	Constitution and enacted law; equality under the law	Public reactions (including abstract ideals of natural law)

*Legitimation refers to "claims of legitimacy" on the part of the rulers and limitation to "claims for quid pro quo" on the part of the ruled. The two claims are antithetical and the outcome of the interaction is uncertain. Terms like "legitimacy" or "social contract" are avoided, because they are too definitive and lend themselves to the fallacy of misplaced correctness.

ers and who remained tied to the ruler through contract and personal loyalty (feudalism, sub-contracting). In this setting, the legitimation of rule also depends upon the interaction between a ruler, those who help him govern the realm, and the subject population. Ordinary people were recognized to be in an inferior position and were excluded from all political participation, but nevertheless custom sanctioned some of their claims. Under traditional authority, rulers and subjects must come to terms with opposite and frequently conflicting imperatives. As rightful incumbents, rulers insist on their time-honored prerogatives, but such insistence may lead to "too many" transgressions of ancient usage and thus jeopardize the claim to legitimacy. In the ideal case, the ruler's prerogative, though sanctioned by tradition, is limited by the usages and rights which are also sanctioned by tradition. Conversely, subjects insist on their traditional rights, but too much insistence verges on disloyalty and treason. It was in this context that the early recruits to an industrial work-force justified rioting by an appeal to their "ancient rights" which were denied them by their employers under the pressures of industrialization.

Thirdly, legal authority. The concept is related directly to individual ownership of property and the entrepreneurship of early industrialization. Under legal authority, all persons are equal before the abstract rules of that authority. That is, each person is the equal of every other solely in his legal capacity, of which the law takes cognizance. The great asset of this approach lies in the fact that every official can exercise the authority of office only on the basis of formally legal commands.

> The typical person in authority, the 'superior,' is himself subject to an impersonal order by orienting his actions to it in his own dispositions and commands. (This is true not only for persons exercising legal authority who are in the usual sense 'officials,' but, for instance, for the elected president of a state.)[7]

Under a system of rules, appointed officials rather than disciples, servants or retainers are charged with the task of implementation, while the people are no longer followers or subjects, but citizens who possess formal rights of participation. Legitimation of legal authority resides in the constitution which contains the basic authentication of the law-making process and in the laws and regulations which are the product of that process. Formally, all citizens became equal before the law, as voters who have the right to elect representatives and as individuals who possess the same formal rights as everyone else. These formal rights were meaningful symbols of emancipation as long as the laws of the ancient regime protected privileges and the inherited inequalities of the traditional status-order. But when these privileges and inequalities decline, formal equality before the law revealed itself as a claim that benefited those best able to make use of it, and that excluded the vast majority of the disadvantaged. The great liability of this approach lies in the fact that in his civic, economic and social capacities the individual is left to fend for himself. The legitimation of legal authority therefore found its limits wherever public reactions focused on the discrepancies between formal equality and substantive inequality. For example, in England, entrepreneurial ideologies were developed to cope with both, the denial of traditional rights and the conflicts between property-interests and the claims of those disadvantaged by industrialization.

After publishing *Work and Authority* in 1956 I studied Max Weber's work more intensively and came to recognize that my own materials had gone beyond those encompassed by his types of domination. The analysis of entrepreneurial ideologies in eighteenth and nineteenth century Russia raised some questions about the appropriateness of "traditional authority." Russian history seemed to allow for little differentiation between "ancient usage" and the "ruler's prerogative" so that there was little room for the development of "traditional rights" which could limit the latter. Weber had discussed this "variant" and had allowed for it by such categories as "patrimonialism" and "Sultanism." But if this permitted the inclusion of the Russian "case" under traditional authority broadly interpreted, the facts of Soviet rule pose more difficult problems of interpretation, which I consider in Chapter 10 and Vol. 2, Chapter 15.[8] At this point I turn to a reinterpretation of social protest in the era of industrialization.

SOCIAL PROTEST RECONSIDERED

Work and Authority in Industry put special emphasis upon the civic position of the work-force and this issue is of continuing interest wherever industrialization is initiated.

> Industrialization in its early phase poses a very general problem. It is accompanied by the creation of a nonagricultural work force which is usually forced to bear the consequences of great social and economic dislocations. These dislocations terminate the traditional subordination of the 'lower classes' in the preindustrial society. Though this development varies considerably with the relative speed and with the social setting of industrialization, its result is that the 'lower classes' are deprived of their recognized, if subordinate, place in society. A major problem facing all societies undergoing industrialization is the civic integration of the newly created work force.[9]

Tocqueville had recognized that in the interval between an accepted system of inequality and a new system of equality "no one knows exactly what he is or what he may be or what he ought to be." In such a setting masters and servants become ill-natured and intractable. The lines that divide right from might have become confused and authority is indistinguishable from oppression. Society is undergoing a revolutionary upheaval in which "the reins of domestic government dangle between [masters and servants] to be snatched at by one or the other."[10]

In *Work and Authority* I discussed the role which the English and Russian ruling classes had played in coping with the problem of political mobilization. A comparative study of the "ideologies of management in the course of industrialization" necessarily dealt with the approach of different ruling classes to the disruption of traditional subordination among the people. But subsequently, my interest shifted to the other side of the coin, namely the civic integration of the newly emerging industrial work-force or, failing that, the cumulation of that revolutionary potential which Tocqueville had discerned in the spread of equalitarian ideas.

Then as now, it seemed to me useful to combine Tocqueville's insight with that of Marx, though in a way that was not fully compatible with either. Tocqueville saw that the transition from the old inequality to a new equality generated a revolutionary potential. He did not identify that potential with any particular group, but rather with the disturbance of social relations by equalitarian claims. And he emphasized strongly that the individualism associated with conflicting expectations would diminish social solidarity and endlessly multiply individual demands for governmental assistance. An unprecedented concentration of governmental power would be the outcome. On the other hand, Marx emphasized the formation of groups under the impact of industrialization and their growth of class-consciousness. Where Tocqueville saw social relations disturbed by equalitarian claims, Marx saw these claims denied by economic exploitation, which was the basis for all other forms of exploitation. Marx also believed that workers protested their lack of social recognition. But he dismissed all claims to traditional rights as "false consciousness" and staked everything upon a revolutionary overthrow which would recreate on a collective level that sense of self in productive work which capitalist exploitation had destroyed.

My own initial conclusion was that

> industrialization tends to create a revolutionary potential as a consequence of the problems engendered in the early phase of industrialization. The resolution of these problems may take a long time. Partial resolutions of the problem only lead to partial dissipations of the revolutionary potential. . . . In such cases the unresolved problems of the early phase linger on long after economic enterprises have been well developed. The revolutionary potential of the proletariat will disappear, on the other hand, where this work force is more or less rapidly reincorporated in the national community. . . . Societies differ in this capacity and willingness to accord civic recognition to an 'internal proletariat' (Toynbee).[11]

In this approach I sided with Tocqueville in an emphasis on the civic problem of self-respect arising from the disruption of a traditional order. I also followed him in seeing "revolution" not as an *event* that had occurred once and for all (or would occur again in the future), but as an enduring condition of change (which he attributed to the failure of institution-building in France based on the idea of equality.) At the same time, I sided with Marx in seeing the importance of industrialization, of class-formation and colonialism as the conditions which continually engendered unrest and protest against social and economic injustice. By combining these two perspectives one might be able to bring into one coherent account the possibility of civic integration (as in England), the phenomenon of partial integration (as in Germany and France), the case of Russia where the impact of industrialization and of Western ideas had engendered a cumulation of revolutionary energies, and even the protest movements in colonial countries which had suffered their own long-standing disruption of traditional social orders and won opportunities for independence through the mounting disarray of the colonizing powers.

Thoughts along these lines suggested themselves through a growing impatience with two prevalent intellectual tendencies, the reductionist elimination of political life and the generalization of "capitalism" as the master-cause of change in the last five hundred years. Some sociologists and political scientists share with classical Marxism the belief that political behavior is explained by the social status of the individuals and groups involved. Certainly, economic interest and social experience often help to make political behavior more intelligible. "But by analyzing the social determinants of political behavior we should not inadvertently explain away the very facts of political life."[12] In this respect Tocqueville saw farther than Marx although he had none of Marx's theoretical grasp. Tocqueville recognized the give and take of human interaction as the foundation of institutions. Accordingly, he gave full attention to the sentiments and opinions of people, which Marx tended to dismiss as "false consciousness" that would be "eliminated" by the historical movement. Marx was too ready to extrapolate from observed tendencies of early industrialization—no doubt out of a desire (based on philosophical constructions) to locate an historical force for a final solution of human ills. But if there are no final solutions (and Marx was inconsistent in implying that there were), then one is forced to be more patient with the proximate solutions that are available through more or less enduring institutional structures.

At the same time, it does not make good sense to attribute all changes of the last four or five centuries to "capitalism." "Old societies" have been disrupted more or less coercively as European commercialism and Christian missionary activity, the emergence and demonstration effects of industrial economies, and finally the ideals of the French revolution have had successive repercussions in all parts of the world. This revolutionary process began with the first empires built by Portugal and Spain in the late fifteenth century, a process which Marx aptly described as "primitive accumulation." With the decolonization of most African and Asian societies that process is entering its final phase only since World War II. So conceived, the main locus of this protracted revolutionizing process is shifted away from the conflicts endemic to "capitalism" and towards conflicts which have arisen wherever commerce, industry, scientific and technical discoveries as well as general ideals have overturned established social relations and political structures. "Capitalism" is merely one of several sources of disruption, among other reasons because the ideal of equality has religious roots that antedate modern economic developments. In this way, attention can be focused on a revolutionary process since the sixteenth century in which peasant uprisings and workers' protests are of a piece with nationalist movements and the vanguard-role of intellectuals. These protean movements are noteworthy less for their group- or class-characteristics than as varied reactions to having lost one's place in an established order of things and hence of seeking, often desperately, for a new basis of personal and collective self-respect. Such sentiments are not defined solely by a person's relations to the work-process and the use of his faculties in that process. They are defined, rather, by the network of interactions with significant others in which a man's occupational role is an important source of identity, but only one of many.

With these modifications it becomes possible to encompass two movements of thought and action—the quest for citizenship and nationalism—which did not have a place either in Tocqueville's scheme or in Marx's. In *Nation-Building and Citizenship* I followed the interpretation of citizenship which T.H. Marshall developed for England. Marshall had distinguished between civil, political and social rights. Civil rights refer to the principal concerns of the French revolution: liberty of person, freedom of speech, thought and faith, the right to own property and conclude valid contracts, and the right to justice. Political rights involve the franchise and an access to public office unrestricted by particularistic legal disabilities (such as titles, birth, inheritance, etc.). In turn, social rights refer to minimum-standards of security and welfare as well as to minimum-opportunities of education.[13] Marshall analyzed the development of these rights in successive stages of English history from the eighteenth to the twentieth centuries. My own treatment examined the right of association (a civil right), the right to an elementary education (a social right), the franchise and secret balloting (political rights) on a comparative basis for several Western European countries.[14] Some of these rights were granted only in response to cumulative political pressure, others resulted from preventive governmental reforms. And some rights were indistinguishable from duties: the right to an elementary education also involves the duty to attend school, and under social security the rights to benefits are inseparable from the obligation to register and make contributory payments. Thus, the extension of the rights of citizenship is a complex process which belies the simplified image of rights granted solely in response to protests against the denial of rights.

It seems possible to combine these perspectives with an analysis of nationalism. The extension of citizenship always involves claims for participation and/or benefits. Implicitly at least, these claims are demands for recognition by the society at large. Those previously excluded claim a right to be heard and those who suffer deprivation claim a right to a minimum level of existence which alone would make their participation possible. Such claims are typically addressed to the ruling institutions of society, thus reflecting an aspiration to belong to the national society as a going concern. Fundamentally, this is a nationalist motivation which has prompted labor movements to identify themselves with "their country" at crucial points in the history of working classes in industrial societies. Only where this drive to achieve recognition is frustrated for too long, i.e., where "the nation" does not hold out the promise of civic integration, there demands will arise for a restructuring of society so that a proper recognition or integration can be achieved. So conceived, the freedom or independence movements in colonial countries are of a piece with the agitation of peasants and workers in the colonizing countries, for in both cases it is a quest for civic recognition or for a society in which such recognition becomes possible.

STATES AND SOCIETIES RECONSIDERED

These perspectives on social protest and nationalism during the nineteenth century have suggested lines of inquiry with which I am concerned today. I shall indicate how *Work and Authority* together with its sequel *Nation-Building* provide a framework of interpretation for my current studies.

Agitation for extension of the rights of citizenship presupposes the existence of a nation-state, i.e. an institutional structure in which major functions of governmental authority are centralized while all adult citizens are *individual* bearers of rights and duties. Broadly speaking, the movements of social protest and nationalism seem to fall into two phases. In their early stages they call forth passionate commitment to high ideals which are typically articulated by intellectuals. The intensity of commitment and articulation is concomitant with the generalization of a grievance, be it foreign occupation, economic exploitation, or the denial of political and social rights.[15] But passionate commitment moves on to other goals once independence is won, exploitation alleviated, or the previous denial of rights terminated by appropriate constitutional or legal changes. As long as the right to vote was restricted, those who were denied that right felt that exclusion branded them as second-class citizens. But once full citizenship is achieved, the right to vote appears as a matter of course and the satisfactions derived from its exercise seem minimal.

When the right to vote is taken for granted, nothing can quite recapture that passionate fellow-feeling which had united those who had joined in the movement to extend the suffrage. In much the same way, nationalist movements are capable of arousing paroxysms of fraternal enthusiasm. But once the nation-state is established, this sense of community becomes for many a matter of routine and consensus at the national level acquires an impersonal quality which does not satisfy the craving for fraternity.[16] This is one reason why the issue of alienation has accompanied the whole development of the nation-state since its inception in the eighteenth century.

Another reason for the persistence of this issue is the decline of solidarity in secondary groups. Tocqueville was among the most discerning in emphasizing that centralization of government was accompanied by the decline of estate-society with its hierarchy of ranks and hence by the social isolation of the individual citizen. And he related the two by showing that this social isolation would prompt the individual in his need to turn to the government for help and hence enhance its centralization of power still further.

> As in periods of equality no man is compelled to lend his assistance to his fellow men, and none has any right to expect much support from them, everyone is at once independent and powerless. These two conditions, which must never be either separately considered or confounded together, inspire the citizen of a democratic country with very contrary propensities. His independence fills him with self-reliance and pride among his equals; his debility makes him feel from time to time the want of some outward assistance, which he cannot expect from any of them, because they are all impotent and unsympathizing.

And in a footnote to this passage Tocqueville analyzes the mechanism involved somewhat further:

> It frequently happens that the members of the community promote the influence of the central power without intending to . . . There is always a multitude of men engaged in difficult or novel undertakings, which they follow by themselves without shackling themselves to their fellows. Such persons will admit, as a general principle, that the public authority ought not to interfere in private concerns; but, by an exception to that rule, each of them craves its assistance in the particular concern on which he is engaged and seeks to draw upon the influence of the government for his own benefit, although he would restrict it on all other occasions. If a large number of men applies this particular exception to a great variety of different purposes, the sphere of the central power extends itself imperceptibly in all directions, although everyone wishes it to be circumscribed.[17]

From the perspective of the 1830s, Tocqueville perceived individualism in this literal fashion, but in other contexts he emphasized the principle of voluntary association, especially among Americans in contrast to Frenchmen. His prescription was that men must cultivate the "art of associating together" where the equality of conditions is increased, i.e. where a man is no longer *"compelled* to lend his assistance to his fellow man" and no longer has "any *right* to expect much support from them."[18] The individual suffers from social isolation where he is no longer obliged to belong to those "mutual aid" associations of an estate society which protected his rights only if he fulfilled his duties. No association can recapture the intense reciprocity of rights and duties that was peculiar to these corporate jurisdictions.

But there is a lacuna in Tocqueville's approach. He failed to see that men would associate together not just for the "vast multitude of lesser undertakings" performed every day, but specifically for the purpose of enlisting governmental assistance in the advancement of their major economic interests. That is to say, he *did not connect* the two tendencies he observed: the growth of voluntary associations and the "craving for governmental assistance."[19] When these two tendencies are combined (as is characteristic of the advanced industrial societies in the West), one can discern *historical types* of authority that should be distinguished as clearly as may be from Weber's *ideal types* (or universal principles) discussed previously.

In making this point I tread on uncertain ground, because terminology in this field is undeveloped, the tendencies referred to point to the future as well as the past, and the distinction between historical and ideal types is difficult to handle properly. The last point requires special emphasis. Naturally, Weber drew on his own background in proposing his tripartite typology. "Charisma" or the "gift of grace" derives from the Christian tradition; "tradition" evokes connotations of European feudalism; and "legality" is a specifically Occidental phenomenon. But in reaching for a higher level of abstraction, Weber's intention was clearly to divest these terms of as much of their historical peculiarity as possible and still retain a vocabulary that could be understood. Certainly, personal (including charismatic) authority occurs outside the Christian context. Traditional authority is not confined to the usages of European feudalism (Weber himself enumerated a three-fold classification of feudalisms with seven sub-types). And legal authority or the adjudication of disputes in accordance with rules acknowledged as binding prior to the dispute can be found in all parts of the world. Until a more comprehensive and less culture-bound terminology becomes available, it will be well to retain this one, aware of its limitations and of the fact that such universal principles are programs of research rather than ready-to-use labels which are somehow self-explanatory.

Weber himself was aware that the *political foundations* of legal authority were changing in his lifetime and they have changed further since his day. To bring these changes into focus it is best to treat legal domination as an aspect of the nation-state and then subdivide it in terms of transformations of the political structure.[20] The nation-state has reached its full development only since the French revolution. It is best to define the state in terms of this modern type,

> ... but at the same time in terms which abstract from the values of the present day, since these are particularly subject to change. The primary formal characteristic of the modern state are as follows: It possesses an administrative and legal order subject to change by legislation, to which the organized activities of the administrative staff, which are also controlled by regulations, are oriented. This system of order claims binding authority, not only over the members of the state, the citizens, most of whom have obtained membership by birth, but also to a very large extent over all action taking place in the area of its jurisdiction. It is thus a compulsory organization with a territorial basis. Furthermore, today, the use of force is regarded as legitimate only so far as it is either permitted by the state or prescribed by it ... The claim of the modern state to monopolize the use of force is as essential to it as its character of compulsory jurisdiction and of continuous operation.[21]

In this classification, Weber's ideal type of legal domination is subdivided into two, roughly successive phases and thus brought closer to the historical configurations as we know them. (The second phase is subdivided further under b1 and b2 because these subordinate types exist concurrently and the distinction between them is a matter of emphasis in different sectors of modern Western societies.)

This schema of legal domination as an *historical* type can be elaborated, depending on different purposes of analysis and on further developments. The terms used are non-technical, but "representation," "referendum," and "plebiscite" require a special comment. ("Pillarization" is explained below.) As used here, representation refers to delegates (or agents) who participate in public decision-making on behalf of a constituency of voters, interest-groups, etc. Referendum refers to the direct vote on a public issue by all qualified voters. In practice, both principles become attenuated. Delegates interpose their judgment of what is best for their constituency, their own political survival, and the community at large, except when they are bound by an imperative mandate. And referenda on public issues are often supplemented or replaced by plebiscites, i.e. by appeals to consent through acclamation or by the tacit assumption that such acclamation is forthcoming or will not be withheld. The three concepts remain distinct in that representation always interposes an interpreting agent between public sentiments and governmental decision-making, referenda always provide the public with a choice, while plebiscites always involve the direct acclamation of a public act by the people at large. As an ideal type, legal domination presupposes *some* balance between the representation of interests, choice by referenda, and rule by acclamation. Thus, under traditional-legal authority, representation by notables claims to speak in the best interest of the people. Under legal authority, the

TABLE 2
Legal Types of Domination in Nation-States

1 Ratification of Authority	2 Politics	3 Staff	4 People	5 Legitimation	6 Limitation
a. Traditional-legal (emphasis on representation as a perogative)	Notables as the natural leaders of the community	Bureaucrats often recruited from privileged strata	First and Second-class citizens	Enacted law; lower-class status retains legal liabilities	Public reactions under close surveillance
b1. Legal (emphasis on balance between representation, referendum, and plebiscite)	Mass parties organize the electorate; at the same time the representation of "organized interests" develops	Bureaucrats (recruited under formal merit system)	Citizens organized for mass participation in election campaigns *minus* the unaffiliated	Constitution and enacted law; formal equality before the law	Public reactions ranging from individual complaints to mass demonstrations; appeals range from private interests to abstract ideals of natural law
b2. Pluralist (emphasis on mixture of representation, referendum and plebiscite, but with more stress on representation)	Mass parties organize the electorate at the same time "pillarization," based on interest- and affinity-groups plays an increased role in public decision-making	Bureaucrats / / Group representatives	Citizens organized segmentally *minus* the unorganized	Constitution amd enacted law; wide-spread consultation with organized interests; co-optation of private organization for quasi-public functions	Same as under b1, but special importance of organized interests in decision-making, e.g., "veto-groups" (Riesman)

interposition of judgments by designated representatives is balanced at several levels by opportunities for the direct expression of public sentiment. And under pluralist authority, decision-making by representatives (if not in legislatures, then through interest-groups) gains at the expense of plebiscitary participation. Still, for legal domination to endure some balance is needed if decision-making is to combine informed judgments with the direct impact of public demands.[22]

The changes of legal domination (from a to b1 and b2) are relatively uncomplicated, at least in outline. During the French Revolution, the debates in the constitutional assembly made clear that equality before the law did not mean equality of political participation. Despite some moves towards universal suffrage, the franchise remained tied to property ownership as it did throughout the nineteenth century in most Western countries. (The United States is an exception in this respect.) Also, balloting was public rather than secret for varying lengths of time so that in practice voting was greatly affected by the wishes of notables who dominated the community, both socially and economically. In practice, politics remained the preserve of an elite, public officials were often recruited from the higher social strata, and only those who were in a position to participate actively in public affairs could be considered first-class citizens.

Much of this changed with the extension of the franchise and the introduction of the secret ballot. Political parties developed in response to the need for organizing the people in periodic election campaigns. As a consequence, political participation spread beyond the circle of notables. Some could combine a public career with their type of work (especially lawyers); others managed to live "off" politics rather than "for" it, as Weber put the distinction between plebeian and aristocratic politicians. And where active politics recruited men from many social strata, the demand for equal access to public employment rose apace. Thus, civil service reform is directly related to the demand for equal opportunity that arose with widespread political participation. If no invidious distinctions were to be made concerning the right to vote, then no rationale remained concerning exclusion from public service—except educational qualifications related to the performance of duties in office. But as indicated earlier, the extension of the franchise (and of access to public office) made these political rights appear less attractive than they had been as long as they were denied. And the work of political parties to mobilize the public for mass participation found its limits in the lack of interest among those who remain unaffiliated despite efforts to organize them.

In the advanced industrial societies of the West the politics of mass parties continues to the present and I see no reason to anticipate changes in this respect. Indeed, there is evidence that some communist parties (such as those of

France and Italy) seek to accommodate themselves in the interest of becoming acceptable partners in coalition governments. But within this framework of mass-politics another tendency is discernible, which Dutch sociologists have called *verzuiling*, or pillarization.

> The phenomenon of *verzuiling* is by no means confined to politics. Each denominational bloc has set up a whole array of organizations encompassing practically every sphere of social life. Schools and universities, radio and television corporations, trade unions, health and welfare agencies, sport associations, and so on, all fit into the *zuilen* system. . . . The final aim of the confessional blocs can perhaps be described best as 'segmented integration': they aspire to participate in all national decision-making and to benefit fully from all national facilities while at the same time maintaining internal unity and cohesion.[23]

This segmentation of the public has developed nowhere as far as it has in Holland, but elements of this process are discernible in many societies. Early on, the German Social Democratic Party responded to its ostracism under Bismarck by a proliferation of associations which allowed the individual member to pass from the cradle to the grave under party-sponsorship. Wherever the Catholic Church or fundamentalist Protestant denominations have retained their hold on the faithful, they have developed similar affiliated organizations. Likewise, political parties, trade unions, business firms and others have frequently sponsored organizations providing a mixture of sociability, services and benefits to which members or employees (and their families) have exclusive access. At still other levels, organizations farm out their own work to other organizations, whether business firms hire organizations to manufacture parts, do accounting and public relations, etc., or governments contract for public work to be carried out by what one writer has called "quasi non-governmental organizations."

In tendencies of this kind, Tocqueville's two principles of individualism and voluntary association appear to be joined. Associations are formed (by individuals or organizations) on the basis of common interests or common affinities to provide services, obtain benefits and participate in decision-making processes. But Tocqueville's individualism has been left behind by a development through which the representatives of organized interests come to work in close symbiosis with each other and with government officials.[24] For some sections of the public this development has gone so far that the segmental organization of citizens (in interest- or affinity-groups) is on a par with, or even exceeds, the importance of political parties. Political parties attain their peak activity during election years, interest organizations operate on a continuous basis. But the non-voter may also be the non-joiner, thus compounding the disabilities of those who are left behind in an organizationally managed society. The question for the future is how in such a society common public inter-

ests can be made to prevail over the purposes of "organized interests."
Nineteenth-century liberalism and socialism assumed that technological advance and increased productivity would resolve short-run conflicts between
individual and public interests. Probably, this assumption was always doubtful, but in the twentieth century it has become quite unrealistic. And where the
repercussions of technological advance and increased productivity are de-
leterious or may become so, a system of legal authority based on individualistic premises may be severely strained.[25]

The use of atomic bombs to end World War II and the subsequent counter-
cultural agitation of the 1960s raised apprehensions which affected the American belief in progress and with it the trust in technology and business. Managers and their spokesmen have responded to these circumstances by yet
another change of vocabulary, indicating their awareness of environmental issues and further elaborating upon the social and psychological attributes of
men in an organized context.[26] Authority relations in industrial enterprises are
based upon the ownership and management of private property. Hence, a
study of changes in American managerial ideologies fits into the on-going development of legal authority on which I have commented.

Let us now turn to the plebiscitarian type of domination in nation-states,
specifically Communist dictatorships.[27] As in other *historical* types, these
systems combine charismatic, traditional and legal elements, and over time
their configuration is subject to structural changes without losing its distinctive characteristics. But this historical type is clearly outside Weber's tripartite
division and one may well ask whether the old terminology of charisma, tradition, and legality is applicable at all, or more specifically whether any ad-
mixture of these terms would fit the plebiscitarian case. Weber did not live to
witness such one-party dictatorships, but his terms are surprisingly suitable.
In the case of the Soviet Union, Lenin was clearly a charismatic leader and the
preservation of his body continues to this day as a symbolic authentication of
the regime. Annually, the great event of the 1917 revolution is celebrated in
ceremonies of rededication, and citations from the classic writings of Marx,
Engels and Lenin remain a symbol of ideological purity. Such facts are too
familiar to require elaboration. With the passage of time, the power of such
symbolic persuasion has probably diminished and recent or current rulers are
"routinized" heirs to a revolutionary inspiration. Yet from that inspiration
they retain the claim to be the unquestioned fountainhead of political (and
spiritual) truth. As rulers of a large empire, their every utterance is not to be
challenged, while those below are made responsible for the implementation of
the "party line." Thus, plebiscitarian regimes are founded upon the *principle*
of absolute commands, on the one side, and absolute responsibility for their
implementation, on the other. But as always, practice differs from principle:
depending on circumstances and strategies commands may not be pressed to

TABLE 3
Plebiscitarian Types of Domination in Nation-States

	1 Ratification of Authority	2 Politics	3 Staff	4 People	5 Legitimation	6 Limitation
a.	Plebiscitarian (mixture of representation and plebiscite but representation becomes nominal and plebiscite decisive)	Single-Party Dictatorship with subordinate bureaucratic interest constellations (e.g., military, secret service, heavy industry, etc. at central as well as regional levels)	Party-Cadres // Bureaucrats	"The People" (Workers, Peasants, and Intellegents) *minus* their enemies (defined by class, race, or party-line)	Vanguard-party "representing the people" and their historic movement (based on principle of equal liability of mobilization)	Emigration, withdrawal from participation, and cumulative reactions to shifts of party line
b.	Same as under a.	Single-Party Dictatorship symbiotic with bureaucratic interest constellations (e.g., military, secret service heavy industry, etc. at central as well as regional levels)	Same as under a. but party and bureaucratic personnel have become technically proficient	Same as under a.	Same as under a. but reinforced by seccessful industrialization nationalist appeals, and promises of peace and equality	Same as under a. but higher levels of education add new dimensions ranging from clandestine critiques (*Samizdat*) to evaluations of official policies based on the expertise of bureaucratic interest constellations at central as well as regional levels

the limit just as subordinate organizations may get away with a good deal of evasion. In Weber's tripartite division, the staff most characteristically charged with the impersonal implementation of specific commands is a bureaucracy, while only disciples of a charismatic leader dedicate themselves to follow him in his mission. Under modern conditions, plebiscitarian regimes tend to combine features from both the charismatic and the legal complex. The rulers of such regimes give specific directives as if they were in legal authority, but make each of these directives absolute as if they held charismatic authority. Under legal authority, theirs would be the ultimate responsibility. But by making their commands absolute, they evade that responsibility and shift the blame for failure onto the executive agencies. In turn, these agencies are organized bureaucratically while being called upon to show the loyal dedication of charismatic disciples. And when called to account, such agencies can try to evade their (bureaucratic) responsibility by pointing to the absolute commands which they have merely obeyed. There are seeds of danger in all exercise of authority. But today we know that on occasion in this particular combination the different dangers of charisma and of bureaucracy have been compounded and escalated at a disastrous cost to all humanity.

Still, the application of Weber's categories is not enough. A schematic representation may be helpful again in order to interpret plebiscitarian domination as an historical type.

Plebiscitarian authority embodies the historical mission of a transcendent collectivity. It cannot be bound either by the inspirations of personal authority, the benevolent authoritarianism of traditional authority, or the rule-bound dictates of science and "rational planning," although all these elements may play a role. The ideal type of plebiscitarian regime depends on the principle that all decision-making is concentrated at the apex of the single party and all responsibility for failure is attributed to the echelons of party and government below that apex. Only such concentration can ensure that the true vanguard of the people (as interpreted by the leading cadre of that vanguard) will fulfill the historic mission of the world-proletariat. The party-leadership alone interprets the mandate of the people while the elected representatives provide the leadership with the "evidence" of public acclamation.

Where such regimes are established, they typically duplicate the established hierarchy of government officials by a second hierarchy of party-cadres. The relations between these two hierarchies fluctuate with changing policies. The main point is that party-cadres are typically charged with intervening in the ordinary conduct of affairs on an emergency basis. They are employed to implement commands emanating from the decision-making center of the party which has the prerogative of overruling other centers of decision-making on an ad hoc basis. This double hierarchy of authority develops systematically what are, one suspects, incipient tendencies in all types of authority, namely the effort to supervise subordinates by agents especially designated for the purpose. At any rate, a single-party authority exists only when these "agents" are centrally organized themselves, at the beck and call of the central leadership. At the top, decision-making is monopolized on behalf of the people conceived as a more or less undifferentiated whole. "The people" are contrasted sharply with an ever-present collective enemy whose identity varies with the party-line, but whose omnipresence is a mainstay of the simulated combat-conditions with which the civil order is imbued ideologically. As a matter of principle, everyone is equally liable to be mobilized so that privacy or diminished effort are literally interpreted as treason, i.e., as evidence of having gone over to the omnipresent internal enemy. On a mass-scale, plebiscitarian rule finds "limits" only in passive resistance, and since any failure is presumptive evidence of disloyalty, passive resistance is suspected widely indeed. But such regimes must also get the work done. And in the absence of more direct sources of information changes of party-line are prompted by evidence that bottlenecks have developed from the implementation of previous directives. Frequent changes of party-line (each being asserted with equal vehemence) are bound to produce cumulative reactions among the people subjected to such conditions.

Much of this remains true of Communist regimes today. Nevertheless, conditions have changed in the period of de-Stalinization (since the 20th Party Congress of 1956) and in East Germany especially since the building of the wall in 1961. An analysis appropriate at that earlier time is no longer valid empirically and my schematic presentation tentatively suggests the directions in which change has taken place. In East Germany, that change has been dramatic. Since the end of World War II, the country had lost approximately one sixth of its population by emigration to West Germany. Clearly, a regime facing such a drain of its manpower was in jeopardy and could be expected to maximize pressure upon its people. Until the building of the wall in 1961, East Germany was reputed as the most "Stalinist" country of Eastern Europe and some of that reputation lingers on even today. No other country (except North Korea) faces the "capitalist enemy" quite so directly and such agreements as have been reached between the two Germanys since 1972 were in part the result of Russian pressure upon the German Democratic Republic (GDR). The relaxation of dictatorial measures has remained quite limited (as it has in the Soviet Union in the post-Stalin period), but some relaxation clearly has occurred. An empirical examination of this change is beyond the scope of this essay, but it is legitimate to ask in what way changes of this kind may be accommodated within the ideal type of plebiscitarian domination.

In fact, a parallel question applies to all ideal types of domination. Under personal authority, a leader's demand for complete personal devotion (based on his exceptional qualities and his sense of mission) is always at odds with his followers' hope for some sign of his gift and its special powers. Under traditional authority, the ruler's prerogative based on ancient usage is always at odds with his subjects' claims to traditional rights, also based on ancient usage. Under legal authority, laws and directives broadly derived from the constitution are always at odds with some public reactions based on particular interests and/or abstract notions of justice. Also, commands and public reactions are pressed home with varying intensity depending upon circumstances. Such tensions are managed from case to case without nullifying the broad applicability of the type of authority in question.

These considerations apply to plebiscitarian types of domination as well. Here, too, it is claims against expectations, because all authority relations are bilateral and only unrelenting coercion borders on the unilateral.[28] The single party proclaims itself the vanguard of "the people," a transcendent collectivity which only the party itself knows how to interpret. Though the people are differentiated in many respects, party-ideology represents them symbolically as a unit with an historic mission. This mission demands the participation of everyone. The party-cadres are a principal instrument of such public mobilization. But conditions fluctuate even when this structure remains intact. Concretely, after the wall was built, the constant jeopardy of mass-defection ceased and the GDR regime undertook a massive drive to catch up with modern technology.[29] Under these new conditions, how does a single-party authority restructure and/or relax its mobilization drives without relinquishing either its complete control over the party-apparatus or its ability to resume maximum pressure when the party-line calls for such pressure? Also, how is this restructuring and/or relaxation handled when "the people" find their situation literally inescapable (as in the Soviet Union), while successful technological change offers increasing opportunities to the technical cadres? For specialists on countries in the Soviet orbit these and related questions rank high on their agenda.

All authority-relations have in common that those in command cannot fully control those who obey. To be effective, authority depends on the assumption that subordinates will follow instructions in terms of the spirit rather than the letter of the rules. Two things are implied here: that the subordinate will adopt the behavior alternatives selected for him, and that he will give his "good will" to carrying out his orders. As this formulations suggests, "good will" involves judgment and initiative. If these are withheld by a "withdrawal of efficiency" (Veblen), a slavish clinging to the letter of the rules, or active sabotage, then the subordinate uses his judgment for purposes of his own.[30] Passive resistance and the regime's need for cooperation can increase both, the social isolation of party activists and the tremendous pressure to which they were subjected by the regime. East German party-cadres were told that the word "impossible" is banished from the language, that "what was correct yesterday is already outdated and incorrect today." In other words, they were made to realize that advancement depends upon compliance and maximum performance, and in case of doubt compliance was rated higher. By simulating combat-conditions in peace-time, the regime concentrated all power at the top and pushed all responsibility downwards. Under these conditions it was only natural if party activists clung to the letter of their rules, even at the risk of alienating others and failing to perform as expected. For the alternative was to be suspected of disloyalty or treason. This condition remains an aspect of single-party rule. But this condition also produces mindless agitation, empty conformity, the failure of any feedback-information that could be of use to the regime, and hence the necessity to shift the party-line repeatedly in response to the cumulative inefficiencies produced by overconformity to the previous dispensation. In the post-Stalin period efforts have, therefore, been made to come to terms with these drawbacks of single-party authority—albeit in a way that will preserve the integrity of the regime as presently constituted. Typically, party-cadres have been instructed to develop initiative, to combat empty conformity by showing true leadership qualities, etc. At the highest levels it may also have taken the form of new accommodations between the Politburo and the elites of various executive bureaucracies such as the military, heavy industry, the secret service, and so on. The analysis of these changes goes beyond the scope of this essay but is not, I believe, incompatible with its results. Probably, these regimes cannot return to their Stalinist past. New personnel techniques in the party are efforts to cope with the mounting disutilities of the earlier methods, the rising articulation of critical judgments in high quarters and, in relations with "the public," the increasing social distance between the party and the people. But these measures to shore up single-party authority are not indications of its dissolution. For the time being, one can only hazard the guess that a transformed type of plebiscitarian domination (b) is in the making and we simply do not know how far this transformation can be developed within the plebiscitarian framework.

THEORETICAL PERSPECTIVES

In this section I have attempted to provide a framework in which structures of authority can be studied in more empirical detail. But this elaboration assumes the existence of the nation-state and that assumption is of limited applicability.

Today we face a world in which the expansion of European ideas and institutions has placed the task of nation-building on the agenda of most countries, whether or not they are ready to tackle the job. . . . We may well face a period in history in which fragments of nation-building—like the quest for a national culture, the unification of language, the detribalization of a population, the assimilation of ethnic communities, the formalization of laws, the elimination of corruption, the maintenance of order, the demilitarization of quasi-autonomous groups, and a thousand other issues—are tackled piecemeal and without immediate prospect of a definitive outcome. In that perspective the dominant experience of our generation appears to be that the unanticipated repercussions of European expansion were effective enough to undermine or destroy existing social frameworks, but often not nearly effective enough to provide viable, structural alternatives.[31]

It is probably idle for now to develop speculative typologies for the structures of authority that may emerge from this world-wide travail. Much of our knowledge in these matters is retrospective, as Hegel knew: "The owl of Minerva spreads its wings only with the falling of the dusk." However, it is not idle to state in what spirit our study of these problems should proceed.

Social theories are trial presentations of the world, not subject to decisive tests of verification. To me it has always seemed that idle curiosity and scientific advance were insufficient grounds of choice for the social theorist. Neither the productivity of his quest for knowledge nor its benefits are sufficient for the kind of self-absorbed preoccupation which has often proved so productive in the natural sciences. At the same time it is obvious that many choices have been made for us. We are all unwitting legatees of a development which witnessed the expansion of Western civilization around the world. Neither contrition nor slashing indictments of our own tradition can undo the effects of that expansion or be persuasive to its victims and their heirs. At the same time and inevitably, we continue to utilize the intellectual framework which itself was shaped by that expansion and remains an important reservoir of analytic tools even for the people on the peripheries, in countries that are "old societies and new states." This is the context in which we can perform a service when we reexamine our conceptual apparatus with the idea of making it more generally applicable.

To this end it may be helpful if I conclude this essay in a more personal vein. Comparative historical studies, conceived in a sociological perspective, have been my main scholarly preoccupation. My German background and emigration to the United States gave an impetus in this direction. The experience of teaching at American universities provided another incentive. From my days of teaching in the College at the University of Chicago in the 1940s I was impressed by the mounting distance between teachers and students, as specialization and technical expertise became the dominant focus of the social sciences. Only a small minority of our students would become professional social scientists and even many of these were likely to be teachers rather than researchers. The vast majority would become white-collar workers of some kind and what did we have to offer them? Indeed, what would be the outlook of social scientists proper, if they knew more and more about less and less, to use that hackneyed phrase? Certainly, such disparagement makes a travesty of the enormous effort with which dedicated men and women have sought to advance valid and reliable knowledge in the social sciences and I want no part of the anti-intellectualism that has been manifest so often. But every intellectual stance exacts its price in missed alternatives. And where so many colleagues were engaged in advancing specialization, there was room for some of us to go in another direction.

But synthetic analyses can be no more random than specialized inquiries and my efforts have been guided by leading questions in turn. Why have I been so concerned with structures of authority? The answer goes back to the shattering experience with which I began. I was seventeen years of age when Hitler's conquest of power destroyed the ordered world in which I grew up. Since then much scholarly work has taught us how precarious and ill-constructed that world had been, but for me this knowledge does not efface the abstract significance of that experience. No social order is possible without authority, but authority can be used for good or ill. This is the root metaphor on which my attention has been riveted ever since.

In examining some of the problems suggested by that metaphor I have been guided by several related considerations. Under favorable conditions authority may be benign, but it cannot function without inequality. The division is deep between the few who exercise authority and the many who acquiesce, between the "elite" and the "masses." Nevertheless, there are limits to what authority can do: the enormity of Hitler's power impressed me no more than the abyss of his defeat. For however extreme coercion becomes and however unilateral power-relations seem to be between the few and the many, there is always interaction. I remembered Georg Simmel's example from some ancient text that at the building of the pyramids ten thousand slaves under the whip would voice their protest by murmuring in unison. Reflections of this kind give an inkling of the perplexities of action. Authority entails inescapable hazards not only because it is bound up with inequality, but because it must steer a course between being too forceful and not being forceful enough, between the arrogance of power and the failure of nerve. And at the level of social action, the same perspective can be applied to the relations between ideas and interests. As Otto Hintze has written,

> Everywhere the first impulse to social action is given as a rule by political and economic interests. But ideal interests lend wings to these real interests, give them a spiritual meaning, and serve to justify them. Man does not live by bread alone. He wants to have a good conscience as he pursues his life-interests. And in pursuing them he develops his capacities to the highest extent only if in so doing he serves a higher rather than a purely egoistic purpose. Interests without such 'spiritual wings' are lame; but on the other hand, ideas can win out in history only if and insofar as they are associated with real interests.[32]

This Weberian notion of conflicting imperatives has many ramifications.

In the context of authority it means a never-ending tension between rule-observance and individual interests. There can be no legal order without rules and hence there must be functionaries (judges, officials, policemen) who insist that the rules be followed. But rules are general, they do not take account of specific circumstances, and they work many hardships upon the lives of individuals. Because of this discrepancy, my father maintained that lawyers must exhaust to the full the legal possibilities of defense, if the individual is to be protected against the necessary rigidities of rule-making. Something like this is also manifest in the relations between politics and social structure. There are a thousand constraints arising from the givens of geography, resources, the legacies of history and the social organization of economic life. All these impose an impersonal structure of limits upon society. But active men also endeavor to shape and reshape their lives closer to their heart's desire. Subject to constraints though it is, politics is a part of that reshaping and represents a chance of freedom in a sea of necessities. Much the same may be said of culture. The accident of birth places everyone into contexts that are not of his making. Only through the formation of habits will he become a functioning adult and, for good or ill, habits impose indispensable rigidities that derive in part from what our culture takes for granted. But as John Dewey pointed out, habits facilitate as well as limit; under favorable conditions they allow us to explore the possibilities of action by enabling us to take so much for granted. And like individuals, cultures can achieve their high points of creativity only because so much culturally conditioned behavior is routine.

The recognition of such conflicting imperatives has formed a constant background of my work: I see it as an indispensable attribute of scholarship in the social sciences. Each intellectual construction has its achievements and the costs bound up with those achievements. And to the extent that one can use this insight properly, attention to both perspectives is an important methodological tool. But this type of rationalism has a moral dimension which should be made explicit. The ancient Greeks taught that the wise man faces up to the eternal mutability of fortunes. In good times and bad, he should be mindful of the opposite extremity of the human condition. This stoic view of our predicament is difficult to accept for legatees of the Enlightenment. Even the skeptics among us believe in the possibilities of reason, though a century of wars and revolutions and the growing complexities of civilization have cast a shadow over the earlier confidence. In a world of conflict and uncertainty we are perhaps learning to live with proximate solutions. But hope continues that knowledge can contribute its share to help make such solutions viable rather than inconclusive.

NOTES

1. See my essay "How I Became an American Sociologist," in Vol. 2, Ch. 2.

2. There may be logical and psychological reasons why classifications by two, or multiples of two, recur as frequently as they do. However, it is also possible that this tendency has historical roots, going back to the origins of Christianity with its dualistic distinctions between heaven and hell, God and Satan, orthodoxy and heterodoxy, a world of light and a world of darkness. The second volume of *Embattled Reason* will contain two unpublished essays on early Christianity, which explore the religious world-view which militates against the pluralism of Pagan or, say, of Hindu beliefs. The legacies of the Biblical view of history in the Western intellectual tradition have been traced by Karl Loewith, *Meaning in History* (Chicago: University of Chicago Press, 1949).

3. Max Weber, *Economy and Society* (tr. and ed. by Guenther Roth and Claus Wittich; New York: The Bedminster Press, 1968), I, 212. Cited below as Weber, *E&S*.

4. Ibid., III, 954.

5. For a further systematization of Weber's analysis of domination cf. Wolfgang Schluchter, *The Rise of Western Rationalism* (tr. with an introduction by Guenther Roth; Berkeley: University of California Press, 1981), chp. V.

6. *E&S*, I. p. 241.

7. *E&S*, I, p. 217.

8. Two years after completing *Work and Authority in Industry* I wrote "Industrialization, Ideologies and Social Structure" with which I replaced the earlier concluding chapter in the second edition of the book. In revised form that essay was included in the first edition of *Embattled Reason* (1970) and with still further revisions in my Heidelberg lectures, *Force, Fate and Freedom* (Berkeley: University of California Press, 1984), chp. 4. The materials discussed in that essay are here related more directly to Weber's types of authority and the question of whether and how dictatorial rule can be fit into a framework of changing relations between state and civil society. A certain amount of overlap remains in Ch. 10 below.

9. Reinhard Bendix, *Work and Authority in Industry* (New York: John Wiley & Sons, 1956), p. 434.

10. Alexis de Tocqueville, *Democracy in America* (New York: Vintage Books, 1954), II, p. 195.

11. See *Work and Authority*, p. 437.

12. Reinhard Bendix and Seymour M. Lipset, "Political Sociology," *Current Sociology*, VI (1957), p. 85.

13. See T.H. Marshall, *Class, Citizenship and Social Development* (Garden City: Doubleday & Co., 1964), pp. 71-72.

14. Reinhard Bendix, *Nation-Building and Citizenship* (New York: John Wiley & Sons, 1964), pp. 80-101.

15. Georg Simmel developed this observation in his discussion of "the negative character of collective behavior" in Kurt Wolff, ed., *The Sociology of Georg Simmel* (Glencoe: The Free Press, 1950), pp. 396-401.

16. For these people the personal commitment to the nation recaptures some of its former intensity only in national emergencies or in confrontations with other cultures. For others, of course, patriotism remains an important part of their conventional creed but even then it becomes a sentiment for special occasions, not the all-consuming passion of a nationalist movement. See my *Nation-Building and Citizenship*, op. cit., pp. 136-38.

17. Tocqueville, *Democracy in America*, op. cit., II, pp. 311-12.

18. Ibid., II, pp. 114-18 where Tocqueville discusses the "use which Americans make of public associations in civic life."

19. The passage linking self-interest to individualism and the centralization of government should be compared and contrasted with Tocqueville's more famous praise of townships in new England (I, pp. 68-101) and his analysis of public and civil associations (II, pp. 114-28). Though he saw that demands by individuals could lead to the expansion of government, he did not see that such demands by associations would lead to even more expansion.

20. In what follows, I confine myself to a discussion of legal and plebiscitarian authority as political sub-types of the nation-state. It is awkward to use the term "legal authority" both in a universal and a historical sense, but I try to make the difference clear by the addition of qualifying adjectives and in the commentary below. Weber was well aware of the need for such sub-classification and although some of his phrases like "patrimonial bureaucracy" are rather *ad hoc*, he also made more systematic attempts. For his sub-classification of traditional and charismatic authority cf. Weber, *E&S*, *op. cit.*, III, pp. 1070-73, 1159-63.

21. See Weber, *E&S*, *op. cit.*, I, p. 56.

22. For the distinction between the representative and the plebiscitarian principle I am indebted to Ernst Fraenkel, *Die Repräsentative und die Plebiszitäre Komponente im Demokratischen Verfassungsstaat* (Heft 219-220 of Recht und Staat; Tübingen: J.C.B. Mohr, 1958), passim. The use of this distinction is my own.

23. Johan Goudsblom, *Dutch Society* (New York: Random House, 1967), pp. 32, 124.

24. Comprehensive, comparative surveys of this material are contained in Joseph Kaiser, *Die Repräsentation organisierter Interessen* (Berlin: Duncker & Humblot, 1956), passim, and, more recently, Klaus von Beyme, *Interessengruppen in der Demokratie* (München: R. Piper Verlag, 1980), passim.

25. Note the convergence on this question between a conservative and a Social-Democratic spokesman in Irving Kristol, "Capitalism, Socialism, and Nihilism," *The Public Interest*, No. 31 (Spring, 1973), pp. 3-16 and Richard Löwenthal, "Mit dem Sozialismus überleben," *Die Zeit* (April 20, 1973), pp. 3-5.

26. For an analysis of American managerial ideologies since the "human relations" movement of the 1930s cf. Alexander Bergmann, "The Evolution of Managerial Attitudes towards Organizational and Environmental Responsibilities" (Ph.D. Dissertation, School of Business Administration, University of California, Berkeley, 1973).

27. My formulation is confined to the Soviet case. I recognize that eventually it is necessary to find formulations abstract enough to apply to other single-party systems as well, but I have not attempted this here.

28. I say "borders" because even coercion is a human act with the torturer seeking in some way to elicit signs of affection (though not necessarily in relation to his victim) and the tortured seeking in some way to relieve their agony by some token of a *quid pro quo* for their suffering. But these extremities of the human condition need not be considered here.

29. Of course, the psychological impact of West German prosperity on the East German population remained a threat and other threats like the Hungarian uprising and the short-lived Dubcek regime in Czechoslovakia probably had the effect of keeping the degree of relaxation quite limited. Other studies and especially Peter Ludz, *Parteielite im Wandel* (Köln: Westdeutscher Verlag, 1968), passim, with its analysis of a "consultative-authoritarian" regime, have examined the relevant developments.

30. My formulation is indebted to Herbert Simon, *Administrative Behavior* (New York: The Macmillan Co., 1959), p. 125 and passim, who has replaced Chester

Barnard's "zone of indifference" by the more appropriate "zone of acceptance," which is defined as "a general rule which permits the communicated decision of another to guide his [the subordinate's] own choices... without deliberation on his own part on the expediency of those premises." To this it is necessary to add a "zone of judgment" pertaining to the execution of the accepted directive. In *Work and Authority*, I call this phenomenon the worker's (or subordinate's) "strategy of independence." My use of the term "good will" is derived from the "work according to rule" strike of English postal workers in 1962 which a union official explained by saying: "What we are doing is merely withdrawing our good will." See *Time Magazine* (January 19, 1962), p. 22.

31. Bendix, *Nation-Building and Citizenship*, *op. cit.*, pp. 300-301. There are also signs that in the established nation-states new questions arise, as supernational organizations both public and private involve citizens in more than one framework of allegiance.

32. Otto Hintze, "Kalvinismus und Staatsräson in Brandenburg zu Beginn des 17ten Jahrhunderts," *Historische Zeitschrift*, vol. 144 (1931), p. 232.

PART III
Studies of Modernization

Stages of Modernization

Introduction to Part III

One imagines that every language distinguishes between past and present and adds evaluative overtones to both terms. A German etymological dictionary tells us that by 500 AD the Latin adjective *modernus* referred to anything that originated a short time ago. Tenth-century Japanese had a word for up-to-date (*Imamekashi*). The word "modern" occurs in German for the first time as a foreign loan word by 1727 in the sense of "new." The Oxford Dictionary records many uses of "modern," pertaining to present or recent times as distinct from the remote past, whether the reference is to the arts or to fashion, linguistic uses like idioms or technical and scientific innovations.

By contrast, the term *modernization* seems to be of recent origin. It evokes not merely the contrast between past and present, but also a conscious effort to shed the past and embrace the present. Modernization in this sense means to bring theory and practice up to date, to make them over in accord with the present state of the art in every field of endeavor, considered on a world scale.[1] In effect, it is often hard to distinguish modernization from Westernization, not because of ethnocentrism but because modern science and technology as well as industrialization originated in Western Europe and gave a few of the European countries a headstart. Wherever this sense of modernization has spread—and it did so first of all within Europe, the age-old contrast between past and present is conceived as a challenge calling for speedy action, if failure is to be avoided. The word "modernization" conveys some feeling of urgency on the part of those who do not want to be out of date compared with those who are up to date. But if such invidious emulation has occurred throughout history, why is the term we use of such recent origin?

The answer may be that social change of the recent past has a special character, if the word *recent* is interpreted broadly enough. It is *accelerated* change which marks this departure, coming into its own through the scientific revolution. The life-time of Copernicus (1473-1543) may be used as a convenient benchmark. During the sixteenth and seventeenth centuries Western European explorations overseas followed hard on the heels of the first scientific breakthroughs. Then outward geographic expansion was followed by the quickening of economic and demographic growth, beginning in the last decades of the eighteenth century. The facts to which modernization refers were in evidence long before the term was coined. Early scientific and technical advances were directly associated with the construction of fortifications and the development of weapons. Overseas explorations were often associated with piracy and the use of force in capturing raw materials and markets. Industrial advances depended not only on innovations and trade, but on technical espionage abroad, the employment of foreign craftsmen and government subsidies. Some early uses of the adjective "modern" refer to weapons and techniques of navigation, as if to remind us that modernization involved national rivalries and frequent wars. Eventually, colonial empires were established that started with isolated European settlements but eventuated in conquests and partitions of countries and continents.

Though the timing of new words and modifications of older ones are hardly precise, one can be more specific with regard to the accelerations to which modernization refers. World population provides one measure. It took millennia for the population to rise to one billion by 1825, but only one hundred and five years to reach the second billion (1930) and only thirty years to reach three billion. In the early 1980s world population stood at 4.8 billion or almost twice the number of 1950. Though the causal chains are very complex, it is still true that Western medicine and sanitation have been a main cause of such rapid growth.

Another measure of acceleration is the period of time it takes for the proportion of the agricultural work force to decline. During much of human history between eighty and ninety percent of the work force was employed in agriculture. In the United States that proportion was already down to fifty-one percent by 1870; it fell to twelve percent by 1960 and has declined further since then. In Japan, another highly industrialized country today, the agricultural work force declined from eighty-five to sixty percent between 1872 and 1960. By 1980, an average of only twenty-three percent of the work force was employed in agriculture in *all industrial* countries. In the same year, the corresponding proportion in *all developing* countries was seventy-one percent. During the period of rapid population growth, a high proportion of the labor force in agriculture has gone together with low productivity and wide-spread poverty, if not outright starvation. The resulting contrast between industrial and developing countries is great and increasing. The Gross Domestic Product per capita was $650 per annum for all developing countries, to use that standard euphemism again. For all industrial market economies (thus excluding the non-market economies of Eastern Europe), the corresponding figure was $10,440 per annum. Again the causal chain is complex, but the early breakthroughs of Western Europe I have mentioned and the industrialization which followed were and remain a root cause of these stark inequalities all over the world. Though the build-up of these enormous contrasts in well-being has been in the making for some four centuries, it has been brought to public awareness especially since World War II.[2]

The situation I have described was *not* my primary concern when I began my comparative socio-historical studies. Instead, I was preoccupied with the problem of totalitarian rule which had forced me to emigrate from Germany when I was twenty-two. From this experience I derived an intense interest in the uses and abuses of authority. The contrast between the place of public and private authority in Germany and the United States caught my attention early on. And since the defeat of Hitler in World War II left the Soviet Union as the main example of this type of rule, it was natural to concentrate on the Russian case. Two other considerations helped me to define my research interest initially. One was that my interest in authority led me to the study of large-scale organizations, public and private. The other was a holdover from an early preoccupation with Marxism, a natural byproduct of having grown up in Berlin. This holdover consisted in my case in the study of ideas, specifically ideas about authority. By combining these interests I came to analyze entrepreneurial and managerial ideologies in the course of industrialization, a formulation of my subject which pointed me in the direction of comparative historical research. As ideas, such justifications of private authority are not very interesting, but they evidently appealed to the entrepreneurs and managers who headed enterprises of all kinds. They were ideas directly linked to the work-organization of large numbers of people, and hence exemplified Marx's unity of "theory and practice," albeit in a field he considered self-evident: "the ruling ideas of the age." They proved to be a part of modernization, as I discovered in the course of my study.

I had derived major clues for *Work and Authority in Industry* from the writings of Max Weber. After completing the book, I became chairman of my department and compensated for my increased administrative duties by concentrating on a detailed study of Weber's work. The result of that study was *Max Weber, An Intellectual Portrait*, published in 1960. In a way, this was not only a self-administered continuation of my education, but also the foundation of my interest in the comparative study of modernization. For it led me to a year's study in India and Japan, which resulted in my next comparative historical study, *Nation-Building and Citizenship* (1964). The last book in this series was *Kings or People, Power and the Mandate to Rule*, published in 1978.

This sequence of my work bears on the essays which follow. All of them were written after the major studies were completed, further reflections on the work I had done. Inadvertently, they also exemplify in my own experience the cumulative causation of life-careers which I characterized as a basis of association in civil societies (see Chapter 8). As my interest shifted from totalitarian rule to modernization, I found that I had committed myself to the study of Western societies to an extent that limited my ability to move farther afield than India and Japan in the study of non-Western societies, as I would have liked to do, had I been younger. Though I have read more widely, the fact is that too much time spent on any one set of subjects limits the time left for others. I have had to make do with exploiting my understanding of Western societies, India and Japan for an understanding of the modernization problem world-wide. The result is more knowledge of past, and less knowledge of present, "modernizations" than I would have liked. My hope is, nevertheless, that my explorations of the past and present on a comparative basis will be found useful by scholars who are able to go beyond my limited vision.

NOTES

1. I take this meaning of "modernization" from Brockhaus Wahrig, *Deutsches Wörterbuch* (Stuttgart: Deutsche Verlagsanstalt, 1982), IV, 709. See also Friedrich Kluge, *Etymologisches Wörterbuch der deutschen Sprache* (Berlin: Walter de Gruyter, 1963), 483 and Ivan Morris, *The World of the Shining Prince* (Harmondsworth: Penguin Books, 1969), 38.
2. The figures in this paragraph are taken from Simon Kuznets, *Modern Economic Growth* (New Haven: Yale University Press, 1966), 106-107 and from *World Development Report* 1984 (New York: Oxford University Press, 1984), passim.

10

INDUSTRIALIZATION, IDEOLOGIES, AND SOCIAL STRUCTURE

Introductory Note[1]

Since World War II, American social scientists have become preoccupied with the industrialization of underdeveloped areas. Considering the recent history of our disciplines, this is a relatively novel undertaking. It involves the study of social change in complex social structures on a comparative basis. One approach to such a study consists in the selection of a social problem encountered in several societies but resolved differently in each. The problem chosen for analysis in my book *Work and Authority in Industry* (1956) was that in the course of industrialization employers and their spokesmen developed ideas in order to justify the exercise of authority over the workers and enhance the latter's obedience and efficiency.[2] I have called the ideas which relate to these two issues entrepreneurial ideologies in the early phase of industrialization and managerial ideologies, when economic enterprises are fully developed.

The first part of the following essay gives an overview of the questions to be addressed. The second part summarizes the changes of ideology that have occurred in Anglo-American and in Russian civilization over a two-hundred year period. The third part deals with the historical significance of ideologies of management and the fourth with the empirical and theoretical significance of ideologies of management. The two concluding sections deal with the problem of bureaucratization and with the difference between totalitarian and non-totalitarian forms of subordination in industry.

CHANGES IN IDEOLOGY

At the inception of industrialization in England an ideology of traditionalism prevailed; John Stuart Mill called it the "theory of dependence." According to this view the laboring poor are children, who must be governed, who should not be allowed to think for themselves, who must perform their assigned tasks obediently and with alacrity, who must show deference to their superiors, and who—if they only conduct themselves virtuously—will be protected by their betters against the vicissitudes of life. This interpretation of authority is self-confirming and self-serving.[3] But it sets up the presumption that the dependence of the poor and the responsibility of the rich are the valid moral rules of the social order. In the course of industrial development these ideas were gradually modified. As the responsibility of the rich was increasingly rejected by the advocates of laissez-faire, the dependence of the poor was turned from an inevitable into a self-imposed fate. As it was "demonstrated" that the rich cannot care for the poor without decreasing the national wealth, it was also asserted that by abstinence and exertion the poor can better their lot. The same virtues, which in the eighteenth century were extolled so that the lowly will not aspire above their station, were praised by the middle of the nineteenth century because they enable a man to raise himself by his own efforts.

In England, and even more in America, this praise of effort led toward the end of the nineteenth century to an apotheosis of the struggle for existence. The militant language of an ethics of the jungle was applied to the relations between employers and workers. Riches and poverty merely reflect difference of ability and effort. The employer's success is evidence of his fitness for survival, and as such justifies his absolute authority over the enterprise. This assertion of authority has a clear-cut meaning only as long as most managerial functions are in the hands of one man. The idea becomes ambiguous as the use of expertise in enterprises increases and the managerial function becomes subdivided and specialized. Just when employers claimed absolute authority over their enterprises, the "scientific management" movement sought to give them expert advice on what to do with that authority. Under these circumstances the doctrines of Social Darwinism gradually lost their appeal, in part because changes in industrial organization gave rise to a changing imagery of men in industry. From the Gilded Age to the 1920s, workers and managers were self-evident failures or successes in a struggle for survival, in which they were the recalcitrant objects or the exasperated originators of managerial commands. Today they have become individuals-in-groups whose skills must be improved and allocated systematically and whose productivity must be maximized by appropriate attention to their psychological makeup. Thus, over the past two hundred years, managerial ideologies in Anglo-American civilization have changed from the "theory of dependence" to laissez-faire, to Social Darwinism, and finally to the "human relations" approach.

In the Russian development we also find the assertion of paternal authority and of child-like dependence, and in much the same terms as in England. But in Russia this ideology of traditionalism was a very different thing from what it was in England because of the Tsar's assertion of supreme authority over all the people. This authority remained intact regardless of how many privileges the Tsar granted to the landlords and regardless of how rarely he interfered in fact with the use and abuse of these privileges. Ideologically the Tsar maintained his preeminence through repeated assertions concerning his paternal care and responsibility for all of "his" people. Through repeated petitions and sporadic revolts the people used this Tsarist claim in order to obtain redress for their grievances against landlords and employers. Also, because of the early centralization of authority under the Muscovite rulers, the whole distribution of wealth and rank among the aristocracy turned upon the competition for favors at the Court and hence reenforced the Tsar's supremacy.[4]

During the second half of the nineteenth century this pattern of Tsarist autocracy had far-reaching consequences. The dislocations incident to the emancipation of the serfs (1861) and the development of industry brought in their train assertions of absolute authority by the employers, efforts of the workers to organize themselves, and sporadic attempts of the government to regulate the relations between them. Although ostensibly acting on an equitable basis, the government in fact supported the employers against the workers. Much of this is again broadly familiar from the English experience; but Russia's historical legacies prevented the shift in ideology which has been described for England. As long as Tsarist autocracy remained intact neither the rejection of responsibility by the Tsar and the ruling strata nor the demand for the self-dependence of the workers developed. Instead, the Tsar and his officials continued to espouse the ideology of traditionalism. Quite consistently, Tsarist officials sought to superintend both employers and workers in order to mitigate or suppress the struggles between them. That is, the officials aided *and* curbed the employers' exercise of authority as well as the workers' efforts to formulate grievances and organize protest movements.

Tsarist autocracy was overthrown in the Russian revolutions of 1905 and 1917. Although vast differences were brought about by the revolution, the managerial ideology of tsarism lived on in a modified form. In theory, Tsarist officials had regarded employers and workers as equally subject to the will of the Tsar; loyal submission to that will was the mark of good citizenship. In theory, Lenin believed that all workers were equal participants in the management of industry and government; their loyal submission to the Communist party represented their best interest and expressed their sovereign will. The logic of Lenin's as of the Tsarist position is that under a sovereign authority the same person or organization can and should perform both subordinate and superordinate functions. For example, Soviet labor unions approach the ideal of workers' control of industry when they are called upon to participate in the management of industry. But they also function in a managerial capacity when they inculcate labor discipline among their members under the authoritative direction of the Communist Party.

Ideologically this position is defended on the ground that the party represents the historical interests of the proletariat against the short-run interests of individuals and factions. In this orientation one can still see survivals of

Tsarist autocracy since all wisdom and responsibility reside in a small group or indeed in one man who, like the Tsar, knows better than private persons what is the good of all, and cares for the well-being of the people. But there is also an important difference. The leaders of the Russian revolution were faced with the task of developing self-discipline and initiative among workers if a suitable industrial work-force was to become available.[5] They proceeded to inculcate these qualities by the direct or indirect subordination of everyone to the discipline of the Communist party. This policy continued the Tsarist tradition by making all matters the object of organizational manipulation rather than of personal striving; but it also represented a break with the past in that it was no longer restricted to personal submission.

HISTORICAL SIGNIFICANCE OF IDEOLOGICAL CHANGE

What are the historical implications of this analysis of managerial ideologies? All industrialization involves the organization of enterprises in which a few command and many obey. The ideas developed by the few and the many may be considered a symptom of changing class relations and hence a clue to an understanding of industrial societies.[6]

Historically, ideologies of management became significant in the transition from a pre-industrial to an industrial society. The authority exercised by employers was recognized as distinct from the authority of government. This was a novel experience even in Western Europe where there was precedent for such autonomy in other institutions. The industrial entrepreneurs were "new men" rather than a ruling class buttressed by tradition. This was also the period during which the discipline of sociology originated. Under the impact of the French revolution society came to be conceived in terms of forces that are independent from, as well as antagonistic to, the formal institutions of the body politic. Some early elaborations of this key idea enable us to see the historical significance of ideologies of management.

The authority of employers rests on the contractual acquisition of property, which the eighteenth century philosophers made the conceptual basis of the social order. In Rousseau's view that order ought to be based on a general will which presupposes that the individual acts for the whole community. In such a society, as George Herbert Mead has pointed out, " . . . . the citizen can give laws only to the extent that his volitions are an expression of the rights which he recognizes in others, . . . [and] which the others recognize in him. . . ."[7] This approach provides a model for a society based on consent so that the power of rule-making is exercised by all and for all. This foundation of society upon a "general will" was directly related to the institution of property. As Mead has stated,

If one wills to possess that which is his own so that he has absolute control over it as property, he does so on the assumption that everyone else will possess his own property and exercise absolute control over it. That is, the individual wills his control over his property only in so far as he wills the same sort of control for everyone else over property.[8]

Thus, the idea of reciprocal recognition of rights specifically presupposed the equality of citizens as property-owners.

This implication gave pause to some eighteenth and nineteenth century philosophers. They noted that the reciprocity of rights among property owners based on freedom of contract does not apply to the relations between employers and workers. As early as 1807 the German philosopher Hegel formulated the problematic nature of this relationship in a manner which anticipates the modern psychology of the self, just as Rousseau's "general will" anticipates the sociological analysis of interaction. Hegel maintains that men come to a recognition of themselves through a process whereby each accepts the self-recognition of the other and is in turn accepted by him. That is, each man's sense of identity depends upon his acceptance of himself. In Hegel's view this reciprocity is lacking in the relation between master and servant. The master does not act towards himself as he acts towards the servant; and the servant does not do towards others what his servitude makes him do against himself. In this way the mutuality of recognition is destroyed and the relations between master and servant become one-sided and unequal.[9]

In Western Europe this inequality of the employment-relationship coincided with the ideological and institutional decline of traditional subordination. Yet while the old justifications of subordination crumbled and new aspirations were awakened among the masses of the people, their experience of inequality continued. According to Tocqueville this problem had a differential impact upon masters and servants. In the secret persuasion of his mind the master continues to think of himself as superior; but he no longer recognizes any paternal responsibilities toward the servant. Still, he wants his servants to be content with their servile condition. In effect, the master wishes to enjoy the age-old privileges without acknowledging their concomitant obligations. And the servant rebels against his subordination, which is no longer a divine obligation and is not yet perceived as a contractual obligation.

> Then it is that [in] the dwelling of every citizen . . . a secret and internal warfare is going on between powers ever rivals and suspicious of each other: the master is ill-natured and weak, the servant ill-natured and intractable; the one constantly attempts to evade by unfair restrictions his obligation to protect and to remunerate, the other his obligation to obey. The reins of domestic government dangle between them, to be snatched at by one or the other. The lines that divide authority from oppression, liberty from license, and right from might are to their eyes so jumbled together and confused that no one knows exactly what he is or what he may be or what he ought to be. Such a condition is not democracy, but revolution.[10]

In the nineteenth century men like Hegel, Tocqueville, and Lorenz von Stein pointed out that the spread of equalitarian ideas was causing a transition in the relations between masters and servants. This transition may be called a crisis of aspirations. In Tocqueville's words the servants "consent to serve and they blush to obey. . . . [They] rebel in their hearts against a subordination to which they have subjected themselves. . . . They are inclined to consider him who orders them as an unjust usurper of their own rights."[11] As a consequence most European countries witnessed the rise of a "fourth estate" which struggled against existing legal liabilities and for basic civil rights, above all the right to suffrage. In a parliamentary debate on Chartism, Disraeli remarked that this struggle was invested with a degree of sentiment usually absent from merely economic or political contests. To the extent that such complex movements can be characterized by a common denominator this sentiment referred, I think, to the workers' quest for a public recognition of their equal status as citizens.[12] Where this and other rights became accepted, such recognition compensated for the continued social and economic subordination of the workers and thus assuaged the crisis of aspirations. Moreover, the political utilization of these civil rights could lead to a recognition of basic social rights. Today these are embodied in the institutions of social welfare characteristic of many Western democracies.[13] The initial crisis of aspirations continued, on the other hand, where civil rights were rejected or where their acceptance was postponed for too long, leading either to an eventual revolutionary upheaval as in Tsarist Russia, or to a more or less damaging exacerbation of class-relations as in Italy and France.

The question of nineteenth century Europe concerned the terms on which a society undergoing industrialization will incorporate its newly recruited industrial work force within the economic and political community of the nation. Ideologies of management are significant because they contribute to each country's answer to this question. In England the workers were invited to become their own masters, if they did not wish to obey; in Russia they were told that their subordination was less onerous than it seemed, because their own superiors were also servants of the almighty Tsar.[14]

EMPIRICAL SIGNIFICANCE OF IDEOLOGIES[15]

What are the implications of this approach? Ideologies of management may be considered indexes of the flexibility or rigidity with which the dominant groups in the two countries were prepared to meet the challenge from below. This "preparedness" or collective tendency to act is analogous to the concept of character-structure in the individual: it may be defined as an "inner capacity" for re-creating similar lines of action under more or less identical conditions.[16] The ideologies of management, which reflect this "inner capacity," naturally provoke new challenges and these in turn lead to new managerial responses, so that at the societal level there is a replication of the action-reaction process so typical of interaction among individuals.

An analysis of this process must deal with those explicitly formulated ideas that are as close as possible to the collective experience of employers and workers. This social philosophizing of and for the ordinary man as a participant occurs at a level somewhere between his attitudes as an individual and the sophisticated formulations of the social theorist. Such philosophizing is exemplified by what Andrew Ure wrote in his *Philosophy of Manufactures* or by what public-relations men for General Motors say in their pamphlet *Man to Man on the Job*. The serious analysis of such documents is at variance with the prevailing tendency to dismiss them as obviously biased and hence unworthy of consideration on their own terms. In this respect Marx was a forerunner of the intellectuals born in the 1850s and 1860s. Freud, Durkheim, Pareto, and others searched for some underlying principle or force that could explain the manifest beliefs and actions making up the external record of individual and collective behavior.[17] Accordingly, ideologies of management might be dismissed because they *merely* express a class-interest, or because they do not reveal the *real* attitudes of the employers, or because they disguise *actual* exploitative practices, or because all this talk tells us nothing about man's behavior and his personality structure. These various objections have in common an intellectual preoccupation with covert forces that can explain the manifest content of the social world.

Modern social science owes to this intellectual tradition many important insights, but also many of its aberrations. Where the phenomena of the social world are treated merely as the reflection of "hidden forces," speculation easily becomes uncontrolled while observable evidence is dismissed as "irrelevant" or "uninteresting" on theoretical grounds. The difficulty is familiar in Marx's theory of history which treated the "false consciousness" of the workers as an epiphenomenon that was bound to be superseded in the course of history. Similarly, the Freudian approach devalues a behavioristic study because it deals with the appearance rather than the underlying motivations of social action. Again, the use of organic analogies in the study of society treats all actions as dependent adjustments to other actions (or environmental conditions). Consequently this approach devalues all deliberate and innovative activity, which is yet another dependent adjustment. In inexpert hands these approaches lead to a cavalier construction of the evidence which can always be more easily imputed to the "underlying determinants" than analyzed in detail on its own ground.

Yet human experience occurs at this phenomenological level—and the study of ideologies of management illustrates that it can also provide an approach to our understanding of the social structure.[18] The managerial interpretations of the authority relationship in economic enterprises together with the workers' contrast-conception concerning their collective position in an emerging industrial society constitute a composite image of class relations which has changed over time and which differs from country to country. Each ideological position may be examined in terms of its logical corollaries as these relate to the authority of the employer and in a wider sense to the class position of employers and workers in the society. Where these corollaries create major problems for the complacent self-interest of the group, one may expect the development of tensions, and perhaps of change, ideologically and institutionally.[19]

Such ideologies are in part expediential rationalizations for the problems confronting the entrepreneur, and in part the result of cumulative response-patters among social groups. In this way ideologies are formulated through the constant interplay between current contingencies and historical legacies. Although "men make their own history under circumstances directly given and transmitted from the past," Marxian dogmatism consistently sacrificed the first to the second part of this generalization.[20] Accordingly, ideologies of management can be explained only in part as rationalizations of self-interest; they also result from the legacy of institutions and ideas which is "adopted" by each generation much as a child "adopts" the grammar of his native language. Historical legacies are thus a part of the social structure: they should not be excluded from a discipline that focusses attention upon the persistence of group-structures. In the following section an attempt is made to show the / link between historical legacies and the structure of industrial societies by relating ideologies of management to the bureaucratization of industry.

IDEOLOGIES, INDUSTRIAL BUREAUCRACY, AND TOTALITARIANISM

Since the eighteenth century Anglo-American and Russian civilizations have witnessed a growing managerial concern with the attitudes as well as the productivity of workers. It is possible to relate this change of ideology to a large number of the developments which constitute the transition from an early to a mature industrial society. The changing structure of industrial organizations was only one of these developments. Yet the bureaucratization of economic enterprises is of special importance for any attempt to "interpret the difference of fact and ideology between a totalitarian and nontotalitarian form of subordination in economic enterprises."[21] Bureaucratization is also especially suitable for a comparative study of authority relations in industry, since it involves comparable processes in two such different civilizations as England and Russia. This choice of focus deliberately eschews a comprehensive theory of society in favor of selecting a problem which, if suitable for comparative analysis, will also lead to an analysis of social structure. For, if comparable groups in different societies confront and over time resolve a common problem, then a comparative analysis of their divergent resolutions will reveal the divergence of social structures in a process of change.

Problems of a systematic management of labor come to the fore where the increasing complexity of economic enterprises makes their operation more or less dependent upon an *ethic of work performance*. That is to say, management subjects the conditions of employment to an impersonal systematization, while the employees seek to modify the implementation of the rules as their personal interests and their commitment (or lack of commitment) to the goals of the organization dictate. As everyone knows, there is no more effective means of organizational sabotage than a letter-perfect compliance with all the rules and a consistent refusal of the employees to use their own judgment. "Beyond what commands can effect and supervision can control, beyond what incentives can induce and penalties prevent, there exists an exercise of discretion important even in relatively menial jobs, which managers of economic enterprises seek to enlist for the achievement of managerial ends."[22] In the literature on organizations this exercise of discretion by subordinates is known by a number of terms: Veblen called it the "withdrawal of efficiency"; Max Weber referred to it as the bureaucratic tendency towards secrecy; Herbert Simon might call it the "zone of non-acceptance." I have suggested the phrase "strategies of independence" so as to get away from the negative connotations of the other terms, since the exercise of discretion may serve to achieve, as well as to subvert, the goals of an organization.

Now, the great difference between totalitarian and nontotalitarian forms of subordination consists in the managerial handling of this generic attribute of all authority relations. In some Western countries management presupposed a common universe of discourse between superiors and subordinates. Managerial appeals to the cooperation of subordinates have ranged from evangelism and the tough-minded laissez-faire approach of eighteenth century England to the latest refinement of the "human relations" approach. Whether good faith existed is less important than that such appeals were made, though it is probable that in England and the United States large masses of workers in one way or another accepted managerial authority as legitimate even if they were indifferent to, or rejected, the managerial appeals themselves.[23] In Russia, on the other hand, historical legacies did *not* encourage a comparable universe of discourse. From the time of Peter the Great to the period of rapid industrial growth in the last decades preceding World War I appeals were addressed to the workers' duty of obedience towards all those in positions of authority. These appeals assumed the workers' bad faith and lacking sense of

duty. Accordingly, officials and managers attempted to eliminate the subordinates' strategies of independence.

This managerial approach is related to the totalitarian type of bureaucratization. In such a regime the will of the highest party authorities is absolute.
The party may disregard all formal procedures as well as its own previous
rulings. Where norms may be changed at a moment's notice, the rule of law is
destroyed. Totalitarianism also does away with a single line of authority. Totalitarian regimes use the hierarchy of the party in order to expedite and control at each step the execution of orders through regular administrative channels. The object is to prevent officials from escaping inspection while compelling their intensified effort to implement orders. A totalitarian government
is based, therefore, on two interlocking hierarchies of authority. The work of
every factory, of every governmental office, of every unit of the army or the
secret police, of every cultural or social organization is programmed, coordi-
nated, and supervised by some agency of government. But it is also prop-
agandized, expedited, criticized, spied upon, and incorporated in special
campaigns by an agency of the totalitarian party, which is separately responsible to higher party authorities.

The rationale of this double hierarchy can be stated within the framework of
Max Weber's analysis of bureaucracy. An ideally functioning bureaucracy in
his sense is the most efficient method of performing large-scale organizational
tasks. But this is true only if the tasks involve more or less stable norms which
maintain the rule of law and an equitable administration of affairs. These conditions are absent where tasks are assigned by an omnipotent *and* revolutionary authority. Under the simulated combat conditions of a totalitarian regime
the norms that govern conduct need not stay put for any length of time, although a drive for maximum achievement is directed at each goal in turn. In
response, subordinates use their devices of concealment for the sake of systematic, if tacit, strategies of independence. They will do so for reasons of
convenience, but also because the directives of the regime are "irrational"
from the viewpoint of expert knowledge and systematic procedure.[24] The
party, on the other hand, seeks to prevent such strategies of concealment. This
is the rationale of a double hierarchy of government, which places a party
functionary at the side of every work unit in order to prevent concealment and
apply pressure. The two hierarchies would be required, even if all key positions in government and industry were filled by party functionaries. For a
functionary-turned-worker or official would still be responsible for "overful-
filling" the plan, while the new party functionary would still be charged with
keeping that official under pressure and surveillance.[25]

In this way totalitarianism replaces the old system of stratification by one
based on criteria of activism and party orthodoxy. The ethic of work performance on which this regime relies is one of material incentives and of a political supervision that seeks to prevent evasion from below as well as from

above. For example, the collective "bargaining" agreements of Soviet industry are in fact declarations of loyalty in which individuals and groups pledge themselves publicly to an overfulfillment of the plan. The subsequent organization of public confessions, the manipulation of status differences between activists and others, the principle of collective leadership, and further devices seek to maximize performance and prevent the "withdrawal of efficiency." The individual subordinate is surrounded almost literally. Aside from ordinary incentives he is controlled by his superior and by the party agitator who stands at the side of his superior; but he is also controlled "from below" in the sense that the social pressures of his peer group are manipulated by party agitators and their agents. This institutionalization of suspicion and the consequent elimination of privacy are justified on the ground that the party "represents" the masses, spearheads the drive for Russian industrialization, and leads the cause of world communism.

A comparative analysis of social structures pays attention to the historical continuity of societies as well as to the concatenation of group structures and deliberate, self-interested action in the process of social change. Studies of managerial ideologies provide an example of such analysis. During the last two centuries Anglo-American and Russian civilizations were characterized by an increased managerial concern with the attitudes of workers. In Western civilization authority relations between employers and workers remained a more or less autonomous realm of group activity even where the "human relations" approach replaced the earlier individualism. In Russia the employment relationship has been subjected throughout to a superordinate authority which regulated employers and workers. Superiors could be transformed into subordinates or (more rarely) subordinates into superiors, when governmental policies seemed to warrant such action.

This comparison has a specific historical rationale. Ideologies of management became significant when the equalitarianism of property owners, brought to the fore by the French revolution and by the legal codifications which followed, was contrasted with the inequality of the employment relationship. A heightened awareness of this inequality coincided with the decline of traditional subordination of the lower classes and hence with aspirations for social and political as well as legal equality. In England these demands for equal rights of citizenship on the part of the lower classes eventuated in a painful reconstitution of class relations; in Russia the same demands were rejected and finally led to the revolutions of 1905 and 1917.

Ideologies may be considered indexes of a readiness to act, which together with the ideological responses of other groups can provide us with a clue to the class relations of a society. Ideologies are an integral part of culture, which should be analyzed on its own terms as an index of the social structure, much as the neurotic symptoms of an individual are analyzed as an index of his personality. Such ideologies are rationalizations of group interests, they

are circumscribed by historical legacies, and their logical and empirical implications provide clues to a country's developing social structure.

Studies of managerial ideologies are also suitable for a comparison of totalitarian and non-totalitarian regimes. All industrial enterprises undergo a
process of bureaucratization and all bureaucracy involves the use of discretion
in the execution of commands. The Anglo-American and the Russian traditions have differed in terms of whether or not managerial appeals have presupposed the good faith of subordinates. Where that supposition has not been
made, the drive for industrialization has employed a double hierarchy of government. The purpose is to apply maximum pressure on subordinates and to
forestall their evasion of commands by supplementing executive with political
controls at every point in the chain of command.

English, American, and Russian industrialization have been marked by
bureaucratization, and bureaucratization certainly threatens the development
of initiative. The Soviet case also illustrates that this threat may provoke
countermeasures. One might speak of an institutionalization of initiative in the
totalitarian party and speculate that the dynamic drive of the Soviet regime can
be jeopardized if the regime were to relax the simulated combat conditions
which justify that drive.

NOTES

1. An earlier version of this essay, given in response to the MacIver prize of the
   American Sociological Association (1958), was published in the *American
   Sociological Review* XXIV (1959), pp. 613-23. The present revision was first
   published in the original edition of *Embattled Reason* (New York: Oxford University Press, 1970), pp. 187-202.
2. Reinhard Bendix, *Work and Authority in Industry* (New York: John Wiley and
   Sons, 1956). A second edition was published by the University of California Press
   in 1974.
3. The laboring poor are asked to prove their virtue by obedience, but they are also
   told that their dependence results from a natural inferiority. Similarly, the ruling
   classes are said to be responsible for the deserving poor, and if they do not meet
   this responsibility, it is only, they say, because the poor who suffer are not deserving.
4. In Russia the landed aristocracy never succeeded in making itself the unavoidable
   intermediary between the ruler and the people, in contrast with Western Europe
   where the ruler's administrative and juridical authority ended in effect at the
   boundaries of the estate, though this contrast merely states the end-result of protracted struggles over the division of authority. Cf. Max Weber, *Economy and
   Society*, trans. and ed. by Guenther Roth and Claus Wittich (New York: The
   Bedminster Press, 1968), III, pp. 1064-68.
5. Lenin's statement that "the Russian is a bad worker" and his advocacy of the
   Taylor system and of electrification as the road to socialism are indicative of the
   fact that the problems of complex industrial reorganizations came to the fore at
   once. Cf. Bendix, *Work and Authority in Industry*, pp. 206-207 for the relevant
   citation.

6. See ibid., pp. xvii-xviii, 1-2.
7. George Herbert Mead, *Movements of Thought in the Nineteenth Century* (Chicago: University of Chicago Press, 1936), p. 21.
8. Ibid., p. 17.
9. Georg Friedrich Wilhelm Hegel, *Phänomenologie des Geistes* (Leipzig: Felix Meiner, 1928), pp. 143, 147. My paraphrasing attempts to convey Hegel's meaning without use of his language. The relevant passages are readily accessible in C.J. Friedrich, ed., *The Philosophy of Hegel* (New York: Modern Library, 1953), pp. 399-410.
10. Alexis de Tocqueville, *Democracy in America* (New York: Random House, 1945), II, p. 195. Some phrases in the preceding paragraph are taken from this chapter of Tocqueville's work.
11. Ibid.
12. See Bendix, *Work and Authority, op. cit.*, pp. 34-46, 150-62. I deal with this aspect in more detail in Chapter 9 above and in *Nation-Building and Citizenship* (2nd ed.; Berkeley: University of California Press, 1977), pp. 89-126.
13. For a perceptive analysis of this development see T.H. Marshall, *Class, Citizenship and Social Development* (Garden City: Doubleday & Co., 1964), pp. 65-122. The statement in the text refers specifically to England. Social rights have been instituted in other ways, sometimes in order to withhold the establishment of civil rights as in Imperial Germany.
14. An expanded statement of this point will be found in Bendix, *Work and Authority*, pp. 174-90.
15. This section repeats points made in Chapters 5 and 7 in a theoretical context. Its purpose is to show their relevance for empirical studies.
16. The quoted phrase occurs in Burckhardt's definition of the objective of culture history, which "goes to the heart of past mankind (because) it declares what mankind *was, wanted, thought, perceived*, and *was able to do*. In this way culture history deals with what is constant and in the end this constant appears greater and more important than the momentary, a quality appears to be greater and more instructive than an action. For actions are only the individual expressions of a certain inner capacity, which is always able to recreate these same actions. Goals and presuppositions are, therefore, as important as events." See Jacob Burckhardt, *Griechische Kulturgeschichte* (Stuttgart: Alfred Kroener, 1952), I, p. 6.
17. Cf. H. Stuart Hughes, *Consciousness and Society* (New York: A.A. Knopf, 1958) which gives a perceptive analysis of this "generation."
18. By "ideologies" I do not refer to attitudes of the type that can be elicited in a questionnaire study, but to the "constant process of formulation and reformulation by which spokesmen identified with a social group seek to articulate what they sense to be its shared understandings." See *Work and Authority, op. cit.*, p. xxii. I call these articulations "ideologies" in the specific sense of "ideas considered in the context of group-action." All ideas may be analyzed from this viewpoint; hence I depart from the identification of "ideologies" with false or misleading ideas.
19. For example, at the turn of the century American employers asserted their absolute authority over the workers but this assertion lacked content until the bureaucratization of industry brought to the fore experts who worked out methods for the exercise of authority. Again, the Tsar's assertion of authority over all the people inadvertently encouraged the peasants to appeal to the Tsar for redress of grievances. This procedure is adapted from that used by Max Weber in his sociology of religion.

20. The sentence immediately following this quotation reads: "The tradition of all the dead generations weighs like a nightmare on the brain of the living." See Karl Marx, *The 18th Brumaire of Louis Bonaparte* (New York: International Publishers, n.d.), p. 13. I do not accept this polemical exaggeration, since traditions are enabling as well as disabling, but the emphasis upon the impact of cultural tradition on current ideologies is more in line with the facts than the effort to explain the latter solely in terms of the problems the businessman encounters in his work. Such an interpretation leads to an elimination of ideological changes, and of differences between ideologies, since all ideologies are in this sense responses to the strains endemic in modern society. Cf. Francis X. Sutton, et. al., *The American Business Creed* (Cambridge: Harvard University Press, 1956), passim, where the change of business ideologies over time is denied and where these ideologies are explained in exactly the same terms as nationalism and anti-capitalism. See also the comments of Leland Jenks, "Business Ideologies," *Explorations of Entrepreneurial History*, 10 (October 1957), pp. 1-7.

21. *Work and Authority, op. cit.,* p. xx.

22. *Work and Authority, op. cit.,* p. 251. To avoid a possible misunderstanding I add that this assertion, which is elaborated in ibid., pp. 244-51, is in my judgment compatible with the endeavor to put managerial decision making on a more scientific basis. The substitution of machine methods for manual operations is obviously an on-going process that has greatly curtailed the areas of possible discretion, although machine methods also create new opportunities for discretionary judgments. But while these methods and organizational manipulations may curtail and reallocate the areas in which discretion is possible or desired, and may in this way achieve greater efficiency, they cannot, I believe, eliminate discretion.

23. Cf. *Work and Authority, op. cit.,* pp. 248-49, for a fuller statement.

24. Hence they will do so even for the purpose of achieving the objectives of the party itself. Cf. Joseph Berliner, *Factory and Manager in the USSR* (Cambridge: Harvard University Press, 1957) which documents that the most successful Soviet managers use subversion to implement plan goals as well as for their personal convenience. This fact suggests that "good faith" can be inculcated in many ways, even by the systematic distrust of all subordinates, provided of course that the distrust has a higher rationale, such as the utopian and nationalist ideology of Russian communism.

25. A case study of totalitarianism in the context of industrial relations is contained in *Work and Authority, op. cit.,* Chap. 5. For a generalized treatment of this approach to totalitarianism cf. Bendix, *Nation-Building and Citizenship, op. cit.,* Chap. V. See the elaborations of the foregoing contrast in Vol. 2, Ch. 15.

11

SOCIAL STRATIFICATION AND THE POLITICAL COMMUNITY

Introductory Note

The following paper was published in 1960, four years after the publication of *Work and Authority in Industry*, the same year in which my book on Max Weber appeared, and four years before the publication of *Nation-Building and Citizenship*. I reprint it here, because it is a piece in transition, showing how I was trying to grapple with my change of interest from totalitarianism to modernization, from civic incorporation of the working class to the larger questions of citizenship, from the interpretation of authority in the context of employment relations to an analysis of the larger relations between public authority and aggregations of interest groups, from managerial ideologies to the problems of the political community.

In 1960, I was forty-four and the paper also shows how I tried to grapple with the realization that my preoccupation with totalitarianism had to give way to the awareness that as a social scientist of the late twentieth century I had to start coping with the enormous inequalities burdening the world. At the same time I felt handicapped by the time spent on studying the economically advanced countries. Rather than attempt to study an economically backward country intensively, I used the opportunity of a fellowship to spend a year in India and Japan, to begin to understand a very poor country of our time and an advanced country outside the Western context. The paper, however, was written before I undertook this exploratory travel (1961-1962). It therefore reflects an effort, not fully conscious at the time I am sure, to rethink the Western experience I had studied, in order to see whether past modernizations held any lessons for the "developing" countries of our century, and if not, why not. In reprinting this essay I have only altered phrases that on re-reading appear to have been mistaken expressions of what I wanted to say. I suppose few writers can resist the temptation of re-stating what they had wanted to say more correctly or adequately than they did twenty-five years earlier. I have resisted this temptation as best I could.

The essay remains a document of transitions. To make my relative change of interest and orientation as explicit as possible, I have allowed repetitions of themes in the essays of Parts A and B to remain unchanged. They are unavoidable in a collection of essays written over many years and ordered thematically so that kindred thoughts appear in different contexts. The reader should be aware that the essay contains anticipations of *Nation-Building and Citizenship* (1964) and of *Kings or People, Power and the Mandate to Rule* (1978).

THEORETICAL PERSPECTIVES

In the developing areas of the world new class-relations emerge, as one after another country tries to develop independent political institutions and initiates economic growth. In the "developing areas" of Europe a comparable process took place since the French Revolution and during much of the nineteenth century. This essay seeks to enhance our understanding of the modern problem by a re-examination of the European experience with special reference to the relation of social stratification and the political community in the nation-state.[1]

This re-examination has a theoretical purpose. The social and political changes of European societies provided the context in which the concepts of modern sociology were formulated. As we turn today to the developing areas of the non-Western world, we employ concepts that have a Western derivation. In so doing one can proceed in one of two ways: by formulating a new set of categories applying to all societies or by rethinking the categories familiar to us in view of the transformation and diversity of the Western experience itself. This study adopts the second alternative in the belief that the insights gained in the past should not be discarded lightly and that a reassessment of the Western experience may aid our understanding of the developing areas of the non-Western world.

The problem before us is the transformation of Western Europe from the estate-societies of the Middle Ages to the absolutist regimes of the eighteenth century and thence to the class-societies of popular sovereignty in the nation-states of the twentieth century. In the course of this transformation new class-relations emerged, the functions and powers of centralized national governments increased and all adult citizens acquired formal legal and (at a later time) political equality. Attempts to understand this transformation gave rise to social theories that were necessarily a part of the society they sought to comprehend. Though their scientific value is independent of this fact, our understanding is aided when we learn how men come to think as they do about the society in which they live. Such self-scrutiny can protect us against the unwitting adoption of changing intellectual fashions; it can alert us to the limitations inherent in any theoretical framework. Since the present essay deals with social stratification in relation to the political community, a critical assessment of some of the assumptions implicit in studies of this relationship constitutes a part of our inquiry.

A glance at the history of social thought since the Renaissance suggests that this relation has been viewed in terms of three perspectives: that society is an object of government, that politics and government are a product of society, and thirdly that society and government are partly interdependent and partly autonomous spheres of social life.[2]

Inevitably, this division of social theories since the Renaissance is arbitrary. Each of the three orientations can be traced back much farther; and there are many linkages among these orientations which blur the distinctions between them. But it is also true that these perspectives have recurred in the history of social theory and that they provide us with useful benchmarks for the reconsideration of "society and the state" which is the particular purpose of this essay.

The idea that society is an object of state-craft goes back in the Western tradition to the medieval tracts containing "advice to princes." From an education of character designed for the sons of rulers this idea was developed into an instrument of state counsel by Machiavelli. In the eighteenth century Montesquieu drew upon this tradition in his theory of law in which he combined the old precepts of state-craft by a personal ruler with an analysis of the social and physical conditions which would facilitate or hinder the exercise of authority under different systems of rule.[3] A view of society as an object of state-craft was closely related to the rise of absolutism in Europe, as Friedrich Meinecke has shown in his study of ideas concerning "reasons of state" and the rights and duties of rulers.[4] In this intellectual perspective a high degree of passivity on the part of society had been presupposed. The masses of the people were excluded from all political participation and became an object of governmental attention primarily as a source of tax revenue and military recruitment. Accordingly, this intellectual perspective lost its appeal wherever absolutism declined and political participation on the part of the people at large increased, although in inchoate form it has come back into fashion through the growth of the welfare-state.

As attention came to be focused on the conditions facilitating or hindering the ruler's purpose, "Machiavellism" gradually blended with the second perspective, the idea that politics and government are products of society. In post-Renaissance Europe this idea came to the fore in the attacks of the Enlightenment philosophers on the established privileges of the church and the aristocracy. These privileges were seen as unjust usurpations arising from the vested interests of established institutions, while politics appeared as a by-politics, its application to the past politicized history. With unabashed forthrightness writers like Voltaire surveyed and judged past events in terms of the eighteenth century concept of a universal human nature and its inherent morality. By distributing praise or blame among contestants of the past they made history appear as a story of ever-changing conflicts among vested inter-

made history appear as a story of ever-changing conflicts among vested interests, suggesting that all governments are mere by-products of contemporary
partisanship.

During the eighteenth century such judgments were made in the belief that
"man" was endowed by God with certain universal moral attributes. During
the nineteenth century this belief and the theory of natural law were replaced
increasingly by attempts to develop a scientific study of human nature and the
political community. A key figure in this transition was Henri de Saint-
Simon, who proposed to make morals and politics into a "positive science"
by basing both on the study of physiology which concerned the truly universal
properties of man. In this way speculation would be replaced by precise
knowledge with the result that political problems would be solved as simply as
questions of hygiene.[5] The outstanding feature of this approach was the tendency to reduce the manifest diversity of social and political life to some underlying, basic element, that presumably could be understood with scientific
precision. During the nineteenth century ever new elaborations of this reductionist approach were advanced, from proposals of a "sociology" based upon
biological facts through various explanations in terms of climate, race and the
struggle for survival to Marx's theory of history as ultimately determined by
the imperative that men "must be able to live, if they are to 'make history.' "
Many of these theories of society accepted the scientific optimism of the
nineteenth century and assumed that a knowledge of the "underlying" forces
of society or nature provided the clue to human power and that in one way or
another such knowledge could be translated into action.

The third intellectual perspective, that society and government are partly
interdependent and partly autonomous spheres of social life, deserves more
extended consideration, since it reflects (and provides insight into) the structural transformation of Western societies which is the focus of this essay. Here
again we may begin with the Enlightenment, especially with those
philosophers who emphasized the cleavage between bourgeois *society* and the
state. That cleavage existed as long as each man's private concerns were at
variance with his duties as a citizen. It was towards a solution of this problem
that Rousseau made his many attempts to reconcile man in the "state of nature" whose virtues and sentiments were as yet unspoiled by civilization, and
man as a citizen who must subordinate himself to the community but without
doing violence to his dignity as a man.[6] This speculative contrast between
man's potential morality and his actual conduct, and this effort to base the political community on the first rather than the second, were replaced in the
nineteenth century by explanations which accounted for man's ethical
capacities *and* his actual behavior in terms of human nature in society.

An outstanding example of such an explanation is found in the work of
Emile Durkheim, which illuminates both the theoretical perspective of

liberalism and the transformation of Western society which is examined below. As a sociologist Durkheim wished to study morality empirically, a phenomenon arising "naturally" from the group-affiliations of the individual. But as a political liberal Durkheim also knew that such group-affiliation would obliterate the personality of the individual, unless the state intervened to guarantee his freedom. It will be seen that in this way Durkheim altered and continued the tradition of the Enlightenment; for him society itself was the "state of nature" for each individual, but as such it was also differentiated from the legal order and representative government of the "civil state."

From the beginning of his work Durkheim was concerned with a scientific analysis of the moral problems raised by the Enlightenment. He praised Rousseau for developing a construct of the *civil state* or society that was superimposed on the "state of nature" *without doing violence to the latter*. But he also criticized Rousseau's conception of the individual person as isolated, which made it difficult to see how any society was possible.[7] Durkheim applied a similar criticism to the utilitarian doctrine, which indeed he regarded as inferior to the Enlightenment tradition in that it made the social nexus entirely dependent upon the exchange relationship of the market while abandoning the earlier concern with the moral pre-conditions of the civil state.[8] The supposition underlying these approaches, that a basic conflict existed between "man in nature" and "man in society," appeared to Durkheim to be factually incorrect. By a study of the exterior social constraints which compel individuals to act alike regardless of personal motivation he proceeded to demonstrate that society was possible because man was naturally social. In a series of studies of suicide, the family, crime, religion and the division of labor he showed that the moral norms governing individual behavior originated in each person's group-affiliation and hence that Rousseau had been wrong in postulating a conflict between man in a "state of nature" and man in society. In other words, Durkheim "solved" Rousseau's problem by making the individual completely subordinate to society.

> Every society is despotic, at least if nothing from without supervenes to restrain its despotism. Still, I would not say that there is anything artificial in this despotism: it is natural because it is necessary, and also because, in certain conditions, societies cannot endure without it. Nor do I mean that there is anything intolerable about it: on the contrary, the individual does not feel it any more than we feel the atmosphere that weighs on our shoulders. From the moment the individual has been raised in this way by the collectivity, he will naturally desire what it desires and accept without difficulty the state of subject to which he finds himself reduced.[9]

Thus, if society is jeopardized, this is due not to a hypothetical conflict between society and the individual, but to a state of *anomie* in which his group-affiliations no longer provide the individual with norms regulating his conduct in a stable fashion. Where such group-norms are weakening as in modern society, the social order can be rebuilt only on the basis of strengthened group-norms. Accordingly, Durkheim concluded his studies with the proposal of a new corporatism, based on modern occupational groups, so that "the individual is not to be alone in the face of the State and live in a kind of alternation between anarchy and servitude."[10]

As these studies progressed Durkheim continued to espouse the "moral existence of the individual." As a life-long liberal he was not willing to postpone this humanistic component to the indefinite future, as Marx had done. And as a sociologist he had demonstrated both man's fundamentally social nature and the seemingly inevitable tendency of increasing "individual variations" as the division of labor increased and the "common conscience" of the group became more general and permissive.[11] But if individualism is inevitable sociologically, why be concerned with safeguarding it politically? This combination of a sociological determinism with political liberalism arose, because like Tocqueville, Durkheim became concerned with the *secular transformation of group-constraint*. The associational ties of the province, the parish and the municipality one after another lost their significance for the individual. "In the structure of European societies," he observed, a "great gap" had been created between the state and the individual.[12] Durkheim's proposal to bridge this "gap" by a new corporatism did not provide a political solution to the problem, as he himself recognized. The individual would be saved in this way from anomie and loneliness vis-à-vis the state, but he would also be oppressed by the secondary group to which he belonged.

Durkheim's answer to this question deserves extensive quotation, since it is not generally familiar.

> In order to prevent this happening, and to provide a certain range for individual development, it is not enough for a society to be on a big scale; the individual must be able to move with some degree of freedom over a wide field of action. He must not be curbed and monopolized by the secondary groups, and these groups must not be able to get a mastery over their members and mould them at will. There must therefore exist above these local, domestic—in a word, secondary—authorities, some overall authority which makes the law for them all: it must remind each of them that it is but a part and not the whole and that it should not keep for itself what rightly belongs to the whole. The only means of averting this collective particularism and all it involves for the individual, is to have a special agency with the duty of representing the overall collectivity, its rights and its interests, vis-à-vis these individual collectivities . . .
>
> Let us see why and how the main function of the State is to liberate the individual personalities. It is solely because, in holding its constituent societies in check, it prevents them from exerting the repressive influences over the individual that they would otherwise exert. So there is nothing inherently tyrannical about State intervention in the different fields of collective life; on the contrary,

it has the object and the effect of alleviating tyrannies that do exist. It will be argued, might not the State in turn become despotic? Undoubtedly, provided there were nothing to counter that trend. . . . The inference to be drawn from this comment, however, is simply that if that collective force, the State, is to be the liberator of the individual, it has itself need of some counter-balance; it must be restrained by other collective forces, that is, by those secondary groups. . . . *And it is out of this conflict of social forces that individual liberties are born.*[13]

For these reasons Durkheim defined that political society as "one formed by the coming together of a rather large number of secondary social groups, subject to the same one authority which is not itself subject to any other superior authority duly constituted."[14]

Durkheim's sociological theories do not prepare us for this political solution of his problem.[15] The emancipation of the individual from the "despotism of the group" appears in the bulk of his work as a result of the increasing division of labor and the related attenuation of custom and law. Though as a political liberal Durkheim valued this "range of individual development," as a social philosopher he feared its consequences for social morality where these consisted in the isolation of the individual and the loss of regulative norms of conduct (anomie). Accordingly he sought to safeguard the individual against the dangers of anomie by his re-integration in the "secondary groups" of society (corporations based on the occupational division of labor). Yet at the same time he called on the aid of the state to preserve individual liberties against the "despotism" with which these groups would seek to control the individual. Implicit in this approach is, therefore, a "dualism" whereby man's psychological and moral attributes are explained in terms of his membership in the society, while the society as a whole is characterized by an overall process (the increasing division of labor), which accounts among other things for man's capacity to alter these attributes through state-intervention in the interest of justice.[16]

This incongruity between Durkheim's sociological and political theories was symptomatic of the liberal tradition in the nineteenth century. Even the classic formulation of this tradition contained, as Elie Halévy has shown, two contradictory principles. Arising from the division of labor in a market-economy man's "propensity to truck, barter and exchange one thing for another" tended to reveal a "natural identity of interests" which enhanced unaided the general interest of society. Yet the quantity of subsistence is insufficient to allow all men to live in abundance and this insufficiency is aggravated by the failure of men voluntarily to limit their numerical increase. Hence it follows, by an exception to the first principle, that the State should protect the property of the rich against the poor as well as educate the latter so that they will restrain their instinct of procreation. In this way the State acts to ensure the "artificial identification of interests."[17]

Thus, the liberal tradition in its classic or its Durkheimian version is characterized by a "dualism" according to which society and government constitute two interdependent, but partially autonomous spheres of thought and action. From a theoretical standpoint this tradition is unsatisfactory because it constantly shifts from the empirical level, as in the analysis of market-behavior or the individual's group-affiliation, to the ethical and political level, as in the demand that the state should act to prevent the undesired consequences of market-behavior or group-affiliation. Still, historically, this perspective can be explained by the unquestioned fact that the societies of nineteenth and twentieth century Europe witnessed a juxtaposition between society as an aggregate of interrelated groups and the nation-state with its identifiable institutional structure.[18]

STRUCTURAL PERSPECTIVES

Medieval Political Life

In turning now from theoretical perspectives to problems of social structure it will prove useful to begin, however sketchily, with the pre-conditions of representative government in the West.[19] In the problematic relations between the "estates" and the power of the royal government, say since the eleventh and twelfth centuries, we have to do with group-formations in society and the exercise of legitimate authority and hence with the relation between society and government which was discussed above in chapters 6 and 8.[20]

Characteristic of the political communities of this early period was the fundamental assumption that the personal ruler of a territory is a leader who exercises his authority in the name of God and with the consent of the "people."[21] Because he is the consecrated ruler and represents the whole community, the "people" are obliged to obey his commands; but he in turn is also responsible to the community. This idea of a reciprocal obligation between ruler and ruled was part of an accepted tradition; it can be traced back to ancient Roman and Germanic practices, was greatly strengthened by Christian beliefs, but became formal law only very gradually.[22]

These characteristics of medieval kingship were closely related to the political conditions of royal administration. Each ruler possessed a domain of his own which he governed as the head of a very large household. On the basis of the economic resources derived from this domain, and in principle, on the basis of his consecrated claim to legitimate authority, each ruler then faced as his major political task the maintenance of his authority over a territory, which as often as not was indistinguishable from the extension of his domain. In their efforts to solve this task secular rulers necessarily had to rely upon those elements of the population which by virtue of their possessions and local authority were in a position to aid the ruler financially and militarily, both in extending his territory and in exercising his rule over the inhabitants. From a pragmatic political standpoint this was a precarious expedient, since such aid of local notables could enhance their own power as well as that of the ruler.

As a result, secular rulers typically sought to offset the drive towards local autonomy by a whole series of devices which were designed to increase the personal and material dependence of such notables on the ruler and his immediate entourage.[23] This typical antinomy of the pre-modern political community in Western Europe became manifest with every demand by secular rulers for increased revenue and military service. And to the extent that such demands were followed up by administrative measures, local notables typically responded by uniting into estates that could exact further guarantees or increases of their existing privileges by way of compensating for the greater services demanded of them.

A second characteristic of medieval political life was, therefore, that certain persons and groups were exempted from direct obedience to the commands issued by, or in the name of, the ruler. This "immunity" guaranteed that within the delimited sphere of their authority these persons and groups were entitled to exercise the legal powers of government. This institution goes back to the privileged position of the royal domains in Imperial Rome, a privilege which was subsequently transferred to the possessions of the church, the secular local rulers (i.e. the landed nobility under feudalism) and during the eleventh and twelfth centuries to the municipalities. This system of negative and positive privileges (which may be called "immunities" and "autonomous jurisdiction") became the legal foundation of representative government in Western Europe, because it accorded positive, public rights to particular persons and groups within the political community. This institution of public rights on the part of certain privileged subjects is more or less unique to Western Europe. Perhaps the most important factor contributing to this development was the fundamental influence of the church, which through its consecration of the ruler and through the autonomy of its organization restrained the power of secular rulers and re-enforced the political autonomy of the secular estates.[24]

In this setting a political life in the modern sense could not exist. Rather, the political community consisted of an aggregate of more or less autonomous jurisdictions, firmly or precariously held together by a king to whom all lords and corporate bodies owed allegiance, and under whose strong or nominal rule they fought or bargained with him and with each other over the distribution of fiscal and administrative preserves. Consequently, politics at the "national" level consisted for the most part of a species of "international" negotiations among more or less autonomous jurisdictions within the confines of a country that sometimes possessed only a precarious cultural and political unity.

In such a polity the coalescence of interests among individuals was not based on voluntary acts, but on rights and obligations determined by birth, such that each man was—at least in principle—bound to abide by the rules pertaining to his group lest he impair the privileges of his fellows. Classes or status-groups in the modern sense could not exist, because joint action occurred as a result of common rights and obligations imposed on each group by law, custom, or special edict. Thus, every group or social rank encompassed the rights and obligations of the individual person. Under these conditions a man could modify the personal and corporate rule to which he was subject only by an appeal to the established rights of his rank and to the benevolence of his lord, although these rights might be altered collectively in the course of conflicts and adjustments with competing jurisdictions. As Max Weber has stated,

> the individual carried his *professio juris* with him wherever he went. Law was not a *lex terrae*, as the English law of the King's court became soon after the Norman Conquest, but rather the privilege of the person as a member of a particular group. Yet this principle of 'personal law' was no more consistently applied at that time than its opposite principle is today. All volitionally formed associations always strove for the application of the principle of personal law on behalf of the law created by them, but the extent to which they were successful in this respect varied greatly from case to case. At any rate, the result was the coexistence of numerous 'law communities,' the autonomous jurisdictions of which overlapped, the compulsory, political association being only one such autonomous jurisdiction in so far as it existed at all . . .[25]

In Western Europe this medieval political structure of more or less loosely united congeries of jurisdictions was superseded gradually by absolutist regimes marked by a relative concentration of power in the hands of the king and his officials and by a gradual transformation of the king's relation to the privileged estates.[26] The variety and fluidity of conditions under these absolutist regimes were as great as under the feudal political structure. For example, the nation-wide powers of the king developed much earlier in England than on the Continent, partly as a legacy of the Norman conquest. However, the insular condition with its relative ease of communication together with legal traditions antedating the conquest both in Normandy and in England also made for an early and effective growth of "countervailing" powers. None of the Continental countries achieved a similar balance with the result that their absolutist political structures revealed either a greater concentration of royal power and correspondingly a greater destruction of the estates as in France or an ascendence of many principalities with some internal balance between king and estates but at the expense of overall political unity, as in Germany. Still, by the eighteenth century, most European societies were characterized by absolutist regimes in which the division of powers between the king and oligarchic estates as represented by various "constituted bodies" was at the center of the political struggle.[27]

The French Revolution with its Napoleonic aftermath destroyed this system of established privileges and initiated the mass democracies of the modern world. We can best comprehend this major transformation of the relation between society and the state if we leave the complicated transitional phenomena to one side and focus attention on the contrast between medieval political life and the modern body politic which has emerged in the societies of Western civilization. To do so, it will prove useful to take the work of Tocqueville as our guide.

Tocqueville's Interpretation of "The Great Transformation"

Tocqueville's analysis has power because it covered a very long time-period, because the French Revolution unquestionably marked a transition despite all equally unquestioned continuities, and because in his admittedly speculative fears about a tyranny of the future he used a "logic of possibilities" that enabled him to cope intellectually with contingencies he could not predict. By extending the scope of his analysis he made sure that he was dealing with genuine distinctions between different patterns of social relations and political institutions at the beginning and the end of the time-span he chose to consider.

In his famous study of the French Revolution Tocqueville showed how the *ancien régime* had destroyed the century-old pattern of medieval political life by concentrating power in the hands of the king and his officials and by depriving the various autonomous jurisdictions of their judicial and administrative functions.[28] In pointed contrast to Burke's great polemic against the French Revolution Tocqueville demonstrated that in France the centralization of royal power and the concomitant decline of corporate jurisdictions had developed too far to make the restoration of these jurisdictions a feasible alternative. The nobility no longer enjoyed the rights it had possessed at one time, but its acquiescence in royal absolutism had been "bought" by a retention of financial privileges like tax-exemption, a fact which greatly intensified anti-aristocratic sentiment. Through the royal administrative system of the *intendants* the rights of municipal corporations and the independence of the judiciary had been curtailed in the interest of giving the government a free hand in the field of taxation with the result that the urban *bourgeoisie* was divested of local governmental responsibility and the equitable administration of justice was destroyed. Noblemen thus preserved their pride of place in the absence of commensurate responsibilities, urban merchants aped aristocratic ways while seeking preferential treatment for themselves, and both combined social arrogance with an unmitigated exploitation of the peasants. In lieu of the balancing of group-interests in the feudal assemblies of an earlier day each class was now divided from the others and within itself with the result that "nothing had been left that could obstruct the central government, but, by the same token, nothing could shore it up."[29]

Tocqueville's analysis was concerned explicitly with the problem of the political community under the conditions created by the French Revolution. He maintained that in the medieval societies of Western Europe, the inequality of ranks was a universally accepted condition of social life. In that early political structure the individual enjoyed the rights and fulfilled the obligations appropriate to his rank; and although the distribution of such rights and duties was greatly affected by the use of force, it was established contractually and consecrated as such.[30] The Old Regime and the French Revolution destroyed this system by creating among all citizens a condition of abstract equality, but without providing guarantees for the preservation of freedom. Hence, Tocqueville appealed to his contemporaries that a new community, a new reciprocity of rights and obligations, must be established and that this could be done only if men would combine their love of equality and liberty with their love of order and religion. This admonition arose from his concern with the weakness and isolation of the individual in relation to government. Because he saw the trend towards equality as inevitable, Tocqueville was deeply troubled by the possibility that men who are equal would be able to agree on nothing but the demand that the central government assist each of them personally. As a consequence the government would subject ever new aspects of the society to its central regulation.[31]

Here is Tocqueville's famous paradox of equality and freedom. Men display an extraordinary independence when they rise in opposition to aristocratic privileges. "But in proportion as equality was . . . established by the aid of freedom, freedom itself was thereby rendered more difficult of attainment."[32] In grappling with this problem Tocqueville used as his base-point of comparison an earlier society in which men had been compelled to lend assistance to their fellows, because law and custom fixed their common and reciprocal rights and obligations. As this society was destroyed the danger arose that individualism and central power would grow apace. To counteract this threat men must cultivate the "art of associating together" in proportion as the equality of conditions advances, lest their failure to combine for private ends encourage the government to intrude—at the separate request of each—into every phase of social life.[33]

We can learn much from these insights. Tocqueville was surely right in his view that the established system of inequality in medieval society had been characterized by an accepted reciprocity of rights and obligations, and that this system had been destroyed as the *ancien régime* had centralized the functions of government. The French Revolution and its continuing repercussions leveled old differences in social rank and the resulting equalitarianism posed critical issues for the maintenance of freedom and political stability. Again, he discerned an important mechanism of centralization when he observed that each man would make his separate request for governmental assistance. In contrast to this tendency as he observed it in France, Tocqueville commended the Americans for their pursuit of private ends by voluntary association, which would help to curtail the centralization of governmental power.

It is necessary, of course, to qualify these insights in view of Tocqueville's tendency to read into modern conditions the patterns of medieval political life. At an earlier time, when landed aristocrats protected their liberties or privileges by resisting the encroachments of royal power, the centralization of that power appeared as an unequivocal curtailment of such liberties. Today, however, that centralization is an important bulwark of all *civil* liberties, though by the same token government can infringe upon these liberties more effectively than before, as Tocqueville emphasized time and again. The collective pursuit of private ends, on the other hand, is not necessarily incompatible with an increase of central government, because today voluntary associations frequently demand more rather than less government action in contrast to the medieval estates whose effort to extend their jurisdictions was often synonymous with resistance to administrative interference from the outside. In contrast to Tocqueville, Durkheim clearly perceived this positive aspect of modern government and, correspondingly, the dangers implicit in group-control over the individual.

> It is the State that has rescued the child from patriarchal domination and from family tyranny; it is the State that has freed the citizen from feudal groups and later from communal groups; it is the state that has liberated the craftsman and his master from guild tyranny . . .

> [The State] must even permeate all those secondary groups of family, trade and professional association, Church, regional areas and so on . . . which tend . . . to absorb the personality of their members. It must do this, in order to prevent this absorption and free these individuals, and so as to remind these partial societies that they are not alone and that there is a right that stands above their own rights.[34]

Important as these qualifications are, they should not make us overlook the reason why Tocqueville's interpretation of the "great transformation" was illuminating.[35] By contrasting an earlier condition of political life, the transformation brought about by the *ancien régime*, the new condition of equality ushered in by the French Revolution, and the possibility of a new tyranny in the future, Tocqueville was concerned with "speculative truths" as he called them. This simplification of different social structures enabled him to bring out the major contrasts among them, and these are not invalidated by the short-run and more deductive analyses that went astray. As I see it, Tocqueville's work becomes intellectually most useful, if we attempt to develop within his overall framework a set of categories that may enable us to handle the problem of the modern political community, which he discerned, in closer relation to the empirical evidence as we know it today.[36]

To do so it will be useful to summarize the preceding discussion. Medieval political life consisted in struggles for power among more or less autonomous jurisdictions, whose members shared immunities and obligations based on an established social hierarchy and on a fealty relation with a secular ruler consecrated by a universal church. By the middle of the eighteenth century this pattern had been replaced by a system of oligarchic rule, in which the king exercised certain nation-wide powers through his appointed officials while other important judicial and administrative powers were pre-empted on a hereditary basis by privileged status-groups and the "constituted bodies" in which they were represented. In contrast to both patterns modern Western societies are characterized by national political communities, in which the major judicial and executive functions are centralized in the hands of a national government, while all adult citizens participate in political decision-making under conditions of formal equality in the more or less direct election of legislative (and in some cases executive) representatives. Centralization, on the one hand, and formally equal political participation, on the other, have given rise to the duality between government and society discussed above in theoretical terms.

The Problem of the Modern Political Community

Centralization means that such major functions as the adjudication of legal disputes, the collection of revenue, the control of currency, military recruitment, the organization of the postal system and others have been removed from the political struggle in the sense that they cannot be parceled out among competing jurisdictions or appropriated on a hereditary basis by privileged status-groups. Under these circumstances politics is no longer a struggle over the distribution of the national sovereignty; instead it has tended to become a struggle over the distribution of the national product and hence over the policies guiding the administration of centralized governmental functions.

One unquestioned corollary of such centralization is the development of a body of officials, whose recruitment and policy execution were separated gradually from the previously existing involvement of officials with kinship loyalties, hereditary privileges and property interests.[37] A second corollary of centralization has been a high degree of consensus at the national level. In the political communities of Western nation-states no one questions seriously that functions like taxation, conscription, law enforcement, the conduct of foreign affairs, and others, belong to the central government, even though the specific implementation of such functions is in dispute.[38] The "depersonalization" of governmental administration and the national consensus on the essential functions of government have resulted in national political communities characterized by a *continuous* exercise of central authority. This continuity is not affected by the individuals filling governmental positions or the conflicts of interest among organized groups which affect the legislative process. Accordingly, a national government of the modern type represents a more or less autonomous principle of decision making and administrative implementation.[39] For Durkheim it was the state which alone could guarantee the "moral existence" of the individual, and in his judgment the state was capable of having this effect because it is "an organ distinct from the rest of society."[40] Presumably, people as members of a political community regard the overall jurisdiction of this organ as inviolate, because they believe in the achievement and orderly revision of an overall reciprocity of rights and duties, whatever the particular political vicissitudes of the moment.

In the modern political community, consensus (or a workable reciprocity of rights and obligations) is strongest at this national level, although as such it possesses an impersonal quality that does not satisfy the persistent craving for fraternity or fellow-feeling. But this emergence of a national consensus concerning the functions of the national government has been accompanied also by a decline of social solidarity at all other levels of group formation. Classes, status groups and formal associations arise from the coalescence of social and economic interest, other groups are formed on the basis of ethnic and religious affiliation; in some measure these collectivities are reflected in voting behavior. Yet none of them involves a consensus comparable to the acceptance by all citizens of the idea that the national government possesses sovereign authority.

This is not a new issue. From the very beginning of the modern political community, say, since the great debates of the eighteenth century, social and political theorists have complained of the loss of social solidarity, for which the vast proliferation of associations has not appeared to be a proper palliative. When writers like Tocqueville and Durkheim stressed the importance of "secondary groups," they did so in the belief that such groups could counteract both the isolation of each man from his fellows *and* the centralization of government. Yet much of this analysis remained at a level where considerations of policy and an element of nostalgia merged with considerations of fact, especially in the ever-recurring, invidious contrasts between traditionalism and modernity.[41] Despite the eminent names associated with it, we should discard this legacy of obfuscation. The "great transformation" leading to the modern political community made the decline of social solidarity inevitable, because (if so complex a matter can be stated so simply) no association based on a coalescence of interests or on ethnic and religious affiliation could recapture the intense reciprocity of rights and duties that was peculiar to the "autonomous jurisdictions" of an estate society. The reason is that in these "jurisdictions," or "law communities" (*Rechtsgemeinschaften*) as Max Weber called them, each individual was involved in a "mutual aid" society, which protected his rights only if he fulfilled his duties. This great cohesion within social ranks was above all a counterpart to the very loose integration of a multiplicity of jurisdictions at the "national" political level. In this respect the absolutist regimes achieved a greater integration through centralized royal administration and the people's loyalty to the king, although the hereditary privileges appropriated by Church and aristocracy also subjected the ordinary man to the autocratic rule of his local master. Where such hereditary privileges replace the "law communities" of an earlier day, the privileged groups achieved considerable social cohesion, but the people were deprived of what legal and customary protection they had enjoyed and hence excluded even from their former, passive participation in the reciprocity of rights and obligations.[42] Modern political communities have achieved a greater centralization of government than either the medieval or the absolutist political systems, and this achievement has been preceded, accompanied, or followed by the participation of all adult citizens in political life (on the basis of the formal equality of the franchise). The price of these achievements consists in the diminished solidarity of all "secondary groups."

This "price" is a by-product of the separation between society and government in the modern political community. Whereas solidarity had been based on the individual's participation in a "law community" or on his membership in a privileged status group possessing certain governmental prerogatives, it must arise now from the social and economic stratification of society aided by the equality of all adult citizens before the law and in the electoral process.[43] On this basis exchange relations and joint actions may develop to the exclusion of "governmental interference" or in quest of governmental assistance or with the aim to achieve representation in the decision making bodies of government.[44] Though it certainly has an impact on the national government, individual and collective action on this basis does not account for the governmental performance of administrative tasks, or, in the larger sense, the continuous functioning of the national political community.

In the societies of Western civilization we should accept, therefore, the existence of a genuine hiatus between the forces making for social solidarity independently of government and the forces accounting for the continuous exercise of central authority in the national political community.[45] This existing pattern is the result of a slow and often painful process. As the central functions of the national government became gradually accepted, organized groups within the society demanded representation in this national political community. Accordingly, "political community" refers not only to the central functions of government and the consensus sustaining them, but to the much more problematic question whether and how the groups arising within the society have achieved a national reciprocity of rights and obligations. For at the beginning of European industrialization in the nineteenth century new social groups were in the process of formation and had yet to learn (in the words of Tocqueville) what they were, what they might be, or what they ought to be, in the emerging national community of their country.

IMPLICATIONS FOR A COMPARATIVE STUDY OF SOCIAL STRUCTURES

During the eighteenth and nineteenth centuries the societies of Western civilization industrialized and became democratic. We should utilize the knowledge gained from this experience as we turn today to a study of the "developing areas" of the non-Western world. This task is difficult because our theories of the "great transformation" in the West have been inevitably a part of that transformation as well. In an effort to disentangle these theories of change from the change itself the preceding discussion has separated the theoretical reflections of this transformation from a consideration of changes in the institutional structure. While retaining the contrast between medieval and modern society it has discarded the nostalgia so often associated with that contrast. And it has utilized the distinction between society and the state in view of its analytical utility and the institutional duality which exists in this respect in the "developing areas" of yesterday and today.[46] In this concluding section I attempt to reformulate this contrast in general terms so as to facilitate a comparative study of social structures.

My thesis is that for our understanding of "society" and "the state" in the nations of Europe since the French Revolution the third perspective (mentioned above in Part I) is most useful, if it is considered as an analytical framework rather than as the political theory of liberalism. In the utilitarian contrast between the "natural identity" and the "artificial identification of interests," in Durkheim's concern with group-interaction and state-interference, or, to cite an American example, in W.G. Sumner's distinction between "crescive" and "enacted" institutions we have repeated references to two types of human associations. One of these consists in affinities of interest which arise from relations of kinship, the division of labor, exchanges on the market place and the ubiquitous influence of custom. The other consists in relations of super- and sub-ordination which arise from the exercise of instituted authority and compliance with its commands.[47] The distinction refers to a universal attribute of group-life in the sense that, however interrelated, these two types of human association are not reducible to each other.[48] From an analytical viewpoint it is necessary to consider "society" and "the state" as interdependent, but autonomous spheres of thought and action which coexist in one form or another in all complex societies, although the separation of these "spheres" is perhaps the greatest in modern Western societies.[49]

The generality of this distinction suggests that it lends itself to a comparative study of types of interrelation between social structure and the political community. In medieval Europe two such types were "competing" with each other as Machiavelli pointed out:

> Kingdoms known to history have been governed in two ways: either by a prince and his servants, who, as ministers by his grace and permission, assist in governing the realm; or by a prince and by barons, who hold positions not by favour of the ruler but by antiquity of blood. Such barons have states and subjects of their own who recognize them as their lords, and are naturally attached to them. In those states which are governed by a prince and his servants, the prince possesses more authority, because there is no one in the state regarded as a superior other than himself, and if others are obeyed it is merely as ministers and officials of the prince, and no one regards them with any special affection.[50]

Government as an extension of the royal household and government based on the fealty between landed nobles and their king and leader thus represented two types of social structure as well as two types of instituted authority.

Again, in the societies of Western civilization at the beginning of the present era this duality between society and the state is reflected in two far-reaching developments, which were eventually followed by a third. A market economy emerged based on contract or the ability of individuals to enter into legally binding agreements, while gradually the exercise of governmental authority was separated from kinship ties, property interests and inherited privileges. These developments occurred at a time when the determination of governmental policies and their administrative implementation were confined to a privileged few. But in the course of the nineteenth century this restriction was reduced and eventually transformed through the extension of the franchise, the growth of bureaucracy and of professionalism.

If we consider these developments in retrospect we can summarize their effects on society and the state. The growth of the market economy and the adoption of universal franchise have given rise to interest groups and political parties which mobilize collectivities for economic and political action and thereby "facilitate the interchange between . . . the spontaneous groupings of society" and the exercise of authority.[51] On the other hand, the "depersonalization" of governmental functions has accompanied a centralization of legislative, judicial and administrative decision-making and implementation which now facilitates the "reverse interchange" between the state and society.[52] The efficacy of these "interchanges" will vary not only with social cleavages and party-structures as Lipset has shown, but also with the "depersonalization" of government and the propensities of rule-abiding behavior among the people at large. On the whole, Western societies are characterized in these respects by a cultural tradition which ensures the containment of group-conflicts within a gradually changing constitutional framework, a high degree of probity in office and popular compliance with rules. But it is well to remember that even in the West the centralization of government and the democratization of political participation have on occasion created a hiatus that has proved more or less intractable. A striking case in point is the Italian experience with its "negative interchange" between society and the state, as exemplified by the "anti-government organization" of the Sicilian *Mafia* which among other things "protects" the society against governmental encroachments.[53] An extreme case like this serves to remind us that all Western societies have had to grapple with a duality that ranges from the juxtaposition of private concerns and public obligation in each citizen to the juxtaposition of solidary groups based on common interest and appointed officials acting in their authorized capacity.

To say that this hiatus is bridged by "interchange" from both sides only refers to the end-product of a prolonged balancing of group interests and formal institutions. In this respect the great issue of the nineteenth century had to do with the question whether and on what terms the disfranchised masses would be accorded the rights of national citizenship. The resolution of this issue could be eased *or* complicated through the continued confinement of politics to an elite of notables and through the natural as well as legal obstacles standing in the way of effective political organization. The balance between oligarchic resistance and popular political activation, the rise of central power and the later development of citizenship on the part of all adults posed the problem of how a new reciprocity of rights and obligations could be established *at the national level*. In several European countries this problem of a national political community came to the fore at a time when the "new" social classes of employers and workers began to make their bid for political participation and to cope as well with the problem of their reciprocal rights and obligations. Ideological controversy was at its height as these and other groups became capable of organized action and as long as they were denied their bid for equal participation in the political process. But as one after another social group has been admitted to such participation, they have in each case used their newly acquired power to pressure the national government into enacting and implementing a guaranteed minimum of social and cultural amenities. In this way a new reciprocity of rights and obligations among conflicting groups could be established by the "welfare state" at the national level and where this has occurred ideological controversy has declined.[54]

Clearly, this statement does not apply to the "developing areas" of the world today. Instead, we are witnessing the formal mobilization of the "voiceless masses" through elementary education, voting, and modern means of communication, while at the same time trying to control the consequences of that mobilization. This means that all the cleavages of the social structure are given political articulation simultaneously, while governments attempt to plan economic development and provide the minimum essentials of public welfare. If it be argued that such governments possess only an uncertain authority and relatively little experience, it will be answered that they must make the attempt nevertheless because only on this basis will the mobilized masses positively identify themselves with the new nation.[55] As a consequence of these conditions, ideological controversy is waged with unparalleled intensity, while political leaders attempt to establish a functioning governmental machinery and protect it against the continuous assault of politics and corruption.

In their increasing preoccupation with the "developing areas" of Asia and Africa since World War II Western scholars have had to grapple with the applicability of concepts which had been formulated in the context of Western experience. Since a simple application of these concepts is found wanting the further we move away from that experience, it is not surprising that some scholars decide to discard them altogether in an attempt to comprise in one conceptual scheme all political phenomena, Western and non-Western. The spirit of this enterprise is best conveyed in the following quotation:

> ... the search for new concepts ... reflects an underlying drift towards a new and coherent way of thinking about and studying politics that is implied in such slogans as the 'behavioral approach.' This urge towards a new conceptual unity is suggested when we compare the new terms with the old. Thus, instead of the concept of the 'state,' limited as it is by legal and institutional meanings, we prefer 'political system'; instead of 'powers,' which again is a legal concept in connotation, we are beginning to prefer 'functions'; instead of 'offices' (legal again), we prefer 'roles'; instead of 'institutions,' which again directs us toward formal norms, 'structures'; instead of 'public opinion' and 'citizenship training,' formal and rational in meaning, we prefer 'political culture' and 'political socialization.' We are not setting aside public law and philosophy as disciplines, but simply telling them to move over to make room for a growth in political theory that has been long overdue.[56]

In this approach politics is to be considered a universal phenomenon and as a result the distinction is discarded between societies which are "states" and those which are not, and that just at a time when leading groups in the "developing areas" are directly concerned with the organization of states and the development of governmental machinery.[57]

The preceding discussion has suggested that this is not a new problem even in the Western experience. The rise of absolutism promoted the centralization of governmental power. But no one reading the record of mercantilist regimes can avoid the conclusion that the efficacy of that central power was often as doubtful as is the efficacy of highly centralized governments in the "developing areas" of today. Again, the destruction of many intermediate centers of authority and the consequent emancipation of the individual through the institution of a national citizenship inevitably accentuated all existing cleavages within the society by mobilizing the people for the electoral struggle over the distribution of the national product. Thus, centralization of power and national citizenship gave a new meaning to the duality between society and the state, as Tocqueville observed long ago, and as we have occasion to witness in the "new nations" of the non-Western world today. It may be true, of course, that some of these "developing areas" are confronted by such an accentuation of cleavages within their social structure and such a lack of effective government, that anarchy reigns, or a political community can be established only by a "tutelary democracy" or a dictatorship as safeguards against anarchy. Meagre resources in the face of staggering tasks, the relative absence of a legal and governmental tradition, and the precipitous political mobilization of all people greatly increase the hazards even aside from the additional aggravation of the Cold War. The efforts to cope with these difficulties certainly command our earnest attention and no one can be sure of their outcome. In view of that uncertainty we should try to preserve the insights we have gained from the Western experience into the social foundations of government *and* the political foundations of society. If a balance is achieved between these perspectives we may be able to utilize our knowledge for an understanding of contemporary social change.

NOTES

1. The two terms used in the title of this paper were chosen in preference to the more conventional terms "society" and "state," although the latter are used in the text as well. My reason is that "social stratification" emphasizes as "society" does not the division of individuals into social ranks which provide the basis of group-formation that is of interest here. The term is used in this very general sense with the understanding that individuals who differ from one another are united into groups by a force that overrides the differences existing between them, as T.H. Marshall put it in his definition of "class." "Political community" in turn emphasizes the consensus between governors and governed within the framework of a polity while the term "state" puts the emphasis upon the administrative aspect of government, at any rate in English usage. Both aspects must be considered together, but I do not wish to emphasize government administration in the title.
2. For easy identification it would be desirable to label these three approaches, but it is awkward to do so since every label has misleading connotations. "Society as an object of state-craft" may be considered a Machiavellian approach, but his perspective is also characteristic of the social-welfare state which is not "Machiavellian" in the conventional meaning of that term. Government considered as a "product of society" might be called the sociological perspective, but this is also characteristic of Marxism which should not be identified with sociology, and then there are sociologists like Max Weber and Robert MacIver who do not adhere to this view. The theory of a partial dualism between society and government is a characteristic feature of European liberalism, but to call it the "liberal orientation" carries overtones of a specific political theory which need not be associated with this approach. In view of such difficulties I have decided to avoid convenient labels and repeat the three phrases mentioned in the text.
3. The development suggested here is traced in Friedrich Meinecke, *Die Entstehung*

des Historismus (München: R. Oldenbourg, 1946), ch. III. The partly scientific orientation of Machiavelli and Montesquieu is discussed in Leonard Olschki, *Machiavelli the Scientist* (Berkeley: The Gillick Press, 1945) and Emile Durkheim, *Montesquieu and Rousseau* (Ann Arbor: University of Michigan Press, 1960).

4. See Friedrich Meinecke, *Die Idee der Staatsräson* (München: R. Oldenbourg, 1925), passim. The work is available in English translation under the title *Machiavellism*. The relation between this concern with "reasons of state" and the development of factual knowledge about society is discussed in Eli Heckscher, *Mercantilism* (New York: Macmillan Co., 1955), II, pp. 13-30, 269 ff. and Albion Small, *Origins of Sociology* (Chicago: University of Chicago Press, 1925). See also C.J. Friedrich, *Constitutional Reasons of State* (Providence: Brown University Press, 1957).

5. Quoted in Frank E. Manuel, *The New World of Henri Saint-Simon* (Cambridge: Harvard University Press, 1956), p. 135. Professor Manuel shows how this theme recurs in ever new formulations throughout Saint-Simon's writings.

6. Karl Löwith has shown that this contrast goes back to ancient Greek and Christian ideas and he has traced the development of this theme during the nineteenth century. See his book *Von Hegel zu Nietzsche* (Zürich: Europa Verlag, 1941), pp. 255-65 and ff. See also the judicious restatement of Rousseau's position in R.R. Palmer, *The Age of the Democratic Revolution* (Princeton: Princeton University Press, 1959), pp. 119-27.

7. Emile Durkheim, *Montesquieu and Rousseau*, pp. 65, 137, and passim.

8. See Emile Durkheim, *The Division of Labor in Society* (Glencoe: The Free Press, 1947), pp. 200-206 and passim.

9. Emile Durkheim, *Professional Ethics and Civic Morals* (Glencoe: The Free Press, 1958), p. 61. Published for the first time in 1950 in a Turkish edition of the French manuscript, these lectures were delivered by Durkheim in 1898, 1899 and 1900 at Bordeaux and in 1904 and 1912 at the Sorbonne. As will be shown below, these lectures contain Durkheim's political theory and their repeated delivery together with the well-known preface to the second edition of *The Division of Labor* (published in 1902) indicate that for Durkheim this aspect of his work was of great importance. It is a symptom of the "sociologizing" tendency of our own time that this political aspect has been neglected or ignored by most scholars who have been influenced by Durkheim's sociological theories.

10. I take this telling phrase from Marcel Mauss's introduction to Emile Durkheim, *Socialism and Saint-Simon* (Yellow Springs: The Antioch Press, 1958), p. 2. Durkheim's elaboration of his views on the corporate society may be found in the second preface to his *The Division of Labor*, pp. 1-31. Cf. especially the following summary statement of his position: "A society composed on an infinite number of unorganized individuals, that a hypertrophied state is forced to oppress and contain, constitutes a veritable sociological monstrosity . . . Where the State is the only environment in which men can live communal lives, they inevitably lose contact, become detached, and thus society disintegrates. A nation can be maintained only if, between the State and the individual, there is intercalated a whole series of secondary groups near enough to the individual to attract them strongly in their sphere of action . . . " ibid., p. 28. In the preceding account I have only restated in the briefest compass the familiar themes of Durkheim's work. The best analytical exposition of these themes is contained in Talcott Parsons, *The Structure of Social Action* (Glencoe: The Free Press, 1949), ch. VIII-XI, though this

statement was written before Durkheim's unpublished lectures on the state became available.

11. Emile Durkheim, *The Division of Labor*, pp. 283 ff.
12. Ibid., pp. 27-28, 218-19.
13. Emile Durkheim, *Professional Ethics and Civic Morals*, pp. 61-63. My italics.
14. Ibid., p. 45. This formulation is indebted to Montesquieu and Tocqueville.
15. Cf. the reference to this paradox in E. Benoit-Smullyan, "The Sociologism of Emile Durkheim and His School," in H.E. Barnes, ed., *An Introduction to the History of Sociology* (Chicago: University of Chicago Press, 1948), pp. 518-20.
16. See *Division of Labor*, pp. 386-88.
17. Elie Halévy, *The Growth of Philosophical Radicalism* (London: Faber and Faber, 1928), pp. 90-91, 118-20, 489-91, and passim.
18. Today, I would generalize this juxtaposition in theoretical terms. My reasons have been stated above in chapter 8.
19. The following statement relies on the work of Otto Hintze, "Weltgeschichtliche Bedingungen der Repräsentativverfassung," *Historische Zeitschrift*, CXLIII (1930), pp. 1-47 and by the same author, Typologie der ständischen Verfassungen, *Historische Zeitschrift*, CXLI (1929), pp. 229-48. Hintze's contributions are corroborated and extended in Dietrich Gerhard's "Regionalismus und Ständisches Wesen als ein Grundthema Europäischer Geschichte," *Historische Zeitschrift*, LCXXIV (1952), pp. 307-37. Cf. the further discussion of this theme below in Chapter 13.
20. This characteristic feature of medieval political life will be contrasted below with the problematic relation between social stratification and the political community in modern Western societies.
21. The quotation marks refer to the ineradicable ambiguity of this term in medieval society. The "people" were objects of government who took no part in political life. Yet kings and estates frequently couched their rivalries in terms of some reference to the "people" they claimed to represent. In fact, "consent of the people" referred to the secular and clerical notables whose voice was heard in the councils of government. See the discussion of this issue in Otto Gierke, *Political Theories of the Middle Ages* (Boston: Beacon Press, 1958), pp. 37-61. It may be added that this ambiguity is not confined to the Middle Ages, since all government is based in some degree on popular consent and since even in the most democratic form of government the "people" are excluded from political life in greater or lesser degree. These differences of degree, as well as the qualities of consent and participation are all-important, of course, even though it may be impossible to do more than formulate proximate typologies.
22. Cf. Max Weber, *Law in Economy and Society* (Cambridge: Harvard University press, 1954), ch. V and passim.
23. In his analysis of traditional domination Max Weber distinguished patrimonial from feudal administration, i.e., the effort of rulers to extend their authority and retain control by the use of "household officials" or by their "fealty-relationship" with aristocratic notables of independent means. These two devices are by no means mutually exclusive, since "household officials" were usually of noble birth and in territories of any size demanded autonomy, while "feudal" notables despite their independence frequently depended upon the ruler for services of various kinds. Contractual obligations as well as elaborate ideologies buttressed the various methods of rule under these complementary systems. For an exposition of Weber's approach cf. R. Bendix, *Max Weber, An Intellectual Por-*

trait (Garden City: Doubleday and Co., 1960), pp. 334-79, which is based on Weber, *Wirtschaft und Gesellschaft* (Tübingen: J.C.B. Mohr, 1925), II, pp. 679-752.

24. A systematic analysis of this role of the church is contained in Max Weber, *op. cit.*, II, pp. 779-817. A brief resume of this chapter is contained in Reinhard Bendix, *Max Weber*, pp. 320-26. For a detailed historical treatment of the consecration of secular rule cf. Ernst Kantorowicz, *The King's Two Bodies* (Princeton: Princeton University Press, 1957). See also the summary statement in chapter 13 below.

25. Weber, *Law in Economy and Society*, p. 143. In this connection it should be remembered that the privileges or liberties of medieval society were associated with duties that would appear very onerous to a modern citizen. Also, these individual or collective "privileges" frequently resulted from compulsion rather than a spontaneous drive for freedom, as is vividly described in Albert B. White, *Self-government at the King's Command* (Minneapolis: University of Minnesota Press, 1933). The title itself illuminates the combination of royal power *and* compulsory local autonomy, which was typical in England, but not found to the same extent elsewhere in Europe. Still, the privileges of an estate also had the more ordinary meaning of rights (rather than duties), and this was true to some extent even of the lower social orders. Cf. the discussion of this problem by Herbert Grundmann, "Freiheit als religiöses, politisches und persönliches Postulat im Mittelalter," *Historische Zeitschrift*, CLXXXIII (1957), pp. 23-53. A detailed case-study of medieval political life is contained in Otto Brunner, *Land und Herrschaft* (Brünn: Rudolf M. Rohrer Verlag, 1943).

26. Cf. note 22 above for a reference to Weber's distinction between feudalism and patrimonialism as the two aspects of "traditional domination" which were present throughout the European Middle Ages. The development towards absolutist regimes is best seen, therefore, as a relative shift of emphasis in western European institutions, which varied from country to country.

27. For a comparative account of this political structure in eighteenth century Europe cf. Palmer, *The Age of the Democratic Revolution*, ch. III and passim.

28. Alexis de Tocqueville, *The Old Regime and the Revolution* (Garden City: Doubleday and Co., 1955), pp. 22-77. For a modern appraisal of the survival of corporate and libertarian elements under the absolutist regimes of the eighteenth century cf. Kurt von Raumer, "Absoluter Staat, Korporative Libertät, Persönliche Freiheit," *Historische Zeitschrift*, CLXXXIII (1957), pp. 55-96.

29. Alexis de Tocqueville, *op. cit.*, p. 137.

30. Ibid., pp. 15-16.

31. See above chapter 9, p. 213-14 for a discussion of Tocqueville's point in relation to the growth of "organized interests." I touch on the same point below, but omit the quotation I used here originally to avoid repetition.

32. Alexis de Tocqueville, *Democracy in America* (New York: Village Books, 1954), II, p. 333.

33. Cf. ibid., pp. 114-132.

34. Emile Durkheim, *Professional Ethics and Civic Morals*, pp. 64-65.

35. A fuller critical appraisal of Tocqueville's facts and interpretations is contained in the essay by George W. Pierson, *Tocqueville in America* (Garden City; Anchor Books, Doubleday and Co., 1959), pp. 430-77, though Pierson slights Tocqueville's theoretical contribution which is emphasized in the text.

36. A further theoretical note is in order here. No one doubts the relevance of the distinction between a feudal order and an equalitarian social structure, which

Tocqueville analyzed. In any study of social change we require some such long-run distinction so that we can know whence we came and where we may be going, though distinctions of this kind may be tools of very unequal intellectual worth. But while it is the merit of long-run distinctions that they enable us to conceptualize theoretically significant dimensions of social life (within the same civilization over time or between different civilizations), it also follows that these distinctions will become blurred the more closely we examine social change in a particular setting and in the short-run. The following discussion will suggest some concepts that are designed to "narrow the gap" between the long and the short run and hence reduce to some extent the reliance on deductions which characterized Tocqueville's work. But I doubt that the gap can be closed entirely, because in the short-run we are bound to fall back upon Tocqueville's method of logically deduced possibilities of social change, even if we can go farther than he did in comparing actual changes with these artificial benchmarks. Two rules of thumb should be kept in mind, however. One is that this partly inductive and partly deductive study of social change in the short-run should not lose sight of the long-run distinctions, for without them we are like sailors without compass or stars. The other is that this retention of the long-run distinctions imparts a dialectical quality to the analysis of short-run changes. Since we do not know where these changes may lead in the long-run we must keep the possibility of alternative developments conceptually open and we can do this by utilizing the dichotomous concepts so characteristic of sociological theory. For suggestions along these lines cf. the chapters in Part Two above. This perspective is greatly indebted, of course, to the work of Max Weber.

37. Max Weber's well-known concept of "bureaucracy" is based on the assumption that this process of separation of modern from patrimonial administration has been completed. See his *Essays in Sociology* (tr. and ed. by H.H. Gerth and C.W. Mills; New York: Oxford University Press, 1946), ch. VIII. For an exposition of the contrast between patrimonial and bureaucratic administration see R. Bendix, *Max Weber*, pp. 419-20. An admirably clear, comparative study of administrative history, in which this process of separation is traced since the middle of the seventeenth century, is contained in Ernest Barker, *The Development of Public Services in Western Europe, 1660-1930.* (New York: Oxford University Press, 1944).

38. Admittedly, these matters are in flux and in this respect significant differences exist within Western civilization. Still, no one can be in doubt in the instances in which this fundamental assumption has come into question, as in the American Civil War or more recently in the critical conflict between the national government in France and the French settlers in Algeria. The Southern opposition to school-integration is *not* a comparable development, I believe, since even in the more extreme cases it was combined with an acceptance of national jurisdiction on which there is no sharp disagreement. The rejection of such national jurisdiction is exemplified by the recent history of Lebanon (as seen from the vantage point of 1986). Chapter 9 above contains an attempt at systematizing state-society relations over time.

39. Neither medieval political life nor the absolutist regimes of the eighteenth century nor yet many of the "developing areas" of the modern world knew or know a government of this type, because adjudication and administration were and are decentralized, personal, intermittent, and subject to a fee for each governmental service.

40. E. Durkheim, *Professional Ethics and Civic Morals*, pp. 64, 82.

41. For a survey of this line of thought, disguised as it is in theoretical disquisitions, cf. Robert A. Nisbet, *The Quest for Community* (New York: Oxford University Press, 1953).
42. Tocqueville tended to obscure this distinction by identifying this reciprocity in the earlier estate societies of medieval Europe with the later symbiosis of absolutist rule and aristocratic privilege, though he was quick to point out how absolutism tended to undermine the aristocratic position. On the increase of aristocratic privileges just prior to the French Revolution cf. Palmer, *op. cit.*, I, ch. II-IV.
43. Max Weber has characterized the contrast as follows: "In the legal systems of the older type all law appeared as the privilege of particular individuals or objects or of particular constellations of individuals or objects. Such a point of view had, of course, to be opposed by that in which the state appears as the all embracing coercive institution. . . . The revolutionary period of the 18th century produced a type of legislation which sought to extirpate every form of associational autonomy and legal particularism. . . . This . . . was effected by two arrangements: the first is the formal, universally accessible, closely limited, and legally regulated autonomy of association which may be created by anyone wishing to do so; the other consists in the grant to everyone of the power to create law of his own by means of engaging in private legal translations of certain kinds." Max Weber, *Law*, pp. 145-46.
44. Demands for representation are difficult to distinguish from demands for privileged jurisdictions or outright benefits, because representation in decision-making bodies may be used to obtain these privileges or benefits. It is clear at any rate that voluntary associations are not the unequivocal counter-weight to centralized power for which Tocqueville was searching in his study of American society. Instead, voluntary associations frequently demand governmental assistance even where they reject it in principle, and in this respect they act in much the same way as individual manufacturers tended to do a century ago according to Tocqueville's observations. Voluntary associations are a protean phenomenon. They are evidence of consensus within the society, especially where they pursue private ends as an alternative to governmental assistance and regulation. But they may also be evidence of dissensus within the national political community, in so far as they enlist the national government in the service of parochial interests, and hence seek to secure from the government privileges that are denied to other groups.
45. Incidentally this hiatus is reflected in the very widespread and sanguine juxtaposition of patriotism with the extreme selfishness of individuals and groups.
46. The term "state" is needed to designate the continuing political identity of the nation irrespective of the governments embodying this identity from time to time. Where monarchical institutions have survived they represent this identity separately from the ruling government. Such institutional separation is not possible under democracies. In this discussion the terms "state" and "political community" or "polity" are used interchangeably, since all three refer with different emphasis to the apparatus and the consensus sustaining the continuous political identity of the modern polity. The emphasis here differs slightly from that of footnote 1 above. The theoretical bases for the historical typology discussed here were analyzed above in chapter 8.
47. Like all such distinctions there is a good bit of overlap between the two types. Affinities of interest which arise from the social structure forever engender relations of super- and sub-ordination, while the exercise of instituted authority forever produces, and is affected by, affinities of interest.
48. Hence, the ideas that society is an object of state-craft or that all governmental in-

48. Hence, the ideas that society is an object of state-craft or that all governmental institutions are the product of social forces represent perspectives which are useful only as long as their partiality is recognized.

     In a recent article Raymond Aron states the case against the Comtean as well as Marxian tendency to reduce all politics and government to forces arising from the socio-economic sub-structure. "Contre l'un et l'autre, nous avons appris que la politique est une catégorie éternelle de l'existence humaine, un secteur permanent de toute société. Il est illégitime de se donner, par hypothèse, l'élimination de la politique en tant que telle ou de caractériser une société par sa seule infrastructure." See Raymond Aron, "Les sociologues et les institutions représentatives," *Archives européennes de sociologie*, I (1960), p. 155. The present analysis is in agreement with this position and I assume that Professor Aron would agree that the sociological level of analysis likewise possesses a certain autonomy. Perhaps it is symptomatic for the modern climate of opinion in the social sciences that the most elaborate systematization of social theory to date acknowledges society, culture and personality, *but not politics*, as relatively autonomous levels of analysis. Cf. Talcott Parsons, E.A. Shils et.al., *Toward a General Theory of Action* (Cambridge: Harvard University Press, 1951), pp. 28-29. Cf. also the learned critique of this reductionist tendency in Sheldon S. Wolin, *Politics and Vision* (Boston: Little, Brown & Co., 1960), chs. IX-X.

49. As I see it, this is the viewpoint from which Max Weber developed the analytical framework of his posthumously published work *Wirtschaft und Gesellschaft*. The fundamental distinction of that work is not the one between "economy" and "society," but between society and domination and hence between groups arising from the pursuit of "ideal and material interests," on the one hand, and relations of super- and sub-ordination arising from beliefs in legitimacy, administrative organization and the threat of force. For details of this interpretation cf. my book *Max Weber*, passim. A lucid exposition of the fundamental assumptions of this approach is contained in Robert MacIver, *The Web of Government* (New York: Macmillan and Co., 1947), ch. XIII.

50. Niccolò Machiavelli, *The Prince and the Discourses* (New York: The Modern Library, 1940), p. 15.

51. See S.M. Lipset, "Party Systems and the Representation of Social Groups," *Archives européennes de sociologies*, I (1960), p. 51. In this article Professor Lipset presents comparative materials of the interrelation of different representative systems with different social structures.

52. Cf. Philip Selznick, *TVA and the Grass Roots* (Berkeley: University of California Press, 1949), which may be considered a case-study of this "reverse interchange."

53. Cf. the analysis by E.J. Hobsbawm, *Social Bandits and Primitive Rebels* (Glencoe: The Free Press, 1959), ch. III. See also Roger Vailland's novel *The Law* which illustrates the anarchical propensities through which either formal compliance with, or the symbolic re-enactment of, the law is used to subvert all "rule-abiding behavior."

54. There is, thus, a close relationship between this *gradual* establishment of "social rights" and the decline of ideology, although it must be kept in mind that this decline in the West may be the consequence of the Cold War and the rise of ideology in the rest of the world as much as it is the result of the welfare-state. Different aspects of this complex phenomenon are discussed in T.H. Marshall, *Citizenship and Social Class* (Cambridge: University Press, 1950), ch. I; Otto Brunner, "Das

Zeitalter der Ideologien," *Neue Wege der Sozialgeschichte* (Göttingen: Vanden-hoeck and Ruprecht, 1956), ch. IX; E.A. Shils, "Ideology and Civility," *Sewanee Review*, LXVI (1958), pp. 450-80; Daniel Bell, *The End of Ideology* (Glencoe: The Free Press, 1960), Part III; and S.M. Lipset, *Political Man*, (New York: Doubleday and Co., 1960), pp. 403-17.

55. For a comparative analysis of the cleavages facing the "new nations" and the re-lated liabilities of government cf. E.A. Shils, "Political Development in the New States," *Comparative Studies in Society and History*, II (1960), pp. 268-82, 379-411.

56. Gabriel Almond, "A Functional Approach to Comparative Politics," in Gabriel Almond and James S. Coleman, eds., *The Politics of the Developing Areas* (Princeton: Princeton University Press, 1960), p. 4.

57. The concept "state" is discarded on the curious ground that it is based on a dichotomy which is incompatible with the existing continuity of the phenomena. Professor Almond suggests that with reference to the "developing areas" only the political "input" functions will be analyzed because the formal governmental structure ("output" function) is usually not well developed. This decision would seem to reintroduce the distinction which was discarded. Cf. ibid., pp. 12, 17.

12

TRADITION AND MODERNITY RECONSIDERED

Introductory Note

Many themes discussed in Chapter 11 were taken up at greater length in my book *Nation-Building and Citizenship* (1964, 1974). Prominent among these were two concerns. One was to get a clearer understanding of the differences between medieval and modern political structures in Western Europe. If the concept of "modernization" was to have any clear meaning at all, that had to be found where this process had occurred for the first time, and where it seemed to be beyond dispute. One part of that process was in the field of law and administration. The term *Nation-Building* referred to two sides of one transformation: the destruction of inherited privilege which included the expropriation of quasi-public functions from private ownership, and correspondingly the appropriation of those functions by a national government. This process is referred to more commonly as the centralization of governmental authority in the name of the people.

The second major concern—and the other part of the process—involved the emergence of citizenship. Prior to the "democratic revolutions" of the seventeenth and eighteenth centuries, all government was in the hands of an elite of rulers, clergymen and nobles. Usually, the urban patriciate belonged to this elite as well. The rest of the people were subjects. But following these revolutions, which R. R. Palmer has analyzed in all the Western countries where they occurred, subjects were turned into citizens. In principle, royal government by the grace of God was superseded by national government based on a popular mandate. Popular sovereignty or the voice of the people was replacing the grace of God (*vox populi, vox dei*) as the basic legitimation of governmental authority. But the change of principle was put into effect very gradually. The universal suffrage established by the French revolution was extended only to all male residents of the country, 25 years or older, who enjoyed a degree of economic security. Not only foreigners and children, but women and all economic dependents who paid no taxes were excluded from the franchise. The process whereby the franchise was extended to men younger than 25, to economic dependents, and eventually to women lasted for more than a century.

This extension of the franchise was one aspect of modernization. There were many others: urbanization; industrialization; the demographic transition from high birth- and death-rates and very rapid population increase to lowered death-rates and eventually lowered birth-rates and moderate or minimal population growth; a massive shift of employment from agriculture to manufacturing and services; scientific and technological change resulting in a transformation of human capacities that revolutionized the quality of human life in all its aspects, and much more besides. When one considers the developments since World War II: the defeat of Hitler's Germany, the political bifurcation of Germany and Korea between the superpowers of the world, the technical revolution in communication, decolonization and the rapid increase in the number of newly sovereign, but very poor countries, etc., it is hard to say what further results this massive process of "modernization" may produce. It is also difficult to subsume all of these changes under the heading of this one word. There is a sense in which change has been loosed upon the world with no prospect that such rapid transformations will come to an end, that "modernization" will result in "modernity." Yet, in the United States, where much of the effort to cope with these changes intellectually has come to be located, and where the sense of "being modern" is probably at its height, the spirit of moving forward, the belief in progress, the idea that with luck and effort solutions will be found where problems arise as they do in the wake of all these advances—in the United States it seemed especially important to reflect on the ever-repeated and often invidious contrast between tradition and modernity.

That is the context in which I came to write the following essay. Along the way I explored the meaning of "modernization," or rather some aspects of that meaning, in Japan, the Soviet Union, and India since independence. But having done so in addition to my reexamination of the Western-European case, I felt the need to come to terms with the frame of reference, the nearly bifurcated view of the world, which had become the fashion of the day

In reprinting this essay in this volume, I have omitted major sections dealing with the history of ideas and a critique of recent studies of modernization, respectively. Instead, I concentrate on the conceptual problems of studying modernization comparatively.[1]

MODERNIZATION

The term *modernization* became fashionable after World War II. The word reflects the discontinuities of interest which have marked the work of American social scientists in recent decades. Before the war, American scholars devoted their primary attention to the study of American society. Even if one considers the tremendous popularity of theories of social evolution in the United States before the 1920s, one is struck by the fact that these theories were largely applied in Social Darwinist fashion to an interpretation of the competitive economic struggle. The predominant American concern was domestic, in contrast with the trend in Europe where these theories were employed to interpret the encounter between the advanced industrial societies of the West and the peoples and cultures of colonial and dependent areas in Africa and the Orient. With the notable exception of anthropologists, this intellectual insularity of American social scientists may be related to America's anticolonial heritage, just as the renewed interest in comparative studies of social change may be related to America's world-wide political involvements since the Second World War.

A steadily increasing number of social scientists have become concerned with non-Western areas, especially with regard to problems of "modernization." A case in point is changing emphases in the field of history. Students used to learn the history of their own country in considerable detail, whereas the histories of other countries were presented more selectively, or not at all. Today, teachers of history no longer adhere to this position as firmly as they did some two generations ago. In notable instances they have familiarized themselves with the histories of non-Western countries and through team-teaching have presented students with comparative studies as well. Moreover, a series of publications has focused on problems of generalization in historical studies. Though preoccupation with national history remains predominant, many scholars so preoccupied are nevertheless concerned with problems of conceptualization in history, which are of central interest to social scientists.[2]

As so often with newly coined or readapted words, *modernization* has many meanings. One's first impulse in the 1980s—the word "modern" in the sense of "up-to-date" derives from a fifth-century Latin root—is to think of technical innovations like jet-travel, space-exploration, and nuclear power. On second thought one is likely to take in the whole era since the eighteenth century when inventions like the steam engine and the spinning jenny provided the major impetus for the industrialization of societies. Since this economic transformation coincided with the independence of the American colonies and the French revolution, "modernization" also evokes associations with democratization, that is the destruction of inherited privilege and the creation of the nation-state with its centralization of government and the extension of the franchise (or national citizenship).

These changes since the eighteenth century initiated a transformation of society comparable in magnitude to the transformation of nomadic peoples into settled agriculturalists some 10,000 years earlier. Till the mid-eighteen hundreds more than eighty percent of the world's labor force was engaged in agriculture. Some two centuries later that proportion still holds true for many "third world" countries. But meanwhile, in the industrialized countries, the agricultural work-force has fallen below fifty percent, reaching low figures like ten to twenty percent in countries with the longest history of industrialization. By 1950, in Great Britain, the proportion of the labor force in agriculture reached a low of five percent.[3]

Wherever it has occurred, this manifold modernization of societies originated in social structures marked by inequalities based on kinship ties, hereditary privilege and established (frequently monarchical) authority. By virtue of their common emphasis on a hierarchy of inherited positions, premodern or traditional societies have certain elements in common. The destruction of these features of the old order and the consequent rise of equality are one hallmark of modernization; hence the latter process shows certain uniformities. These changes in the social and political order were apparent before the full consequences of the industrial revolution were understood. As a result, most (if not all) thinkers of the nineteenth century

> ... exhibit the same burning sense of society's sudden, convulsive turn from a path it had followed for millennia. All manifest the same profound intuition of the disappearance of historic values—and, with them, age-old securities, as well as age-old tyrannies and inequalities—and the coming of new powers, new insecurities, and new tyrannies. . . .[4]

And, as Professor Nisbet adds, "Sociology in Europe was developed almost wholly around the themes and antitheses cast up by the two revolutions and their impact upon the old order."[5] Although we owe many insights to this intellectual tradition, it is also true that those antitheses give an oversimplified view of tradition, of modernity, and of the transition from one to the other. Oversimplification resulted from ideological interpretations and undue generalizations of the European experience. Today, a more differentiated and balanced analysis of modernization should be possible; the following discussion is presented as a contribution to that end.

Its first part deals with basic assumptions of a comparative approach to sociological analysis. In the second part I turn to a consideration of concepts of limited applicability, propositions that are true of more than one and less than all societies. Its last and main part applies these general considerations to a restructuring of the contrast between tradition and modernity. My objective is to retain that contrast, but to divest it of the misplaced ideological interpretations which have been associated with it.

ASSUMPTIONS OF COMPARATIVE SOCIOLOGICAL ANALYSIS

At least three divergent approaches to the study of historical change can be distinguished. The older, evolutionist approach tended to be classificatory. It assumed that the less developed countries would follow the "steps and sequences of change" through which the more developed have passed already. Culture traits, or even a whole country at a given time, are assigned to a specific stage of development. Once this is done, it is possible to assess the progressive or regressive significance of ideas and actions, either because the future or next state is "known" in advance, or at least because it seems plausible to classify the past of the developed countries for purposes of such retrospective evaluation. To be sure, evolutionist theory is no longer expounded in such simplistic terms. Scholars have become more cautious than their predecessors. Concepts of differentiation or increasing complexity are substituted for the idea of progress, and allowance is made for multilinear developments and the reversal or omission of "stages."[6] But while these modifications go far, it is not clear that the original theory has been abandoned. The proliferation of synonyms for "change," such as "development" or "modernization," with their several adjectives, warns us that this is an area of uncertainty and confusion; the new vocabulary often employs older theories of evolution uncritically.

Related to this older approach, but more modern in its nomenclature, is the view that societies should be analyzed as natural systems. In this perspective a social structure appears as an interrelated, functioning whole with systemic prerequisites, properties, and consequences, which may be identified as a unit that maintains or changes itself in order to survive as such. I have commented on this view in chapter 6, but wish to refer here to one modern tendency related to, but not identical with, this wholistic or systemic approach. I refer to the social-engineering approach, which is oriented toward planned social change. In its view, analysis should aim at the discovery of critical independent variables, since control of these will entail predictable changes in the dependent variables. Indebted to images derived from controlled experiments or from medical practice, this approach is less classificatory than the older evolutionist theory and less organicist than systems theory proper. But, like these theories, its simplifying assumptions and test of truth depend upon a *ceteris paribus* treatment of historical constellations. For example, the record of economic growth in the developed countries is employed as a model, however provisionally, so that historical preconditions reappear as logical prerequisites without which growth cannot occur. In this way the engineering approach comes close to the natural-systems approach in that both operate with the concept of "indispensable prerequisites," though the engineering approach is perhaps more candid in generalizing from the Western experience.[7]

Comparative analysis of historical change attempts a closer approximation to the historical evidence than is possible on the assumptions of evolutionism, or of systems theory, or of social engineering. As a result, it promises less in the way of prediction and in the way of guiding social actions towards defined goals. Whether this sacrifice is permanent or temporary remains to be seen. Studies of social change in complex societies may hold in abeyance the tasks of causal analysis and prediction while concentrating on the preliminary task of ordering the phenomena of social change to be analyzed further. This task can be characterized by reference to the meaning of change and of social structure.

At the risk of oversimplification, I shall assume that, at a minimum, considerations of change involve two terminal conditions, so that the word "change" refers to the differences observed before and after a given interval of time. Since the future is uncertain, studies of historical change deal in the first place with past changes, the better to understand what the contrasts between before and after are and how they have come about. Naturally, it is hoped that a better understanding of historical changes will contribute to a fuller exploration of developmental possibilities, perhaps even to constructive action, but the relations between knowledge and action are complex and should not be prejudged.

Studies of change, then, depend upon contrasts between social structures before and after change has occurred. Without knowledge of how a later social structure differs from an earlier one, we do not know what changes to look for and explain. This is one reason why studies of this kind use familiar concepts such as feudalism, democracy, totalitarianism, etc., despite the many justified criticisms leveled against these terms. Such concepts express something we want to express, namely, that in some over-all and important, but rather general, sense, an old social structure has passed away and a new one has taken its place. Dissatisfaction with such conventional terms is understandable, but it is no solution to substitute universal terms for these concepts of limited applicability. Almond has suggested, for example, that "interest aggregation" is a term that cuts across all the conventional distinctions between political systems and hence can be applied universally.[8] Such a term has the utility of prompting us to look for "interest aggregation" in unfamiliar social structures to which our conventional terms do not apply, but it does not dispense with the utility of terms such as "class" or "estate" which already differentiate—however approximately—more familiar types of "interest aggregation." I suspect that we shall invent new terms to fit the unfamiliar types of "interest aggregation" once we have analyzed them sufficiently, for concepts are the result of inquiry as much as they are its precondition.

What, then, is meant by "social structures" and how do we study them comparatively?

Social structures retain certain of their characteristics while individuals come and go. The specification of such enduring characteristics involves abstractions from observations of behavior and from historical evidence. On this basis, studies of social change should be able to state that one type of social structure has ceased to prevail and another has taken its place. Yet to make such an assertion involves the hazards demonstrated by the debates concerning Max Weber's ideal type. Definitions of structures such as feudalism, bureaucracy, etc., usually take the form of enumerating several distinguishing characteristics. Such enumerations necessarily "freeze" the fluidity of social life, as Weber himself emphasized. They say nothing about the strength or the prevalence of a given characteristic, nor do they say anything about structures in which one or another element of the definition is missing. The result has been uncertainty. Abstractions are needed to define the characteristics of a structure and thus they remove the definition from the evidence. Conversely, when we approach the evidence "definition in hand," we often find its analytic utility diminished, because the characteristics to which it refers are in fact neither unequivocal nor general.[9]

Concretely: impersonal definition of rights and duties is one of the distinguishing criteria of bureaucracy. But "impersonal definition" has meant many things: the rights and duties of the classic Chinese bureaucrat and of an English official in the administrative class are worlds apart, even if both are impersonally defined. Nonetheless, the criterion is indispensable if we are to find all instances of bureaucracy or properly identify those instances we do find. Then we will want to know how general and important the phenomenon of impersonal definition is in a given case. Typically, this involves us in the task of analyzing the methods by which the rights and duties of officials are defined, and the degree to which these definitions correspond to behavior. That analysis will reveal the characteristic discrepancy between formally stipulated methods and actual implementation, and that discrepancy will raise questions about the utility of the criterion ("impersonal definition") with which we started. Thus the criterion employed simplifies the instances to which it applies, and hence its analytic application poses difficulties. The dilemma is genuine, but there are proximate solutions.

Examination of comparative studies suggests, it seems to me, that definitions of social structures are contrast conceptions. Implicitly or explicitly, we define feudalism, capitalism, absolutism, caste system, bureaucracy, and other such terms by contrast with what each of these structures is not. For example, fealty ties are contrasted with contractual ties, absolutist-centralized with feudal-decentralized authority, caste with tribe or estate, impersonal with personalized administration, the unity of household and business with their separation, etc. My suggestion is that contrast conceptions are indispensable as a first orientation (they serve a function as bench marks), which introduces analysis but should not be mistaken for analysis.

Since social structures are defined by several characteristics, more than one contrast conception may be found analytically useful. The choice depends in good measure on the purpose of the inquiry and the historical context. In the emergence of modern bureaucracy, as Weber defined it, the recruitment of officials and their exercise of authority were emancipated from the direct intrusion of kinship relations and property interests. This aspect was prominent as long as hereditary privileges prevailed, but has declined in importance along with the rise of egalitarianism in all spheres of modern life. The exclusion of "every purely personal feeling" remains a valuable desideratum and a proximate characteristic of official conduct but this condition may not do as much today to insure administrative impartiality as it did when government by a social elite encouraged the intrusion of family loyalties and property interests upon the conduct of public business. That is, recruitment to official positions on the basis of impersonal criteria and the separation of office and incumbent remain characteristics of bureaucracy, but the changed structure of modern politics has altered their significance. For certain purposes it would be useful, therefore, to formulate an early and a later type of bureaucracy, which would take account of this altered environment of government administration.

In this view, the definition of a social structure in terms of a cluster of traits can serve only as a first approximation. On closer inspection, every such trait proves to be an abstraction from the contentions among groups of men. The fealty relation between king and vassal is one of the defining characteristics of feudalism. But the contentions over reciprocal rights and obligations between these classes of men are resolved in a variety of ways without thereby divesting that relation of the quality of fealty. In this way, social structures are defined by a set of issues which comprise the characteristic areas of contention among the constituent groups of a society. If we then say that one social structure has ceased to exist and another has taken its place, we mean that the terms of reference have changed by which issues are defined, relationships maintained, or contentions resolved. This is the meaning, it seems to me, of Tocqueville's classic specification of the contrast between a feudal and a democratic society.[10]

One corollary of these considerations is that concepts of social structure should be used in two forms. By bureaucracy we mean a depersonalized form of governmental administration, but we know that depersonalization is a matter of degree. Hence we use "bureaucracy" when we wish to contrast one type of administration with another, and "bureaucratization" when we wish to emphasize that the new term of reference ("depersonalized personnel selection") continues to be problematic, an issue whose every resolution creates new problems as well. Similarly, one can distinguish between democracy and democratization, nation and nation-building, centralized authority and the centralization of authority, etc. Such usage will create linguistic problems from time to time. For example, Max Weber's usage of *Vergesellschaftung* instead of *Gesellschaft* had much the same purpose that I suggest here, and it is not exactly usual in German either. Whatever the linguistic difficulties, we should keep the substantive distinction in mind.

By defining social structures in terms of a set of issues, we not only avoid the reification of concepts but make them "operational." If, in this way, we reformulate Max Weber's definition of bureaucracy, we obtain a specification of the issues over which individuals and groups contend in their effort to realize their ideas and maximize their chances, however they define these. The consequence of such contentions is a development in the direction of bureaucratization or debureaucratization, as the case may be. Analysis of such contentions can account for the changing strength of the "traits" which characterize a social structure, but are "never twice the same."[11]

A third corollary is a reformulation of the concept of equilibrium. Having been taken over from feedback mechanisms such as the thermostat or from biological analysis, the term is widely used by social scientists who employ the concept of social system. Such systems are believed to survive as long as they are in condition of equilibrium or return to it. The idea has merit in the very general sense that we combine with the concept of social structure the notion of some stability and identity over time. We must account for such stability as exists. However, I do not consider the concept of equilibrium useful for this purpose, because it is not the social structure or the system that maintains itself in "equilibrium," whatever that means, but men, who, by their actions (however conditioned), achieve a certain degree of stability or fail to do so. Here the definition of social structure in terms of a set of issues helps, because it points to the contentions through which individuals and groups achieve a measure of accommodation or compromise between conflicting imperatives.

Here may be the place also to comment briefly on a problem raised by a German and by an English historian, both of whom warn us against the dangers of substituting inevitably arbitrary categories for the terms in which the historical participants themselves think about the questions at issue.[12] The point is well taken, I believe, and the definition of social structure suggested here allows us to take account of this subjective dimension. But it is also necessary to go beyond that dimension and define the social structure which eventually results from all these contentions; and that cannot be done in subjective terms alone. Indeed, some abstractions and arbitrariness will be unavoidable in order to freeze the fluidity of historical change for purposes of obtaining bench marks, as suggested earlier. It may be that the deliberate employment of static *and* dynamic terms, for example bureaucracy and bureaucratization, democracy and democratization, etc., provides a way of conceptualizing both the group contentions that are an essential part of change and the altered social structures which from time to time result from that change.

The points discussed may now be considered in relation to the comparative analysis of historical change, and specifically of the "steps and sequences of change in the processes of nation-building and national integration." Ideally, we should be able to consider all such changes in the same terms, and there is a powerful intellectual legacy which invites us to do so. That legacy goes back to the contrast between tradition and modernity which was first formulated in the Romantic period and has been reformulated ever since. Familiar dichotomies such as status and contract, *Gemeinschaft* and *Gesellschaft*, folk and urban society, and others have been given their most systematic formulation in Talcott Parsons's scheme of pattern variables. The utility of these distinctions has been diminished, in my opinion at least, by a tendency toward reification. Nineteenth-century evolutionary theory, for example, imputed to the different aspects of a society "a strain of consistency with each other, because they all answer their several purposes with less friction and antagonism when they co-operate and support each other."[13] Modern reformulations of this idea in terms of systems theory and equilibrium are more sophisticated no doubt, and have an impressive array of analogies to draw on, yet they continue to attribute a "strain of consistency" to social structures such that the "frictions and antagonisms" between the several traits will diminish—in the famous long run.[14]

On these assumptions it is certainly possible to consider all societies in comparative terms, irrespective of time and space. This approach has been most fully developed with regard to the social and psychological consequences of industrialization, and in the field of national integration with regard to the study of the central value system.

For the scholar interested in comparative studies, the alternative to this approach is to think in terms of concepts applicable to some, rather than all, societies. This strategy of analysis proceeds in the belief that concepts of universals—even if useful for certain orientating purposes—are so emptied of content that they require specifications in order to be applied to some body of evidence, and these specifications are concepts of more limited applicability. Examples: interest aggregation is a universal concept, whereas class, estate, political party, etc., are more limited; goal-attainment is universal, but administration by disciples or bureaucrats or patrimonial servants is limited, and so on. By "concepts of limited applicability," I mean concepts that are usefully applied to more than one society for a period whose approximate beginning and end are themselves an object of research. Such delimitation is always debatable. But, however difficult in detail, I doubt that it is useful, for example, to speak of class in the absence of a formal legal equality and the freedom of movement and expression that goes with it, or of political parties in the era of politics among cliques of notables, or of the nation-state in the absence of a monopoly of legitimate coercion in the hands of government—although in these and other cases the qualifying criterion is a variable as well as a contrast conception, as discussed earlier. These considerations are equally applicable to "nation-building." The concept "nation" requires delimitation against a period and condition to which it does not apply, and it may be that, with variations in such preconditions, different types of nationhood will have to be formulated. A nation is always in the process of change, for example in the extent to which consensus prevails or different sections of the people have formally equal rights—hence the phrase "nation-building."

With regard to any such change, whether it is the "building" of a nation-state or modernization in any of its meanings, the specification of an early and a late condition is necessary, the "before-and-after" model to which I referred. It is useful, therefore, to lay down some methodological guidelines for the study of social change which follow from the preceding discussion.

METHODOLOGICAL GUIDELINES

As indicated, the word "change" refers to the differences observed before and after a given interval of time. Without knowing in what respects a later social structure differs from an earlier one, we would not know what changes to look for and explain. Accordingly, we are obliged to characterize the earlier, traditional and the later, modern social structure by two lists of mutually disjunctive attributes. And therein lies the dilemma we face, for the ideal types constructed in this way are *not* generalizations. An example may make this clearer. Talcott Parsons has contrasted the particularism of a traditional with the universalism of a modern society, one set of attributes among many. Suppose we apply this contrast. Medieval European society was certainly particularistic in many respects, yet one of its major components was the universalism of the Christian faith and the institutions of the Catholic church. Even in India, where Hindu religion and the caste system fostered an extreme particularism, the basic cultural themes of karma and reincarnation spread throughout the sub-continent. Evidently, particularism characterizes traditional societies only in some respects, whereas in others tradition is combined with universalism. By the same token, the universalism of rights based on an impersonal assessment is very widespread in modern society, and in many respects this is unequivocal. All American citizens have the right to vote, and to exercise that right they must prove their citizenship, their age and enter the registry of voters. The same universalism applies to school attendance at the elementary level. But when it comes to college admissions, a whole series of particularistic considerations enter in, among which the universalistic criterion of scholarly achievement is only one of many. So, tradition is particularistic but there are also universalist elements; modern society is universalist, but there are also particularistic elements. That is what Weber meant when he said that ideal types "simplify and exaggerate" the evidence.

The same disjunction between ideal types and the empirical world is found in studies of change. Weber was explicit on this point:

> *Developmental* sequences too can be constructed into ideal types and these con-
> structs can have quite considerable heuristic value. But this quite particularly
> gives rise to the danger that the ideal type and reality will be confused with one
> another.

The reason for this confusion is clear. In *constructing* a developmental sequence from tradition to modernity we will use illustrative materials in order to
make evident what we mean, and thereby we may be seduced into mistaking
the sequence of types for the course of events.

> The series of types which results from the selected conceptual criteria appears
> then as an historical sequence unrolling with the necessity of a law. The logical
> classification of analytical concepts on the one hand and the empirical arrange-
> ment of the events thus conceptualized in space, time, and causal relationship,
> on the other, appear to be so bound up together that there is an almost irresistible
> temptation to do violence to reality in order to prove the real validity of the con-
> struct.[15]

Accordingly, one methodological guideline should simply be to understand
why this confusion is widespread, and how it may be avoided.

In operating with a "before-and-after" model of social change, one has
difficulty in resisting the view that the two sets of attributes distinguishing the
earlier from the later social structure constitute generalizable systems of empirically interrelated variables. But in adopting this view, we ignore that each
list of attributes is ideal-typical. If we are to avoid mistaking ideal types for
accurate descriptions, we must take care to treat the clusters of attributes as
hypothetically, not as actually, correlated. We need these clusters to distinguish between social structures, we illustrate them by historical examples, but
these are still abstractions, constructs that should be used as tools of analysis.

That these cautions are often ignored may be illustrated by reference to two
related and quite common lines of reasoning. One of these has to do with the
notion of "prerequisites." Beginning with the contrast between tradition and
modernity (in one of its many versions) the analyst takes all the basic traits of
modernity to be prerequisites of modernity, a procedure which implies that
regardless of time and place all countries must somehow create all the conditions characteristic of modernity before they can hope to be successful in their
drive for modernization. But

> obviously, some of the factors listed are not prerequisites at all, but rather
> something that developed in the course of industrial development. Moreover,
> what can be reasonably regarded as a prerequisite in some historical cases can be
> much more naturally seen as a product of industrialization in others. The line
> between what is a precondition of, and what is a response to industrial develop-
> ment seems to be a rather flexible one.[16]

Such a distinction could be made only if the specific processes of industrialization are analyzed. However, causes and consequences tend to become confused, if instead a uniform process is assumed such that countries entering upon industrialization at a later time will repeat in all essentials the previous industrialization of some other country.

Another line of reasoning involves an undue generalization of a limited historical experience (rather than working back from present characteristics to necessary prerequisites). For example, the decline of kinship ties and the concomitant rise of individualism were aspects of Western modernization. Today we are learning how many meanings and exceptions were in fact compatible with this overall tendency, though these are quite properly ignored when we construct an ideal typical sequence. But, rather than using that sequence as an analytical tool to show how and why actual historical developments deviate from it, we use it to make contingent predictions about the future of "developing" societies.[17] To be sure, no one is likely to say simply that these societies will develop; he states instead that they will not develop unless kinship ties decline. There are at least three things wrong with this procedure: (a) it ignores the exaggerations and simplifications which went into the ideal type in the first place, and hence blinds us to the role which kinship ties and collectivism played in the modernization of Western Europe; (b) it also blinds us to the possible ways in which kinship ties and collectivism might be, or might be made, compatible with the modernization of other areas (tacitly we have misused the ideal type as a generalization); (c) it diverts attention from the very real possibility that modernization may never arrive at modernity, so that terms like "development" or "transition" are misnomers when applied to societies whose future condition may not be markedly different from the present. As Wilbert Moore has pointed out in a similar context:

> The manner in which history prevents its own replication creates difficulties in generalizations that will unite historical and contemporary experience and deal with diversity that optional paths of change introduce.... In addition to minimum, required sequences and results, what is needed, and is mostly not at hand, is the construction of limited-alternative or typological sequences where total generalization is improper.[18]

Strictures of this kind were already expressed by Gerschenkron in 1952.

The impetus to generalize even where generalization is improper derives in part from the desire to put policy directives on a "scientific" basis, and from the indispensability of ideal types in studies of social change. The fact that time and again the distinction between tradition and modernity has been oversimplified does *not* mean we can dispense with that contrast entirely. Studies of social change are not possible without a "before-and-after" model of the social structure in question.

The contrasts between pre-modern and modern social structures may be reformulated along the several dimensions that are conventionally distinguished in the analysis of social structures. The problem of the causal interrelation among these dimensions is one of empirical research which cannot be replaced by logical deductions, as long as the evidence argues against the assumption of one uniform process of modernization. Nor is it proper to turn the two attribute-checklists by which we may distinguish tradition from modernity into two systems to which certain properties are imputed. For in this way a set of separate or separable attributes is transformed into the structural propensities of a collective entity. Such reification is closely related to the moralism and scientism that has characterized many reactions to industrialization. Only assiduous attention to the liabilities and assets of both tradition and modernity can avoid the ideological implications of the ideal-typical contrast between the two configurations. Otherwise, we merely nurse the discontents of industrial society by contrasting the liabilities of the present with the assets of the past.

To avoid this pitfall, it is useful to summarize the preceding discussion in explicit contrast to the received conventions of sociology. Social structures may be distinguished by the solidarities they achieve. Typically, traditional societies achieve intense solidarity in relatively small groups isolated from one another by poor communication and a backward technology. These groups create for their individual participants an intensity of emotional attachment and rejection which modern men find hard to appreciate and which most of them would find hard to tolerate. Typically, modern societies achieve little solidarity in relatively small groups and by virtue of advanced communication and technology these groups tend to be highly interdependent at an impersonal level. In this setting individual participants experience an intensity of emotional attachment and rejection at two levels which hardly exist in the traditional society, namely in the nuclear family at its best and worst, and at the national level where personal loyalties alternate between being taken for granted in ordinary times and moving up to fever pitch during national crises or other direct confrontations with alien ways of life.

Analogous considerations apply to the invidious personification of modernity and tradition. For example, the stultifying effects of the division of labor became a major theme of social philosophers from the beginning of industrialization. Generations of writers have reiterated the theme with different contrasting images of man ranging from the "aristocrat" and the "medieval craftsman" to the several versions of "the Renaissance man" of protean capacities who has been the daydream of intellectuals from Goethe's Wilhelm Meister and Baudelaire's *Dandy* to Herbert Marcuse's "Multi-dimensional Man."[19] This romantic utopia of intellectuals in an era of industrialization must be taken seriously indeed, since the ideal images of a culture affect the changing social structure. But the idea of unlimited creativity by "the individual" or "the people" is as much a chimera as is that of a womb-like security and warmth in human relations attributed to a bygone age. These are projections of the discontents of intellectuals with a civilization that induces in them an intense ambivalence between elitism and populism—a point to which I return in chapter 14.

The contrast between tradition and modernity may be recast accordingly. It is probably true that traditional societies are characterized by universally accepted cultural norms. But this goes together with the subservience of men of letters to the church and to private patrons, and with the prevalence of illiteracy in the general population. It is, therefore, not accidental that terms like "ideology," and "intellectuals" originated in Europe during the eighteenth century, when traditional beliefs were challenged, men of letters were emancipated from their previous subservience and literacy increased along with printed materials and a market for literary products. The universal cultural norms of traditional society also go together with a low level of productivity and communication and with a consequent fragmentation of the social structure in economic, legal, and political terms. One implication of this fragmentation is the prevalence of force and fraud and of jurisdictional disputes among a large number of solidary groups which depend for their cohesion not only on common norms but also on the imperatives of self-help and defense.[20] In each of these solidary groups and in the polity as a whole, society tends to be divided sharply between rulers and ruled. Those of gentle birth have a disproportionate share of the wealth, privileged access to positions of formal authority, enjoy sociability, leisure, and culture, whereas the bulk of the population lives in the drudgery of physical labor and in poverty, without access to literacy, culture, or positions of influence, and without recognized means of airing their grievances. In this setting the term "society" is applied only with difficulty, since the people themselves live in fragmented subordination, while their rulers constitute "the society" because they are the persons worthy of note in the country. These attributes may suffice as a contrast-conception for a reformulation of modernity.

It is probably true that modern societies are characterized by relatively few cultural norms that are universally accepted, and this goes together with a relative emancipation of men of letters and a nearly universal literacy in the general population. Structural differentiation in technology and communications has led to high levels of productivity and a high degree of impersonal interdependence. Associated with this interdependence are the attributes of the nation-state which were noted earlier. The adjudication of legal disputes, the collection of revenue, the control of currency, military recruitment, the postal system, the construction of public facilities, and others have been removed from the political struggle among competing jurisdictions and have become the functions of a national government. Another and related characteristic of modern society is the process of fundamental democratization by which "those classes which formerly only played a passive part in political life" have been stirred into action.[21] The old division between rulers and ruled is no longer clear-cut, since the ruled have the vote, and the rulers are subject to formal controls at many points. Status distinctions no longer coincide with hereditary privileges. In this setting the term "society" is appropriately applied to all people in a country who constitute that society by virtue of their interdependence and equality as citizens.

The foregoing discussion has attempted to "de-ideologize" the conventional contrast of tradition and modernity. At this general level the contrast holds good for many societies that have undergone a process of modernization. Most "traditional societies" lack means of rapid communication so that the bulk of the population lives in relatively small enclaves isolated from one another. However, if one goes beyond such generalities, one is obliged also to go beyond the simple contrast discussed here. What is true of *all* traditional societies is by the same token not very illuminating about any one of them. As noted earlier, a key feature of the European experience was the tie-in of universal cultural norms with the organization of the Church and hence with the enduring, if rather unstable balancing of centralizing and decentralizing tendencies of government which culminated in the development of representative institutions.[22] In countries like Russia and Japan universal cultural norms came to prevail in a manner that is quite different from this Western-European pattern. The study of social change in these societies would, therefore, require a more specific conceptualization of the contrast between tradition and modernity, in order to be analytically useful. The general contrast here discussed should be only the beginning of analysis, though often it has been mistaken for analysis itself.

Another limitation becomes apparent when one applies these concepts to colonial and post-colonial societies. Can any colonial society be said to have the characteristics of "tradition"? Does it have universally accepted norms? And since the prevailing norms surely do not apply to the subject population, in what sense can one in fact speak of one society? To contrast the past and present social structure one should take account of at least two traditions: the native tradition and the tradition of a dual society created by the colonizing country. Analogous questions apply to the European frontier settlements abroad, as in the United States, Canada, Australia, and New Zealand, but here the native populations were not strong enough to create the problem of a dual society, while the imported culture of the European settlers already represented a major break with the medieval tradition. The point of these comments is to suggest that several models of change are needed and are preferable to any attempt of forcing all types of change into the Procrustean bed of the European experience.

That ideal types of social change are of limited applicability, makes them more, not less useful. Once the weakness of the most general formulation as well as the limitations of the Western-European model are observed, it is then appropriate also to recognize the utility of focussing attention on the area in which the breakthrough to modernity was achieved first. The following analysis attempts to spell out the implications of this breakthrough and to interpret the process of modernization in the light of the foregoing discussion.

MODERNIZATION IN COMPARATIVE PERSPECTIVE

Theoretical Orientation. As European societies approached the "modern era," men of letters came to think about differences of social rank with an awareness of a new society in the making. Although political and ideological rather than scholarly, these ideas about modern society have strongly influenced the concepts with which social scientists have approached the study of modernization. At this point it is useful to state the common denominator of this intellectual tradition in terms of three related tenets.

A. The industrial revolution in England and the contemporary political revolution in France had a profound cultural impact, frequently leading men of letters to formulate pervasive and invidious contrasts between the old and the new social order. As a result "tradition" and "modernity" came to be conceived in mutually exclusive terms, not only as a conceptual aid but also as a generalized, descriptive statement about the two, contrasting types of society. Related to this approach is a conception of each type of society as a social system, characterized by the functional interdependence of its component parts and a balance of forces among them. Hence, "traditional" and "modern" societies appear as two types of societies, each with its own, built-in tendency towards self-maintenance or equilibrium.

B. From the vantage-point of Europe in the late eighteenth and early nineteenth centuries, both revolutions and much of the social change that followed appeared as phenomena that were internal to the societies changing. This mode of explanation goes back to influences emanating from Plato and characteristic of Western philosophy down to the present.[23] In the late eighteenth century this intellectual tradition was reflected in interpretations of the growth of commerce and industry. Specifically, many writers of the period considered the division of labor a major factor in promoting social change. To a man like Adam Ferguson (1723-1816) that growth depended ultimately on the subdivision of tasks, which determined the ideas and actions of men, provided the basis for the difference between social classes, and gave rise to political actions.

The view that social change is the product of internal social forces has a certain basis in historical fact, difficult as it is to separate facts from reflections upon them. Most observers of early industrialization thought economic change the primary factor, whether they believed that governmental measures reflect that change, as the radicals did, or that these measures were needed to avert its worst consequences, as the conservatives did. In England, the work of the classical economists enhanced this consensus, because opposition to mercantilist policies argued for less regulation of economic affairs and hence for a secondary role of government. As governmental controls over the economy were reduced, as guild regulations were abandoned, as labor mobility increased along with population, trade, and manufacture, it became very plausible to consider that society and economy possess a "momentum" of their own, while government merely responds to the impact of social forces. At this time, office holding was still a form of property ownership so that the idea of authority as an adjunct of ownership partly described the society. In addition, the industrial revolution first occurred in England; among the continental countries England (along with Holland) lacked an absolutist tradition with its basis in a standing army, and she was also characterized by a more permeable upper class than the countries of the Continent. It was indeed a unique constellation of circumstances which gave new emphasis to the old view that social change is internal to the society changing, that social change originates in the division of labor, and that, consequently, government or the state are products of the social structure. It may be suggested that this intellectual perspective unduly generalizes from a very limited phase of the English experience.

Accordingly, both the intellectual tradition of Europe and the specific historical constellation at the end of the eighteenth century encouraged explanations of social change which emphasize the continuity and interconnectedness of changes *within* society, a tendency which was reinforced when modern nationalism came into its own. As a result a certain lawfulness was attributed to the social structure, while the relative autonomy of government and the impact of external factors upon every society were ignored or minimized. Paradoxically, this perspective also prevailed during a period of absolutist regimes, of European overseas expansion and of world-wide industrialization, when societies were increasingly subject to influences from abroad in contrast to the relative integrity of national societies in Western Europe. This cultural and historical background may help to account for the prominence of explanations which attribute change to a society's internal functional differentiation, such as the increasing division of labor, an observation that can alert us to the limitations of this intellectual perspective without questioning its analytic utility in the proper context.

C. The third tenet asserts that ultimately industrialization will have the same effects wherever it occurs. This follows, or appears to follow, from a combination of assumptions rather loosely linked with the preceding points. Where the causes of social change are conceived as intrinsic to a society, industrialization (and, more vaguely, modernization) is considered to have certain necessary and sufficient prerequisites without which it cannot occur. Conversely, once these prerequisites are given, industrialization becomes inevitable. The same reasoning is applied to the consequences of the process. Once industrialization is under way, it has certain inevitable results. In the long run, modernity will drive out tradition and fully industrialized societies will become more and more alike.

The three tenets mentioned here are closely related. Their common basis is the conception of society as a structure arising from a fixed set of preconditions and characterized by mutually reinforcing attributes which make the change of the structure appear as an inevitable modification of interrelated variables. This conception of society is closely related to the theory of social evolution, though that theory is not of direct concern to the present discussion.[24] But the three assumptions of social system, internal differentiation, and developmental inevitability form a coherent approach to the study of industrialization from which the approach to be discussed below will now be distinguished.

A. Against the view that tradition and modernity are mutually exclusive, I wish to maintain that even the two revolutions of the eighteenth century are best understood as culminations of specific European continuities, i.e. that "modern" elements were evident long before the modern era. (By the same token the European tradition, and English society particularly, had distinctive attributes not found in other civilizations.) The point may be illustrated with regard to the bases of social action. Kinship ties, religious beliefs, linguistic affiliations, territorial communalism, and others are typical forms of association in a traditional social order. None of these ties or associations have disappeared even in the most highly industrialized societies; to this day the relative decline of "traditional" and the relative ascendance of "modern" solidarities remain or recur as social and political issues. But some of the old ties or associations were weakened by the ascendance of Christianity, others by the Renaissance and Reformation, and others still in the course of the struggles between absolutist rulers and the estates. It may be recalled that Max Weber's lifework documents the proposition that Christian doctrine and the revival of Roman law militated against familial and communal ties as foci of loyalty which compete with the universal claims of legal procedure and the Christian faith. The ethical universalism of the Puritans and its subsequent secularization were later links in this chain of preconditions. By these prior developments in Western Europe men were freed very gradually for such alternative solidarities as those of the nuclear family, social class and national citizenship. In my view there was indeed a breakthrough to a new historical era, but this was the result of continuities reaching back to classical antiquity, which came to a head in a specific time and place owing to the very particular conditions of English society in the seventeenth and eighteenth centuries. This element of continuity was neglected by men of letters who interpreted the emerging industrial society in terms of a cultural conflict between tradition and modernity. However, in other respects continuity was emphasized.

B. Against the conception of change as intrinsic I wish to maintain that following the breakthrough in England and France every subsequent process of modernization has combined intrinsic changes with responses to extrinsic stimuli,[25] and has involved government intervention as a prominent feature of that process. The modernization of societies is *not* to be understood primarily as a result of internal changes in which governments play at best a secondary role. The great lacunae of the interpretations here opposed is their failure to account for the diffusion of ideas and techniques, the prominent role of government, and the rising tide of nationalism, all of which have accompanied the process of industrialization throughout.

The point is a general one. All complex societies have an internal structure and an external setting. Likewise, all complex societies possess a formal structure of governmental authority which differs from, and is relatively independent of, the group formations arising from the social and economic organization of society. For analytic purposes it is legitimate to separate these dimensions and to neglect one or another of them, if this seems indicated by the problem under consideration. But in the comparative study of modernization, and especially one that focuses attention on problems of social stratification, such neglect seems inadvisable. The influence of modernization on the means of communication is international in scope, so that we should attend to the external setting of societies, even where our primary focus is on changes internal to their social structures. Moreover, the secondary or dependent role of government resulted from very particular historical circumstances, and should not be considered a general, theoretical proposition. The facts are that intellectuals have played a major role in helping to transform the social structure of backward societies and have done so more often than not in reference to prior economic and political developments abroad. Likewise, government officials have played a major role in the development of economic resources, or have supported and implemented an institutional framework in which such a development became easier. To be sure, these are possibilities, not certainties. But to neglect the rather independent role of intellectuals or governmental officials in the process of modernization is to subscribe to the Marxian view that the international setting, the political structure and the cultural development of a society depend in the long run on its organization of production.

C. Against the concept of industrialization as a largely uniform process of structural change I wish to emphasize the importance of diffusion and of government "intervention" for an understanding of this process. England was the first country to industrialize and in Marx's view she exemplified the "laws of capitalist development." In his preface to the first edition of *Capital*, Marx declared England to be the classic ground of the capitalist mode of production. England was more developed industrially than other countries. As they enter upon the path in industrialization, these other countries will undergo developments comparable to those of England because of the tendencies inherent in the capitalist organization of production. Marx made this prediction on the assumption that the same organization of production generates everywhere the same or similar transformations of social classes and the political structure. As an empirical proposition, this assumption is false. Once industrialization had been initiated in England, the technical innovations and the institutions of the economically advanced country were used as a model in order to move ahead more rapidly than England had; and also as a warning so as to mitigate or even avoid the problems encountered by the pioneering country. Marx himself noted this possibility, but did not consider it seriously. He declared that his analysis of the advanced country could only help to "shorten the birthpangs" of similar developments in other countries, for the capitalist mode of production is governed by the same laws or inevitable tendencies wherever it occurs.

Again, the point is a general one. Industrialization itself has intensified the communication of techniques and ideas across national frontiers. Taken out of their original context, these techniques and ideas are adapted so as to satisfy desires and achieve ends in the receiving country. Certainly, such adaptation is affected at every point by the resources and economic structure of the country, but Marx tended to make necessities out of contingencies. He did not give full weight to the historical traditions which affect the social structure of every country and with it the capacity of a people to develop its opportunities. Nor did he consider that this structure is modified materially by the international transmission of techniques and ideas and by attempts to control the process and repercussions of industrialization politically. Against the view that industrialization has the same effects wherever it occurs, I wish to maintain the importance of timing and sequence as crucial variables. Once industrialization has occurred anywhere, this fact alone alters the international environment of all other societies. There is a sense in which it is true to say that because of timing and sequence, industrialization cannot occur in the same way twice.

Accordingly, studies of modernization should be guided by two considerations which have been neglected in the past. Although it is true that certain consequences follow from an increasing division of labor, these are embedded in the *particular* transition from a pre-industrial to an industrial structure which distinguishes one society from another. The social structure of a country's "transitional phase" should, therefore, be a primary focus of analysis rather than dismissed as a survival of the past. In addition, modernization, once it has occurred anywhere, alters the conditions of all subsequent efforts at modernization so that "the late arrivals cannot repeat the earlier sequences of industrial development."[26] Both considerations, the significance of the transition and the demonstration effects of "earlier sequences," preclude an evolutionary interpretation of modernization.

The reorientation I propose considers the industrialization and democratization of Western Europe a singular historic breakthrough, culminating a century-long and specifically European development. But modernization brings about special discontinuities by virtue of is expansive tendencies so that the relation between the intrinsic structure and external setting of societies assumes special significance. Thus, the internal, historically developed structure of a country and the emulation induced by economic and political developments abroad affect each country's process of modernization.

Towards a Definition of Modernization. My objective is to define the term so that it refers to change during a specific historical period. I want to show that throughout the designated period the process of change has certain overall characteristics. At the same time I emphasize the distinction between "modernization" and "modernity." Many attributes of modernization like widespread literacy or modern medicine have appeared, or have been adopted, in isolation from the other attributes of a modern society. Hence, modernization in some sphere of life *may* occur without resulting in "modernity." Uncertainty concerning their future existed in the past history of all presently industrialized countries, just as it exists at present in the so-called developing countries. Recognition of this uncertainty provides a better basis for the comparative study of modernization than the alternative assumption that industrialization has the same prerequisites and results wherever it occurs.

In thus preferring uncertainty to a generalizing, systemic analysis we deal in effect with two approaches to the study of social change. The *retrospective* approach employs a "before-and-after" model of society, i.e. some variant of the contrast between tradition and modernity. Such models are indispensable aids in an analysis of social change, which can start from a knowledge of past changes, though with the cautions suggested earlier. The *prospective* approach cannot employ such a model directly, because it seeks to deal with future contingencies. This second approach may still employ the available "before-and-after" models, but its emphasis will be on the diversity of modern societies in the search for clues to the process of transformation. I adopt this approach for the remainder of the discussion.

By "modernization" I refer to a type of social change which *originated* in the industrial revolution of England, 1760-1830, and in the political revolution in France, 1789-1794. One can set the inception of the changes here considered differently, and this is in fact advisable for certain purposes. The expansion of Europe, for example, antedated the late eighteenth century; some aspects of modernization like the diffusion of modern weapons can be traced back to the fifteenth century.[27] Also, particular antecedents of modernization can be traced back very far, as in the instance of printing or of representative institutions or ideas of equality, and many others. Nevertheless, there are reasons of scale which make it advisable to separate the transformations of European societies and their world-wide repercussions since the eighteenth century from earlier economic and political changes. Reference was made at the beginning to the massive transformation of agriculture, initiated in the eighteenth century. Similarly, the fundamental elitism of societies prior to the eighteenth century has been replaced, albeit gradually, by a "fundamental democratization" (Mannheim), and this change may again be traced to beginnings in the eighteenth century. Also, the distinction between the literate and the illiterate was beginning to break down in the course of the eighteenth century with the slow spread of both literacy and printed matter.[28] These three transformations of the economic, political, and social order may suffice as an indication that it is useful to treat the eighteenth century as a breakthrough to a new historical era, at any rate in studies of modernization.

The economic and political "breakthrough" which occurred in England and France at the end of the eighteenth century, put every other country of the world into a position of "backwardness." Indeed, the same may be said of the two pioneering countries. The economic transformation of England provided a "model" for France, while the political revolution of France instantly became a major focus of political debate in England. Ever since, the world has been divided into advanced and follower societies. With reference to the eighteenth and early nineteenth centuries, it is appropriate to have this formulation refer to England and France as the "advanced" countries and all others as follower societies, even though the statement would have omitted earlier pioneering areas such as Holland or Venice. But since that time the process has ramified much further. Follower societies of the past such as Russia or China have become advanced societies, which are taken as models by the satellite dependencies of Eastern Europe or by some African and Asian countries that have won their independence since World War II. Each of the countries that has come to play the role of "pioneer" with regard to some follower society has a history of externally induced changes, though with the success of modernization the emphasis on this extrinsic dimension may become less salient than it was at an earlier time. Accordingly, a basic element in the definition of modernization is that it refers to a type of social change since the eighteenth century, which consists in the economic or political advance of some pioneering society and subsequent changes in follower societies.[29]

This distinction implies a shift in intellectual perspective. Sociological theory commonly conceives of change as slow, gradual, continuous and intrinsic to the societies changing. This view is more or less appropriate as long as we confine ourselves to the enduring characteristics of a social structure which may aid or hinder the modernization of society. As suggested earlier, it is quite appropriate to the interpretation of change in European civilization, and this was the intent of Max Weber's question concerning the combination of circumstances to which the rationalism of Western civilization can be attributed. However, once the two eighteenth century revolutions had occurred, subsequent social changes were characterized by a precipitous increase in the speed and intensity of communication. Ideas and techniques have passed from "advanced" to "follower" societies, and to a lesser extent from "follower" to "advanced" societies. Within a relatively short historical period there are few societies which have remained immune from these external impacts upon their social structures.[30]

Diffusion of ideas and techniques is the byproduct of expansion by "advanced" societies, but it occurs even in the absence of expansion because of the economic and political breakthrough in eighteenth century Europe. As Gerschenkron has pointed out, leading strata of "follower" societies respond to this breakthrough by introducing the most modern, capital-intensive technology, in order to close the "gap" as rapidly as possible.[31] This tendency is part of a larger context:

> ... one way of defining the degree of backwardness is precisely in terms of absence, in a more backward country [or "follower" society as I have termed it here], of factors which in a more advanced country serve as prerequisites of development. Accordingly, one of the ways of approaching the problem is by asking what substitutions and what patterns of substitutions for the lacking factors occurred in the process of industrialization in condition of backwardness.[32]

Such substitutions are believed to represent shortcuts to "modernity." They are part of the effort to avoid the difficulties encountered in the modernization of the "advanced" country. This idea of the "advantages of backwardness" did not originate with Leo Trotsky (as has sometimes been supposed) but was expressed already in the late seventeenth century.[33] All aspects of modernity are up for adoption simultaneously, and it depends upon available resources, the balance of forces in the "follower" society, and the relative ease of transfer which aspects will be given priority. The fact that such items as medication, printed matter, educational innovations, political practices like the franchise are more easily transferred than advanced technology requiring heavy capital investment is another aspect of the divergence of processes of modernization.

Many writers have observed that in this setting of "follower societies" governments play, or attempt to play, a decisive role. The special utility of this perspective for comparative studies of modernization is evident from a recent, comprehensive analysis of English, French, and German industrialization since the eighteenth century. In that context, David Landes states that for the governments of Europe "industrialization was, for the state, a political imperative."[34] Governments may be more or less successful in meeting the imperatives confronting them, and their attempts to do so will be affected throughout by the structural attributes of their societies. Generally speaking, governments attempt to play a larger role in the modernization of relatively backward than of relatively advanced societies. This generalization applies to "follower societies" since the eighteenth century, and because most societies of the world are (or have been) in that category, the proposition is perhaps only another aspect of modernization, i.e. of the distinction between the two types of societies. The difference can be of strategic importance for modernization, because "follower societies" are by definition lacking in some of the elements of modernity found in "advanced societies." Where governments manage to provide "functional equivalents" or "substitutes" for these missing elements, they may succeed in reducing the backwardness of their societies, but this presupposes a relatively effective government which itself is an attribute of modernity or advance.[35]

Here again a major shift in intellectual perspective is implied. The view that government is an integral part of the social structure, but may have the capacity of altering it significantly, is not in the mainstream of social theory. The opposite view is more common, that formal government and its actions are epiphenomena, the product of forces arising from the social and economic structure of society. This view is related to the "emanationist" and "evolutionary" intellectual tradition and was reinforced, as noted in chapter 11, by a particular historical constellation in early nineteenth century Europe. Writers of otherwise incompatible political views agreed that government is an epiphenomenon, and this uncommon agreement still influences modern social thought. Yet in studies of modernization it is more useful to consider social structure and government, or society and the state, as interdependent, but also relatively autonomous, spheres of thought and action.[36]

The gap created between advanced and follower societies and the efforts to close it by a more or less *ad hoc* adoption of items of modernity produce obstacles standing in the way of successful modernization.[37] In his discussion of the "new states" that have come into being since World War II. E. A. Shils has characterized these obstacles as a series of internal, structural cleavages:

> It is the gap between the few, very rich and the mass of the poor, between the educated and the uneducated, between the townsman and the villager, between the cosmopolitan or national and the local, between the modern and the traditional, between the rulers and the ruled.[38]

Though such tensions exist in "advanced" states as well, they are far more

pronounced not only in the "new states" of today but also in the follower
societies of the past which can be ranked, albeit roughly, by their degree of
backwardness.[39] The analogy between "backward" or "underdeveloped"
social structures then and now should not be pressed too much, since the Continental countries possessed many cultural and economic attributes that were
relatively favorable to modernization. But it is also true that during the
nineteenth century there was a gradient of backwardness within Europe such
that the countries to the East paralleled the "gaps," found in the "new states"
of today, more closely than the countries of Western Europe.[40]

The analogies or parallels noted here are especially close at the cultural
level. For the "gap" created by advanced societies puts a premium on ideas
and techniques which follower societies may use in order to "come up from
behind." Educated minorities are, thereby, placed in a position of strategic
importance, while the always existing gulf between the educated and the un-
educated widens still further. In a world marked by gradations of backwardness the comparative study of modernization must attend to the "reference society" that becomes the focus of attention in the follower society, especially
for the educated that seek to utilize advanced ideas and techniques in order to
"catch up."[41] Here one can see at a glance that a focus on the distinction between advanced and follower societies, and on the communications-effects of
modernization, necessarily gives prominence to the role of intellectuals and of
education, whereas ideas about social change focusing on the internal division
of labor necessarily made much of standard social classes like workers and
capitalists. It is as typical of backward countries to invest heavily in education
in order to "bridge the gap," as it is for an intelligentsia to develop and engage in an intensified search for a way out of the backwardness of their country.[42] A typical part of this search consists in the ambivalent job of preserving
or strengthening the indigenous character of the native culture while attempting to close the gap created by the advanced development of the "reference
society or societies."[43]

Four aspects of the process of modernization have been distinguished in the
preceding discussion:

a. Reasons of scale suggest that since the eighteenth century the external
setting of societies, and especially the "gap" created by the early industrialization of England and the early democratization of France, have imparted
to the "degree of backwardness" the special significance of a "challenge" to
modernization.

b. In their endeavor to bridge this "gap" leading strata of follower
societies typically search for substitutes to the factors which were conditions
of development in the advanced countries. Within the limitations imposed by
nature and history all aspects of modernity (as developed abroad) are up for
adoption simultaneously, and the problem is which of the adoptable items

represents a shortcut to modernization. Since the achievement of "modernity" is not assured, it is part of this process that the adoption of items of modernization may militate against "modernity," or may be irrelevant to it.

c. This common setting of follower societies in turn imparts special importance to government. Typically, governments attempt to play a major role in modernization at the same time that they seek to overcome the sources of their own instability which arise from the special tensions created by backwardness.[44]

d. The division of the world into advanced and follower societies, together with the relative ease of communication, puts a premium on education as a means to modernization, which is more readily available than the capital required for modern technology. Education and modern communications also encourage the development of an intelligentsia and a cultural product which—as Wilhelm Riehl noted as early as 1850—is in excess of what the country can use or pay for.[45] This recurrent phenomenon is reflected in a mushrooming of efforts to overcome the backwardness of the country by attempts to reconcile the strength evidenced by the advanced society with the values inherent in native traditions.

Comparative Aspects of Social Stratification. This concluding section outlines a program of comparative study dealing with stratification in relation to modernization. In the past that study has contrasted tradition and modernity in "either-or" terms and emphasized changes internal to the society studied and largely determined by the division of labor. The present analysis emphasizes the continuity of social change insofar as the contrast between a social structure then and now is an artifact of conceptualization. But modernization may have a disrupting effect on changing patterns of stratification, due to the hiatus between advanced and follower societies. Governmental intervention is another possible source of discontinuity, since authority structures are relatively autonomous. In other words: although social change is a continuous process, it is often affected by factors conventionally considered extrinsic to the social structure. In a process of modernization relations among groups are exposed to such "extrinsic" influences, although other aspects of the social structure (e.g. the family) may be less affected in this manner. Typically, the modernization of societies is accompanied by a nation-wide redefinition of rights and duties. Individuals and groups respond not only to the actions and beliefs of others, but also to the images of such group-relations derived from prior developments in their reference-society. The following discussion attempts to show that these general points bear directly on the study of social stratification.

The simplified contrast between tradition and modernity shows us that medieval society was ruled by a landowning aristocracy and capitalist society by a bourgeoisie owning the means of production. If one conceives of the transition from tradition to modernity as the decline of one set of attributes and the rise of another, one gets the simple picture of a declining aristocracy and a rising bourgeoisie. Possibly Marx has contributed more than anyone else to this conception. His interpretation of the bourgeoisie as the collective, histori- cal agent which "created" the revolutionizing effect of modern industry, has produced a tendency to read a "rising bourgeoisie" back into the last thousand years of European history.[46] The broad effect of this tendency has been to make the merchants of pre-eighteenth-century Europe into direct pre- cursors of nineteenth-century industrial entrepreneurs and to fasten upon them a corresponding degree of striving and social protest, when in fact they fit quite well into the social structure of feudal Europe. The effect is also to ante- date the decline of the aristocracy by some centuries in order to provide room for the rising bourgeoisie.[47] But the changes of social stratification in the course of industrialization do not present the simple picture of a declining aristocracy and a rising bourgeoisie.

In most European countries the social and political pre-eminence of pre- industrial ruling groups continued even when their economic fortunes de- clined, and the subordinate social and political role of the "middle classes" continued even when their economic fortunes rose. In Europe this pattern applies rather generally to the period of transition to an industrial society. Here is how Joseph Schumpeter puts the case with reference to England, while pointing out that in modified form the same applies elsewhere:

> The aristocratic element continued to rule the roost *right to the end of the period of intact and vital capitalism*. No doubt that element—though nowhere so ef- fectively as in England—currently absorbed the brains from other strata that drifted into politics; it made itself the representative of bourgeois interests and fought the battles of the bourgeoisie; it had to surrender its last legal privileges; but with these qualifications, and for ends no longer its own, it continued to man the political engine, to manage the state, to govern. The economically operative part of the bourgeois strata did not offer much opposition to this. On the whole, that kind of division of labor suited them and they liked it.[48]

In the modernization of Europe, aristocracies retained political dominance long after the economic foundations of their high status had become impaired and after alternative and more productive economic pursuits had brought bourgeois strata to social and economic prominence. The "capacity to rule" obviously varied among the several aristocracies, as did the degree to which other strata of the population tended to accept their own subordinate position. In Europe, these legacies were eroded eventually, but only after the transition to an industrial society was affected by the general pattern to which Schum- peter refers. This pattern of a continued political dominance by traditional ruling groups even under conditions of rapid modernization reflects an earlier condition of the social structure, when families of high social and economic status had privileged access to official positions while all those below the line of gentility were excluded. Pre-modern European societies were characterized by a vast number of status-differences and clashes of interest of all kinds, but by only "one body of persons capable of concerted action over the whole area of society." [49] That is, a tiny, possessing minority of the well-born was capable of concerted action and hence constituted a class, while the whole mass of unorganized and, under these conditions, unorganizable persons were set apart by their common lack of access to positions of privilege. Accordingly, European societies conformed at one time to a pattern in which class and authority were more or less synonymous terms, but this identity diminished in the course of modernization and was replaced eventually by the principle of separation between office and family status. [50]

This equalization of access to public employment is an aspect of modernization which makes sense of the assumptions we bring to this field of study. In modern sociology, government employment is not considered a basis, or an index, of social stratification. Rather, government employment (even in high positions) is seen as a dependent variable, for example when we examine the distribution of public officials by social origin. Yet this perspective presupposes the separation of government office from the claims a family can make by virtue of its social status and economic position. This separation is less applicable in an earlier phase of European societies, and today it is less applicable in the follower societies that are economically backward. There, governments play, or attempt to play, a major role in the process of modernization, as we have seen. Under these conditions government employment provides one of the major bases of social mobility, economic security, and relative well-being. In fact, in economically backward countries the government is one of the major economic enterprises. Hence, government officials partake of the prestige of ruling, even if their positions are humble. And in view of the power at the disposal of government, access to government office and influence upon the exercise of authority are major points of contention—in the personalized sense characteristic of societies in which inter-action is kinship-oriented. [51] While this importance of government employment is associated with economic backwardness and the weakness of middle strata in the occupational hierarchy, it can also divert resources from uses which might overcome these conditions. In the absence of viable economic alternatives government employment itself becomes a major basis of social stratification, [52] although these new polities frequently institutionalize plebiscitarian, equalitarian principles in the political sphere. This identification of class with authority differs, of course, from the elitism of medieval European societies, in which only a privileged minority had access to positions of authority.

The preceding sketch suggests perspectives for the comparative study of ruling classes in the process of modernization. Within the European context it focuses attention on the continued importance of traditional ruling groups throughout the period of modernization. In this respect, further study would have to differentiate between the relatively accommodating development in England and the much more conflict-ridden development of other, follower societies. At the same time, I have suggested that the modernization of Western societies generally shows a gradual separation between governmental office and family status. The continuity between tradition and modernity remains a characteristic of social change throughout, for even the increasing differentiation between office and family in Western Civilization reveals a variety of historically conditioned patterns. There is no reason to assume that future developments elsewhere will be more uniform. The comparative study of ruling groups in the process of modernization can thus combine the three themes, mentioned above: the continuity of change, the effect of extrinsic influences on the changing role of ruling strata, and the relative separation between government and social structure. The same themes may be combined in the study of other social groups.

The patterns of action and reaction which characterize a society's changing structure come most readily into focus as one moves from the top to the bottom ranks of the social hierarchy. Here one may use the simplified contrast between tradition and modernity as a point of departure, because the rise of political participation by the lower strata is a characteristic feature of modernization. In medieval Europe lower strata, fragmented in household enterprises of a patriarchal type, existed side by side with a ruling class characterized by wealth, high status and high office. Karl Marx has analyzed this condition effectively with regard to the French peasantry:

> The small peasants form a vast mass, the members of which live in similar conditions, but without entering into manifold relations with one another. Their mode of production isolates them from one another, instead of bringing them into mutual intercourse. The isolation is increased by France's bad means of communication and by the poverty of the peasants . . . . Each individual peasant family is almost self-sufficient; it itself directly produces the major part of its consumption and thus acquires its means of life more through exchange with nature than in intercourse with society. The small holding, the peasant and his family; alongside them another small holding, another peasant and another family . . . . Insofar as there is merely a local interconnection among these small peasants, and the identity of their interests begets no unity, no national union and no political organization, they do not form a class. They are consequently incapable of enforcing their class interest in their own name, whether through a parliament or through a convention. They cannot represent themselves, they must be represented. Their representative must at the same time appear as their master, as an authority over them, as an unlimited governmental power, that protects them against the other classes and sends them the rain and the sunshine

from above. The political influence of the small peasants, therefore, finds its final expression in the executive power subordinating society to itself.[53]

Probably, Marx would have agreed that this analysis of peasants in nineteenth century France applied *mutatis mutandis* to the small craftsmen of the towns, to the manorial estates as well as to the independent peasant freeholds in medieval Europe. The family-based enterprise fragmented the lower strata into as many units of patriarchal household rule over family, servants, and apprentices. On the other hand, the heads of households would join with others in guilds, exercise authority in official capacities, join in the deliberation of representative assemblies, and thus constitute a "class" or "classes" in the sense of groups capable of concerted action.

In this setting "fundamental democratization" refers to the whole process of class-formation by which the fragmentation of the lower strata is gradually overcome, not only to the extension of the franchise. Geographic mobility increases, literacy rises along with the diffusion of newspapers, patriarchal rule and household enterprises decline as conditions of work lead to an aggregation of large masses of people in economic enterprises providing opportunities for easy communication.[54] As Marx noted, these conditions gave rise to trade unions, political organizations, and a heightened class-consciousness due to repeated conflicts with employers. He was too preoccupied with "industry" to note that other groups than workers and other means of communication than direct contact at the place of work might come into play.[55] He was also too committed to an evolutionary perspective with its emphasis on the eventual decline of the aristocracy to note the importance of the beliefs which upheld the legitimacy of the traditional "ruling class" even in an industrializing society. Large masses of people at the bottom of the social hierarchy retained their loyalty to the established order, even in the face of the physical and psychological deprivations so suddenly imposed upon them.[56]

This loyalty is evident in the numerous references to the real and imaginary rights enjoyed under the old order. Populist protest based on such references meant, among other things, the demand for equality of citizenship. That equality was proclaimed by the legal order and by the appeals to national solidarity in an era of well-publicized empire-building, but in practice it was denied by the restriction of the franchise, the dominant ideology of class-relations, and the partisan implementation of the law. The rising awareness of the working class in this process of "fundamental democratization" reflects an experience of *political alienation*, a sense of not having a recognized position in the civic community of an emerging industrial society. During the nineteenth century nationalism was so powerful in part because it could appeal directly to this longing of the common people for civic respectability, a longing which was intensified by acute awareness of development in other countries. When this quest was frustrated and as ideas of the rights of labor spread during the nineteenth century, people turned to the socialist alternative of building a new civic community to which they too could belong.[57] This general interpretation of working-class agitation in Europe may be contrasted with the problems encountered today under conditions of greater economic backwardness and greater advance abroad.[58]

In employing the English development as the prototype of later developments in other countries, Marx mistook the exception for the rule, a consideration which applies to his analysis of an emerging working class. As English workers attained a level of group-consciousness in the late eighteenth and early nineteenth centuries, they became aware of England's preeminent position as a world-power. In follower societies the lower strata rise to an awareness of the relative backwardness of their society. Also, early working-class agitation in England occurred in an anti-mercantilist context which militated against protective legislation during a transitional period of greatly intensified deprivations. In follower societies the greater reliance on government makes social legislation a natural concomitant of early industrialization.[59] In England the work-force in the early factories was separated effectively from the land, and population increase in the countryside as well as the city roughly corresponded to the increasing demand for labor. In many follower societies the work-force retains its familial and economic ties to the land and population increase in city and country is well in advance of the demand for labor.[60]

These contrasts vary with the degree of industrialization achieved locally and the degree of governmental control over internal migration, to mention just two relevant considerations. The permanent separation of workers from their ties to the land obviously facilitates the growth of class consciousness and of political organization in Marx's sense of the word. On the other hand, a continuation of these ties may result either in a weak commitment to industry (and hence weak group solidarity), and/or in the emergence of segmental peasant-worker alliances in urban and national politics. Where this latter alternative exists, one can begin to appreciate how important it is to consider such phenomena in their own right, rather than treat them as transitions that are expected to disappear with increasing modernization. We do not know after all what forms modernization might take where separation between town and countryside fails to occur, at least for a considerable period of time.[61]

Having considered ruling and lower strata, I wish finally to turn to a brief analysis of education and intellectuals, again using the guidelines of the preceding discussion. In the case of England, education had been a privilege associated with high status until, in the course of religious controversies, several sectarian groups instituted private school systems so as to preserve the integrity of their beliefs. The idea of making education available beyond these narrow circles immediately raised the question of danger to the social order because workers and peasants would learn to read and write. This apprehension is quite understandable when one considers that the basic dividing line between those who officially ranked as "gentlemen" and the vast majority of the people was identical with the division between the literate and the illiterate. Still, the social mobilization of the population due to commerce and industry undermined the old hierarchy of ranks. The effort of ensuring that people would retain their old regard for rank led to the gradual spread of education with a strong emphasis on religion. This spread of education was not unlike the parallel problem of military conscription: both were aspects of a "fundamental democratization" which gave unprecedented political importance to people who could read and—in times of emergency—had guns.[62]

These issues are transformed in follower societies which seek to achieve the benefits of an industrial society, but by a speedier and less costly transition than occurred in England. In these societies popular and higher education seem to provide the easiest shortcut to industrialization. By this means the skill level of the population is raised while the highly educated increase their capacity of learning advanced techniques from abroad. For these reasons governments in follower societies usually push education, even though in so doing they also jeopardize their own political stability. They may attempt to avert such dangers through restrictions of the franchise, censorship, control of associations, etc. One can differentiate between follower societies of the nineteenth and the twentieth centuries in terms of degrees and types of control over a mobilized population.

Such contrasts in the role of education are paralleled by contrasts in the role of intellectuals. Many educated persons engage in intellectual pursuits from time to time, but the term "intellectuals" is usually (if vaguely) restricted to those persons who engage in such pursuits on a full-time basis and as free professionals rather than "hired hands."[63] Intellectual pursuits occur in all complex societies, but "intellectuals" as a distinct social group emerged as a concomitant of modernization. In Western Europe men of letters underwent a process of emancipation from their previous subservience to the Church and to private patrons, because industrialization created a mass public and a market for intellectual products. The whole process was one of great complexity, but it can be simplified for present purposes. Intellectuals tended to respond to their emancipation by a new cultural elitism, and to the new mass-public by responses which vacillated between a populist identification with the people and a strong apprehension concerning the threat of mass-culture to humanistic values.[64] These responses were quite incongruent with the dominant materialism of advanced industrial societies, so that intellectuals experienced a social and moral isolation. During the nineteenth century the great economic and political successes of advanced European societies reinforced, rather than assuaged, the isolation of those intellectuals who took no direct part in that success and questioned the cultural and personal worth of those who did. To the extent that this estrangement resulted from the emancipation and consequent elitism of intellectuals, as well as from their ambivalent reaction to a mass public, it must be considered a concomitant of modernization.[65]

The response of intellectuals briefly sketched here was largely internal to the most advanced societies of Europe. But the breakthrough achieved by the industrial and political revolutions of England and France made other countries into follower societies. The economic advance of England and the events of the French revolution were witnessed from afar by men who rejected the backwardness and autocracy of their own country. Under these conditions cultural life tends to become polarized between those who would see their country progress by imitating the "more advanced countries," and those who denounce that advance as alien and evil and emphasize instead the wellsprings of strength existing among their own people and in their native culture. Both reactions were typified by the Westernizers and the Slavophils of Tsarist Russia, but the general pattern has occurred again and again. It has been a mainspring of nationalism and of movements for national independence. In this setting intellectuals do not remain estranged witnesses of a development carried forward by others; they tend to turn into leaders of the drive towards modernization.[66]

This discussion has endeavored to provide a framework for the comparative study of modernization and inequality. Such studies have been influenced for too long by a stereotype derived from the Marxian tradition. According to this stereotype, history is divided into epochs, characterized by a predominant mode of production and, based upon it, a class structure consisting of a ruling and an oppressed class. Each epoch is further characterized by a typical sequence of changes in the relations between the two major classes. In the early phase the dominant mode of production is established by a class in its period of revolutionary ascendance. For a time this class is progressive. Its economic interests are identical with technical progress and human welfare, and hence, on the side of liberating ideas and institutions. Eventually however, such an ascending class becomes a ruling class. From a champion of progress in its period of ascendance the class has turned into a champion of reaction in its period of dominance. Increasingly, the ruling class resists changes which would endanger its entrenched position. But meanwhile, within the structure of the old society, a new class has been formed from the ranks of the oppressed, who have no such vested interests and who in due time will overthrow that old structure in order to make way for the material progress which has become technically possible. Within the European context this grandiose simplification appeared to account for the feudal powers of resistance, the progressive, rising bourgeoisie and its gradual transformation into a reactionary ruling class, and finally the class of the oppressed proletariat which has a world to win and nothing to lose but its chains.

It is quite true, of course, that Marx modified this scheme to allow for leads and lags in interpreting the actual historical developments of his time. These modifications may have appeared all the more persuasive because of the passionate moral and intellectual conviction with which Marx adhered to the basic assumptions of the scheme itself. This conviction, I have suggested, was part of the European intellectuals' response to the crisis in human relations brought about by the rise of an industrial society, a response which suggested an "either-or" confrontation between tradition and modernity with its many ramifications.

A critical awareness of this intellectual heritage can assist the reorientation needed in the comparative study of stratification. It prompts us to recognize that the contrast between tradition and modernity is itself part of the evidence we should consider. This intellectual response to the rise of industry has been an aid or hindrance (as the case may be) in each country's modernization, typically marked by the emancipation of men of letters and by the manner in which they assessed their country's backwardness relative to the advances of their reference-societies. Once the unwanted legacies of this intellectual response are discounted, as I have attempted to do in this essay, a rather different approach to the study of modernization emerges.

The division of history into epochs, like the distinction between tradition and modernity, is a construct of definite, but limited utility. These constructs will vary with the purpose of inquiry. While we have found it useful to consider late eighteenth-century Europe as an historical turning point, it is recognized that the process of modernization which reached a crescendo since then, is coextensive with the era of European expansion since the late 15th century, or the "Vasco da Gama era" as Carlo Cipolla has called it. If we want to explain this historical breakthrough in Europe, our emphasis will be on the continuity of intra-societal changes. If we wish to include in our account the worldwide repercussions of this breakthrough and hence the differential process of modernization, our emphasis will be on the confluence of intrinsic and extrinsic changes of social structures. Both emphases are relevant for the comparative study of stratification.

Within this broad context the rise of new social structures as of technical innovations appears as a multifaceted process, not exclusively identifiable with any one social group. Typically, the pioneers of innovation seek the protection of ruling groups rather than defy them, provided of course that such groups exist and can provide protection. The outcome of this process varies with the pressure for innovation and the degree to which given ruling groups themselves participate in innovation or feel jeopardized by it. At any rate, the emphasis upon the continuity of ruling groups in the era of modernization is a first corollary following from the rejection of the "either-or" image of tradition and modernity.

A second corollary involves what Karl Mannheim has called the "fundamental democratization'' of modern society. The contrast between the monopoly of rule by a tiny minority of notables and the principle of universal suffrage in modern nation-states is striking and unquestioned. But the growth of citizenship which occurs in the transition from one to the other, involves highly diverse developments in which the relative rights and obligations of social classes are redefined, as the political process interacts (more or less autonomously) with the changing organization of production. In the era of modernization this interaction can be understood best if proper attention is given to the international setting as well as the internal differentiation of social structures.

In the end it may appear—from a mid-twentieth-century view-point—that the growth of citizenship and the nation-state is a more significant dimension of modernization than the distributive inequalities underlying the formation of social classes. In that perspective Marx's theory of social classes under capitalism appears as a sweeping projection of certain temporary patterns of early nineteenth-century England. Not the least argument favoring this conclusion is the growth of the welfare state in the industrialized societies of the world, which in one way or another provides a pattern of accommodation among competing social groups as well as a model to be emulated by the political and intellectual leaders of follower societies.[67] My object has been to provide a framework which can encompass these contemporary developments as well as the modernization processes of the past.

NOTES

1. The omitted sections are readily available in three places: *Comparative Studies in Society and History*, IX (April 1967), 292-346; *Embattled Reason* (New York: Oxford University Press, 1970), 250-314; *Nation-Building and Citizenship* (2nd ed.; Berkeley: University of California Press, 1977), Part III. It seems more in keeping with the presentation of my approach—the main purpose of this edition of selected essays, as stated in the beginning—to confine this reprinting of "Tradition and Modernity Reconsidered" to the alternative approach I have proposed. To do this effectively, my revision also draws on my essay "The Comparative Analysis of Historical Change," in Tom Burns and S.B. Saul, eds., *Social Theory and Economic Change* (London: Tavistock, 1967), 67-86 (reprinted in Reinhard Bendix and Guenther Roth, *Scholarship and Partisanship* (Berkeley: University of California Press, 1971), 207-24.
2. Note the two Bulletins of the Social Science Research Council dealing with the relations between history and the social sciences: *Theory and Practice in Historical Study: A Report of the Committee on Historiography* (New York: Social Science Research Council, 1946), Bulletin 54, and *The Social Sciences in Historical Study: A Report of the Committee on Historiography* (ibid., 1954), Bulletin 64. See also Louis Gottschalk, ed., *Generalizations in the Writing of History* (Chicago: University of Chicago Press, 1963). The statement in the text is especially well illustrated, however, by the many contributions of historians published in the pages of *Comparative Studies in Society and History* (edited by Sylvia Thrupp).

3. See Carlo M. Cipolla, *The Economic History of World Population* (Baltimore: Penguin Books, 1964), pp. 24-28. By focusing attention on the technical and economic effects of the process, Cipolla provides a comprehensive formulation of what is meant by industrialization. Nothing like that clarity can be achieved with regard to "modernization," which is more inclusive and refers, albeit vaguely, to the manifold social and political processes that have accompanied industrialization in most countries of Western civilization. The following discussion contains contributions towards a definition of "modernization."

4. See Robert A. Nisbet, *Emile Durkheim* (Englewood Cliffs: Prentice-Hall, 1965), p. 20.

5. Ibid., p. 21 n.

6. Cf. the contributions by Talcott Parsons, "Evolutionary Universals in Society," *American Sociological Review*, 29, 1964, 339-57; R.N. Bellah, "Religious Evolution," *American Sociological Review*, 29, 1964, 358-74; and S.N. Eisenstadt, "Social Change, Differentiation, and Evolution," *American Sociological Review*, 29, 1964, 375-86.

7. Lerner suggests that, since rising output per head depends especially upon a people's willingness to change, politicians are well advised to promise economic benefits only after people have changed their ways in the requisite direction. He is silent, however, on how politicians can be induced to act in this manner, or on how people are likely to change in the absence of promises, or why in the movements for independence the value of independence has priority over the value of economic growth. Cf. Daniel Lerner, "Comparative Analysis of Processes of Modernization," paper submitted to International Social Science Council Round Table on Comparative Research, Paris, April 22-24, 1965. Unpublished.

8. G.A. Almond and J.S. Coleman, eds., *The Politics of the Developing Areas* (Princeton: Princeton University Press, 1960), 38-45 and passim.

9. These and related issues are discussed in Arthur Schweitzer, "Vom Idealtypus zum Prototyp," *Zeitschrift für die gesamten Staatswissenschaften*, 120, 1964, 13-55. The article will be useful even to those who do not follow all of Schweitzer's stimulating suggestions.

10. I have used this and other suggestions of the literature in my elaboration of this point in *Nation-Building and Citizenship*.

11. I use the example of bureaucracy since, in *Nation-Building and Citizenship, op.cit.*, 107-15, I have formulated the implications of the general points made here. Similar points are suggested elsewhere in that volume with regard to the contrast between patrimonialism and feudalism, the plebiscitarian and the representative principle in a democracy, the double hierarchy of government in totalitarian regimes, the relation between central and local authority in Indian history. None of these other concepts is as clearly worked out as the concept of bureaucracy.

12. See Otto Brunner, *Neue Wege der Verfassungs- und Sozialgeschichte* (Göttingen: Vandenhoeck und Ruprecht, 1968) and E.P. Thompson, *The Making of the English Working Class* (London: Gollancz, 1963; New York: Pantheon, 1964). In his major work, *Land und Herrschaft* (Vienna: Rudolf M. Rohrer, 1959) and *Adeliges Landleben und europäischer Geist* (Salzburg: Otto Müller, 1949), Otto Brunner reanalyzes feudalism in terms of the legal, economic, and ethical categories employed by those directly involved in feudal relationships, but the volume of essays puts this perspective in the larger context of European social history. Thompson, for this part, wishes to restore the meaning of the term "class" and accordingly he rejects abstract definitions. Class, he says (*op.cit.*, 9), is a histori-

cal phenomenon "which *happens* when some men, as a result of common experiences, feel and articulate the identity of their interests as between themselves and as against other men whose interests are different from theirs." Note, incidentally, that the same point is made despite the rather marked difference in political orientation of the two authors.

13. W.G. Sumner, *Folkways* (Boston: Ginn, 1940), 5-6.
14. It is a short step from this thought to a metaphoric language which attributes actions of various kinds to society, the famous fallacy of misplaced concreteness against which Whitehead warned.
15. Max Weber, *The Methodology of the Social Sciences* (Glencoe: The Free Press, 1949), p. 101, 102-103.
16. Alexander Gerschenkron, *Economic Backwardness in Historical Perspective* (New York: Frederick A. Praeger, 1965), p. 33. My indebtedness to Gerschenkron will be evident throughout; in several respects my analysis represents a sociological extension of points first suggested by him in the context of economic history.
17. Ibid., p. 40. Cf. also Gerschenkron's critical discussion of Rostow along similar lines in Rostow, ed., *The Economics of Take-Off, op. cit.*, pp. 166-67. See also for a related discussion Albert O. Hirschman, "Obstacles to Development," *Economic Development and Cultural Change*, XIII (1965), pp. 385-93.
18. Wilbert Moore, *The Impact of Industry* (Englewood Cliffs: Prentice-Hall, 1965), p. 19. Cf. also the same writer's earlier monograph on *Social Change* (Englewood Cliffs: Prentice-Hall, 1963), Chap. V. Similar critiques of evolutionism are contained in the writings of S. N. Eisenstadt, esp. in two recent essays "Social Change, Differentiation and Evolution," *American Sociological Review*, XXIX (1964), pp. 375-86; and "Social Transformation in Modernization," ibid., XXX (1965), pp. 659-73.
19. See Cesar Grana, *Bohemian Versus Bourgeois* (New York: Basic Books, 1964), passim, for a sympathetic analysis of this imagery. Herbert Marcuse's *One-Dimensional Man* (Boston: The Beacon Press, 1964) appeared too late to be included in Grana's concluding analysis.
20. It may well be the present-day absence of a need for self-help and defense which makes the closely knit solidarity of such groups appear oppressive to a modern observer, especially if he discounts the romanticism of past interpretations. By the same token, it may be the absence of that need for collective self-help and defense which weakens the solidarity of groups in modern societies and allows for the development of individualism. The older pattern often arose from the imposition of taxes in return for privileges, which necessitated the organization of communities for self-help and defense; Max Weber discussed this device under the concept of "liturgy." Cf. Max Weber, *The Theory of Social and Economic Organization* (New York: Oxford University Press, 1947), pp. 312-13. A society like the Russian in which this older pattern was preserved up to the present may well engender customs and attitudes markedly different from those that are familiar to us today. For an insightful discussion of these customs and attitudes see Wright W. Miller, *Russians as People* (New York: E. P. Dutton, 1961), Chap. 5.
21. See Karl Mannheim, *Man and Society in an Age of Reconstruction* (New York: Harcourt, Brace & World, 1941), p. 44.
22. See above chapter 11 and chapter 13 below.
23. For the link between the theological conception of emanation with theories of social evolution and functionalism cf. Arthur Lovejoy, *The Great Chain of Being,*

op. cit.; Karl Loewith, *Meaning in History* (Chicago: University of Chicago Press, 1949); and the comprehensive historical treatment in Robert A. Nisbet, *Social Change and History* (New York: Oxford University Press, 1969), passim. The intellectual tradition discussed in these works has been criticized very effectively by Ernest Gellner, *Thought and Change* (Chicago: University of Chicago Press, 1964), passim. Gellner's analysis corroborates the present discussion at several points.

24. This summary is related to my reply to Talcott Parsons in chapter 6 above.
25. So, of course, did the initial development of England, depending as it did on intense competition with Holland. The point that social structures cannot be understood by exclusive attention to their internal developments is a general one. See Otto Hintze, "Staatsverfassung und Heeresverfassung," in *Staat und Verfassung* (Göttingen: Vandenhoeck & Ruprecht, 1962), pp. 52-83. The essay was published originally in 1906.
26. See Milton Singer, "Changing Craft Traditions in India," in Wilbert Moore and Arnold Feldman, eds., *Labor Commitment and Social Change in Developing Areas* (New York: Social Science Research Council, 1960), p. 262.
27. Carlo Cipolla, *Guns and Sails in the Early Phase of European Expansion, 1400-1700* (London: Collins, 1965), passim.
28. The changes in literacy and the availability of printed matter are surveyed for England in Raymond Williams, *The Long Revolution* (London: Chatto and Windus, 1961), pp. 156-72.
29. The terms of that distinction do not stay put. Before the "modern" period England was a "follower" society while Holland and Sweden were "advanced," especially in the production of cannons. Cf. Cipolla, *Guns and Sails, op. cit.*, pp. 36-37, 52-54, 87n. In the twentieth century the Russian revolution, the fascist regimes, and the Chinese revolution have added their own modifications of this distinction. Singer, *op. cit.*, pp. 261-62 refers to the same distinction by speaking of "early" and "late" arrivals, but I wish to emphasize the sense of pioneering or backwardness that has animated people in "advanced" and "follower" societies. These terms refer to the evaluations of the participants rather than to my own assessment of "progress" or "backwardness."
30. There are those who consider societies closed systems. They would counter this diffusionist argument with the contention that societies are not passive recipients of external stimuli, but select among them in accordance with the dictates of their internal structure. This interpretation is an extension of the equilibrium model and as such a secular version of the original, theological belief in "pre-established harmony." That older view was as compatible with the existence of evil in a divinely created world as the functionalist interpretation is compatible with the existence of conflict and change. Neither view is compatible with the possibility of a self-perpetuating disequilibrium, or cumulative causation as MacIver has called it.
31. Gerschenkron, *op. cit.*, pp. 26, 44, and passim.
32. Ibid., p. 46.
33. Cf. the analysis of this complex of ideas in the work of Gottfried Wilhelm von Leibniz (1646-1716), especially the interesting contacts between Leibniz and Peter the Great with regard to the modernization of Russia, in Dieter Groh, *Russland und das Selbstverständniss Europas* (Neuwied: Hermann Luchterhand Verlag, 1961), pp. 32-43.
34. David Landes, "Technological Change and Development in Western Europe,

1750-1914," in H. J. Habbakuk and M. Postan, eds., *The Cambridge Economic History of Europe: The Industrial Revolution and After* (Cambridge University Press, 1965), Vol. VI, Part I, p. 366.

35. Note the frequency with which "political unity" appears as an index of modernity in the several lists of attributes presented in Marius Jansen, ed., *Changing Japanese Attitudes Towards Modernization* (Princeton: Princeton University Press, 1965), pp. 18-19, 20-24, and passim.

36. For a discussion of this point cf. chapter 8 above.

37. On the "ad hoc diffusion" of items of modernity cf. the illuminating discussion by Theodore H. von Laue, "Imperial Russia at the Turn of the Century," *Comparative Studies in Society and History*, III (1961), pp. 353-67; and Mary C. Wright, "Revolution from Without?" *Comparative Studies in Society and History*, IV (1962), pp. 247-52.

38. Edward A. Shils, "Political Development in the New States," *Comparative Studies in Society and History*, II (1960), p. 281.

39. Gerschenkron, *op. cit.*, pp. 41-44.

40. Cf. Landes, *op. cit.*, pp. 354, 358.

41. The concept "reference society" has been chosen in analogy to Robert Merton's "reference groups." Cf. Robert Merton, *Social Theory and Social Structure* (Glencoe: The Free Press, 1957), pp. 225 ff.

42. Cf. the succinct overview of the "intelligentsia" by Hugh Seton-Watson, *Neither War Nor Peace* (New York: Frederick Praeger, 1960), pp. 164-87. See also Bendix, *Nation-Building, op. cit.*, pp. 231 ff. and chapter 14 below.

43. The most sensitive analysis of this bifurcation I have found in the literature is the study by Joseph Levenson, *Modern China and its Confucian Past* (Garden City: Doubleday & Co., 1964), passim. Cf. also Cipolla, *Guns and Sails, op. cit.*, pp. 116-26.

44. Cf. the analysis of these tensions by Edward A. Shils, "Political Development in the New States," cited above.

45. Cf. the chapter on "Die Proletarier der Geistesarbeit" in Wilhelm Riehl, *Die Bürgerliche Gesellschaft* (Stuttgart: J. G. Cottasche Buchhandlung, 1930), esp. pp. 312-13.

46. For a vigorous critique of this tendency cf. J. H. Hexter, *Reappraisals in History* (New York: Harper & Row, 1963), passim. Note also the cautionary comments regarding the problem of historical continuity in Gerschenkron, *op. cit.*, pp. 37-39.

47. For a more balanced assessment of the European bourgeoisie, cf. Otto Brunner, *Neue Wege der Sozialgeschichte*, pp. 80-115.

48. Joseph Schumpeter, *Capitalism, Socialism, and Democracy* (New York: Harper and Bros., 1947), pp. 136-37. See also pp. 12-13 for a more generalized statement. Substantially the same observations were made by Frederick Engels in 1892, but the political primacy of the aristocracy and the secondary role of the bourgeoisie appeared to him only as a "survival" which would disappear eventually. See Frederick Engels, *Socialism, Utopian and Scientific* (Chicago: Charles H. Kerr, 1905), pp. xxxii-xxxiv. For an empirical study cf. W. L. Guttmann, *The British Political Elite* (New York: Basic Books, 1963).

49. Cf. Peter Laslett, *The World We Have Lost, op. cit.*, p. 22 and passim.

50. Cf. Ernest Barker, *The Development of Public Services in Western Europe, 1660-1930* (London: Oxford University Press, 1944), pp. 1-6 and passim.

51. Cf. Clifford Geertz, "The Integrative Revolution," in Geertz, ed., *Old Societies*

and New States (Glencoe: The Free Press, 1963), pp. 105 ff. Cf. my article "Bureaucracy" in the *International Encyclopedia of the Social Sciences*, 1968 edition.

52. Cf., for example, the statement that "In Egypt the middle class has been weak in numbers and influence, and civil servants have comprised a large proportion of it." Morroe Berger, *Bureaucracy and Society in Modern Egypt* (Princeton: Princeton University Press, 1957), p. 46.

53. Karl Marx, *The 18th Brumaire of Louis Bonaparte* (New York: International Publishers, n.d.), p. 109.

54. See John Stuart Mill, *Principles of Political Economy* (Boston: Charles C. Little and James Brown, 1848), pp. 322-23.

55. Cf. the analysis of growing class consciousness among workers in Karl Marx, *The Poverty of Philosophy* (New York: International Publishers, n.d.), pp. 145-46; but note also the evidence adduced by David Mitrany, *Marx against the Peasants* (London: Weidenfeld and Nicolson, 1951), passim.

56. To discount such beliefs because they disappeared eventually is no more plausible than to make the aristocracy's role decline in advance of its eventual demise. Cf. the discussion of the "traditionalism of labor" in my book *Work and Authority in Industry* (2nd ed.; Berkeley: University of California Press, 1974), pp. 34 ff.

57. For a full statement of this interpretation cf. Bendix, *Nation-Building, op. cit.*, pp. 61-74, and chapter 9 above.

58. As always, the contrast is not absolute. During the nineteenth century, as one went eastwards in Europe, one encountered certain parallels to the "underdeveloped syndrome" of today, namely an increased importance of government and rather weakly developed middle strata. Cf. the illuminating statement by David Landes: "The farther east one goes in Europe, the more the bourgeoisie takes on the appearance of a foreign excrescence on manorial society, a group apart scorned by the nobility and feared or hated by (or unknown to) a peasantry still personally bound to the local *seigneur*." See Landes, *op cit.*, p. 358.

59. The debate concerning the deprivations of early English industrialization continues. But whatever its final resolution in terms of the changing standard of living, there is probably less disagreement on the psychological repercussions. The separation of the worker's home from his place of work, the novelty of a discipline which previously had been associated with the pauper's workhouse, the brutalization of work conditions for women and children merely by the shift away from home, and related matters constitute the impressive circumstantial evidence. Note also that the statement in the text makes sense of Germany's pioneering in the field of social legislation as an attribute of an early follower society.

60. Cf. Landes, *op. cit.*, pp. 344-47 for a summary analysis of the labor supply problem in the English industrial revolution in terms of the current state of research. These findings can be contrasted readily with comparative materials on various follower societies contained in Wilbert Moore and Arnold Feldman, eds., *Labor Commitment and Social Change in Developing Areas, op. cit.*, passim.

61. Note that Marx and others with him considered that separation as a prerequisite of capitalist development. Cf. the discussion of the distinctive position of workers in African countries by Lloyd A. Fallers, "Equality, Modernity and Democracy in the New States," in Geertz, ed., *Old Societies and New States, op. cit.*, pp. 187-190. See also Richard D. Lambert, "The Impact of Urban Society upon Village Life" in Roy Turner, ed., *India's Urban Future* (Berkeley: University of California Press, 1962), pp. 117-40.

62. In these respects there are of course striking differences between France and England which can be considered symptomatic of the radical and the conservative approach to education and conscription. For a comparative treatment of these issues cf. Ernest Barker, *The Development of Public Services in Western Europe, op. cit.*, Chaps. 2, 5.
63. The circularity of this statement is unavoidable. In a general sense pursuits engaging the intellect refer to the creation and maintenance (transmission) of cultural values, but each of these terms (cultural values, creation, maintenance, transmission) is the subject of constant debate, and that debate itself is an important intellectual pursuit. Since this debate involves the pejorative as well as appreciative use of these terms, and by that token the endeavor of speakers to "belong" to the positive side of the cultural process (in however marginal a fashion), no one set of defining terms will be wholly satisfactory. In view of this difficulty the most reasonable alternative is to set up a typology of intellectual pursuits and leave the group of persons called "intellectuals" undefined. For one such attempt cf. Theodor Geiger, *Aufgaben und Stellung der Intelligenz in der Gesellschaft* (Stuttgart: Ferdinand Enke Verlag, 1949), pp. 1-24, 81-101.
64. Cf. the case study of this process in England by Leo Lowenthal and Marjorie Fiske, "The Debate over Art and Popular Culture," in Mirra Komarovsky, ed., *Common Frontiers of the Social Sciences* (Glencoe: The Free Press, 1957), pp. 33-112.
65. I avoid the term "alienation" because misuse has made it worthless. For a scholarly treatment of this intellectual response to "bourgeois society" in nineteenth-century Europe cf. Karl Loewith, *From Hegel to Nietzsche*, passim. Cf. also the analysis of the social distance between "intellectuals" and "practical men" in Joseph Schumpeter, *op. cit.*, pp. 145-55. See the further discussion of this problem in chapter 14 below.
66. See Edward A. Shils, "Intellectuals, Public Opinion and Economic Development," *World Politics*, Vol 10 (1958), pp. 232-55.
67. Cf. Gaston Rimlinger, *Welfare Policy and Industrialization in Europe, America and Russia* (New York: John Wiley and Sons, 1971).

13

THE SPECIAL POSITION OF EUROPE

Introductory Note

My studies of modernization led me to the conclusion, elaborated in the preceding chapters, that this multifaceted process cannot be understood apart from the fact that it had started in Western Europe in the era of the Reformation, European explorations overseas and the scientific revolution. Therefore, when I was asked by colleagues to contribute to a series by restating and perhaps developing what was known about the origins and ramifications of inequality, I found myself unable to respond to this request by an analysis of social stratification, to which I myself had contributed in previous years. By this time (around 1970) I had concluded that studies of inequality (social stratification) were flawed as long as their scope remained confined to any one society. True, every known society including the economically most advanced ones were marked by gross inequalities. But in a world in which the poorest strata of American and Western European society were rich by comparison with the poor of Asia or Africa, it did not seem "right" to continue the emphasis where Marx had placed it, on the class struggle within societies. At the time I realized, as noted earlier, that I would have to extend my previous work rather than attempt to change course entirely.

Several other considerations prompted me to make the special position of Europe with its unresolved struggles between kings and aristocrats, the sociology of intellectuals, and the diffusion of ideas between cultures my focus of inquiry. The publication of *Kings or People, Power and the Mandate to Rule* (1978) was the result. Though I had studied Marx's work intensively for many years, the drawbacks of his perspective had come to outweigh its insights, for me at any rate. The working classes of capitalist societies were not the revolutionary force he had predicted. They had a trade-unionist mentality, as Lenin had seen, and their class-consciousness was impeded by their patriotism. The humanistic values inspiring Marx's own work had given way to "man's inhumanity to man," wherever Marxism had become the dominant ideology in one-party dictatorships dedicated to the industrialization of their countries. There Marxism has become an instrument of domination in the hands of the ruling party and bureaucracy; as such it has lost whatever intellectual value it had before. And the Marxisms which have flourished in various economically developed countries have simply not interested me as much as the Marxisms which serve "Third-World Intellectuals" as a veneer for their personal and national aspirations.

Rather than accommodate myself to the fashions of the day, I chose to probe more deeply than before into the antecedents of that breakthrough of sixteenth-century Europe, which as a world-historical constellation has conditioned the inequalities of the world down to the present. The first part of *Kings or People* examines that emerging constellation in terms of the foundations of kingship and aristocratic representation in Japan, Russia, Germany, and England. The following essay on the special position of Europe gives particular attention to the political repercussions of religion and the church as a condition which distinguishes all of Western Europe from other civilizations.

A SHIFT OF EMPHASIS

The particular development of Europe is a central concern in the writings of Max Weber, Otto Hintze, Otto Brunner, and Dietrich Gerhard. In order to take these exemplary analyses into account without repeating them, I will accentuate several aspects of these earlier discussions in a different framework. My attempt presents a summary view of familiar ideas, but at the same time a shift of emphasis in our current view of the special path of Europe.

A qualification and a motto will assist me in this effort. The qualification refers to the title, which should actually be "the special path of Western Europe," or perhaps even the special path of Holland, England and France, and—with some further qualifications—of Central Europe as well. This point was worked out in two of Otto Brunner's essays dealing with differences in agrarian conditions and in the bourgeoisie of Western Europe and Russia. Max Weber and other researchers of his generation had already pointed out the structural difference between West German and East Elbian peasants and farm laborers. In addition, the social structures of Spain and Italy should be distinguished from those of northwestern Europe, a distinction which however has not been given the same attention by social historians as the East-West comparison.[1] Our topic, in any event, is the special position, or special path, of Western Europe—with certain provisos concerning intra-European differences that will have to be omitted here in the interest of simplicity.

Now my motto. At the end of his essay on objectivity, Weber noted that the theories and ideas that guide research are subject to change. In making this observation, Weber's intent was not to advocate either a "chase after ever new perspectives and conceptual constructs," or "the insatiable appetite" of 'fact grubbers' for ever more file material, statistical tomes, and surveys." But at certain times the leading ideas and theories do change, even if one avoids such largely unproductive fads of intellectual life. To quote Weber:

> But at some point the atmosphere changes. The significance of viewpoints that had been utilized without reflection, becomes uncertain—the path is lost in the twilight. The light of the great cultural problems has moved on. Then science also prepares to change its standpoint and conceptual apparatus, and to look at the stream of events from the heights of thought.[2]

One can attribute the slight pathos of these sentences to the style of the time, and substitute for them Thomas Kuhn's notion of paradigm change. The question remains whether such a change in guiding ideas is beginning to take shape in our current view of the special position of Europe.

I think the answer is yes. The discussion about the Western-European origins of capitalism is over two hundred years old, if one goes back to Adam Smith. By now it is sufficiently clear that capitalism can develop in a number of quite different ways, albeit on the assumption of its prior development in Western Europe. It has also become common knowledge that the ways and means of capitalist development in Japan and Russia were different from those in Western Europe. Since the Second World War we have also observed rapid capitalist developments in Singapore, South Korea and Taiwan—not to mention Hong Kong and the development of the Arabic peninsula that was fueled by the demand for oil. The diversity of capitalist developments has been analyzed in a number of ways which are not under discussion here. I do doubt, however, that a comprehensive analysis of that diversity can be obtained by always referring back to the unique West European origins of capitalism. Indeed, the *consequences* of those origins of capitalism are far more important by now than the fact that this breakthrough occurred in Western Europe.

The capitalist development of Western Europe certainly remains intellectually significant because many of the so-called developing countries have not achieved a comparable breakthrough in economic rationality, but would prefer to attain comparable economic results. However, a breakthrough that occurred centuries ago in Western Europe helps these countries very little. One can grasp the practical irrelevance of the West European experience for the problems of economic development of the present day when one reads of a new agricultural fundamentalism in Africa and elsewhere of the "white elephants" of development programs which can be found from Bangladesh to Zambia.[3] A Protestant ethic *without* the spirit of capitalism may well have something to do with such failures, but this aspect of the problem will not be addressed here.

What then is the guiding idea that should direct our contemporary interest in the special position of Western Europe? My answer to this question makes use of an old idea, but our interest in it has probably been revived by contemporary experience. I am concerned with the close connection among kinship relations, politics and religion. A personal experience may clarify the point at issue. During a stay in India over twenty years ago, an experienced Indian anthropologist explained to me that the strength of familial bonds in her country could only be broken if individual Indians got a chance—through economic development or public welfare measures—to make their way without the support of their families. To make sure this observation is not misinterpreted in a romantic-communal sense, I remind readers of the cases (reported also in the West) in which young Indian brides were doused with kerosene and burned by their mothers-in-law, because the bride's family refused to grant an increase in her dowry. The context which lies at the base of these family situations can also be applied to politics more broadly conceived, for example to the prevalence of military dictatorships in many of the so-called developing countries. In my opinion this phenomenon cannot be understood in terms of Weber's category of patrimonialism, nor can it be interpreted simply as the personal hunger for power on the part of reactionary military officers. Instead, it is more likely that the armies (and frequently also the governments) of very poor countries offer one of the few avenues for individuals to move up in society. These opportunities for social advancement are so thoroughly exploited through family patronage and corruption that one has to view them as a special form of political-economic enterprise. For in many cases these are armies whose function consists not in defending borders and waging war but rather in controlling the domestic population. And these are governments in which individuals use public office for their own private gain. It should be noted that these distinctions themselves—between waging war and police action, between the "public" and "private" use of office, and the like—are among the foundations of the special position of Europe.

I have mentioned a shift in emphasis concerning the special position of Europe, using materials already generally familiar to us. The analysis will be presented in three steps. In the limited space available here, I can only lay the groundwork for a discussion that would have to be pursued in detail with reference to the extensive literature.

1. First I will move Weber's main thesis on the Protestant Ethic from its religious-sociological to a religious-political context. I will refer to a path-breaking but little-known work by Herbert Schöffler from 1932.

2. Using this religious-political perspective I will then search for the special position of Western Europe not in the Reformation, but rather in the early Christian tensions between kinship relations and a community of faith, between state and church.

3. Finally, on this basis I will follow Otto Hintze in his interpretation of the roots of a representative constitution in Western Europe, and try to show why the West European path faces great obstacles in many parts of the world.

ENGLISH PURITANISM IN ITS POLITICAL SETTING

Max Weber linked economic activities calculated in terms of expenditures and profits with the notion of predestination in English Calvinism. The promise of salvation held a significance for people of the 16th century that is unimaginable for us today. At the same time, however, a person's uncertainty of whether or not he was one of God's "chosen" people evoked in him a state of fear about his fate after death that is equally unimaginable for us.

Out of this context emerged the cultural foundations of the spirit of capitalism: the rationalization of daily life and the denial of sensual pleasure. One must use each moment of life given by God, so that on the day of judgment one can account for one's self-denying use of God's gifts. This explains, for example, the pastoral advice in this period that people should keep a diary, and maintain it meticulously, in order to record their use of every waking hour as well as note their sleeping hours, so that the latter not exceed the minimum necessary for health.

The details of this context, and the entire "Protestant Ethic" literature, have been critically examined by Gordon Marshall.[4] On the basis of this comprehensive study, I am convinced that Weber laid out in exemplary fashion the ideal-typical consequences of the doctrine of predestination. My emphasis here is on "ideal-typical." Even in a deeply religious culture one cannot assume homogeneity in religious motivation for an entire population. In my view, Weber's analysis leaves open the question of how the causal link between a religious doctrine and the economic activity of believers is to be understood in detail. Weber himself must have sensed this gap, for in his essay on the Protestant sects he partially addressed it in his reference to the social pressure exerted by the community of believers on the individual. Credit worthiness and recommendations to neighboring communities depended on the irreproachable conduct of a puritan life. In this respect Herbert Schöffler provided what I consider a more persuasive and more general answer by linking Weber's hypothesized religious fear closely with the political history of England in the sixteenth century.

I will briefly review Schöffler's main theses:

1. There was no religious reformer comparable to Luther or Calvin in the English Reformation.

2. Various anti-Catholic predecessors notwithstanding, the Reformation was initiated by Henry VIII with the Act of Supremacy of 1534 and the subsequent dissolution of the Catholic monasteries.

3. The non-religious, political-economic motives for this state act were probably apparent to contemporaries, although printed comments on this issue are not to be expected, because they would have amounted to treason and would have been severely punished.

4. Schöffler emphasizes the vacillating religious policies of the Anglican church which, despite Luther's influence, continued to follow the old English-Catholic church order in its liturgical rules of 1549. The primary characteristics of the English Reformation were, on the one hand, the King as sovereign, a secular jurisdiction rather than a clerical one, as well as a Bible

translation in the vernacular, and, on the other hand, sporadic changes in the church's position on theological questions.

5. Most importantly, from 1534 until Edward VI's death in 1553 the Anglican system was in effect. This made all remaining *Catholics* papists and therefore also traitors of their King and country. Edward's rule was followed by the five-year reign of Mary Tudor (1553-1558), a strict Catholic ruler. This suddenly made all *Anglicans*—previously loyal to the King—not only heretics but traitors as well. After that came the reign of Elizabeth I (1558-1603), subjecting all remaining Catholics to the suspicion of treason once again. One can characterize the psychological state on which Weber focused one of "salvation panic," if one views, as Schöffler does, the religious state of the individual as tenuous and imperiled in the context of the variety of theological positions and sect formation of that period. In this way I think one has a religious-political basis for making a causal connection between theological doctrine and the everyday behavior of people, including their economic ethos.[5]

With these few observations I want to suggest that the economic ethos of the world religions—one of the critical factors in the special position of Europe—should be seen in its religious-political context. The point here, as I said, is a shift in emphasis. Weber discussed this connection in his typologies, but he did not make it the center of his analysis in *The Protestant Ethic and the Spirit of Capitalism*.

And now I ask readers to make a great leap from the Reformation of the sixteenth century to the period of early Christianity. For the special position of Western Europe is closely related to the development of the church, especially to the religious-political separation of faith from people's familial and ancestral bonds, that is, from their kinship relations.

POLITICAL ASPECTS OF EARLY CHRISTIANITY

The Bible as a whole is pervaded by a tension between a particularistic morality and a universal ethic based on a shared belief. On one side is the idea that those who believe in God are his chosen people; on the other, the idea that the God of this one people of believers will benefit all other people through his judgment and grace.

The clearest expression of the particularistic ethic is found in the Deuteronomic distinction between the brother and the stranger. "Unto thy brother thou shalt not lend upon usury" it says there (5 Moses 23:20-21), but unto the stranger you can do so with a clear conscience. One can attribute this double standard to a social order which drew a sharp moral distinction between an individual's kinship affiliations and his impersonal relations with resident aliens or kin groups of enemies. The motto is generosity toward kin, but usury and war, that is all otherwise disallowed means, toward all aliens and enemies.

The clearest expression of the contradiction between this morality among brothers and the universal ethic of believers comes from the post-apostolic period during the closing decades of the first century. The written text of the New Testament is commonly dated at this time. In this period, the Christian movement constituted a very controversial minority, which put its universalistic beliefs in sharp opposition to the particularistic in-group morality not only of the Jews but of all non-Christians. In a letter to the Galatians Paul writes (3:25): "But after that faith is come, we are no longer under a schoolmaster" of the law, which of course refers to the Jewish observance of the law. Mention is made of "the children of God by faith" (Gal. 3:26). Where this faith prevails, there is "neither Jew nor Greek, ... neither bond nor free, ... neither male nor female" (Gal. 3:28). Elsewhere, in his letter to the Ephesians, Paul writes of this brotherhood of man between those who "were afar off, and to them that were nigh."

18. For through him we both have access by one Spirit unto the Father.
19. Now therefore ye are no more strangers and foreigners, but fellow citizens with the saints, and of the household of God;
20. And are built upon the foundation of the apostles and prophets, Jesus Christ himself being the chief corner stone;
21. In whom all the building fitly framed together groweth unto an holy temple in the Lord;
22. In whom ye also are builded together for an habitation of God through the Spirit.

Equality in Jesus Christ takes the place of ethnic-cultural, social and even sexual distinctions, that is, precisely those distinctions that were generally dominant in the Roman population.

The distinction in Deuteronomy between the brother and the stranger thus contrasts with the early Christian distinction between believers and the pagan enemy, that is the non-believers of the ancient popular cults. In his commentary against usury, *De Tobia* (ca. 377), Ambrosius, Bishop of Milan (340-397) justified war against non-believers who do not belong to the community. According to Ambrosius, Deuteronomy can only be understood in connection with the just war of the chosen people against the clans of the promised land. You should exact usury from the stranger, writes Ambrosius, but not from your brother. All men are your brothers, *insofar as they are brothers in the faith* and comply with the law of Rome. Ambrosius was a militant church father who knew how to exploit the Deuteronomic standard of opposing kin-groups for the Christian cause.

> Who is the stranger but the Amalekite, the Amorite, the enemy. "From him" it
> says "demand usury." It is lawful to impose usury on him, whom you rightly
> desire to harm, against whom weapons are lawfully carried. On him whom you
> cannot easily conquer in war, you can quickly take vengeance with the hun-
> dredth. From him exact usury whom it would not be a crime to kill. He fights
> without a weapon who demands usury, he who revenges himself upon an enemy
> without a sword, who is an interest collector from his foe. Where there is the
> right of war, there also is the right of usury.[6]

Here the resident alien is put on an equal footing with the non-believer. Ambrosius' goal was to overcome the distinction in Deuteronomy between
brother and stranger by having all men become brothers in faith.

The idea of forming a community, founded solely on a common faith was a
tremendous innovation. This is reflected especially in the first epistle of Peter
(1 Pet. 2:1-10). There, believers are symbolized in changing images as
"new-born babes" and as a "living stone" with which to build a "spiritual
house," but who are a "stone of stumbling and a rock of offense" to the
non-believers. Then the new believers are characterized as a chosen generation, like the Jews before them, but naturally with emphasis on their fundamental uniqueness:

> 9. But ye are a chosen generation, a royal priesthood, an holy nation,
>   a peculiar people; that ye should shew forth the praises of him who
>   hath called you out of darkness into his marvelous light;
> 10. *Which in time past were not a people, but are now the people of
>   God;* which had not obtained mercy, but now have obtained mercy.

A people created solely by a shared faith and the grace of God implied the
complete devaluation of all traditional social distinctions. Small wonder that
the people of the Roman Empire protested against this innovation and played a
major role in the early persecutions of Christians. It made some sense, therefore, when Tacitus accused the Christians not only of superstition, but also
tagged them with "opinions inimical to the community" (*odio humanis
generis*). Pagans thought of themselves as godfearing people who were even
familiar with the idea of the one God, albeit in a non-Christian version. The
Christian rejection of the traditional popular pieties, which among others
sanctified kinship relations, appeared to pagans as atheism and hateful blas-
phemy.[7]

Early Christianity thus substituted a community based on shared beliefs for
the kinship ties of the individual, at any rate in principle. In fact this idea was
realized only in the course of protracted struggles within the Christian movement and against the resistance of a majority of the pagan population.[8] Traditional historiography understandably emphasized the persecution of Christians. However, what matters in this context is to stress that the spread of
Christianity was very limited until the second half of the third century. From a

total population of between 40 and 50 million people, the percentage of Christians in the West Roman Empire barely exceeded five percent, and these were primarily in the cities. (In the East Roman Empire the proportion was probably higher.) The mostly rural population remained in spatial and religious isolation, which makes it probable that the proportion of Christians in the cities was above five percent. One must of course be cautious in using such estimates, for they reflect at best the dimensions of the movement. However, experts agree that the spread of Christianity even at the time of massive persecution of Christians—in the West, with long interruptions between 249 and 306—was still limited. The number of Christians rose rapidly only after the Toleration Edict of Galerius (311) and the Edict of Milan (313). After that the Christianization of the world empire cannot be separated from the establishment of Christianity as the religion of the state.

As early as the fourth century the problem of church and state had become an issue which later developed into one of the most important foundations of the special position of Europe. As mentioned above, the church at the beginning of the fourth century already looked back on a history of internal controversy dating back to apostolic times. Now these controversies assumed a public character. The Toleration Edict of 313 provided for the return of confiscated church property. This led to conflicts between different Christian factions in North Africa. I need not go into the details of the Donatist controversy here, except to note that a series of appeals to provincial authorities and finally several petitions to Emperor Constantine occurred in the course of it. The emperor attempted time and again—through the appointment of various councils of bishops—to settle the conflict and to restore unity to the church, whose protector he was. All attempts on the part of Constantine and his successors failed and the controversy dragged on till the early fifth century. In the meantime, however, a precedent had been established which had significance for the future. For these boards, councils and synods developed inadvertently into quasi-representative institutions, regardless of whether they were called by the emperor, or later by the pope. Moreover, they created the possibility of using synodal authority not only in the arbitration of internal conflicts, but also against the throne, although on the other hand the ruler was also able to make the church subject to them. Both possibilities were tried out as early as the fourth century. Although Emperor Constantine could not prevail in the Donatist conflict, he did play a leading role, even in questions of church doctrine, at the council of Nicea (325), which he had convened. On the other hand, Bishop Ambrosius of Milan, who was mentioned earlier, was able to force Emperor Theodosius I to revoke one of his own edicts of restitution by denying him the eucharist (388). That edict had commanded a bishop to use church funds to pay for a synagogue destroyed by the people.[9]

This special character of the development of the church in Western Europe has to my knowledge no analogue in other civilizations. Two examples illustrate this point. In Russia, Christianity did not spread through a popular movement which then became the state religion after more than 250 years as it did in Western Europe. Rather, Russian Christianity was introduced through the conversion of Princess Olga of Kiev (945-964) and through the dissemination of information about religious practices in other countries. In later phases it developed further through state actions, campaigns in the name of Orthodox belief, and by a Greek clergy which built churches and proselytized despite its limited command of Russian. The sovereignty of the Russian princes over the Orthodox church was insured not only through Greek Orthodox doctrine and the decline of the Byzantine patriarchy. Secular dominance was also reinforced through the growing power of the Muscovite Empire and the subordination of the leader of the Russian church to the Muscovite Dynasty. This contrasts with a country outside Europe such as Japan, in which one can observe an unbroken continuity in the indigenous popular religion. The Japanese empire arose out of struggles among great clans whose leaders also conducted the ceremonies of ancestor-worship and of Shinto. The emperors lost their political authority early on, but not their representative religious function. This is consistent with the national legend of the divine ancestry of the imperial house, which became an enduring element of Japanese culture. This is also consistent with the unbroken, formal subjection of the military governors (Shogunate) to the Emperor, in spite of his powerlessness, even though the governors ruled the country. Finally, this corresponds to the complete dominance of a patriarchal-hierarchic social order, in which every political or military conflict could be translated into a rearrangement of family or pseudo-familial relationships. Neither Russia nor Japan was characterized by a rivalry between political and religious authority.[10]

Here two religious-political points are decisive. The special position of Europe as a whole was a consequence of the origin of Christianity, which broke through the age-old connection between religious cults and the familial and ethnic-linguistic membership of the individual, and established by contrast communities based on shared Christian faith. It should be noted that we are talking only about a break with tradition, not its destruction. Throughout its history the church battled against non-Christian belief systems and loyalties based on kinship. It still does that today, if one considers the pope's recent trip to Africa from this perspective. On the other hand, the tension between church and state is a special characteristic of the West European development, though in this regard one must then also count Poland and Hungary as a part of Western Europe.

REPRESENTATION IN MEDIEVAL EUROPE

I now turn to the development of representative institutions, using as my point of departure the problem of church-state relations, and in particular the

tension-filled history of synodal authority. In doing this I am of course defining the concept of "representation" very broadly. One should keep in mind
that the power relations between church and state were problematic from the
beginning. After the Toleration Edict of Milan (313) it was difficult for the
Emperor to support the church without being drawn into its internal conflicts,
or allowing the authority of the church, which was never clearly defined, to
get the upper hand. At the same time, the church, which soon was growing
larger and richer, confronted the continuous problem of using the state for the
promotion of spiritual interests without allowing that use to degenerate into a
secularization of church interests. Seen from this perspective, priestly celibacy was of decisive importance, especially if one follows Henry Charles Lea
in dating the inception of this institution in the fourth and fifth centuries.[11] The
separation of the entire clergy (and not only the monks) from all hereditary
ties (aside from their solicitation of contributions to the church) reinforced
both the separation of the church from kinship relations as well as the
spiritual-imperial authority of the church itself.

In this interdependent but contentious relationship between state and church
one can see a model of the interdependent but contentious relationship between King and aristocracy that developed later, provided one includes church
dignitaries and the city patriciate on the side of the aristocracy. This model is
summarized best in two quotations, which I take from the excellent comparative study of medieval parliaments by Antonio Marongiu. The king, writes
Marongiu,

> stood out because of his sacerdotal attributes; because he was the first of the
> great vassals; because he was recognized as head of the state by the pope, the
> emperor and other foreign powers; because he continued to administer directly
> large areas within the boundaries of the state, and was in possession of his own
> force of armed men; because he was the supreme representative of judicial au-
> thority, as guarantor of justice and peace, and because fiefs without heirs re-
> verted to him.

But that is only one side. The other is—at any rate in Western Europe—that
the great church leaders, the nobility and the cities

> were no longer ordinary subjects, but possessed economic and legal privileges,
> granted or accepted by the sovereign. . . . They were considered outside the
> "general subordination" of subjects by custom and by the very terms of their
> investiture. They owed fealty, counsel and aid, but in return were exempt from
> all other obligations and impositions. They represented and personified both the
> population of their territories in their relations with the sovereign, and public
> authority within their territories.[12]

This distinction between royal supremacy and the privileged upper strata can
be stripped of its ideal-typical simplification in a similar way as the opposition
between state and church was before. Kings and the privileged elites found

themselves in an ongoing struggle for political power. Though each was dependent on the other, each tried to gain independence from the other, and where possible dominance over it. Marongius' conclusions obviously refer to the result of many centuries of development. These developments have been dealt with in the writings of Otto Hintze and also in my book *Kings or People*.

But what were the conditions under which the special development of Western Europe was prevented elsewhere? Russia and Japan can again serve as examples, even if they cannot provide conclusive evidence. They document conditions leading to developments differing from those of Western Europe, affecting large peoples and their civilizations.

The Greek-Orthodox Christianization of the ten principalities of Kievan Russia began with an act of state. Vladimir the Holy (978-1026) converted on the occasion of a Byzantine petition for military support. His condition was that the sister of the Byzantine Emperor become his wife. This occurred at a time when the great ecumenical councils of the early church (from Nicea 325 to Constantinople 869-70) were already over and fundamental issues of Christian dogma had been settled. Through his marriage to the Byzantine princess the path was cleared for the Greek Orthodox idea of the ruler as representative of Christ on earth, appointed by God. This was a theologico-political enlargement of royal authority, which contrasts with the subordination of the King to divine law characteristic of the West European development. Archbishop Hincmar's statement of 860 to the Frankish King is quoted here by way of example: "You have not created me archbishop of Rheims, but I, together with my colleagues, have elected you to the government of the kingdom, on condition that you observe the laws."[13] Such a statement is unthinkable in the Russian context. The religio-political development of Russia began with the subordination of the church, and this was followed later on by an analogous subordination to the Tsar of the nobility and the city patriciate.

Incipient developments of representative institutions occurred on a local level (*boyar dúma, véche*) at the time of the Kievan principalities, but these institutions grew weak with the decline of those principalities. The chances for autonomous attempts were foiled by the Mongolian invasion in the early thirteenth century and the consequent tribute owed to the Golden Horde. In addition to that tribute and the sporadic interventions of Mongolian troops, there were also military conflicts in the West. One can think of the changing political situation of the Russian principalities as rivaling forces, whose rise and fall between the sack of Kiev in 1240 and the end of the fifteenth century depended on two factors: the fate of Russian petitions at the court of the Great Khan in Sarai and his fickle patronage in the East, and the equally changeable outcomes of the struggles in the West against Sweden, Poland, Lithuania, and the Teutonic Order.

The limited chances of representative institutions and the basic causes of autocracy are certainly related to this tenuous position of the Russian principalities between East and West. The internal battles of the Russian territories were exploited time and again by the Mongols and their Western opponents, each for their own purposes. One calculation reveals that northern Russia experienced 133 invasions and 90 feuds among rivaling principalities in 234 years (1228-1462). Another shows that the northwestern city-state of Novgorod had to defend itself against external attacks on the average every 5 1/2 years during some three centuries between 1142 and 1466. The beginning of the Muscovite Dynasty was the result of rivalries among the Russian princes in Sarai, the taking of office by Iván Kalíta (1325-1341) as principal collector of tribute for the Mongols in all of Russia, and the support by Mongolian troops of Kalíta's battles with his Russian rivals. Finally Kalíta was granted the title of "Grand Prince" by the Mongolian court, which can be seen as the ceremonial foundation of the rise of the Muscovite Dynasty. This ascendence of Moscow depended on successful strategies vis-à-vis the Mongolian overlord in the struggle against assaults from the West and—equally important—against Russian rivals.

The Muscovite rulers could neither rule nor build up their military power without outside help. But with this assistance they succeeded in subjecting the descendants of the great princely and boyar lineages to the condition of personal service. Hence these previously independent lineages were transformed into a service nobility. Wealth and social position came to depend on military or administrative status in the service of the Tsar. Hence members of this nobility ruled at the bidding and on behalf of the Tsar, not on the basis of a right to rule that had been granted to them. Because the citizenry and the clergy were also subordinate to the Tsar, the ascendence of the Muscovite Dynasty was coterminous with the decline of representative institutions of the Kievan period. Accordingly, the provincial assemblies (*zémskii sobór*) of the sixteenth and seventeenth centuries consisted of coopted delegations that were convened to rally opinion in favor of military decisions already taken, to formally enact tax levies, and occasionally to endorse a succession to the throne by acclamation. Petitions to the Tsars did not require an assembly of delegates. This is consistent with the patriarchal conception of the ruler as the father of his people, to whose tutelage one could appeal at any time.

There was no equivalent in Tsarist Russia for the interdependent but contentious relationship between Kings and estates in Western Europe. The details of the Christianization of Russia make it clear that the spread of the new faith did not lead to a direct weakening of kinship relations. This occurred only under circumstances in which the church developed an independent power base. In the Russian case, on the other hand, it may be that the Greek Orthodox mission—through its connection with the old Slavonic language and the idol worship of the saints (icons)—contributed to the popular national union of the Russian Empire, and this despite hierarchic subordination and the continuing influence of Greek clerics.

In conclusion, I want to apply this perspective to Japan. I have mentioned that the Japanese emperor's loss of power vis-à-vis the military governors (the Shogunate) contributed to the strengthening of nature- and ancestor worship. A descendant of the goddess of creation remained the symbolic center of Japanese culture for over a thousand years. The Emperor's purely ceremonial representation had not only cultural significance because it consecrated patriarchal kinship relations. That representation also had material consequences. One result of the Emperor's religious functions as representative of the country was to strengthen the landowning families as the source of wealth and the basis of military power. This led again and again to wars over land and succession at provincial and country-wide levels. Under favorable circumstances Western European conflicts between ruling families could also be worked out through negotiations in various councils, though one naturally has to take into account the pressure of circumstances and the massive use of force as well as the intrusion of foreign relations. Even in isolated Japan there were certainly negotiations in various forms, but they were never institutionalized; even under favorable circumstances conflicts had to be resolved militarily. The very different development of regional interest representation can be seen in the symbolic beginning of the Meiji Restoration. In the so-called Bakumatsu Period (1853-1868) a group of samurai reformers circumvented their regional territorial governors (daimyo) by using the name of these leaders to place their regional territories (han) including the inhabitants at the personal disposal of the Emperor.

This constituted a concerted reorganization of Japanese society, using the Emperor as the symbolic representative of the country, who as such was superior even to the regional lords of these rebellious samurai. For the initiators of this step were a group of Samurai subordinates of the daimyo. At the end of the sixteenth century the ancestors of these Samurai had been deprived of their property and military independence by Hideyoshi Toyotomi; henceforth they became rentiers of modest income but high rank in the fortified cities of their daimyo rulers. But the daimyo themselves, that is the highest nobility in Japan, were made so personally dependent on the Shogunate in Edo under Tokugawa rule (from about 1640) through an ingenious system of alternate residence (sankin-kotai), that they lacked the independence necessary for the development of representative institutions—despite their high rank and great wealth. As in Russia, here again the lack of an independent religious institution (the word ''church'' does not fit Japanese conditions) in the form found in Western Europe, due in part to the religious ideas and institutions of Shinto and of Buddhism.

In the religio-political analysis presented here I come to the already familiar conclusion that the special position of Europe depended as much on the development of representative institutions as on the breakthrough of capitalism. We should keep in mind that these two developments—much as they may appear to converge—came about through quite different causal sequences, each of which has a long historical background. The most recent development of Islamic fundamentalism with its indivisibility between state and religion—should also remind us, how significant such long pre-histories can be for our own time.

Now I want to close my comments with another perspective, to which I can only allude, but without which the shift of emphasis I have proposed would remain incomplete. There is another side to the representative constitution that is as well-known as the negative effects of capitalism, but not often enough linked causally with the special path of Western Europe. Otto Brunner emphasized that princely authority over a territory and its people was based on a readiness to protect the ruler's personal rights by force of arms. This, naturally, was often hardly distinguishable from raids and other warlike enterprises. Brunner's analysis in *Land und Herrschaft* is especially important because it deals with the peculiar causal connection between the legal system and the private exercise of force. If one emphasizes the independence of the church as a constitutive element in the representative order as I have done, one should not neglect to emphasize the war-like side of this element as well. This point calls for an explanation of "desperate brevity," as Schumpeter once put it.

The history of the old church encompassed many controversies between an established orthodoxy and attempts at reform, which appealed to the ideal of early Christianity as the only valid source of the true faith. Examples of this range from the Gnostics and the Montanists through the Donatists of North Africa to the conflict with Pelagianism and beyond. Again and again the church—as an institution legitimized by the apostles—had to build bridges between this early Christian "puritanism" and the moral imperfections of man and society. In its mediating role between heaven and earth the church not only monopolized by proxy the absolution of sins for all Christians, but at the same time made a claim to absolute truth vis-à-vis non-believers or non-Christians. According to the Augustinian interpretation, man's hereditary sinfulness derived from original sin and the consequent expulsion from paradise. In this way, the idea of a community based on a shared faith was transformed into the idea of an inherently sinful mankind. Hence, the church is the only human institution that can transmit to all men the ethical foundation of the Divine Order between the Fall of Man and his salvation in the hereafter. In the end, the idea of original sin became the cornerstone of the church's claim to absolute truth.

The sinfulness of all men and the church's claim to a monopoly on absolute truth finally contributed to the justification of Europe's colonial expansion. An example of this leads us back again to the introduction. The claim to absolute truth, together with missionary duty led to the idea of the just war against non-believers and non-Christians as enemies. The Portuguese discoveries reaching as far as India were justified through a decree sent by Pope Nicholas V in 1454 to Henry the Navigator (1394-1460). It reads:

> Our joy is immense to know that our dear son, Henry, Prince of Portugal . . . inspired with a zeal for souls like an intrepid soldier of Christ, has carried into the most distant and unknown countries the name of God and has brought into the Catholic fold the perfidious enemies of God and Christ, such as the Saracens and the Infidels . . .

> We, after careful deliberation, and having considered that we have by our apostolic letters conceded to King Alfonso, the right, total and absolute, to invade, conquer, and subject all the countries which are under the rule of the enemies of Christ, Saracen or Pagan, by our apostolic letter we wish the same King Alfonso, the Prince, and all their successors, to occupy and possess in exclusive rights the said islands, ports and seas undermentioned, and all faithful Christians are prohibited without the permission of the said Alfonso and his successors to encroach on their sovereignty.

One has to keep in mind that this document was written one year after the Turks seized Constantinople. It was also prompted by Henry the Navigator's petition requesting that the pope sanction Henry's claim to the annexed lands as well as grant the complete remission of sins to all participants in the African discoveries.[14] None of that changes the fact that the pope justified the conquest and subjugation of the enemies of Christ in the name of his apostolic mission.

This papal sanction of the European discoveries and conquests was not only a final consequence of the church's claim to absolute truth. It was at the same time a component of that representative order which was based in part on the autonomy of the church and which contributed markedly to the particular development of Western Europe. The mission of the church outside Europe cannot be separated from the church's century-old struggles for autonomy. Whoever reflects on the special position of Western Europe is obliged to consider both the positive and the negative aspects of that position, and the interrelations between them. The feud as a way of asserting one's rights, which later contributed to the foundation of representative institutions, as well as the missionary imperialism which ushered in and characterized the era of discoveries—these too belong to our picture of the special position of Western Europe.

NOTES

1. It is not necessary to list individually Max Weber's many relevant contributions to the analysis of the special development of the Occident. Otto Hintze's contributions are contained in the first volume of his collected essays. See Otto Hintze,

Staat und Verfassung ed. by Gerhard Oestreich; Göttingen: Vandenhoeck & Ruprecht, 1962), passim. Among Otto Brunner's writings I am thinking especially of chapters 5 and 9-12 in his volume of essays *Neue Wege der Verfassungs- und Sozialgeschichte* (second edition; Göttingen: Vandenhoeck & Ruprecht, 1968). The most recent addition to this inquiry into the special place of Western Europe is Dietrich Gerhard, *Das Abendland 800-1800, Ursprung und Gegenbild unserer Zeit* (Freiburg: Verlag Ploetz, 1985). The original English edition was published as *Old Europe, A Study of Continuity 1000-1800* (New York: Academic Press, 1981). See also Richard Löwenthal (ed.), *Die Demokratie im Wandel der Gesellschaft* (Berlin: Colloquium Verlag, 1963), pp. 164-91, and Hans Albert's unpublished essay, "Der Beitrag Europas, Erbe und Auftrag."

2. Max Weber, *Gesammelte Aufsätze zur Wissenschaftslehre* (Tübingen: J.C.B. Mohr (Paul Siebeck), 1982), 214.

3. Nicholas D. Kristof, "Industrial Dream Fades; Third World Revives Farms," *International Herald Tribune* (July 31, 1985), I,13. The author cites one example of "development failure" in the capital of Togo with its closed oil refinery, a nearly empty 36-story luxury hotel, a closed brick factory, and a leased but nonoperative steel mill.

4. Gordon Marshall, *In Search of the Spirit of Capitalism, An Essay on Max Weber's Protestant Ethic Thesis* (New York: Columbia University Press, 1982), passim.

5. Herbert Schöffler, *Wirkungen der Reformation* (Frankfurt: V. Klostermann, 1960), pp. 189-324. Originally published in 1932. I referred to this study above in chapter 7, pp. 158-59.

6. See Lois Miles Zucker, *S. Ambrosii De Tobia* (Patristic Studies Vol. XXXV; Washington: The Catholic University of America, 1933), 67. For this source and for many ideas, I am indebted to the book by Benjamin Nelson, *The Idea of Usury, From Brotherhood to Universal Otherhood* (second edition; Chicago: University of Chicago Press, 1969), 4.

7. See also the various essays in Gerhard Ruhbach (ed.), *Die Kirche angesichts der Konstantinischen Wende* (Darmstadt: Wissenschaftliche Buchgesellschaft, 1976), passim.

8. Elaine Pagel's *The Gnostic Gospels* (Vintage Books; New York: Random House, 1981) offers an impressive overview of these battles, especially between the growing orthodoxy and the gnostic movement, based on the Nag Hammandi discoveries. Other dimensions of these intra-christian conflicts have been analyzed by Gerd Theissen. See Theissen, *Studien zur Soziologie des Urchristentums* (Tübingen: J.C.B. Mohr [Paul Siebeck], 1979).

9. Henry Chadwick, *The Early Church* (Baltimore: Penguin Books, 1967), 167 and chapter 8 offers a reliable overview of these developments in the fourth century. See also the important recent study by Robert L. Wilken, *The Christians as the Romans Saw Them* (New Haven: Yale University Press, 1984).

10. Here and in what follows I use my characterization in Reinhard Bendix, *Kings or People* (Berkeley: University of California Press, 1978), chapters 3 and 4.

11. Henry C. Lea, *History of Sacerdotal Celibacy* (London: Watts & Co., 1932), 39-60, who dates the first legislation and application of the institution of priestly celibacy between 384 and 401. The book originally appeared in 1867. This dating has not been challenged in modern characterizations, even those that are critical of Lea. See Georg Denzler, *Das Papsttum und der Amtszölibat* (Vol. 5, 1 of Päpste und Papsttum; Stuttgart: Anton Hiersemann, 1973), passim.

12. Antonio Marongiu, *Medieval Parliaments* (London: Eyre & Spottiswoode, 1968), 21.

13. Quoted in Walter Ullmann, *A History of Political Thought* (Baltimore: Penguin Books, 1965), 88.
14. Quoted without source in K.M. Pannikar, *Asia and Western Dominance* (London: Allen & Unwin, 1959), 26-27. A sketch of the geopolitical situation of the papacy around the middle of the fifteenth century is contained in Kleo Pleyer's work, *Die Politik Nikolaus V.* (Stuttgart: W. Kohlhammer, 1927), 13-14 and passim, which shows that Spanish and Portuguese interests were only a small part of the pope's concern. J.H. Parry, *The Establishment of the European Hegemony, 1415-1715* (Harper Torchbooks; New York: Harper & Row, 1961), 31 concludes that the initiative for papal approval of Portuguese expansion came from Portugal. The larger context of the relation between church and state and their politics of expansion has been analyzed by C.R. Boxer, *The Church Militant and Iberian Expansion 1440-1770* (Baltimore: Johns Hopkins University Press, 1978), passim.

14

THE INTELLECTUAL'S ROLE IN THE MODERN WORLD[1]

Introductory Note

At the end of his famous essay on Protestantism, Max Weber states that his intention was not to "substitute for a one-sided materialistic an equally one-sided spiritualistic causal interpretation of culture and of history." I make the same claim and believe, furthermore, that by the end of the twentieth century the whole distinction between materialism and idealism has lost much of its former salience. Just one example underscores this point. Carlo Cipolla has shown that the physical power behind the early European explorations overseas was made available by cannons mounted on sailing ships. These facts have their materialistic side in terms of the capital needed to outfit and provision these sailing expeditions, whether one thinks of the famous explorers like Vasco da Gama or lesser figures like the English pirates harassing the Spanish fleet. But the same facts have their idealistic side as well. Consider the inventions involved like the compass, ship-building designs, the early engineering needed not only for the manufacture of cannon but for their effective mounting on seagoing vessels. And if engineering seems too close to manufacture to be considered idealistic, the same can hardly be said of geographic ideas, astronomy, religious and early national aspirations behind ventures of exploration, though each idea has a material dimension. Then again, venture-capital cannot do without ideas since investments call for decisions among possible alternatives, and so on. This whole debate seems by now hopelessly antiquated, and Weber did a great deal to make it antiquated.

Nevertheless, these point are worth recalling in introducing the concluding discussion of "The Intellectual's Role in the Modern World," written in response to an invitation to speak on this topic at Loyola Marymount University, Los Angeles, in its Charles S. Cassassa Lecture Series, in 1982. It seemed a challenge to try to pull together ideas I had developed on different occasions and provide an overall sketch of the intellectual's role in different parts of the world today. The parts I had worked on separately seemed to fit together in this way; hence, some materials discussed above in Chapter 3 are repeated here.

The reason for this "fit" is my anti-evolutionist position, I believe. If our modern world is divided into advanced, late-comer and third-world countries, and if the contrasts between them indicate in the last analysis a world-history of uneven development, as I have contended, then the last five centuries since the age of exploration have been marked by "intellectual mobilization." Every "advanced" or "developed" country of today was "backward" or "undeveloped" in some respect at one time of its history. Hence, the impulse of men of ideas to do something for their country that would narrow this gap between "development abroad and backwardness at home" was repeated over and over again. Intellectual mobilization of this kind was encouraged or discouraged by men of affairs, depending on where they saw their best chance of advancing their interests. But to the extent that such emulation succeeded and material advances were achieved, to that extent voices were also raised by men of ideas, who saw the dangers of materialism and immorality and decried the evils of the age. This, I think, is one of the enduring paradoxes of the modern era, and the process I delineate in the following paper has not yet run its course. It is a process that is intimately related, albeit in complex ways, to national sentiments and nationalist movements.

The terms of the title invite us to consider what we mean by the "intellectual" and the "modern world," and how these two, multifaceted words may be related to one another. This is a challenge; the risks of so broad a theme are all too evident. In the hope of outlining the main points clearly, I must leave out much that would also be relevant and interesting. My warrant for this attempt is the very proliferation of writings by intellectuals on intellectuals.

I

Here is the way writers for the Oxford Dictionary defined "intellectuals" in 1936: "The class consisting of the educated portion of the population regarded as capable of forming public opinion." No attempt is made to distinguish groups within the "educated portion" and the capacity of forming public opinion is neatly qualified by saying that intellectuals are *regarded* as having this capacity. Whether they do or not is left open. With a deft touch, another, later edition of the Oxford Dictionary reserves the critical use of the word for another term, "intellectualism." Already in 1838 this latter term was defined as "devotion to *merely* intellectual culture or pursuits." The emphasis on "merely" is my own.

Let us now examine American rather than English definitions. In 1934, Webster's Unabridged Dictionary had this entry under intellectuals: "Informed intellectual people collectively; the educated or professional group, class, or party—often derisive." Note that the American definition includes the critical or derisive use of intellectual, which in the English definition is reserved for the special term "intellectualism." By 1961, Webster's had these facets under better control, by which I mean that the pejorative use of "intellectual" has been integrated in the definition. Now we read: "A class of well-educated articulate persons constituting a distinct recognized and self-conscious social stratum within a nation and claiming or assuming for itself the guiding role; an intellectual, social, or political vanguard.'' The ambivalences of American culture are just below the surface of this formulation. Intellectuals are well-educated and articulate, but perhaps also too articulate. They are recognized, but also distinct and self-conscious, perhaps again too much so. They claim the guiding role and perhaps rightly, but then again they assume that role for themselves and perhaps they assume too much. In pointing up these ambivalences I have spelled out the derisive meaning mentioned in 1934. The words used to characterize ''the intellectual'' seem always on the verge of slipping from the positive to an equally possible negative connotation.

This loaded use of ''intellectuals'' is a distinctly American phenomenon. We make a clear distinction, for example, between the adjective ''intellectual'' which has a positive and the noun (pl.) ''intellectuals'' which has a negative connotation. It is as if we always meant ''mere intellectuals'' but dropped the qualifier, because it goes without saying. Harvey McPherson, a lawyer, notes this usage when he stated on one occasion that ''a number of politicians I've known had very considerable intellectual powers, but most of them would have recoiled at the idea that they were 'intellectuals.' '' McPherson's statement is based on long experience in Washington, but it is a little startling to find it corroborated by a bona fide intellectual, the Nobel Prize-winning novelist William Faulkner. Upon receiving the National Book Award in 1955, Faulkner referred in his address to the pursuit of art as ''a peaceful hobby like breeding Dalmatians.'' As artists, he said, we are ''constantly and steadily occupied by, obsessed with, immersed in trying to do the impossible, faced always with the failure which we decline to recognize and accept... [But] this way we stay out of trouble, keep out of the way of the practical and busy people who carry the burden of America.'' Faulkner accepts the dichotomy. The practical people deal with what can be done, artists with what cannot be done but must be attempted anyway.

The dictionary definitions I have cited and others tell us much about the intellectual's role, even when they do not give one neat definition. Intellectuals are recognized as the educated part of the population, variously engaged in independent thinking and the formation of public opinion, sometimes constituting a professional group that is recognized as self-conscious, but also falling short of their leading role in their own eyes and those of others. Intelligent people are respected, but intellectuals as critics are suspect. This usage is biased, because practical affairs and the status quo have their defenders, who are intellectuals every bit as much as the critics. But the one-sided, critical usage prevails, perhaps because in a business civilization practical men hold mere theory in some suspicion, and intellectuals defending that civilization want to avoid designations which undermine their case. At any rate, those striving to do the impossible find fault with the possible, and since people at large remain earthbound and ridden with defects, they repay their critics with derision and contempt. This mutual disrespect between intellectuals and practical people explains the curious fact that many people doing intellectual work are not "intellectuals" in their own eyes or those of others. Engineers, physicians, lawyers, many other professionals try—to use Faulkner's distinction—to do the possible like the other people, who "carry the burden of America." Many of these professionals are highly capable, think independently, and guide public opinion, but few if any are philosophically concerned with "man, society, nature, and the cosmos," which Edward Shils considers the hallmark of "intellectuals" in still another definition. Instead, these men of applied learning are busily engaged in building the technically complex society of today and tomorrow, so that most of them are an integral part of the world which the intellectuals without quotation marks tend to criticize. In the modern world only those educated people are intellectuals, in this narrow sense, who criticize the world of the possible, which is the principal concern of the practical people, including those doing intellectual work. The critique by intellectuals derives from attempting to achieve the impossible, while declining to accept the failure with which such attempts are faced.

Now I have introduced our second conundrum, the "modern world." The current term "the third world," which implies a first and second world as well, makes it easy to be brief, although we all know that these slogans of international politics pretend to a unity and uniformity that does not exist. Leaving this difficulty aside, I shall mean by the "first world" that group of countries which pioneered the development of capitalism in the eighteenth and nineteenth centuries, or as I prefer to call it they pioneered the commercialization of land, labor, and capital. The reference is to the countries of North Western Europe and to their permanent settlements overseas like the United States, Canada, Australia, New Zealand—and South Africa. Japan is an early and perhaps the state of Israel is a late and precarious addition to this list. The "second world" comprises all countries of centrally planned industrialization under Communist rule, which means that I add a political criterion to the fact of more or less successful industrialization. Finally, the "third world" is commonly understood to comprise the poor countries. Only a few of them were represented among the 51 countries which founded the United Nations in 1945. A disproportionate part of the Third World belongs to the 91 additional countries which have joined the UN between 1946 and 1976. Many of them are former colonies which have acquired their sovereignty only recently. But all of the poor countries are "areas of darkness" or "wounded civilizations," as V.S. Naipaul has said of India. Dark and wounded not only in the sense of stark poverty, widespread disease and only isolated pockets of economic advance; dark and wounded also because their populations are exposed to signs of abundance and well-being in countries beyond their frontiers. Dark and wounded finally because these poor countries lack a secure sense of national identity. What then is the intellectual's role in the modern world, subdivided into these three unequal parts, when we define intellectuals as those educated people who criticize the world of the possible? I shall attempt an answer to this question in three parts, because the intellectual's role varies, depending upon which of the three worlds is under discussion.

II

Since I have defined the "modern world" largely in terms of economic development, we can say very roughly that the "first world" became modern in the late eighteenth century. There are phases within this meaning of modernity: we speak of early industrialization, of a first and second and even a third industrial revolution, meaning broadly steam-driven machinery, assembly-line production, and now the age of atomic power and computerization. But in using the "modern world" in this technical-economic sense, we must not neglect the relevant past.

The first world of countries had its beginning in the eighteenth century and so did the intellectuals' critique of the industrial society that was emerging. In his *Essay on the History of Civil Society* (1767), Adam Ferguson declared that nations of tradesmen consist of members who are ignorant of all human affairs beyond their own particular trade. And while he argued that the economic ends of society are best promoted by the mechanical arts, he also said that these arts "thrive best under a total suppression of sentiment and reason" (p. 305). The merchant and the mechanic pay a high price for the economic success produced by their specialization. If this was said by a Scotch moralist who favored the coming of the industrial world, it cannot be surprising that his sentiments were echoed by a poet, P.B. Shelley, who was appalled by its consequences as early as 1821.

> The rich became richer, and the poor have become poorer; and the vessel of the state is driven between . . . anarchy and despotism. Such are the effects which must ever flow from an unmitigated exercise of the calculating faculty. . . . The cultivation of those sciences which have enlarged the limits of the empire of man over the external world, has, for want of the poetical faculty, proportionally circumscribed those of the internal world. . . . The accumulation of the materials of external life exceed the quantity of the power of assimilating them to the internal laws of human nature.

These sentences of Shelley's are moderate in comparison with two devastating declarations by Charles Baudelaire, which were written about 1864 and may be said to summarize Shelley's sentiments with a dash of vitriol added.

In *My Heart Laid Bare*, Baudelaire writes: "The man of letters is the enemy of the world" and, by way of contrast, "To be a useful person has always appeared to me something particularly horrible." Here the conflict between the practical, useful people of the modern world and the critical intellectual appears in an extreme form. Baudelaire is relevant for our theme, because he is one of the originators of the term "modernity." When he used the term for the first time in 1859, he apologized for its novelty, but said that the word was needed to express the peculiarity of the modern artist, who must not only be able to see decay in the human desert of the metropolis, but also detect the hitherto undiscovered, mysterious beauty of that decay. Baudelaire went much further than Shelley, because he asked how poetry was possible at all in a technical and commercialized civilization. Indeed, all the attributes of modern art were anticipated by Baudelaire, each one a challenge to "the practical people who carry the burden" of affairs. Where they emphasize individualism, Baudelaire stresses the depersonalization of the hitherto most personal form of literature, poetry. Where they order and advance the material world, Baudelaire sees it as the marvelous privilege of artistic expression, to make the ugly and horrible beautiful and to fill the mind with quiet joy through rhythmic transformations of its pain.

Baudelaire and the many who followed him had a desperate urge to escape the reality of the practical people who were all around them. To achieve this escape, they used their imagination to decompose the created world, and by reordering the component parts in a manner without precedent they created a new world of their own. A retreat from meaning and coherence is evident in this endeavor. Since the conduct of everyday affairs depends upon the common-sense use of language, opposition to that conduct implies the search for a "new language" which is tantamount to the destruction of grammar and sentence structure. The spirit of this endeavor by the intellectuals is beautifully expressed in T.S. Eliot's *East Coker*: the poet is

> Trying to learn to use words, and every attempt
> Is a wholly new start, and a different kind of failure . . .
> . . .And so each venture
> Is a new beginning, a raid on the inarticulate.

In *Burnt Norton*, Eliot writes that "words strain, crack and sometimes break, under the burden, under the tension." To be usable by the poet, all the old words must be abandoned and a new beginning must be made, a new venturesome raid on the inarticulate. The same idea was expressed in 1935 by Picasso with regard to painting:

> I noticed that painting has a value of its own, independent of the factual depiction of things. I asked myself, whether one should not paint things the way one knows them rather than the way one sees them. . . . In my pictures I use the things I like. I do not care, how things fare in this regard—they will have to get used to it. Formerly, pictures approached their completion in stages. . . . A picture used to be a sum of completions. With me a picture is a sum of destructions.

More examples of this kind could be given, but there is no need. To paraphrase André Gide, the world of the "busy, practical people" imposes itself upon us at every turn, while the intellectuals try to impose their own interpretation on this outside world. The rivalry between these two worlds, one practical and the other imaginative: this is the spiritual drama of our lives in the pioneering countries of modern industry.

This drama has had several phases of which I note two: the decline of bourgeois values and the rising skepticism toward science. On the side of practical affairs we have witnessed in the last hundred years a disintegration of bourgeois culture, whether one considers sexual morality, the work ethic, educational standards, the creative arts, or the manners of everyday life. Bourgeois culture had many drawbacks from which the culture that has taken its place has liberated us. At the same time, the "adversary culture" as Lionel Trilling has called it, has produced many liabilities of its own. One can date this change from the end of the nineteenth century. Perhaps it is better to think of World War I as the watershed, because this prolonged slaughter marked the end of widely accepted standards of conduct and judgment. Then again, one may take the end of World War II as the dividing line. The dating is uncertain, the decline of bourgeois culture is not.

But why attack bourgeois culture if it is in headlong decline? Since the later nineteenth century, art has been characterized increasingly by a retreat from meaning and coherence. That is to say, an ethic of social despair has led by circuitous routes to self-created, hermetic worlds of pure subjectivity in which neither the old romantic ideal of the human personality nor the objects and themes of ordinary experience have a recognized place or meaning. Thus, in the dominant culture of the West a type of sensibility has developed which reacts to the world as a provocation and which is hostile to intellectual positions that retain a belief in the constructive possibilities of knowledge. When a Harvard student wrote in 1969 that "rationality might even destroy our brain cells" or the Yippies declared the year before that in the future society every man would be an artist, they were no longer attacking bourgeois culture as ordinarily understood, but the scientists and technicians who believe with Francis Bacon that "knowledge is for the benefit and use of life." Be it remembered that in the century since 1870 the number of degrees granted at American institutions of higher education has risen from roughly 9,000 to over 1 million, and that from 1963 to 1970 alone the percentage of the scientific population in the work force has risen from 3.6 to 4.7, that is to some 4 million people. Hence, the intellectuals' role in the first world, taking the term in its narrow, critical sense, has come to mean distrust of the belief in progress, while enjoying its benefits and testing to the limit the precarious foundations of human freedom. Need I add that the questions raised by this critique leave none of us untouched, even if the art associated with it leaves us cold?

III

What then can I say of the intellectuals' role in the second world? I shall confine my remarks to Tsarist and Soviet Russia, to simplify matters. According to Robert Tucker of Princeton University, the Russian term "intelligentsia" referred in the nineteenth century to people of all occupations (with the exception of government officials) who shared opposition to the established order and also opposed a regular career, if it was oriented toward personal advancement. They shared a love of the Russian people, preoccupation with the country's backwardness and with ideas as a means of change. By contrast, the *Soviet Encyclopedia* gives the following definition of the same term: "Engineering-technical workers, those engaged in science, art, teaching, medicine and other members of society engaged in mental work." Seemingly, the contrast between the Tsarist and the Soviet meaning of intelligentsia is similar to Faulkner's contrast between those striving for the impossible and the "practical people" who make a country run. But this appearance is deceiving. Tsarist Russia had its practical people and Soviet Russia has its visionaries. Indeed today, both types are present in every society. However, the contrast between the types varies and is important.

In Tsarist Russia, back to the beginning of the eighteenth century, the "practical people" were either public officials, or entrepreneurs (some of them serfs), or landed aristocrats and military men. All these ranks (and their subdivisions) could operate only because they had been entered in government registers and were granted government privileges and assigned government duties. Nearly all worked (or were idle) under governmental directives and supervision. That is the main reason why under the Tsars the intelligentsia opposed the established order *and* regular careers, which depended on official sanction. In Western Europe intellectuals opposed a bourgeois way of life and the "calculating faculty" in the economy and in science; in Russia they opposed the government, often in the name of art *and* science. I should add that in Western Europe bourgeois morals, economic advance and technological change were indigenous developments. In Russia, these same developments were slow in getting started, and when they did, they were linked to the pioneering changes of Western Europe. That linkage was profoundly ambivalent.

A case in point is the literary critic Vissarion Belinsky (1811-1848), who was revered by Russian intellectuals through much of the nineteenth century. Belinksy brought an extraordinary moral passion to bear on such ultimate questions as the purpose of life and the proper moral end of literature. While Tsarist censorship controlled the expression of opinion, it could not prevent writers from endowing abstract literary questions with moral and, by implication, political fervor. The Tsarist police thought Belinsky solely concerned with questions of taste, not with anything that touched on "politics of communism." They thought him wayward but harmless, and yet they considered him with suspicion. Gendarmes attended Belinsky's funeral to keep an eye on his friends and prevent demonstrations. One can see their dilemma. Belinsky deplored that Russian men of letters discussed every idea imported from abroad, and created nothing of their own. With this heady attraction of foreign ideas went a revulsion at the realities of Western bourgeois society and near despair at the condition of the Russian homeland. Belinsky saw a "syphilitic sore" running through French society, but he also said "We are people whose country is a ghost, and we are ghosts ourselves." There is only one way out: "Lose yourself in science and art, love them as the goal and necessity of your life, and not as mere instruments of education and winning success in the world. . . . Love what is good, and you are bound to turn out useful to your country." The idea has been elaborated many times that Tsarist autocracy and censorship, which suppressed or closely controlled all activities of civil society, thereby helped to create a culture in which truth and beauty were endowed with surprising importance and ultimately with political significance.

In part, this political significance of culture arose—paradoxically perhaps—from the very efforts of the Tsarist regime to reform itself. Since the reign of Peter the Great (1685-1725), Tsarist governments were attempting to develop the country. To this end, craftsmen and teachers were imported from Western Europe. Several prominent officials and scientists were of foreign birth. Catherine II (1762-1796) cultivated her contacts with French philosophers, to present an enlightened image to the outside world. The stunning success of Russian arms against Napoleon in 1812 brought Russian officers and men to Western Europe. This was the era of Speransky's attempts at legal reform and of the Decembrist revolt of 1825, organized by army officers with liberal aspirations: both failed. Tsar Alexander II (1855-1881) initiated the emancipation of the serfs of 1861 and under his reign the enrollment of students in secondary schools and universities increased rapidly. Both reforms provided conduits for the influx of Western European ideas, opposition to the autocratic regime spread, there was an unsuccessful attack on the Tsar's life in 1866, and repressive measures followed. It seems that every reform attempted by the government allowed for breathing space to the educated elite of the country, and the intellectuals among them used that space to protest, which led to further repressions and reforms and further protests in a spiral of reciprocal escalation. As Peter Lavrov (1823-1900) pointed out in 1870, the very education of students added to their guilty conscience, because it was "purchased" by the suffering of millions. They could not undo their education, but they could redeem their guilt by using their education to oppose the Tsarist regime which had benefited them. This trauma of Russia's youth led to the assassination of Alexander II, in 1881, producing a much more severe repression than before and still greater traumas at the backwardness of Russia among the country's intellectuals.

A hundred years have passed since that assassination. The military defeat of Russia in the Russo-Japanese war and the first World War were followed by the revolution of 1905 and the Bolshevik revolution of 1917, respectively. In November of 1982, the Soviet Union celebrated the 65th anniversary of the Russian revolution, which was led under Lenin's leadership by a highly organized cadre of professional revolutionaries—many of them intellectuals of middle-class background. During the last 65 years, the early revolutionary elite was transformed into an elite of party functionaries and an aggregate of scientists and technicians largely responsible for the transformation of Russia's economy. Taking just official figures, we get the following contrasts between 1928 and 1981: electricity (in billion Kwhs) from 5 to 1325; steel (in million tons) from 4.3 to 149; oil (in million tons) from 11.6 to 609, and so on. We all know that the record is far less impressive in other branches of industry and altogether dismal in the field of agriculture. In terms of per capita productivity and income the Russian development cannot compare with the major cases of Western industrialization, and Russia's cost in human lives has been staggering. But all this does not alter the success of Russia's industrialization and military build-up. What then of the country's intellectuals, spiritual heirs to the Western critics of bourgeois culture and the Russian critics of Tsarist autocracy?

Their tragedy is that their situation has become much worse in comparison with their predecessors under the Tsars. In 1836, Peter Chaadayev was declared mad by the Tsar himself and subjected to periodic medical inspection, because he had publicly criticized the social and political conditions of Russia. This episode of autocratic paternalism cast a pall over the small circle of artists and writers in Moscow and St. Petersburg, but its notoriety then as now also suggests that it was a rather singular case. Today, hundreds and perhaps thousands of dissidents languish in psychiatric hospitals, because the regime has decreed that their deviation indicates insanity. A similar contrast applies to the matter of censorship. Public debate was closely controlled under the Tsars, as it is under the Soviets. But Tsarist practice allowed a certain leeway and was riddled with inefficiency. It was often possible to evade the prohibition by discussing the problems of Western Europe or of Ancient Society, since every reader understood what was meant. In the Soviet Union, such evasions are more difficult or even impossible, in part because censorship has become tighter and more sophisticated, and in part because Communist orthodoxy applies worldwide, as Tsarism did not. Yet in one respect the result of censorship has been much the same. The suppression of public debate has endowed poetry and literary questions with extraordinary significance for politics as well as for culture. Belinsky's singular devotion to truth and beauty is echoed today when a poetry-reading by Yevtushenko, Voznesensky, and others is attended by audiences numbering in the hundreds and sometimes thousands. The idea that drastic censorship inadvertently endows poetic celebrations of feeling and nature with political significance is reflected in Osip Mandelstam's identification of poetry with power. "If they kill people for writing poetry," he said, " poetry must be powerful."

Thirdly, poverty and oppression evoke ambivalent responses, then as now. Under the Tsars "the West" appeared to Russian intellectuals as lands of wealth and freedom, but marred by shallow materialism and cultural decadence. Yet the defects of "the West" brought no consolation regarding conditions at home. Just as under the Tsars, Slavophils sought to regenerate Russia by turning to her past and Westernizers looked to France or Germany for inspiration, so it is today. From his exile in Zurich and Vermont, Solzhenitsyn appeals to the Politburo to return to Russian tradition and excoriates "the West" for its spiritual decay. Meanwhile inside the Soviet Union, Andrei Sakharov, another Nobel Prize winner, champions the protection of human rights—hardly the main tradition of Russian civilization. And both men are at one in their love of Russia. But in contrast to the Tsarist regime, Soviet Russia has become a world power. If before Russian intellectuals condemned the slovenly and stupid officials of the Tsar, today they condemn the graft and brute materialism of the party bosses which fosters the evasion of law and the growth of very wealthy, but illegal entrepreneurs.

Then as now, the freedom of the West holds powerful attraction to Russian intellectuals, for they live in a thoroughly regimented society which quickly punishes deviations. Today, the Soviet Union is perhaps the most conservative society in the world, but a conservatism based on the success of forced industrialization and the social structure that emerged from it. All symbols of Western culture are suspect, but blue jeans, some Western detective stories, and some jazz music are permitted by the authorities and enjoy a huge popularity. There are some timid imitations of Western modernism in the arts. But it is difficult in modern Russia to point up the dangers of technological advance (let alone of the military build-up), when in addition to one-party rule there are periodic short-falls of agricultural production, basic consumer needs cannot be satisfied, and the existence of American superpower can be used to justify every twist of the party-line. One gets the impression that intellectuals of the second world prize freedom, but confine their critique of technology and individual consumption to the West, while intellectuals of the first world have the luxury of rejecting as a whole what they enjoy in their everyday lives.

The distinction between the two groups becomes clearest perhaps when one considers the agony of intellectuals within the Soviet orbit who become refugees. In their home-country, all power is concentrated in the Politburo and all organizations in society are coopted and controlled by agencies of the Communist party. This control extends to all channels of communication. Under these conditions intellectuals feel, like their predecessors under the Tsars, that they alone speak for the whole country. Persecution confirms them in their view, because persecution proves beyond a doubt that they are not official speakers and, therefore, cannot speak falsely. As long as they remain in Russia, Russian intellectuals identify morally with the ideals of Russian culture and bear the hardships this entails. When one turns to intellectuals of other nationalities in the Soviet Union and within the Soviet orbit, the identification with the people as well as culture and, by implication at least, the anti-Russian note becomes more prominent. Returning from a visit to Poland in 1981, Czeslaw Milosz—the Nobel Prize Laureate for literature in 1980— described an example of this experience:

> Intellectuals, workers, students all spoke the same language. There was true solidarity, for people were united by a common goal. I found that as a poet— and I do not consider myself a very easy poet to read—I had a mass audience in Poland composed of people of various strata of society. Even poems that are rather difficult were understood. That's rare. My poems appeared in 150,000 copies. That's over now [following the military crackdown of December 13, 1981]. A relatively uncensored publishing movement and the free exchange in public opinion are ended. But the human spirit remains.

In the same interview, Milosz stated that he found the United States very difficult to judge. By upbringing and political instinct, he had expected to find allies among American liberals, "but in fact I see we have not many points in common." As a Pole and a revered figure in his country, Milosz may be exceptional, and he is certainly different from Russian refugee intellectuals. But as an exile, he is one of many who must preserve their identity in an alien environment, in which the multiplicity of groups and sympathizers is a constant reminder of the real or imagined wholeness of their native land. The point to note is that many intellectuals of the first world have no comparable identification either with the culture or the people of their native land; they tend to be elitists who despair of popular taste even when their works are bought by the public.

Finally, I turn to the intellectual's role in the Third World. This world of darkness is marked, as I said, by poverty, disease, and isolated pockets of economic advance, in which people lack a sense of identity because they are continually exposed to signs of affluence abroad. In these countries, neither the educated elite, nor representative institutions, nor an economically active middle class are indigenous developments. But such countries are arenas of intellectual mobilization nonetheless, because officials, teachers, literary people, in a word the whole educated minority, tend to coalesce into a class of their own. This class is sensitive to developments beyond their country's frontier and anxious to find a more viable mode of social organization for their native land.

There is a family resemblance between the third world of today and the poor countries of earlier eras. In the sixteenth and seventeenth centuries, English intellectuals and other people reacted to the economic advance of Holland and the Spanish world empire. In the eighteenth century, German writers reacted positively or negatively to the economic and political advance of England and France. In response to the French revolution, German rulers proposed to do for "their" people—by a revolution from above—what the French people had done at high cost by and for themselves. As I have pointed out, Russian intellectuals during the nineteenth century took standards derived from West European developments to form counter-images of Tsarist realities; and in the twentieth century Russian revolutionaries adopted programs and tactics derived from the French revolution and Marxist theory in their overthrow of the Tsarist regime. For a while, the Russian revolution became in turn the reference society for China before and after 1949. But the Chinese under Mao Tse-tung reacted to the model of forced collectivization and industrialization by accepting a slower rate of economic growth, and with a positive emphasis on the peasantry, on reeducation campaigns, and on the importance of subjective commitment as a major cause of change. By linking these policies with the Chinese tradition, they have created a new revolutionary model, which since Mao's death has been modified further.

I believe an archetypical experience underlies the obvious diversity of these examples. In comparison with some advanced country, the intellectuals see their own country as backward. This is a troubled perception, for it identifies strength if not goodness with alien forces and sees weakness if not evil in the land of one's birth. In this setting ideas are used to locate and mobilize forces which will be capable of effecting change and thus redress this psychologically unfavorable accounting. A typical strategy of perception and argument ensues. As viewed by the native intellectual, the strength of the advanced country is formidable, but it is also sapped by false values, corruption, and spiritual decay and therefore should not or cannot endure. At the same time, the weakness of one's native land is pervasive, but the hidden spiritual values of the people are an untapped source of strength which will prevail in the end (whatever the evidence to the contrary may be). Thus, the dominance of the advanced country carries within itself the seeds of its own destruction, while the backward people and the underdeveloped country possess capacities that are signs of a bright future. Behind this strategy lies the simple belief that ultimately the advanced country must be weak because its people are evil, while the backward country must be strong because its people are good.

In the middle of the nineteenth century Russia's best-known exile, Alexander Herzen, wrote that "human development is a form of chronological unfairness, since late-comers are able to profit from the labor of their predecessors without paying the same price." He did not anticipate the enormous price which Russia herself paid for economic development, nor did he, or any of his contemporaries, envisage the far greater problems which the modernizing countries of the Third World face today and in the foreseeable future. This is not a problem which intellectuals of the first or second world can contemplate with equanimity. For the breakthrough to modern technology and economic development occurred for the first time in Western Europe some four centuries ago, it occurred for a second time in Japan in the latter half of the nineteenth century, and it occurred for the third time both in the late Tsarist period and under Communist auspices since the revolution of 1917. In each instance, new inequalities were introduced on a major scale between the countries of economic advance and the many countries that became rapidly more impoverished by comparison. In all too many instances economic advances in one place were used to exploit the resources and increase the relative poverty in other places.

In the twentieth century all of us, but particularly the intellectuals of the Third World, face the consequences of these antecedents. The effort of learning from the development of other countries is beset by difficulties and the cost in human labor and suffering is rising and may have become prohibitive already. Let me sketch the situation in intellectual terms. Every idea taken from elsewhere can be both an asset to the development of a country and a reminder of its comparative backwardness, that is both a model to be emulated and a threat to national identity. What appears desirable from the standpoint of progress often appears dangerous to national independence. The revolution in communications since the fifteenth century has been accompanied by ever new confrontations with this cruel dilemma, and the rise of nationalism has been the response nearly everywhere.

However, nationalism is not in fact a force that easily unifies a country. The old states underwent long periods of intellectual polarization when they had to come to terms with challenges from abroad. Similarly, in the new states the typical response is the polarization of modernizers and nativists. These two camps of intellectuals share the desire to preserve and enhance their native land—and even the hostility to the "advanced country" whose accomplishments they covet nonetheless. A Westernizer like Herzen commented on his affinity with the Slavophils: "Like Janus, or the two-headed eagle, we looked in opposite directions, but one heart beats in our breasts.'' All the same, the division is deep over which path the country should follow.

Perception of advances abroad are reminders of backwardness or dangers and weaknesses at home. Intellectuals attempt to cope with the ensuing dilemma: whether to adopt the advanced model and invite its attending corruptions, or fall back upon native traditions and risk their inappropriateness to the world of power and progress. This dilemma engenders heated debates and ever-uneasy compromises. Men want their country recognized and respected in the world, and to this end they cultivate or revive native traditions. The reconstruction of history is an act of resacralizing authority in the name of the people. It is an appeal to civic loyalty and national brotherhood in lieu of the more divisive attachments to language, ethnicity and religion, because birth in a common homeland makes all people members of one nation sharing equally in its past glories. But the desire to be recognized and respected in the world also calls for the development of a modern economy and government, and this effort at development focusses attention upon ideas and models derived from the advanced society of one's choice.

The drama of intellectuals in the first world consists in the rivalry between the practical and the imaginative approach to the human condition. The drama of the second world consists in the incompatibility between individual freedom and the centralized hierarchy of a one-party state—in the midst of economic advance well in excess of the rate of per capita consumption. The drama of the third world consists in the pain of intellectuals usually educated abroad, who confront the poverty of their land amidst images of plenty abroad, and who struggle against overwhelming odds to define a place for themselves and for their country.

NOTE

1. The substance of this essay was presented as the first Charles S. Cassassa Distinguished Lecture at Loyola Marymount University, Los Angeles, March 4, 1982. The materials for this lecture are derived from three of my earlier publications, though I have not previously formulated the framework developed here. The three publications are: "Sociology and the Distrust of Reason," *American Sociological Review*, vol. 35 (October 1970), pp. 831-843 and reprinted in the present volume as chapter 3 above; "Why Nationalism? Relative Backwardness and Intellectual Mobilization," *Zeitschrift für Soziologie*, vol. 8 (January 1979), pp. 6-13; and *Kings or People* (Berkeley: University of California Press, 1978), ch. 13. All the sources cited are quoted in these publications except for the statement of Harvey McPherson derived from an unpublished paper without title presented at a Conference at the University of Massachusetts, May 9-11, 1974 and the address by William Faulkner, printed in *The New York Times Book Review* of February 6, 1955. The interview with Czeslaw Milosz appeared in *U.S. News and World Report*, January 25, 1982. I am indebted to my colleague, Professor Gregory Grossman, for his criticism and suggestions.

INDEX

Administrative behavior: judgment in, 229-30
Advice to Princes. *See* State(s)
Almond, Gabriel. *See* Functionalism, Legitimacy
Ambrosius, Bishop of Milan: justification of early Christianity, 327-28; relations with Emperor Theodosius, 329
America. *See* United States
American Sociological Association: convention of, 1970, 63; President of, 62
Anti-modernism: "Adversary culture" (Trilling), 345; Baudelaire on 70, 344; Friedrich's analysis of, in modern poetry, 70-71
Aristocracy: Brunner on, 55; French, 138; medieval, 331; Russian, 248; Schumpeter on, 306-07
Aron, Raymond. *See* State(s)
Associations. *See* Interest groups
Auerbach, Erich. *See* Modernization
Auletta, Ken. *See* Citizenship, Class(es)
Authority: double hierarchy of, 246-47; paternal, in Tsarist Russia, 238-39; quid-pro-quo model of, 223-24; types of, 204-08

Bacon, Francis: advocacy of science, 17-18, 64-65, 85-87; on bias and reason, 9, 32-33; goal of science, 8; theory of idols, 23, 27-28, 92
Bailyn, Bernard. *See* Ideology
Barker, Ernest. *See* Modernization, State(s)
Barnard, Chester: on zone of indifference, 229-30
Barth, Hans: analysis of Helvétius by, 33; on Napoleon's polemic against idéologues, 29; traces changing ideas of man and truth, 57
Baruch, Bernard. *See* Science
Baudelaire, Charles. *See* Anti-modernism

Becker, Carl: on modern ideology, 24
Bell, Daniel: on end of ideology, 55
Bellow, Saul: on impotence and personality, 70
Bendix, John: co-author with Reinhard Bendix, 179ff.
Bendix, Reinhard: on civic problem of industrialization, 208; critique of, by Talcott Parsons, 133-36; on Marx and Tocqueville, 209-10; Master's thesis by, 7-8; President of A.S.A., 62; restatement of position by, 203-04; shift of interest from totalitarianism to modernization, 234-35; "Social Science and the Distrust of Reason" by, 8, 61-62; on strategy of independence, 229-30
Berger, Bennett: age-cohort of anxiety, 64; co-author with Bendix, 128
Bergmann, Alexander. *See* Managerial ideology
Berliner, Joseph: on managerial ideology in the U.S.S.R., 250
Bettelheim, Bruno: on adolescent rebellion, 63
Bias: changing ideas of, 9-10; Edmund Burke on, 29-30; Bacon's theory of idols, 27-28. *See also* Prejudice
Bierstedt, Robert: on non-charismatic leadership, 129-30
Birnbaum, Norman: on declining evolutionism among Marxists, 177-78
Blau, Peter: critique of Weber by, 129
Bodin, Jean: on kingship and society, 180-81
Bogdanov, A.A.: on spread of bourgeois ideology, 72-73
Bronowski, J.: on ethics of science, 90-91
Broom, Leonard: definition of primary relations, 130
Brunner, Otto: on aristocratic way of life, 55
Burckhardt, Jacob: on culture history, 249; on great men in history, 172

355

Bureaucracy: critiques of Weber on, 129-30; ideal type of, 120; and patrimonialism, 120-22

Burke, Edmund: Hobbes and, 31-32; on moral discoveries, 56; on prejudice, 29-31, 99; on society as contract, 194

Burke, Kenneth: on perspective by incongruity, 124

Bush, Vannevar: on science and national welfare, 76

Capitalism: critique of, as master cause, 210-11

Categorical imperative: of science, 90-91

Change: and integration, 152-53; religious, 153-54. *See also* Social change

Charisma: breakthrough and routinization, 170-72; Burckhardt on "great men," 172; definition of, 163-64

Christianity: medieval expansion of, 335-36; politics of early, 326-30; spread of, in Russia, 330, 332

Cipolla, Carlo M: on industrialization, 315

Citizenship: Auletta on "underclass," 202; extension of, 211-13, 217-18; T.H. Marshall on civic, political and social rights, 211; national, 197-98; R.R. Palmer on emergence of, 279

Civil society: absence of, in Lebanon, 191; Gabriel Almond on, 177; William Blackstone on, 188; Edmund Burke on, 194; civic position of work force, 208; definition of, 187-91; Duke du Rohan on, 188; and the market, 191-94; and the life cycle, 193ff.; as a problem of industrialization, 208-09

Class(es): Auletta on "underclass," 202; T.H. Marshall's definition of, 271; status-groups and, 119-20; stratification and legitimation, 168-70; E.P. Thompson's definition of, 315-16

Clermont-Tonnere: on Jews as a nation, 189

Coercion: -model of social structure, 161

Cohen, Morris. *See* Paired concepts

Collingwood, R.G.: critique of propositional calculus, 178

Commitment. *See* Participation

Comparative Method: assumptions of, 282-89; and paradigm shifts, 322-24; personal aspect of, 225-26; and social change, 274-75; in the study of modernization, 295-305; Tocqueville on, 126-27

Conflicting imperatives. *See* Dual tendencies

Contrast conceptions. *See* Dual tendencies

Culture: Burckhardt on, 249; decline of bourgeois, 344-46; elites and masses in, 156; as theory and as practice, 157-60; Weber on, as convention, 123-31

Dahrendorf, Ralph: on "homo sociologicus," 196

Darnton, Robert: on writers in French revolution, 140-41

Declaration of the Rights of Man: principles of, 144-45

Demonstration effect: pioneering and follower societies, 137-38

Theory of dependence. *See* Traditionalism

Deutsch, Karl: on communication flows between countries, 130

Dictatorships. *See* Plebiscitarianism, Authority

Domination: types of authority, 204-08

Double hierarchy: *See* Authority

Dual tendencies: concepts of, 124-25; and contrast conceptions of social change, 285-88; from Empedokles to Freud, 113-16; of ideas and interests, 226-27; and Weber's types of authority, 167

Durkheim, Emile: central themes in sociology of, 45-48, 112-13; Freud and, 13-14; Marx, Tocqueville, Weber and, 52; on "normal" crime, 122; on the state and the emancipation of the individual, 263-64, 272; on the study of moral facts, 12-13; as successor to Rousseau and Tocqueville, 254-55; Weber and, 50-52

Dyson, Kenneth: on the "Western State Tradition," 179-80

Eliot, T.S.: "East Coker" and "Burnt Norton" by, 70-71, 344

Elites: and masses, 154-57

Empedokles. *See* Dual tendencies

Encyclopédie, edited by Diderot and d' Alembert. *See* Intellectuals

Entrepreneurs: Schumpeter on industrial, 172

Equality: ideal of, in French Revolution, 145; limited franchise and, 148-49

Evolutionism. *See* Social change

Exchange-model: of social structure, 160-61

Fascism: rhetoric of, 72-75

The Federalist. See James Madison

Ferguson, Adam: on modernization, 343

Fontenelle, Bernard de: on value of the "geometric spirit," 86

Fraenkel, Ernst: on representation and plebiscite, 229

Franchise: extension of, 217-18; limited, and equality, 148-49; universal, in the French Revolution, 279

Franklin, Benjamin: as representative of American colonies, 139

Frederick II of Prussia: on domination of French in Europe, 138

Freemasons: in France, 138; in French Revolution, 141-43; and Mozart's *Magic Flute*, 143; spirit of, 150

Freud, Sigmund: Durkheim and, 13-14; not a Freudian, 19; as iconoclast and emancipator, 66-67; Marx and, 9-12, 34; Saint-Simon and, 35; on society and the family, 190

Friedrich, Hugo: on "dictatorial phantasy" in modern poetry, 70-71. *See also* Anti-Modernism

Functionalism: Almond's terminologial proposal on, 270; critique of, 134-35; Merton on, 132; and paired concepts, 130

Fundamental democratization: Karl Mannheim on, 294, 309

Futurism: manifesto of, 71. *See also* Marinetti, Fillipo

Gerschenkron, Alexander: analysis of backwardness by, 290, 302

Gide, André: on the spiritual burden of our time, 71, 345

Gierke, Otto von: on medieval conception of "the people," 293

Goubert, Pierre: on eighteenth-century France, 186

Goudsblum, Johan: on confessional blocks in Dutch politics, 218. *See also* Pillarization

Haller, William: on spiritual problem addressed in seventeenth-century sermons, 158

Hegel, G.F.W.: on master and servant, 241; and Tocqueville, 241-42

Heller, Erich: on values and the scientific trust in objectivity, 98

Helmholtz, Hermann: on science and specialization as the model, 65

Helvétius, Claude: on prejudice, 33

Hintze, Otto: on ideas and interests, 226

Hirschman, Albert: on "exit, voice, and loyalty," 191-93

Hobbes, Thomas: Burke and, 31-32; definition of reason by, 31

Hofmannsthal, Hugo von: on destructive consequences of abstractions, 74; on real people and fictional characters, 160

Holton, Gerald: on the scientific quest, 88-89

Hughes, H. Stuart: on the generation of scholars born 1850-70, 14, 68-69

Ideology: Bailyn on American, 149; Barth on, and truth, 56-57; Becker on modern, 24; definition of, 25-26, 249; empirical significance of, 242-44, 247-48; end of, 24, 55; of French revolution, 141-43; historical significance of, 240-42; Napoleon on, 29; of science, 86-93; "science of," 29; of traditionalism, 237-38

Industrialization: American interest in, 237; civic problems posed by, 208-09

Integration: and change, 152-53, 170

Intellectuals: definitions of, 340-42, 346; in French Revolution, 139-40; Milosz on Polish response to poetry, 350; Riehl on, 305; role of, 311-12, 320; in Russia, 346-50

Interdependence: -model of social structure, 160

Interest groups: definition of, by H.-J. Varian, 191; development of, 218-19; Tocqueville and Durkheim on secondary groups, 265-66

Jaucourt, Chevalier de: definition of equality by, 145

Jews: as a nation, 189. *See also* Clermont-Tonnere

Jonas, Hans: on contrast between medieval and Baconian view of knowledge, 85-86; on technology and responsibility, 104

Kant, Immanuel: on unsocial sociability, 114
Kerr, Clark: Godkin lectures by, 76
Kierkegaard, Søren: on the search for knowledge, 66-67
Knowledge: Baconian and evolutionist idea of, 18, 85-86; Christian idea of, 84-85; classical idea of, 84; Kierkegaard, Nietzsche, Schopenhauer on the search for, 66-67; medieval and Baconian view of, 85-86; Promethean concept of, 17; purposes of, 3, 83-86; in society, 93-102; sociology and the pursuit of, 77-79; uncertain future and, 127; value of, 5-7, 14-16, 86-93
Kuhn, Thomas: on paradigm shifts, 323

La Chalotais, Attorney General: on Jesuit education and the nation, 189
Lacqueur, Walter: critique of Tucholsky, 75
Laissez-faire: theory of rich and poor, 238
Lakatos, Imre: on philosophy of science, 100
Law. See Legal authority
Legal authority: changes of, in nineteenth century, 214-17; and modern state, 184; viability of, 165-67
Legitimacy: Almond on civic culture, 177; belief in, 161-62; charismatic, 164-65; quid-pro-quo or exchange model of, 162-63, 180-87, 223-24; types of, 204-08
Leighton, Alexander: on scientists and politicians, 61
Lenin: as charismatic leader, 171-72
Linton, Ralph: on culture and the individual, 115-16
Loewith, Karl: on ancient and Christian origins of philosophy of history, 228, 272
Loi le Chapelier: on the unlawfulness of mutual aid societies, 189
Luddites: C.P. Snow on "natural," 66, 68

Madison, James: on factions (Federalist No. 10), 189-90
Managerial ideology: A. Bergmann on American, 229; Berliner on, in U.S.S.R., 250; in England and Russia, 242, 245-46; history of, 240-42; in Tsarist Russia and the Soviet Union, 238-40; Andrew Ure's, 243

Mandeville, Bernard de: "Private Vices, Public Benifits" by, 101
Manichean division: of the world, 62
Mannheim, Karl: on conservative thought, 62-63; on "fundamental democratization," 294, 309; Ideology and Utopia by, 4
Marinetti, Fillipo: Futurist Manfesto by, 71
Marongiu, Antonio: on medieval kingship and aristocracy, 331
Marshall, Gordon: review of "Protestant Ethic" literature, 325
Marshall, T.H.: on civil, political and social rights, 211; definition of class by, 271
Marx, Karl: "bourgeois ideologists" according to, 4; central themes in sociology of, 36-40; "Communist Manifesto" by, 4, 54; critique of theory of revolution by, 308-10, 312-14; Durkheim, Tocqueville, Weber and, 52; on French peasantry, 308-09; Freud and, 9-12, 34; on human agency, 100; as iconoclast and emancipator, 66-67; and Tocqueville, 209-10; on traditionalism, 250
Mass parties: role of, 217-21
Masses: and elites, 154-57
Mead, George Herbert: on property, 240-41; on psychology of the self, 114-15; on Rousseau, 148
Medieval society: expansion of Christianity in late, 335-36; liberty as privilege in, 274; representation in Russian, 332-33
Meinecke, Friedrich: on "reason of state," 253
Membership: in associations, 195-98
Men of letters: in France, 140-41, 144-45. See also intellectuals
Merton, Robert K.: on functionalism, 132; on the growth of knowledge, 20, 56-57
Mill, John Stuart: on the theory of dependence, 137-38. See also Traditionalism
Milocz, Czeslav: on Polish response to poetry, 350
Modernization: Erich Auerback on, of "reality," 55; Ernest Barker on, of the state, 184; buildup of, 137-38; changed sensibility through, 344-46; in comparative perspective, 295-305; Adam Ferguson

on, 343; meaning of, 233-34, 280-82, 300-14, 342-43; political, 264-67; of Western Europe, 252-58; and tradition, 290-95

Montesquieu, Baron de: *pouvoirs intermédiaires*, 196; view of English government by, 138

Napoleon Bonaparte: on ideology, 29

Nation-Building: in the late twentieth century, 224-25

Nietzsche, Friedrich: on the search for knowledge, 66-68

Nisbet, Robert A.: on classical origin of "society as system," 136, 177

Novalis (pseud.): on superiority of poetic knowledge, 68, 70

Order: in society and nature, 8-9

Organized interests. *See* Interest groups

Paired concepts: Morris Cohen on principle of polarity, 128; and functionalism, 130; Maine, Durkheim, Tönnies, MacIver, Redfield on, 117

Palmer, R.R.: on emergence of citizenship, 279

Park, Robert: on competition and communication, 114

Parsons, Talcott: on action theory, 131; critique of Bendix by, 133-36; integration of social theory by, 111, 151; on social system, 128

Participation: disaggregation of, 194-99; extension of citizenship and, 211-13, 217-18; through interest groups, 218-19; through representation, referenda and plebiscites, 215-16; by secret ballot, 217-18

Particularism: ethical, according to Deuteronomy, 326-28

Paternalism: in Mill's theory of dependence, 237-38; in Tsarist autocracy, 238-39

Patrimonialism: and the modern state, 184-85

Picasso, Pablo: interveiw with, 71, 344-45

Pillarization (Verzuiling): in Holland, 218

Plebiscitarian: type of domination, 219-23

Pope Nicholas V: Bull of, to Henry the Navigator, 336

Popular mandate: through representation, referendum and plebiscite, 215-16

Prejudice: Edmund Burke on; 29-30; Helvétius on, 33. *See also* Bias

Price, Don: on self-determination of science, 75, 89

Primary relations: and secondary, 117-19

Property: G.H. Mead on, 240-41

Protestantism: as analyzed in Weber's "Protestant Ethic," 152-60; doctrine and conduct in, 157-60; political setting of English, 325-26; survivals of, 123

Radbruch, Gustav: on action theory in criminal law, 107

Rationalization: as increased rationality, 172-74; as justification, 244

Reason: conventional, 99; definitions of, 31-32; dialectical, 100; imaginative, 98-99; prudence and, 99

Reductionism: definition of, 26; through elimination of politics, 210; theoretical, 10-16

Reference societies: and follower societies, 304; in eighteenth-century France, 138-39; for Tsarist Russia and the "Third World," 349-53

Religion: as a source of change, 153-54

Representation: in the French Revolution, 145-47; in medieval Japan, 334; in medieval Russia, 332-33; and priviledged jurisdiction, 276

Revolution: ideology of French, 141-43; Tocqueville on, 208-09, 241-42

Riehl, Wilhelm: on German intellectuals, 305

Robespierre, Maximilien: revolutionary ideas of, 144-47

Roles: definition of social, 123-24; Simmel on multiple, 152

Romantic: critique of science, 66-68

Rousseau, Jean-Jacques: on government by consent, 146, 181

Routinization: and breakthrough, 170-72

Rustow, Dankwart: definition of charisma, 164

Saint-Simon, Henri de: on politics as a question of hygiene, 33, 99

Salis, J.R. von: on reality of appearances, 4

Schoeffler, Herbert: on political setting of English Reformation, 159, 325-26

Schopenhauer, Arthur: on the search for knowledge, 66-67

Schumpeter, Joseph: on aristocracy, 306-07; on entrepreneurship, 172

Science: advocacy of, 86-93; autonomy of, 89, 97; Bernard Baruch on the perils of, 76; categorical imperative of, 90; changing role of, 75; civic problem of, 90, 93-96; code of conduct for, 91-93; Helmholtz on, 65; Holton on, 88-89; moratorium on, 103; prudence and, 32; public disclosure of, 92; radicalism of, 91-92; and religion, 97-98

Secret ballot. See Participation

Selznick, Philip: definition of primary relations by, 130

Shelley, Percy B: "Defense of Poetry" by, 67-68, 98-99, 343-44

Shils, Edward A.: on the "new states," 303; on sentiment as the measure of man, 72; on utopia of plenitude, 64

Sieyès, Abbé: distinguishes passive and active citizenship, 146; on legal rights of representation, 148; on nation as the source of law, 144; opposes unjust inequality of rights, 145

Simmel, Georg: interaction among individuals, 112; on large social formations, 128; multiple roles of individuals, 152; "negativity" of collective behavior, 228

Simon, Herbert: on judgment in administrative behavior, 229-30

Skocpol, Theda: on "bringing the state back in," 180

Smelser, Neil: on the history of sociology, 152

Smith, Adam: theory of classes by, 189

Snow, C.P.: on two cultures, 65-66; on "natural Luddites," 68

Social change: critique of evolutionist theory of, 137-38; as social evolution, 136-37, 282-83; studies of, 289-95; and Weber's view of evolution, 174-75

"Social Contract": Rousseau's, 146

Social Darwinism. See Struggle for survival

Social fact: definitions of the, 112-13

Social Structure: coherence-models of, 160-61, 284-85; quid-pro-quo or exchange models of, 223-24

Social Systems approach: affinities of, 283; critique of, 134-35, 317

Society: and government, interdependent and autonomous, 254-55; government as a product of, 253-54; as an object of state craft, 253, 277; and the state, 267-69; Sumner on "crescive" and "enacted" institutions, 267; Tocqueville and Durkheim on secondary groups, 265-67

Sociology: authority of knowledge in, 77-79; Smelser on history of, 152

Sovereignty: popular, 144-45; implemented through representation, referendum and plebiscite, 215-16

State: "Advice to Princes," 253; Raymond Aron on politics of the, 27; Ernest Barker's definition of the modern, 184; definition of the, 182-87, 276; functions of the, 183; monopolization of force by the, 185-86; "Reason of," 253; and society, 267-69; Weber's definition of the, 182

Status groups: and classes, 119-20; and religion, 123; stratification of, and legitimation by, 168-70

Strategies of independence: in administrative behavior, 229-30; in totalitarian and non-totalitarian subordination, 245-47

Strauss, Leo: critique of Weber by, 51, 59; on theory and practice in Edmund Burke, 30, 104

Struggle for survival: in industry, 238

Student protest: analyses of, 63-64

Subjectivism: and the loss of language, 68-72

Sumner, William G.: distinction between "crescive" and "enacted" institutions by, 267

Swidler, Ann: on organizations without authority, 186

Teggart, Frederick: Department of Social Institutions, Universiity of California, Berkeley, 8

Thompson, E.P.: definition of class by, 315-16

Tocqueville, Alexis de: central themes in sociology of, 40-45, 114; comparative method in, 126-27; on decline of solidarity, 213-14; Durkheim, Marx, Weber and, 52; on French Revolution, 141, 241-42; and Marx, 209-10; on masters and servants, 241-42; on speculative truths, 125-26; on transformation of European society, 261-64

Toleration: edicts in early Christianity, 329

Totalitarianism. *See* Authority, double hierarchy of; Plebiscitarian(ism)

Tracy, Destutt de: ideology as part of zoology, 29; laws of the human mind, 33; on "science of ideology," 29

Traditionalism: Erich Auerbach on idea of "reality" in, 55; ideology of, 237-38; Marx on, 250; of medieval political life, 258-61; and Mill's theory of dependency, 237-38; and modernization, 290-95; transformation of, in Western Europe, 252-58

Trotzky, Leo: on advantages of backwardness, 302

Tsarist autocracy: and intellectuals, 346-48; paternal authority of, 238-39

Tucholsky, Kurt: critique of, 75

United States: educational expansion in the, 345-46; French view of, 138-39

Universalism: ethical, of early Christianity, 326-30

University of California, Berkeley: Department of Sociology and Social Institutions in, 8

University of Chicago: Department of Sociology at the, 8, 111

Varain, Hans-Josef: definition of private associations by, 191. *See also* Interest groups

Veblen, Thorstein: on "withdrawal of efficiency," 245

Vietnam War: and scholarship, 63

Voltaire, Francois Marie Avouet: compares France and England, 138, 140; image of man of, 8-9; on physics and poetry, 98

Weber, Max: on bureaucracy, 120; central themes in the social theory of, 48-52; on charisma, 163-64; on class and status group, 119-20; on culture as convention, 123, 131; definition of religious behavior by, 154-55; definition of sociology by, 115; definition of the state by, 182, 215-15; Durkheim and, 50-52, 112-13; Durkheim, Marx, Tocqueville and, 52; on methods, 107-08, 322-23; on paradigm shifts, 101; Parsons and, 151-52; on the Protestant Ethic, 152-60; on rationalization, 173-74; on religion and change, 153-54; on "Science as Vocation," 5, 54, 69, 94; on social evolution, 174-75; on types of authority, 204-08

Weisskopf, Victor: on value of scientific state of mind, 88

Weizsäcker, Carl Friedrich von: on crisis and value of science, 91

Western states. *See* State

Wirth, Louis: course on "sociology of intellectual life" by, 4

Withdrawal of efficiency: Veblen's idea of, 245

Work performance: ethic of, 245

Zeno: paradox of, 53, 57

Ziman, John: on the scientific community, 94-95

Zone of acceptance: Herbert Simon's idea of, 229-30, 245

Zone of indifference: Chester Barnard's idea of, 229-30

ABS-8293